D0849945

Moral Combat

This book explores the troubling claim that legal roles force actors to confront one another in moral combat. This claim is implicit in the ordinary assumption that citizens are sometimes morally required to disobey unjust laws while judges are morally required to punish citizens for their civil disobedience. As Professor Hurd demonstrates, the punishment of morally justified actors is commonly thought to be necessary to preserve the rule of law, democracy, and the separation of powers. But inasmuch as our best moral theories cannot tolerate moral combat, they cannot license us to prefer the protection of our institutional values to the protection of the innocent.

In constructing her argument against the common assumption that the law makes citizens, judges, and system designers "moral gladiators," Hurd discusses issues of central importance in jurisprudence, moral philosophy, political theory, criminal law, and the theory of professional responsibility. She engages in a detailed discussion of the authority of law, defending the surprising claim that the law lacks authority to compel persons to do what morality otherwise forbids. She argues that our traditional political commitments to the rule of law, democracy, and the separation of powers cannot justify the punishment of the justified. She also demonstrates that a "role-relative" understanding of our moral obligations is incompatible with both consequentialist and deontological moral philosophies. In the end, Hurd convincingly refutes the possibility of moral combat, and with it the common presupposition that those who assume public roles within a democratic state can fulfill their obligations only by applying the law to those to whom the law properly does not apply.

Moral Combat is a thoughtfully conceived, carefully argued, and provocative book on a very important topic at the junction of legal, moral, and political thought. It will be of interest to moral, legal, and political philosophers as well as to lawyers, judges, and teachers of law and legal ethics who are concerned with the moral obligations that apply to actors within our system of justice.

Heidi M. Hurd is Professor of Law and Philosophy and Co-Director of the Institute for Law and Philosophy at the University of Pennsylvania.

Cambridge Studies in Philosophy and Law

GENERAL EDITOR: Gerald Postema
(University of North Carolina, Chapel Hill)

ADVISORY BOARD

Jules Coleman (Yale Law School)
Antony Duff (University of Stirling)
David Lyons (Boston University)
Neil MacCormick (University of Edinburgh)
Stephen Munzer (U.C.L.A. Law School)
Phillip Pettit (Australian National University)
Joseph Raz (University of Oxford)
Jeremy Waldron (Princeton University)

Other books in the series:

Moral Combat

HEIDI M. HURD
University of Pennsylvania

CAMBRIDGE
UNIVERSITY PRESS

PUBLISHED BY THE PRESS SYNDICATE OF THE UNIVERSITY OF CAMBRIDGE
The Pitt Building, Trumpington Street, Cambridge, United Kingdom

CAMBRIDGE UNIVERSITY PRESS
The Edinburgh Building, Cambridge CB2 2RU, UK10   http://www.cup.cam.ac.uk
40 West 20th Street, New York, NY 10011-4211, USA   http://www.cup.org
10 Stamford Road, Oakleigh, Melbourne 3166, Australia

© Heidi M. Hurd   1999

First published 1999

Printed in the United States of America

Typeset in Palatino 10/12 pt.   *System* QuarkXPress™ [AG]

*A catalog record for this book is available from
the British Library.*

Library of Congress Cataloging-in-Publication Data is available.

ISBN 0 521 64224 8 hardback

For My Children,
Gillian and Aidan

Contents

Contents

Preface

Moral philosophers have often feared that what we must do is in some manner or another inconsistent with what we can do. Some have worried that morality may be literally contradictory: It may command us both to do certain acts and to refrain from doing those acts. Thus some have thought, for example, that we may be both categorically obligated not to kill and categorically obligated to kill in self-defense. If threatened with deadly force, we thus do wrong whatever we do. Others have thought that, while morality may not be contradictory, it may be conflicted: It may impose on individuals obligations that cannot be simultaneously satisfied. Sartre, for example, thought it possible that a man might be obligated both to join the Free French to defend against Naziism and to stay at home to administer to his failing mother.

My worry in this book is not that morality may issue contradictory injunctions or confront us with intrapersonal conflicts. My worry is that morality may require interpersonal combat. It may make one person's moral success turn on another's moral failure. Persons may be morally obligated to prevent others from satisfying their moral obligations and morally compelled to punish others for doing precisely what they should have done.

The fear that morality may be gladiatorial derives from the very common presupposition that those who take on certain roles within our society simultaneously take on unique obligations – obligations that do not burden those outside such roles. For example, personal roles, such as the role of a parent or a spouse, are often defined in terms of special obligations that are owed to those who are near and dear. And it is commonly believed that professional roles give rise to similarly unique obligations. Such is the stuff to which courses in professional responsibility are dedicated. In law schools, students are standardly taught that lawyers and legal officials have reasons to do things, or to refrain from doing things, that others do not have. Thus, while a lawyer may know where the proverbial body is buried, she is bound not to reveal its location – although she could certainly do so were she not the killer's legal representative. And while a judge may believe that a law is unjust, he is not entitled to refuse its application, even if he believes that, were he a citizen, civil disobedience would be in order.

If the role of a judge is defined by a special obligation to protect the rule of law, as is commonly supposed, and if the role of a legal system designer is defined by a unique obligation to preserve democracy and the separation of powers, then we must believe that morality is perspectival. Moral obligations vary from one role to another, so we must check which hat we are wearing to discover the duties that bind us. Yet the claim that morality is perspectival generates a jurisprudential dilemma. A role-relative commitment to the rule of law may compel judges to punish citizens who (free of judicial constraints) justifiably violate the law. And a role-relative duty to preserve democracy and the separation of powers may compel system designers to criticize, discipline, or impeach judges who (free of the duties that bind system designers) act justifiably in acquitting citizens who violate the law without a legal justification or excuse. If our institutional values are role-relative, as has long been assumed, then our most fundamental jurisprudential commitments are in conflict. Either we must countenance the punishment of the justified or we must abandon the common presumption that legal officials are uniquely bound to follow the law out of deference to the rule of law and democracy.

To opt for the first of these alternatives is to admit that actors may be forced to confront one another in moral combat. It is to conclude that, for a judge to be morally successful at fulfilling her obligation to protect the rule of law, she may be forced to punish a citizen whose moral success depends on fulfilling an obligation to violate the law. Alternatively, for a system designer to be morally successful at fulfilling his obligation to protect majoritarian decision making, he may be forced to punish a judge who has justifiably refused to punish a citizen who has justifiably violated the law without a legal justification or excuse.

On the other hand, to opt for the second of the above alternatives is to jeopardize our jurisprudential commitments to the rule of law and the separation of powers. If judges should disregard the law whenever citizens justifiably disobey it, and if those who judge disobedient judges (that is, legal system designers) should refuse to require judicial obedience when it would imply the punishment of justified offenders, then what becomes of the rule of law and democracy? The majority does not rule itself and the powers are not kept separate if individuals can ignore democratically enacted laws whenever those laws fail to achieve morally ideal results.

It is to this dilemma, and the long-standing supposition that it can only be satisfactorily solved by countenancing moral combat, that this book is devoted. Part I draws the contours of the dilemma of legal perspectivalism and traces its roots to three theses: first, that the content of law does not perfectly mirror the content of morality; second, that the content of morality is not relative to the beliefs of individuals or communities; and third, that the law, *qua* law, does not compel our obedience. As I argue, if any of these theses are false, then the dilemma dissipates: Either there are no instances of justified disobedience or it is morally unproblemmatic to punish such disobedience.

Part II is dedicated to detailed defenses of the truth of these theses. Its chapters collectively render the dilemma of perspectivalism a robust one, requiring a solution that does more than deny its premises. Chapter 2 contests the dominant theories of moral relativism, foreclosing the arguments for moral combat that such a metaethical position easily provides. Chapters 3–6 constitute a detailed discussion of the authority that can be justifiably assigned to law, arguing in the end that the law can serve, at most, as a theoretical authority about the content of our (antecedently existing) moral obligations. Chapter 3 disputes the dominant theory of legal authority, which credits law with "practical authority," and hence, with the moral power to compel us to do what morality would otherwise prohibit us from doing. Chapter 4 contests the claim that law can at least be thought to possess "influential authority," that is, the power to give us new reasons for acting that we did not have antecedent to the law's enactment. Chapter 5 rejects the even more modest claim that the law should be thought to possess "advisory authority" – a kind of theoretical authority that derives from the expertise of lawmakers to discern socially optimal arrangements. Chapter 6 provides a defense of the claim that law (not lawmakers) can at best provide us with reliable moral advice, but cannot provide us with any reasons to do what morality otherwise prohibits.

In their detail, Chapters 3–6 constitute a free-standing discussion of the authority of law severable from the project to which the book, as a whole, is devoted. There are, however, two reasons for including these chapters in all their detail. First, it is profoundly tempting to solve the dilemma of legal perspectivalism by denying the possibility of justifiable disobedience, or by adopting a theory of legal authority that trivializes its incidence. Chapters 3–6 provide the most compelling case possible for the claim that the dilemma of legal perspectivalism cannot be solved by insisting that the law has a kind of authority that precludes justified disobedience (or minimizes its occurrence beyond the point of jurisprudential interest). Second, the dilemma of legal perspectivalism emerges from these chapters as the principle problem confronting those who agree that the law cannot compel us to do what morality prohibits. To be able to solve the dilemma of legal perspectivalism without returning to a theory of legal authority that invites the problems recounted in detail in Chapters 3–6 is the most significant challenge to one who assigns theoretical authority to law. One cannot meet this challenge without appreciating both how devastating the objections are to alternative theories of authority and how robust the dilemma of legal perspectivalism turns out to be in the face of those objections.

Those who bear no fondness for moral relativism and who are prepared to assume (if only for the sake of argument) that the law possesses only theoretical authority should feel free to turn from Part I to Part III, thereby avoiding the detailed treatment given to the positions of those who seek to deny the prima facie plausibility of the dilemma of legal perspectivalism. Part III examines the viability of resolving the dilemma of legal perspectivalism by embracing the view that morality can indeed require combat between those within and those outside of legal roles. Its three chapters examine a set of reasons to think that our jurisprudential values provide unique reasons for action to those within legal roles – reasons so weighty that they compel legal actors to preserve the rule of law, democracy, and the separation of powers, even at the cost of punishing the justified. Chapter 7 considers arguments that the prospect of error should prompt citizens, legal officials, and institution designers to grant different degrees of deference to the law. Chapter 8 takes up claims that the rule of law values bind judges and other legal officials in a manner that they do not bind citizens. Chapter 9 considers analogous arguments concerning the weight to be assigned to constitutional values – specifically, the values of democracy and the separation of powers – in decisions of institution designers. The burden of Part III is to articulate and critically appraise the best case for the thesis that the dilemma of legal perspectivalism should be solved in favor of our jurisprudential commitments, even at the cost of moral combat.

Part IV turns the tables and critically examines the arguments for resolving the dilemma of legal perspectivalism by holding fast to the opposite horn of the dilemma. Its chapters advance and evaluate reasons why both consequentialists and deontologists should prefer to sacrifice institutional values rather than countenance the claim that the justified can be justifiably punished. Chapter 10 examines and rejects a set of arguments that attempt to demonstrate how consequentialism can make room for role-relative reasons for action that generate moral combat. Chapter 11 canvasses the most compelling circumstances in which deontologists might find maxims for action that pit actors against one another in moral combat, arguing in each case that our best deontological theory would resist claims that the maxims of morality can be perspectival.

Together, Parts III and IV conspire to make the dilemma of perspectivalism seemingly insoluble: We can make sense of our jurisprudential commitments to the rule of law, democracy, and the separation of powers only by according role-relative reasons for action to legal actors that consign them to moral combat (Part III); but neither of our best moral theories can make sense of moral combat (Part IV). Part V hazards a solution to the dilemma of legal perspectivalism by advancing arguments that reconcile our systemic values with the tenets of both consequentialism and deontology. Chapter 12 demonstrates how one can assign sufficient importance to the rule of law, democracy, and the separation of powers to ensure their systemic protection while refusing to countenance the sort of moral combat between legal actors that has been assumed necessary to preserving these institutions. Chapter 12 closes with a short note concerning the jurisprudential implications of denying that legal actors can engage in moral combat.

Acknowledgments

I am enormously grateful to the many friends and colleagues whose challenging criticisms of my past work motivated this book. Special thanks go to Matthew Adler, David Braybrooke, Stephen Burbank, Richard Craswell, Meir Dan-Cohen, Jacques deLisle, Colin Diver, John Dreher, William Ewald, Samuel Freeman, Richard Fumerton, Ronald Garet, Frank Goodman, Barbara Herman, Leo Katz, Kenneth Kress, Howard Lesnick, David Lyons, Scott MacDonald, Stephen Morse, Eric Posner, Gerald Postema, Joseph Raz, Edward Rock, Kenneth Simons, Jeremy Waldron, Elizabeth Warren, and R. George Wright. I am particularly grateful to Larry Alexander, whose lengthy letters and telephone calls prompted major sections of this book. I am forever indebted to my parents, Carroll and Jeanne Hurd, who set me on the road to ideas when I was very young, and who have provided directions whenever I have lost my way. Most importantly, I thank my husband, Michael Moore, whose indulgence of my decade-long obsession with the questions raised in this book not only inspired much of my thinking about those questions, but also made for treasured years of debate and discussion.

I am very grateful to the faculties who invited me to give workshops on chapters of this book (or on the articles that were their precursors) or who attended conference sessions at which I presented material from the book. I received very helpful comments at Boston University School of Law, University of Chicago Law School, Chicago-Kent College of Law, Cornell Law School, George Washington University National Law Center, University of Iowa College of Law, University of Iowa Philosophy Department, Northwestern University School of Law, University of San Diego School of Law, University of Southern California Law Center, University of Texas School of Law, and Vanderbilt University School of Law. I am particularly indebted to my colleagues at the University of Pennsylvania Law School for

cheerfully enduring yearly workshops on the developing manuscript. Particular thanks go to Colin Diver, Frank Goodman, Stephen
Morse, Howard Lesnick, and Edward Rock, for the very thoughtful
replies that they gave to the work I presented.

I benefited from the careful research assistance and challenging
editorial comments of a number of superb students, including Matthew Biben, Daniel Epstein, Louis Feldman, Halley Finkelstein, Reid
Fontaine, Aaron Katzel, Howard Lager, Angela Pelletier, and Jami
Wyatt. Special thanks also to my secretary, Patricia Meier, for keeping my life organized; to my liaison librarians, Catharine Krieps and
Edwin Greenlee, for their extensive research assistance; and to my
step-daughter, Ellen Moore, for compiling the earliest version of the
Bibliography.

My work on this book was generously supported by the University
of Pennsylvania Law School. I am also grateful to the Rockefeller
Foundation's Study and Conference Center in Bellagio, Italy, for providing me with a spectacular retreat in which to finish the manuscript.

Many of the chapters of this book reflect modified segments of already published works. Chapters 1, 7, 8, and 9 draw from "Justifiably
Punishing the Justified," *Michigan Law Review* 90 (1992), 2203–2324,
and from "The Morality of Judicial Disobedience," *Penn Law Journal*
29 (1993), 22–24. Chapter 2 draws from "Relativistic Jurisprudence:
Skepticism Founded on Confusion," *Southern California Law Review*
61 (Note 1988), 1417–1506. Chapters 3 and 4 draw from "Challenging
Authority," *The Yale Law Journal* 100 (1991), 1611–77. Chapters 5 and
6 draw from "Sovereignty in Silence," *The Yale Law Journal* 99 (1990),
945–1028, and from "Interpreting Authorities," in *Law and Interpretation*, ed. Andrei Marmor (Oxford: Clarendon Press, 1995). Chapters 10
and 11 draw from "Justifiably Punishing the Justified," *Michigan Law
Review* 90 (1992), 2203–2324 and from "What in the World is Wrong?,"
Journal of Contemporary Legal Issues 5 (1994), 157–216. Sections of Chapters 1, 3, 7, 8, 9, 10, and 11 also appear in my doctoral dissertation, *Legal Perspectivalism*, on file at the University of Southern California. I
am grateful to the publishers of my previous work for their permission to reproduce modified segments of it here.

[A]ll law is universal but about some things it is not possible to make a universal statement which shall be correct. In those cases, then, in which it is necessary to speak universally, but not possible to do so correctly, the law takes the usual case, though it is not ignorant of the possibility of error. . . . When the law speaks universally, then, and a case arises on it which is not covered by the universal statement, then it is right, where the legislator fails us and has erred by oversimplicity, to correct the omission – to say what the legislator himself would have said had he been present. . . . And this is the nature of the equitable, a correction of law where it is defective owing to its universality. . . . [W]hen the thing is indefinite the rule also is indefinite, like the leaden rule used in making the Lesbian molding; the rule adapts itself to the shape of the stone and is not rigid, and so too the decree is adapted to the facts.

Aristotle, Nicomachean Ethics

Must the citizen ever for a moment, or in the least degree, resign his conscience to the legislator? Why has every man a conscience, then? I think we should be men first and subjects afterwards. It is not desirable to cultivate a respect for the law, so much as for the right. The only obligation which I have a right to assume, is to do at any time what I think right.

Henry David Thoreau, Civil Disobedience

Part I

The Dilemma of Legal Perspectivalism

Contemporary moral philosophy, political theory, and jurisprudence have converged to create a quite baffling dilemma. This dilemma is generated by the apparent incompatibility of three principles, each of which grounds features of our system of law and government, and each of which carries substantial normative weight. The first I shall call the principle of weak retributivism – a moral principle doctrinally entrenched in American civil and criminal law, which holds that individuals who are morally justified in their actions ought not to be blamed or punished for those actions. The second is the principle of the rule of law – a complex jurisprudential principle that requires law to conform to a set of formal values, such as generality and coherence, as a means of protecting substantive moral values like liberty and equality. The third is the principle of democracy and the separation of powers – a principle of political morality that vindicates the right of majorities to be self-governing by assigning policy-making powers to a democratic legislature and restricting the executive and judiciary to the secondary tasks of policy implementation and application.

These three principles now serve as cornerstones of our legal and political systems. Yet, if they are genuinely incompatible, one or more of them must be abandoned. We must resign ourselves to the punishment of the justified or sacrifice systemic values that have long been invoked to justify our commitment to structural pluralism and rule-governed adjudication.

1

Chapter 1

The Incompatibility of Weak Retributivism, the Rule of Law, and the Separation of Powers

Since our fundamental commitments to weak retributivism, the rule of law, and the principles of democracy and the separation of powers are not in obvious conflict, the dilemma engendered by their mutual defense takes some construction. Let me begin at its seemingly remote beginning.

MORAL CORRESPONDENCE

Consider the following hypothetical. Smith is attacked by a hoodlum while walking her dog through the city park. Smith justifiably believes that her life is in peril, and she is thus forced to choose between killing the hoodlum and being killed or maimed herself. Jones is a jogger who witnesses the hoodlum's attack on Smith. Unable to affect the hoodlum's conduct, Jones must choose between permitting Smith to kill the hoodlum and intervening to prevent that killing. Long is a concession stand owner who also witnesses the event. Long is unable to affect the conduct of either the hoodlum or Smith, and so can only choose between restraining Jones from intervening to prevent the hoodlum's death or allowing that intervention.

The morality of each actor's choice appears to be determined by what I shall call the "correspondence thesis." The correspondence thesis asserts a moral claim about the justification of codependent actions. It holds that the justifiability of an action determines the justifiability of permitting or preventing that action. According to the correspondence thesis, if Smith is justified in killing the hoodlum (as a means of self-defense), then Jones is not justified in intervening to prevent that killing, and, hence, Long is justified in restraining Jones's intervention.

The correspondence thesis rests on the intuition that, since an action cannot be simultaneously right and wrong, it cannot be the case

3

that one actor may be justified in performing an act while another may be simultaneously justified in preventing that act.[1] The intuitive plausibility of the thesis can be cashed out as follows.

Step One: Right action is action that accords with the balance of reasons for action.[2] Reasons for action are objective in the sense that their right-making characteristics are universal. If it is right for one to do an act, it must be right for all others that one do it. If, for Smith, the balance of objective reasons for action favors action A (where A is killing the hoodlum in self-defense), then the balance of reasons in favor of Smith's doing A must be the same for Jones and Long, namely, it must dictate the conclusion on their part that it is right that Smith do A.

Step Two: Where other actors face choices between alternative actions that will or will not thwart action A, the rightness of A entails the wrongness of those actions that will thwart A. For example, Jones faces the choice between intervening to prevent Smith from killing the hoodlum or not intervening. It would be morally anomalous if

---

[1]   As Immanuel Kant argued:

> Each member of the commonwealth has right of coercion in relation to all the others, except in relation to the head of state. For . . . he alone is authorized to coerce others without being subject to any coercive law himself. . . .

> But if there were two persons exempt from coercion, neither would be subject to coercive laws, *and neither could do to the other anything contrary to right, which is impossible.*

Immanuel Kant, On the Common Saying: "This May be True in Theory, But it Does Not Apply in Practice," in *Kant's Political Writings*, ed. Hans S. Reiss, trans. H.B. Nisbet (Cambridge and New York: Cambridge University Press, 1970), 61, 74–5 (emphasis added).

[2]   Joseph Raz puts this principle as follows: "It is always the case that one ought, all things considered, to do whatever one ought to do on the balance of reasons." Joseph Raz, *Practical Reason and Norms*, 2d ed. (London: Hutchinson & Sons, 1990), 36. As Raz makes clear, the phrase "ought all things considered" functions in this principle to indicate "what ought to be done on the basis of all the reasons for action which are relevant to the question, and not only on the basis of the reasons the agent in fact considered or could have considered." Ibid. For similar statements of the conditions of right action, see Stephen Darwall, *Impartial Reason* (Ithaca, NY: Cornell University Press, 1983), 99; John Rawls, *A Theory of Justice* (Cambridge: Harvard University Press, Belknap Press, 1971), 341, 408. For alternative conceptions that epistemically limit the conditions of right action, see Richard A. Fumerton, *Reason and Morality: A Defense of the Egocentric Perspective* (Ithaca, NY: Cornell University Press, 1990), 90–128; Donald Davidson, *Essays on Actions and Events* (Oxford: Clarendon Press, 1980), 21–42. I criticize such alternative conceptions in Chapter 10.

A were the right thing for Smith to do, while preventing A would be the right thing for Jones to do. The objective reasons that constitute the content of morality must make it right (for Jones as for everyone else) that Smith do A, so those same reasons seemingly cannot make it right that Smith not do A. Hence, the balance of reasons for action must demand the permission of justified actions and the restraint of attempts to thwart justified actions.

It is useful at this early stage to stop to consider a series of objections that might be made to the correspondence thesis. By putting these to rest at this point, one can both better appreciate the claim made by the correspondence thesis and forestall future confusion about its implications. First, one might be tempted to resist the correspondence thesis because of the following sort of case. Suppose that Green has grounds for reasonably believing that she is being stalked by a man who seeks to kill her. Suppose further that she reasonably believes that a man who she discovers quietly circling her house is in fact the stalker. She thus reasonably believes her life to be in peril and shoots at the man as he approaches her. However, the man, Brown, is in fact the meter reader for the electric company who is on her property to perform the routine task of monitoring her use of electricity. Reasonably believing his life to be in peril, Brown shoots back, misses, and is killed by another shot from Green.

Is this not a case of two individuals who are each entitled to attempt to prevent the other from doing a justified act? Does this case not demonstrate that the correspondence thesis is false, because the justifiability of Green's conduct does not make it unjustifiable for Brown to resist it, and the justifiability of Brown's conduct does not make it unjustifiable for Green to resist it? Each appears to be justified in attempting to thwart the actions of the other, and, as such, the justifiability of one actor's conduct does not appear to determine the justifiability of the other's attempt to prevent that conduct.

This analysis is initially plausible only because the meaning of the phrase "justified action" is equivocal. The phrase is alternatively employed to capture both right action and nonculpable action. But the conditions of right action and the conditions of nonculpable action are distinct. And the correspondence thesis is a thesis that is solely about the conditions of right action; it is not a thesis about the conditions of nonculpable action. Let me explain.

An individual is nonculpable if she does an action justifiably believing it to be right. Alternatively, an individual is culpable if she

5

does an action believing it to be wrong or unjustifiably believing it to be right.[3] Culpability is thus a condition of an actor's state of mind: It reflects the degree of epistemic justification with which an actor concludes that her actions are right. An actor is epistemically justified in believing an action to be right if, under the circumstances, she has invested a reasonable amount of time, talent, diligence, and resources to acquire information about her circumstances and to determine the demands of morality within those circumstances. She has invested a reasonable amount of time, talent, diligence, and resources at these tasks if, crudely speaking, the costs of investing more of these goods are greater than the costs of a wrong decision discounted by its probability.[4] In the case of Green and Brown, one might well conclude that Green justifiably believed that she was entitled to shoot Brown. She rightly believed that an innocent person is entitled to use deadly force in cases of imminent peril, and, given what she knew of the activities of her stalker, she reasonably concluded that she was in such peril and, thus, that the costs of investing further time to determine more accurately the identity of the unknown man in her garden were sufficiently great as to outweigh the discounted costs of shooting an innocent man. At the same time, Brown justifiably believed that he was entitled to defend himself. He rightly concluded that, as an innocent person, he was entitled to use deadly force to defend himself against imminent peril, and he invested a reasonable amount of time and diligence to determine that Green was indeed placing him in such peril.

The correspondence thesis is plainly false if it is construed as a thesis about the conditions of culpability. Two individuals can justifiably believe that they are each entitled to thwart the actions of the other, because they each can possess sufficiently different amounts of information, time, talent, and resources to make it reasonable for them to entertain different beliefs about what they are each entitled to do. One actor thus may be epistemically justified in believing that she should do an action that another actor is epistemically justified in be-

---

[3] For an extensive discussion of the distinction between wrong-doing and culpability, see Heidi M. Hurd, "What in the World is Wrong?," *Journal of Contemporary Legal Issues* 5 (1994): 157–216.

[4] There are certainly credible accounts of culpability that do not explicitly rely on the kind of cost-benefit analysis that I have employed here For a discussion of these alternative conceptions of culpability and a defense of the claim that even deontologists should employ a cost-benefit theory of culpability, see Heidi M. Hurd, "The Deontology of Negligence," *Boston University Law Review* 76 (1996): 249–72.

lieving that he should thwart. Construed epistemically, it is thus false that the justifiability of an action determines the justifiability of permitting or preventing that action.

However, the correspondence thesis is not an epistemological thesis about the conditions of culpability; it is a metaphysical thesis about the conditions of right action. While culpability is a function of an actor's state of mind, the rightness of an action is a function of the degree to which the action satisfies the objective criteria specified by our best normative theory. The claim made by the correspondence thesis is that the criteria of right action specified by our best moral theory – whatever that moral theory may be – cannot make contradictory actions simultaneously right. While two individuals might be justified in *believing* that it is right to thwart the actions of the other, it cannot in fact be right for each to thwart the actions of the other. If the action of one individual is in fact right, it cannot be simultaneously right for the other to prevent that action.

Thus, while Green and Brown may have reasonably believed that they should shoot one another, only one of them acted rightly in so doing. Since Brown was not in fact attacking Green, Green did not in fact act rightly in shooting Brown. Had she refrained from shooting Brown, an innocent life would have been saved at no cost to her own life. If it is categorically wrong to take an innocent life (according to our best deontological theory), then Green acted wrongly, albeit nonculpably, in shooting Brown, because Brown was in fact an innocent actor. If it is right to maximize the preservation of innocent lives (according to our best consequentialist theory), then Green acted wrongly, because her action took one innocent life without in fact saving others (for her life would have been preserved had she not shot Brown). Once it is clear that the correspondence thesis is not a thesis about culpability, but a thesis about right action, it is clear that hypotheticals such as that involving Green and Brown are not counterexamples to it.

However, it might be thought that, while the previous hypothetical of Green and Brown makes the correspondence thesis plausible for both deontological and consequentialist accounts of right action, the truth of the thesis is in fact theory-dependent. While the thesis might be necessarily true of a consequentialist account of right action, it need not be true of a deontological account of right action. I shall have a great deal to say about this suggestion in Chapters 10 and 11, which are devoted to determining the relative truth of the correspondence thesis for consequentialists and deontologists. At this stage, however, it is worth recognizing the plausibility of the thesis for both types of theorists.

Consequentialists are committed to the claim that right action consists in maximizing good consequences or minimizing bad consequences. Monistic consequentialists embrace a single-valued theory of the good. Thus, utilitarians define the good in terms of human pleasure. Egoists define the good in terms of what will serve the individual's own interests, and virtue theorists define the good in terms of what will make individuals virtuous. Pluralist consequentialists, on the other hand, embrace a multivalued theory of the good. They maintain that the good should be maximized, but then define the good in terms of some complex combination of the previously mentioned types of values.

As a thesis about the conditions of right action, the correspondence thesis appears necessarily true for consequentialists.[5] In our previous tale, in which Smith is attacked by a hoodlum while Jones and Long look on, the death of the hoodlum is a better state of affairs than its only alternative, the death of Smith (assuming, of course, that our best consequentialist theory prefers innocent lives to culpable ones). And it is a better state of affairs not only for Smith, but also for Jones and Long. Since the only criterion of right action for the consequentialist is whether an action promotes good states of affairs, it follows that Smith, Jones, and Long should all promote this good state of affairs. At the very least, it cannot be right on consequentialist grounds for Jones to interfere with Smith's act of self-defense, even if for some reason it is not obligatory of Jones to join Smith in her endeavor.

In contrast to consequentialists, deontologists are committed to the claim that the goodness of an act lies not in its consequences, but in the inherent quality of the act itself. According to deontological moral theories, certain act-types are intrinsically right or intrinsically wrong. Thus, if it is right to preserve an innocent life, one cannot take an innocent life, even if, in so doing, one saves a great many more innocent lives.[6] Contemporary deontologists often cash out this anti-

---

[5]   Chapters 10 and 12 are devoted to a much more extensive analysis of this supposition.

[6]   As Finnis puts it, "one should not choose to do any act which *of itself does nothing but* damage or impede a realization or participation of any one or more of the basic forms of human good." John Finnis, *Natural Law and Natural Rights* (Oxford: Clarendon Press, 1980), 118.

   [This] perhaps unfamiliar formulation . . . is well recognized, in other formulations: most loosely, as "the end does not justify the means"; more

consequentialist claim by describing morality as a set of agent-relative categorical imperatives.[7] Morality directs each agent not to kill an innocent person, even if such a killing will prevent a greater number of killings by others.

A deontological, or agent-relative, theory of morality does not share the characteristic that appears to make the correspondence thesis necessarily true for the consequentialist. It is logically possible that a (certain type of) deontological theory would render the correspondence thesis false.[8] Suppose, for example, that morality contained an agent-relative permission (or obligation) to kill when necessary to preserve one's own life. Under such a moral directive, it would be right for Smith to defend herself by killing her attacker. But suppose that this morality also contained an agent-relative obligation (or permission) to prevent killings by others, even when those killings are in self-defense. Then it would be right for Jones to prevent Smith from (rightly) defending herself. In such a theory, there is no correspondence between what it is right for Smith to do and what it is right for Jones to do.

While such a deontological theory entails the rejection of the correspondence thesis, it does not contain any formal contradiction. Yet its content is highly implausible. Agent-relative morality is still universal: If it is right for Smith to defend her own life, it is right for Jones to defend his own life. The view considered here has to both admit this and contend that it is also right for Jones to prevent Smith from defending her life. The agent-relativity of such a deontological morality prevents these norms of rightness from contradicting one another, but it does not prevent their mutual assertion from being highly untenable. If morality were to combine such maxims, then there would

precisely, though still ambiguously, as "evil may not be done that good might follow therefrom"; and with a special Enlightenment flavour, as Kant's categorical imperative: "Act so that you treat humanity, whether in your own person or in that of another, always as an end and never as a means only."

Ibid., 122, quoting Immanuel Kant, *Foundations of the Metaphysics of Morals*, trans. Lewis W. Beck (Indianapolis: Bobbs-Merrill, 1959).

7　See, for example, Thomas Nagel, *The Last Word* (New York and Oxford: Oxford University Press, 1997), 119–25; Thomas Nagel, *The Possibility of Altruism* (Oxford: Clarendon Press, 1970), 90–5; Thomas Nagel, *The View From Nowhere* (New York: Oxford University Press, 1986), 152–4; Thomas Nagel, *Equality and Partiality* (Oxford and New York: Oxford University Press, 1991), 40, 85–6; Derek Parfit, *Reasons and Persons* (Oxford: Clarendon Press, 1984), 143.

8　Chapter 11, however, constitutes a defense of the claim that a plausible deontological theory would incorporate the correspondence thesis.

be times when we would be forced to confront one another in moral combat. Others would be called on to prevent us from doing what we would be entitled, and perhaps obligated, to do. Morality would make us moral gladiators in an arena in which one's moral success would depend on another's moral failure.

On pain of condemning us to moral combat, it thus would seem that any plausible deontological moral theory would subscribe to the correspondence thesis. If this is true, then the correspondence thesis does not depend for its intuitive viability on any particular moral theory.

LEGAL PERSPECTIVALISM

Compelling as the correspondence thesis appears to be on any plausible moral theory, its intuitive appeal seems to give way when one is forced to take into account role-related considerations. Suppose now that Smith is married to a man who frequently beats her and her three children. She rightly believes that her husband will eventually attempt to kill them all. She also rightly believes that at that point she will be unable to defend any of them. And she rightly believes herself to be unable to secure their safety if they attempt to flee from him. She thus plausibly takes the balance of reasons for action to favor a preemptive strike, notwithstanding the fact that she recognizes and takes seriously the law's refusal to recognize a special battered spouse defense to homicide. She waits until her husband is asleep, enters his bedroom, and fatally shoots him.

Suppose that Jones is a judge who must decide whether to convict or acquit Smith. Jones considers Smith morally justified in shooting her husband, because Jones concurs that the balance of reasons applicable to her choice favored such a killing. But Jones is a judge charged with the task of applying the law, and the law does not permit the acquittal of those who claim self-defense but admit the absence of any imminent threat of harm. Jones, like Smith, must thus decide whether to break the law. He must decide whether to comply with the decision rule that demands punishment of those who kill without a *legal* justification or to break that rule and acquit one who possesses a *moral* justification.[9]

---

[9] It will be useful throughout discussions of legal perspectivalism to invoke the distinction between conduct rules and decision rules coined by Jeremy Bentham

Suppose, finally, that Long is responsible for designing and maintaining our political and legal systems. Among the many tasks required to foster democracy, preserve the separation of powers, maintain law and order, and ensure right action by citizens and officials is the task of appointing and disciplining members of the judiciary. Long, like Jones, recognizes the plausibility of Smith's claim of justification. Long also recognizes that Jones might rightly conclude that he should acquit Smith, notwithstanding the decision rule that requires her punishment. Long thus faces the choice between disciplining Jones, should Jones fail to comply with the decision rule, or licensing the sort of judicial legislation that justified judicial disobedience would represent.

We are now in a position to appreciate the dilemma with which we began. Jones and Long face choices that pit our fundamental moral, political, and jurisprudential values against one another. If the correspondence thesis applies to acts of punishment in the same way that it applies to preventative and permissive acts, then it would seem that Jones should acquit Smith, and Long should not discipline Jones for such an acquittal. It also would seem that the correspondence thesis should be as true of acts of punishment as of acts of prevention,[10] because punishment labels an act as wrong and thus serves to prevent future actors (including the actor who is punished) from performing that act in similar circumstances. If Smith's act is right, it would seem wrong to respond to that act with sanctions that imply either that Smith should not have performed that act or that future actors should not perform the same act in similar circumstances. But if judges like Jones acquit those who are morally justified in breaking the law, what will become of the rule of law? Law seemingly ceases to be law if judges are entitled to rethink its wisdom in every case to which it applies

---

and famously exploited by Meir Dan-Cohen. Conduct rules constitute those rules that are intended to guide the daily behavior of citizens. Decision rules constitute those rules that are intended to guide judges in the adjudication of disputes concerning citizens' behavior. See Jeremy Bentham, *A Fragment on Government and An Introduction to the Principles of Morals and Legislation*, ed. Wilfred Harrison (Oxford: Oxford University Press, 1948), 430; Meir Dan-Cohen, "Decision Rules and Conduct Rules: On Acoustic Separation in Criminal Law," *Harvard Law Review* 97 (1984): 625–30.

[10] But see the extended discussion of this claim in the first section of Chapter 12, which makes clear the potential moral differences between preventing a moral act and punishing a moral act – differences that make it possible that an act can be moral only if punished.

and to disregard it whenever it is inferior to the rule that they would fashion.[11] Also, if system designers like Long refuse to discipline members of the judiciary who disobey democratically enacted decision rules, what will become of democracy and the separation of powers? The majority does not rule itself and the powers of government are not kept separate if single individuals are entitled to substitute their own considered opinions for those of a democratic legislature.[12]

Yet the correspondence thesis applies only if the balance of reasons for action is indeed the same for Jones and Long as it is for Smith. That is, it applies only if it is right for Jones and Long, as well as for Smith, that Smith violate the conduct rule prohibiting homicide in a situation in which there is no fear of imminent harm. The rule of law is secure if there are reasons for action that are applicable to Jones but are not applicable to Smith – reasons that make Smith's conduct wrong for Jones, notwithstanding its rightness for her. Such reasons for action, if sufficiently weighty, might justify the judicial punishment of an admittedly justified offender. And even if such judicial reasons are insufficient to justify Jones' punishment of Smith, our commitment to democracy and the separation of powers is secure if there are reasons for action that are applicable to Long which are not applicable to Jones – reasons that make Jones's acquittal of Smith wrong for Long, notwithstanding its possible rightness for Jones. In such a case, Long might be justified in punishing Jones for justifiably refusing to punish Smith.

However, the cost of preserving our systemic values is the cost of abandoning the principle of weak retributivism – a principle that is indelibly inscribed in our current conception of the conditions of justice. According to this principle, moral desert is a necessary condition of blame or punishment: Morally innocent individuals (individuals whose actions are justified) do not deserve punishment and

---

[11] As Lon Fuller argued, insofar as the substitution of individual judgment constitutes a failure to comply with the "internal morality of the law," it constitutes "no law at all." Lon Fuller, *The Morality of Law,* rev. ed. (New Haven, CT: Yale University Press, 1969), 39.

[12] [G]ood reasons for avoiding the creation of nondemocratic political elites militate against judges being given the authority to modify extant legal rules on the basis of their personal perceptions of what is likely to have the best consequences in the instant case . . . [T]he whole point of the legislative enterprise would be lost if the courts were given the authority to subvert it. Rolf E. Sartorius, *Individual Conduct and Social Norms* (Encino, CA: Dickenson Publishing Co., 1975), 178.

thus should not be punished, even when their punishment might further some welfare goal.[13] The principle of weak retributivism draws

---

[13]   Gerald Postema disputes this understanding of weak retributivism. In his view, weak retributivism makes *legal* desert a necessary condition of punishment, not *moral* desert. That is, retribution is appropriate if one has violated the law in a manner that is neither justified nor excused.

There are at least four problems with this view, each of which is sufficient to justify the conception of retributivism that I have advanced here. First, it seems that those who would agree with Postema's construal of weak retributivism do so for reasons that prove the truth of the construction advanced above. That is, they believe that persons are *morally* obligated to obey the law, and, hence, that those who break the law are morally deserving of punishment. If persons are morally obligated to obey the law, then of course legal desert will be a necessary condition of punishment. But this will be *because* moral desert is a necessary condition of punishment.

Second, Postema's construal of weak retributivism trivializes the constraints that it imposes on judges and legislators. If morality compels us to follow the law, then the fact that a law has been passed settles the question of the desert of a law-breaker. But this means that the legislature can pass any law, without regard to whether the law criminalizes morally deserving conduct, because, once the law is passed, any violation will be morally deserving of punishment. And if every violation is morally deserving of punishment, judges need not concern themselves with the possibility that, by punishing a law-breaker, they will in fact be punishing the innocent.

Third, as a matter of academic sociology, it does not appear that those who have defended weak retributivism have done so on Postema's terms. Strong retributivists like Michael Moore have advanced the weak retributivist thesis precisely as a means of making the application of the sanctions backing law commensurate with conditions of moral blame. As Moore explains, the principle of weak retributivism is to be contrasted with the principle of strong retributivism, which holds that moral desert is not just a necessary, but also a sufficient condition of praise and blame: Morally culpable individuals deserve punishment, and thus should be punished even when their punishment will not serve to advance any welfare goal, e.g., the prevention of crime. For a defense of both principles of retributivism, see Michael S. Moore, "The Moral Worth of Retribution," in *Responsibility, Character, and the Emotions*, ed. Ferdinand Shoeman (Cambridge: Cambridge University Press, 1987), 179–219. It is this stronger claim that distinguishes retributive theories of the criminal law from mixed theories. See Rawls, "Two Concepts of Rules," *Philosophical Review* 64 (1955): 3–4 ("What we may call the retributive view is that punishment is justified on the grounds that wrong-doing merits punishment."). Mixed theorists have generally argued that *moral* desert is a necessary but not sufficient condition of punishment; considerations of utility, for example, must also conspire to demand punishment before its infliction is justified. As Rawls makes clear, his mixed theory is premised on a *moral* conception of desert, because "punishment" of those who are morally innocent is better described as "telishment." John Rawls, "Two Concepts of Rules," 11.

Finally, I devote Chapters 3 through 6 to disputing claims that the law has the (moral) authority to compel us to do what morality otherwise obligates us not to do. If my arguments are persuasive, then Postema's construal of weak retributivism is, on the merits, indefensible. The law cannot bind us to do what we otherwise have reasons not to do, so we cannot deserve punishment solely for breaking the law.

its intuitive strength from the sense that it is morally repugnant to blame or punish individuals who have done precisely what they should have done. To abandon the principle of weak retributivism is to threaten individuals with a catch-22: To escape punishment, they must depart from the balance of reasons for action – and so act immorally; to preserve the morality of their conduct, they must conform to the balance of reasons for action – and so suffer punishment.

Notice that if the correspondence thesis is true, then the principle of weak retributivism becomes but a special case of its application. The morality of an individual's act determines the justifiability or unjustifiability of her punishment, because the balance of reasons that determines the morality of her act is identical to the balance of reasons that determines the morality of her punishment. Insofar as an actor is justified in performing an act, another actor cannot be justified in punishing her for that act.[14]

However, the recognition of role-relative reasons for action puts the principle of weak retributivism in jeopardy, because it entails the indefensibility of the correspondence thesis. If morality requires conduct in accordance with the balance of reasons for action, and if that balance differs between the citizen, judge, and institution designer, then it appears that there may be instances in which the punishment of the justified is itself justified. The most that the principle of weak

---

[14] It is the vindication of the principle of weak retributivism by the correspondence thesis which distinguishes that principle from what Rolf Sartorius has called "the reflection principle." According to the reflection principle, "[w]here an individual has correctly decided that he ought to do X, any higher-order judgment about his decision to do X or his actual act of doing it ought to license or approve of, rather than disapprove of or penalize, the decision and/or the act itself." Rolf Sartorius, *Individual Conduct and Social Norms*, 56–7. The reflection principle, as stated by Sartorius, presupposes that the reasons for action may differ as between an actor and one who judges that actor. It thus constitutes a normative thesis about the sort of judgment that ought to be made concerning an actor's conduct, rather than a conceptual thesis about the sort of judgment which must be made about that conduct. If the correspondence thesis is true, the reflection principle collapses into the principle of weak retributivism. This is because the reasons for higher order judgments about an actor's conduct are identical to the reasons for that conduct; hence, if the conduct is justified, the only justifiable judgment about that conduct is one of approval. It is not because the reasons for judgment include a second-order principle which holds that, notwithstanding the fact that the reasons for conduct and the reasons for judgment about that conduct may be different, the reasons for judgment ought to be calculated *as if* they were identical to the reasons for conduct.

For helpful discussions of Sartorius' reflection principle, see Larry Alexander, "Pursuing the Good – Indirectly," *Ethics* 95 (1985): 323–5; Larry Alexander, "Law and Exclusionary Reasons," *Philosophical Topics* 18 (1990): 10–11.

retributivism can do under role-relative morality is serve as a reason, albeit a possibly weighty one, to refrain from punishing the justified offender.[15] But since such a reason must be added to the balance of reasons for and against punishment, it may be insufficient to compel the acquittal of the justified.[16]

The dilemma is now clear. Either we must give up the principle of weak retributivism (and with it the more general correspondence thesis) and acquiesce to the punishment of justified offenders, or we must give up our traditional understanding of the systemic principles that currently justify our system of adjudication. More precisely, (1) either judges must violate the principle of weak retributivism and punish citizens who justifiably break the law, or they must violate the rule of law and disobey decision rules that require the punishment of the justified; similarly, (2) either system designers must violate the principle of weak retributivism and punish judges who justifiably disobey decision rules (by refusing to punish justifiably disobedient citizens), or they must violate the principles of democracy and the separation of powers by permitting the substitution of individual judicial judgment for the will of a legislative majority.

The first alternative in each of these cases appears to be the inevitable result of embracing the possibility of role-relative morality, or what I shall call "perspectivalism."[17] If institutional roles create

---

[15]   The principle of weak retributivism collapses, under this analysis, into the reflection principle. See ibid.

[16]   I say this on the assumption that the principle of weak retributivism (like the reflection principle with which it is identical on this analysis) cannot function as an exclusionary reason for action. This assumption follows from the arguments that I will make in Chapter 3 on behalf of the claim that exclusionary reasons are conceptually indefensible.

It is important to recognize that if the deontologist considers both the principle of weak retributivism and the role-relative reasons for action unique to citizens, judges, and institution designers to be both intrinsically right-making and at least practically incompatible, then the deontologist will be confronted with moral conflict that can seemingly be resolved only by the sort of moral balancing described here. For a classic discussion of deontological balancing, see W.D. Ross, *The Right and the Good* (Oxford: Clarendon Press, 1930), 16–47. Contrast Barbara Herman, "Obligation and Performance: A Kantian Account of Moral Conflict," in *Identity, Character and Morality: Essays in Moral Psychology*, eds. Owen J. Flanagan and Amelie Oksenberg Rorty (Cambridge, MA and London, England: MIT Press, 1990), 319; Barbara Herman, "The Practice of Moral Judgment," *The Journal of Philosophy* 82 (1985): 414.

[17]   As one theorist has put the perspectivalist thesis:

Decisions taken in full exercise of personal responsibility and individual accountability can lead to varying assessments regarding whether the values they promote order society's affairs so as to advance the human

---

15

new reasons for action (or eliminate otherwise valid reasons for action), the correspondence thesis is false and morality may compel the punishment of the justified. The second alternative appears to be the inevitable result of denying the possibility of role-relative morality. If citizens share with officials an identical set of reasons for action, then the correspondence thesis is true and justifiable disobedience by a citizen will justify disobedience by an official, which in turn will justify approval of that disobedience by a system designer.

SOURCES OF THE DILEMMA OF LEGAL PERSPECTIVALISM

The dilemma of legal perspectivalism would not arise if one of three things were true. First, if the content of the law perfectly mirrored the content of morality, so that citizens and officials were never called upon by law to do anything contrary to the balance of moral reasons for action, then citizens and officials would never be justified in violating the law. The dilemma of legal perspectivalism is a real dilemma only if law and morality are noncongruent.

Second, if metaethical relativism were true, the correspondence thesis would be trivially false. The truth of moral propositions would be relative to the beliefs of individuals (in the case of metaethical subjectivism) or to the beliefs of communities (in the case of metaethical conventionalism). Inasmuch as beliefs can differ, the morality of any given act could differ between individuals or communities. It would thus be trivially true that an actor might be morally justified (given her beliefs) in doing an act that another (occupying a different role) is morally justified (given his beliefs) in punishing. The puzzle generated by the incompatibility of our institutional commitments is therefore significant only if metaethical relativism is false.

Finally, if the law, *qua* law, provided reasons for unconditional obedience, then even if it did not perfectly mirror morality, it would nevertheless preclude justified disobedience by citizens. Indeed, even if

condition. Higher authority may view the situation entirely differently from nonlegislative decision-makers involved in the initial assessment of the appropriateness of a specific actor's behavior.

Rex J. Zedalis, "On First Considering Whether Law Binds," *Indiana Law Journal* (1993): 208.

It is crucial not to confuse a theory of perspectival, or role-relative morality with a theory of metaethical relativism. A theory of role-relative morality is entirely consistent with a theory of metaethical realism. Indeed, the puzzle with which I am herein concerned is only interesting if it is supposed that metaethical relativism is false. I shall argue in Chapter 2 that it is.

the law lacked the power to command unconditional obedience but possessed the power to give generally weighty reasons for obedience, we would not expect that citizens and officials would be justified in breaking the law often enough to generate a jurisprudential crisis of the sort depicted by the dilemma of legal perspectivalism.

It is to the latter two theses that I shall devote Part II. As I shall argue in its chapters, the dilemma of perspectivalism cannot be escaped either by embracing metaethical moral relativism or by defending a theory of legal authority that renders our moral duties subservient to our legal ones, because neither moral relativism nor the theories of legal authority that preclude moral disobedience are defensible. The first thesis is considerably less controversial than these latter two. Inasmuch as its defense provides us with the category of cases with which this book is concerned, it is useful to dispose of it here. We shall then be in a position to take up the presuppositions of the dilemma of perspectivalism with which there is likely to be considerable quarrel.

The content of law fairly plainly fails to cohere with the content of morality even in legal systems, like our own, that make a real effort to pass laws that accord with the demands of morality. To appreciate the possibility that a morally justified actor might be subject to punishment under Anglo-American law, let us consider first the criminal law proper and then turn to civil sanctions under tort law.

Anglo-American penal systems purport not to punish justified offenders. Sometimes this is captured by the fact that many of those who are justified in their actions are not interpreted to be "offenders" at all. The sheriff who arrests a federal mail carrier for murder while that carrier is carrying the mail *literally* "obstructs the mails," but does not *legally* obstruct the mails because his obstruction is justified. Or the sheriff who risks damage to federal property in his attempt to arrest a murderous mail carrier does not *recklessly* risk its damage because legal recklessness amounts to taking a substantial *and* unjustifiable risk.[18] In these cases, the good consequence achieved (that of apprehending a murderer) renders the sheriff's conduct nonpunishable, because the sheriff is said to lack either the *actus reus* or the *mens rea* of the offense in question. Sometimes the refusal to punish such a justified offender is captured by a separate defense, such as the

---

[18] These illustrations are loosely constructed from the facts of *United States v. Kirby,* 72 U.S. (7 Wall.) 482 (1869), in which a county sheriff was prosecuted for obstructing the mail after arresting an on-duty federal mail carrier suspected of murder. I discuss this case further in Chapter 8.

Model Penal Code's "balance of evils" defense: Conduct that is otherwise criminal is not punishable if "the harm or evil sought to be avoided by such conduct is greater than that sought to be prevented by the law defining the offense charged. . . ."[19]

Yet despite the manifest reluctance of the criminal law to punish justified offenders, it will nevertheless demand such punishment in the cases with which I will be concerned in this book. There are at least three classes of persons who cannot avail themselves of any of the legal exceptions that would warrant an acquittal. The first class consists of civilly disobedient offenders – offenders who rightly believe that a law is so immoral that it justifies illegal actions to obtain its repeal. Draft protesters, for example, might rightly think that a war is sufficiently immoral that it justifies them in trespassing into Selective Service offices to disrupt operations. However, the moral justification invoked by these protesters for violating laws on criminal trespass and the destruction of government property are not afforded legal recognition, but instead are held to be preempted by the laws that license the draft.[20]

The second class of justified offenders that our law requires judges to punish consists of offenders for whom the law has created an exception but who fail the conditions of that exception. The battered wife might rightly think that, if she does not kill her husband in his

---

[19] American Law Institute, *Model Penal Code* sec. 3.02 (Proposed Official Draft. N.p.: 1962).

[20] As section 3.02 of the *Model Penal Code* states:

> (1) Conduct which the actor believes to be necessary to avoid a harm or evil to himself or to another is justifiable, provided that:
>
> . . .
>
> (c) a legislative purpose to exclude the justification claimed does not otherwise plainly appear.

American Law Institute, *Model Penal Code* sec. 3.02. See, for example, *State v. Tate,* 102 N.J. 64, 505 A.2d 941 (1986), in which the court held that the necessity defense was unavailable to a quadriplegic who possessed marijuana for medical purposes because a state statute allowing the use of controlled substances under a physician's supervision suggested a legislative intent to exclude the defense.

For useful overviews of the history of attempts by American civil disobedients to justify legally their deliberate and open violations of the law, see Matthew Lippman, "Civil Resistance: Revitalizing International Law in the Nuclear Age," *Whittier Law Review* 13 (1992): 17–105; Martin C. Loesch, "Motive Testimony and a Civil Disobedience Justification," *Notre Dame Journal of Law, Ethics and Public Policy* 5 (1991): 1069–119. As both authors describe, American courts have consistently rejected disobedient defendants' attempts to deny the possession of culpable mens rea, as well as attempts to invoke a mistake of law defense, the necessity defense, or the so-called Nuremburg defense.

sleep, she will be unable to prevent him from taking her life. But she fails to fulfill the conditions of self-defense, because she does not bring about her husband's death while under a threat of imminent harm. In such a case, she may not be civilly disobedient (in the classic sense), because she may believe that the law is (in general) justified in requiring imminent peril as a condition for the use of deadly force, and she may not act in order to bring about any changes in that law. Nevertheless, as in cases of civil disobedience, the law of self-defense preempts her ability to invoke a *legal* justification for her (morally) justified conduct.[21]

The third class of justified offenders who are unable to avail themselves of any legal justifications consists of those offenders whose justification for violating the law is too personal to be given legal recognition by the balance of evils defense or by other exculpatory doctrines. The citizen who finds herself at a red light in the middle of the night while in the middle of nowhere may rightly conclude that, while the inconvenience of stopping is negligible, the danger to herself and others from running the red light is nil. Such a citizen may well be justified in running the red light, but the law will regard her justification as being preempted by the rules of the road.

In each of these three sorts of cases, Anglo-American criminal law demands the punishment of justified offenders. Now consider the civil law. Unlike the criminal law, the civil law by and large does not "punish" justified offenders with civil liability.[22] This is made particularly

---

[21] Thus, according to section 3.02 of the *Model Penal Code:*

   (1) Conduct which the actor believes to be necessary to avoid a harm or evil to himself or to another is justifiable, provided that:

   . . .

   (b) neither the Code nor other law defining the offense provides exceptions or defenses dealing with the specific situation involved. . . .

   American Law Institute, *Model Penal Code* sec. 3.02.

[22] Only those who maintain that the proper purpose of tort liability is to punish culpable defendants can speak of punishing the justified through civil liability without scare quotes. Those who (more plausibly) believe that tort law serves either the goal of corrective justice or the utilitarian goal of maximizing societal welfare must employ the notion of punishing the justified purely metaphorically. If tort law imposes liability on the fully justified, however, the metaphor is apt. But it is not the aptness of the metaphor that is the issue. The issue is whether the dilemma of legal perspectivalism confronts actors in civil cases as well as in criminal cases. And it does if tort law licenses or requires the imposition of tort liability on actors who have acted rightly. It is this latter claim that we are exploring now – a claim that does not depend on any particular theory of tort liability (and certainly not on a retributive theory).

clear by negligence law, which explicitly exempts from liability those who act on the balance of reasons for action. One must pay damages under the law of negligence only if one is unjustified in having taken risks that materialized in harm to a plaintiff.

Tort law is less clear about its refusal to "punish" the justified in cases that invite the application of strict liability. Insofar as tort law imposes liability in these cases without regard to the justification with which an individual caused the plaintiff's harm, it might be thought to "punish" the justified. Thus, for example, in cases like the famous *Vincent v. Lake Erie Transportation Co.*,[23] individuals are justified in using or damaging the property of others, because by so doing they prevent a greater loss to themselves. Yet the law requires that they compensate those who they justifiably injure. In cases that involve harms caused by privately owned wild animals, owners are thought to be justified in keeping the animals so long as they do so nonnegligently. Yet the law nevertheless holds them liable for all injuries that their animals cause.[24] In cases that involve injuries caused by abnormally dangerous activities, such as dynamiting tunnels or transporting gasoline, those who engage in such activities are thought to be justified in so doing if they conduct themselves nonnegligently. But they are nevertheless held liable for all injuries that they cause.[25]

On their face, these sorts of cases certainly seem to suggest that in at least some instances individuals will be civilly "punished" for morally justified conduct. But this suggestion is misleading. While the balance of reasons for action may favor the use of others' property in circumstances of necessity, or the ownership of wild animals, or abnormally dangerous activities, the balance of reasons for action in such cases probably also requires the compensation of those injured. Thus, while defendants in such cases may have justifiably caused harm, they are probably unjustified in their refusal to abide by the civil law that requires compensation for such harm. Put differently, the reasons that judges would have to exact compensation in these cases are reasons for defendants to volunteer compensation to begin with. In such cases, compensation vitiates unjust enrichment gained by the defendant at the plaintiff's expense. If redressing unjust enrichment

---

[23] 109 Minn. 456, 124 N.W. 221 (1910). In this case, the court held a shipowner liable for the loss of a dock owner's dock even though the court found that the shipowner acted reasonably in tying his ship to the dock during a storm.
[24] American Law Institute, *Restatement (Second) of Torts* sec. 509 (N.p.: 1965).
[25] American Law Institute, *Restatement (Second) of Torts* secs. 519, 520.

is a reason for a judge to require compensation, it is a reason for a citizen to offer it.[26] And defendants who in fact *wrongly* refuse to compensate those whom they injure are not *justified* offenders of the civil law. Hence, while judges should require them to compensate those whom they injure, this imposition of liability does not mean that genuinely justified offenders will be held civilly liable, because genuinely justified offenders are those who would be both justified in causing harm and justified in not paying for that harm.

Tort law thus by and large does not make genuinely justified offenders liable. The only exceptions to this are given by cases in which strict liability is imposed on defendants who neither acted negligently nor were personally enriched by conduct that caused harm to a plaintiff. I know of no uncontroversial cases, but some product liability cases have this flavor,[27] as do some cases that involve abnormally dangerous activities pursued for public (rather than private) benefit.[28] In such cases, strict liability is imposed on individuals who have done the right thing and who have not been unjustly benefitted by so doing. Unless morality provides individuals with a reason to pay for all the harms that they cause, these parties seem to have no moral reason to offer compensation to those who are injured by their justified conduct. Insofar as tort law imposes liability anyway, it "punishes" the justified.

It is thus contingently true that, in our legal system, criminal and civil liability is sometimes imposed on actors who act morally. But some would go further. Some would claim that it is necessarily true that, in all legal systems, the content of law must depart from the content of morality. Hence, it is necessarily true that the law will call for the punishment of the justified.

Fred Schauer, for example, has recently argued that legal rules are

---

[26] The thesis that unjust enrichment constitutes a morally legitimate reason for the imposition of civil liability has been advanced by Jules Coleman, *Markets, Morals and the Law* (Cambridge and New York: Cambridge University Press, 1988), 166–201; Jeffrie G. Murphy and Jules L. Coleman, *The Philosophy of Law: An Introduction to Jurisprudence* (Totowa, NJ: Rowman & Allanheld, 1984), 167–89; Jules Coleman, "Moral Theories of Torts: Their Scope and Limits: Part II," *Law and Philosophy* 2 (1983): 5–36; George Fletcher, "Fairness and Utility in Tort Theory," *Harvard Law Review* 85 (1972): 537–73. See also Heidi M. Hurd, "Correcting Injustice to Corrective Justice," *Notre Dame Law Review* 67 (1991): 62–84 (discussing Jules Coleman's unjust enrichment theory of tort liability).

[27] *Seigler v. Kuhlman*, 81 Wash. 2d 448, 502 P.2d 1181 (1973); *Koos v. Roth*, 293 Or. 670, 652 P.2d 1255 (1982).

[28] *Brody v. Overlook Hospital*, 121 N.J. Super. 299, 296 A.2d 688 (1972) (reversal affirmed 66 N.J. 448, 332 A.2d 596 (1975)).

necessarily suboptimal in comparison to moral rules.[29] Legal rules are, for Schauer, a species of prescriptive rules authored to guide the behavior of others.[30] Prescriptive rules are probabilistic generalizations that are inevitably over- and underinclusive.[31] Not all dogs create annoying disturbances, and many things that are not dogs do create such disturbances; hence, a rule prohibiting dogs from public buildings, while probabilistically related to the justification for that rule, is simultaneously over- and underinclusive. As Schauer maintains, "it is logically impossible for a rule to generate a result for a particular case superior to the result that would have been generated in the absence of rules, but . . . it is indeed quite possible for rules to generate results in particular cases that are inferior to those generated without them."[32] As he explains:

> In many cases, indeed in most cases, the result indicated by applying a rule will be the same as the result indicated by directly applying the rule's background justifications. . . . But . . . there will be some cases in which the result indicated by the rule will be inferior to the result indicated by direct application of its justification. Yet these instances will not be accompanied by any offsetting instances in the opposite direction.
>
> . . .
>
> The only standard for measurement would be the one ultimate justification, and thus the result indicated by that justification would by definition be the best for any particular case. Consequently, any rule-indicated result diverging from the justification-indicated result would *eo ipso* be an inferior result.[33]

Schauer's claim that legal rules must necessarily depart from moral rules depends on the assumption that the function of legal rules is to guide action. From this assumption, Schauer reaches his necessity claim in two steps: (1) For legal rules to guide action more effectively than do moral rules, legal rules must be clearer, simpler, and more accessible than are the rules of morality. (2) To possess these features, legal rules must be over- and underinclusive vis-a-vis the more complex, shaded reasons for action that morality provides.

I shall not pursue whether Schauer is correct either in assuming

---

[29] Frederick F. Schauer, *Playing by the Rules: A Philosophical Examination of Rule-Based Decision-Making in Law and in Life* (Oxford: Clarendon Press, 1991), 100–2.
[30] Ibid., 17–37. [31] Ibid., 31–4. [32] Ibid., 101. [33] Ibid., 100–1.

that the function of law is to guide conduct or in calculating that law must necessarily depart from morality to fulfill that function. It is sufficient for our purposes to note that actual legal systems do in fact punish some justified offenders because such systems lack a legal defense for every case in which a disobedient citizen has a moral justification. It follows from this fact alone that, unless the law itself provides citizens with an overriding moral reason to obey the law, there will be cases in which individuals are morally justified in violating the law. And unless moral relativism is our best explanation of the nature of moral judgments, the possibility of such violations suggests that morality is itself deeply paradoxical. If our moral values include our systemic ones, morality may compel some persons to violate the law while simultaneously compelling others to punish them for their fully justified disobedience. That is, morality may pit us against one another in moral combat.

Part II

Sources of the Dilemma
of Legal Perspectivalism

As was made clear in Chapter 1, the dilemma of legal perspectivalism is a product of three presuppositions: (1) that the content of law departs from the content of morality; (2) that the content of morality is not relative to individual or communally held beliefs; and (3) that the authority of law departs from the authority of morality. In Chapter 1, I defended the first of these presuppositions. In this part I shall take up the second and third presuppositions in an attempt to determine whether we must indeed choose between the jurisprudential axioms that the dilemma of legal perspectivalism makes incompatible. In Chapter 2, I shall advance reasons to think moral relativism indefensible. In Chapter 3, I shall demonstrate the indefensibility of the dominant theory of legal authority – the theory of practical authority – which defends the power of law to trump morality in instances in which the two diverge. In Chapter 4, I shall similarly criticize a popular variation on this theory – one which holds that the law, while lacking the power to trump morality, nevertheless possesses influential authority, and so is entitled to such weighty respect that only on the rarest occasions will one be entitled to set it aside in the name of morality. In Chapters 5 and 6, I shall explore two accounts of how law might be evidential of, but not paramount to, morality. I shall defend in Chapter 6 the theory that only morality can obligate us, because law can possess, at most, theoretical authority. If persuasive, the chapters of this part collectively render the dilemma of legal perspectivalism a robust one. That is, they make it clear that we cannot escape a choice between our most basic jurisprudential principles. Either we must abandon the principle of weak retributivism and license the punishment of those who act morally by violating the law, or we must revise our understanding of the obligations imposed on legal actors by our institutional commitments to the rule of law, democracy, and the separation of state powers.

Chapter 2

The Rejection of Moral Relativism

The first presupposition of the dilemma of legal perspectivalism is that moral relativism is an indefensible account of the nature of morals. Were it otherwise, the correspondence thesis would be false and the dilemma posed in Chapter 1 would be illusory.[1] Recall that the correspondence thesis asserts that the justifiability of an action determines the justifiability of permitting or preventing that action. The defense of this thesis relies on two claims. The first claim is that the reasons for action that determine the morality of conduct are objective, in the sense that their right-making characteristics are universal. If it is right for an actor to do an act, it must be right for all others that she do it. The second claim is that, where other persons face a choice between alternative actions that will or will not thwart the actor's course of conduct, the rightness of the actor's conduct entails the wrongness of any actions that will thwart it.

If relativism provides the best understanding of the nature of normative judgments, then the first claim upon which the defense of the correspondence thesis rests must be false, and the dilemma of legal perspectivalism must be without bite. After all, if the morality of an action is relative to the beliefs of either individuals or communities, then, inasmuch as the beliefs of persons and the conventions of communities can differ, so too can the morality of similar or codependent actions. It is simply false that reasons for action are objective, in the

---

[1] While the dilemma of legal perspectivalism presupposes that metaethical relativism is false, it does not presuppose that metaethical realism is true. Some noncognitivists believe that they can duplicate virtually all of the claims made by metaethical realists. See, for example, Simon Blackburn, *Spreading the Word* (Oxford: Clarendon Press, 1984); Jeremy Waldron, "The Irrelevance of Moral Objectivity," in *Natural Law Theory*, ed. Robert P. George (Oxford: Clarendon Press, 1992), 158–87. If they are right, then the question of whether morality is role-relative is as significant for them as for moral realists.

sense that their right-making characteristics are universal. Inasmuch as one actor may believe it right to do act A, while others may believe it wrong for her to do act A, it may be right for the actor to do act A and wrong for others that she do it. It follows trivially that one actor may be morally justified (given his beliefs) in thwarting or punishing an action that another actor (given her beliefs) is morally justified in performing. The puzzle generated in Chapter 1 is thus a genuine one only if moral relativism is false. It is my project in this chapter to advance reasons sufficient to think that moral relativism is indeed false.[2] If persuasive, these reasons bolster the claim that the dilemma of legal perspectivalism is a real one, requiring us either to abandon the correspondence thesis (and its satellite principle of weak retributivism) or to forfeit systemic values that have long been thought unassailable.

FIVE THESES OF MORAL RELATIVISM

Those who defend moral relativism may be making any one of (or any combination of) the following five arguments. First, they may be making the radical metaphysical claim that moral propositions possess no singular truth value: The truth value of moral propositions is relative to the beliefs of the individuals who assert or deny them (in the case of moral subjectivism) or to the conventional acceptance or rejection of them by a given reference group (in the case of moral conventionalism). Hence, what may be right for one may be simultaneously wrong for another in like circumstances. Second, those who describe themselves as moral relativists may be making the quite different metaphysical claim that at least some moral judgments are incommensurable: There literally is no truth of the matter concerning the comparative morality of certain actions. Hence, in at least some cases, there will be no answer to the question of whether an action that thwarts the justified action of another is all-things-considered right or wrong.

Third, and much more modestly, self-described moral relativists may simply be making the empirical observation that persons and communities disagree about morals. Fourth, they may be asserting the epistemological claim that, given the empirical disagreement about

---

[2] I have advanced a more extensive and detailed critique of moral relativism in Heidi M. Hurd, "Relativistic Jurisprudence: Skepticism Founded on Confusion," *Southern California Law Review* 61 (1988), Note.

the truth of moral propositions, the justifiability for asserting moral propositions must be considered relative to the beliefs of those individuals or groups making the assertions. Finally, those who defend moral relativism may be making the semantic point that there exists no language of comparison by which to adjudicate the meaning of moral terms when used by individuals or groups who appear to disagree about moral matters: The term "right" as used by Hitler may have meant something different than the term "right" as used by Ghandi; hence, contrary to appearances, Hitler and Ghandi may not, in fact, have harbored any moral disagreements (although there exists no means of translating their uses of the term "right" so as to establish the truth or falsity of such a suggestion).

Inasmuch as the correspondence thesis is a metaphysical thesis, only the first two of these five theses of moral relativism pose genuine challenges to it. Persons and communities may well disagree among themselves concerning the truth of certain moral propositions (the third empirical thesis), and hence it may not be possible to attain agreement about the rightness of an individual's action – that is, about the balance of reasons for action that determines the morality of that person's conduct.[3] But this fact alone does not establish that such a set of reasons does not objectively exist; it simply means that we cannot now reach agreement about its specification. That we cannot agree about the content of morality in all its fine detail does not entail that we cannot reach reasoned conclusions about the general relationship between moral obligations and permissions – such as, for example, the conclusion embodied in the correspondence thesis that, whatever the content of morality, its provisions cannot make codependent actions morally gladiatorial.

Similarly, the justification with which persons assert moral propositions may well be (and indeed, presumably is) relative to the information and cognitive resources available to them. It may thus be justifiable for one person to defend the morality of an action while it is simultaneously justifiable for another (possessed of different information or cognitive capacities) to contest the morality of that same action (the fourth epistemological thesis). Again, however, this claim alone is insufficient to dispel the thesis that moral disputes have

---

[3] For thoughtful defenses of the thesis that *irreconcilable* moral disagreement (born of irresolvable moral conflict) is compatible with moral objectivity, see Stuart Hampshire, *Morality and Conflict* (Cambridge, MA: Harvard University Press, 1983), 151–5, and Judith Wagner DeCrew, "Moral Conflicts and Ethical Relativism," *Ethics* 101 (1990): 27–41.

determinate right answers. It is thus insufficient to defeat the conclusion of the correspondence thesis that, while two parties may be justified in thwarting each other's actions, one is ultimately right to do so and one is ultimately wrong. Indeed, as I shall argue, since we consider beliefs to be justified to the extent that we think that they come close to approximating what is true, it is impossible to construct a theory of moral justification that does not presuppose an independent theory of moral truth. Thus, when our theory of justification commits us to the view that two persons are each justified in defending conflicting moral judgments, we have reason to attempt to further hone our theory of justification so that it will enable us to declare the true judgment the more justified of the two.

Finally, if the language employed by different persons or groups of persons is incommensurable (the semantic thesis), then it may be impossible to know whether a person who thwarts another's right action does so as a result of moral disagreement, moral confusion, moral ignorance, or moral psychopathy. But the unavailability of a common moral language does not spell the nonexistence of objective criteria of moral action.[4] Hence, it remains fully coherent to assert a moral correspondence between codependent actions while admitting (if necessary) that we may lack a common language by which we can talk about the metaphysics of morals with any guarantee that there will be a meeting of minds.

On the other hand, if either of the first two theses of moral relativism is true, the correspondence thesis is in jeopardy and a defense of legal perspectivalism may pose no dilemma at all. Because it is possible to dispense quickly with the argument against the moral correspondence of codependent actions predicated on the second thesis of moral relativism, let me pursue the above two theses in their reverse order. I will first take up the claim that some moral judgments are incommensurable and, hence, that some codependent actions may lack any moral correspondence. I will then devote the remainder of the chapter to the first thesis, that the truth value of moral judgments can vary between individuals or groups and, hence, that the morality of two actors' codependent actions may not correspond.

---

[4]   As I shall make clear in the third section of this chapter, those defending the first thesis of moral relativism may rely on a theory of semantic relativism to bolster their metaphysical claims. It nevertheless remains their metaphysical claims that challenge the truth of the correspondence thesis, not the semantic claims that they advance in the course of their defense.

MORAL INCOMMENSURABILITY
AND MORAL CORRESPONDENCE

If one believes that things of value, including actions, can be incommensurable, then one may think of oneself as well-equipped to contest the correspondence thesis. If two apparently codependent actions are of incommensurable value, then it cannot be said that the morality of one corresponds with (or in any other way relates to) the morality of the other.

To say that two actions are of incommensurate value is to deny both that one is better than the other and that they are of equal value. Joseph Raz describes "the mark of incommensurability" as a failure of transitivity. As he says:

> We have here a simple way of determining whether two options are incommensurate given that it is known that neither is better than the other. If it is possible for one of them to be improved without thereby becoming better than the other, or if there can be another option which is better than the one but not better than the other, then the two original options are incommensurate.[5]

Raz argues that, where the considerations for and against available alternatives are incommensurate, reason is indeterminate. In such cases, he argues, morality affords persons an extensive sphere of freedom in which they enjoy permissions to choose among mutually incompatible options. "Since it follows that there is no reason to shun one of the alternatives in favor of the other, we are in a sense free to choose which course to follow."[6]

Those who would call themselves moral relativists by virtue of embracing the claim that values can be incommensurate in Raz's sense are employing a bizarre understanding of the concept of relativism. Nothing in the claim that two values are incomparable suggests that their value is relative to anything. Nothing in the claim that reason is indeterminate when confronted with incommensurate options suggests that morality can defy the constraints of reason so as to be contradictory. It is thus, strictly speaking, a misnomer to treat claims of incommensurability as claims of moral relativism. However, since

---

[5] Joseph Raz, *The Morality of Freedom* (Oxford: Clarendon Press, 1986), 325–6. Joseph Raz is, of course, no moral relativist. However, his formulation of the concept of incommensurability might well be employed to defend a skeptical conclusion about the existence of universal right-making characteristics.

[6] Ibid., 334.

those who describe themselves as moral relativists may only mean that they endorse moral incommensurability, I shall pursue the argument from incommensurability as an argument for metaethical skepticism about objective claims of moral correspondence.

There are two conceptions of freedom that self-described relativists might be after in co-opting the notion of incommensurability to defeat the correspondence thesis. First, they might be using the concept of incommensurability to argue that, when actions are of incommensurate value, persons possess *permissions* to engage in them, even if in so doing they will thwart another in doing likewise. Second, they might be using the concept of incommensurability to argue that, when two actions are of incommensurate value, persons are *at liberty* (in a Hohfeldian sense) to engage in those actions, even at the cost of canceling one another's efforts.

The distinction between having a permission and being at liberty is important here,[7] although in the end neither concept enables moral relativists to contest the correspondence thesis. To have a permission to do an act (in the traditional sense in which that piece of moral machinery is employed) is to have a right to do that act. In Wesley Hohfeld's terms, it is to be in a position in which (1) others have no right that one not do the act, and (2) others have a duty not to interfere with one's doing the act.[8] To be at liberty, however, is to have (under a Hohfeldian analysis) merely a privilege to do an act. When one has a privilege to do an act, others have no right that one not do the act, but others also have no duty not to interfere with that act.[9]

Those who seek to use the concept of incommensurability to argue that permissions can compete in ways that violate the correspondence thesis invite conceptual confusion. If permissions constitute rights and rights give rise to duties of noninterference on the part of others (as they do by any standard theory of the nature of rights), then two persons cannot have permissions that license them to act in ways that confound the other's efforts. Thus, while there may be actions of incommensurate value that generate rights on the part of individual

---

[7] This distinction is put to a similar use in Chapter 11 by deontologists who dispute the correspondence thesis by arguing that, while obligations cannot conflict, permissions can. The arguments that I advance here to demonstrate the endurance of the correspondence thesis in the face of claims about moral incommensurability are precursors to those made in Chapter 11 in the face of claims about the asymmetry of obligations and permissions.

[8] Wesley Newcomb Hohfeld, *Fundamental Legal Conceptions*, ed. W.W. Cook (New Haven: Yale University Press, 1919), 36–9.

[9] Ibid., 41.

actors to choose between them, the rights generated cannot justify one actor in doing something that thwarts what another actor has a right to do. In short, one cannot contest the correspondence thesis by invoking the concept of moral incommensurability to make sense of conflicting moral rights.

Those who seek to use the concept of moral incommensurability to argue for competing privileges invite less obvious confusion. If one has a Hohfeldian privilege to do an act, then others have no right that one not do the act. But others may still have a right to interfere with one's act, and in such a case one has no right that they not intervene. The correspondence thesis appears to be at risk, because the liberty that licenses one to act does not imply an absence of liberty on the part of another to prevent one's act.

The problem that confronts those who would employ the concept of moral incommensurability to generate (Hohfeldian) privileges that violate the correspondence thesis is that the actions so privileged lack moral value of any sort, while the correspondence thesis is about the relationship between actions that possess moral value. Liberties of the Hohfeldian sort define arenas of amoral action. Actors within such arenas are not bound by any maxims of action – they are genuinely at liberty. They have no obligations, but they also have no rights. Hence, when in a state of liberty (conceived of in Hohfeldian terms), actors are both unconstrained and unprotected by morality. That their actions may conflict is thus of no normative importance, because their actions are of no normative importance. They are the actions of those in a moral state of nature. Because the correspondence thesis is a thesis about the conditions of moral action, it is neither troubling, nor even surprising, that it is inapplicable to amoral actions.

In the end, then, an appeal to the incommensurability of values to generate skeptical arguments against the correspondence thesis fails. Some actions may well be of incommensurate value, and reason may well be indeterminate when one is choosing among a set of such actions. But if the indeterminacy of reason generates a right to choose among various incommensurate options, then it must be the case that those options do not include actions that would prevent others from pursuing options to which they have a right. Similarly, if the indeterminacy of reason generates a (Hohfeldian) privilege to choose among various incommensurate options, then it must be the case that those options are not of moral importance, and hence it must be the case that any choice that conflicts with another's choice is not a violation of the correspondence thesis.

Thus, the correspondence thesis cannot be challenged by those who predicate a theory of moral relativism on a theory of moral incommensurability. As such, the dilemma of legal perspectivalism, relying as it does on the correspondence thesis, remains as confounding as before. If the correspondence thesis is right, then judges should abide by the principle of weak retributivism and refuse to punish citizens in circumstances in which their legal violations are morally justified. However, if judges substitute moral judgments for legal rules whenever the law departs from morality, judges become legislators, and the rule of law, democracy, and the separation of powers become institutionally unattainable goals.

METAETHICAL RELATIVISM
AND MORAL CORRESPONDENCE

A more promising means of denying the grip of the dilemma of legal perspectivalism by rejecting the correspondence thesis is available to those who defend the first, more radical thesis of moral relativism – the thesis that all moral propositions lack a determinate truth value. It is this metaethical claim that captures the conventional meaning of the phrase "moral relativism," and it is this claim that is typically made by those seeking to dispute the objectivity of moral judgments by defending the ontological relativity of moral propositions. On this theory, the truth value of moral propositions is relative to a particular set of beliefs.

Metaethical moral relativism captures two sorts of theories: subjectivist theories and conventionalist theories. A *subjectivist* maintains that the truth of moral judgments is relative to the beliefs of those individuals who assert or deny them. A *conventionalist* believes that the truth of moral propositions is relative to the beliefs or conventions of a reference community. Thus, while an individual cannot be wrong about the morality of an action on a subjectivist theory (except to the extent that she may be wrong about her own beliefs), an individual can be wrong about the morality of an action on a conventionalist theory, because her beliefs can fail to comport with the conventions of her community. In part out of concerns for economy, and in part because conventionalism is the more prevalent of the two versions of radical moral relativism (because most theorists think that individuals can make moral mistakes), I shall concentrate on conventionalist theories of ethics. The arguments advanced both for and against such theories, however, are for the most part applicable to subjectivist theories as well.

Metaethical moral relativists of either stripe dispute the objectivity of moral judgments, and so argue, for example, that it is both morally right that our ancestors kept slaves and morally wrong for us to do so today. Similarly, active euthanasia is morally right for the Inuit today, but simultaneously morally wrong for the British. Abortion is morally right for those who are pro-choice, and morally wrong for those who are pro-life. As William Frankena says:

> [W]hat is right or good for one individual or society is not right or good for another, even if the situations involved are similar, meaning not merely that what is thought right or good by one is not thought right or good by another . . . but that what is *really* right or good in the one case is not so in another.[10]

And as Phillipa Foot argues, "Local truth is the only substantive truth that we have, and it is this truth that we tacitly claim for our [moral] opinions when we express them."[11] We must recognize, she says, that if moral relativism is true, then "judgments opposed to our own are true by some other peoples' standards as ours are true by ours, and . . . there is no choosing between them on objective grounds."[12] Whether relative to local community standards or to the standards of the individual, moral judgments must proceed "without the slightest thought that [those] . . . standards are 'correct'."[13]

It follows easily from a metaethical theory of moral relativity that the correspondence thesis is false. Inasmuch as codependent actions may be conventionally believed to be morally asymmetrical by those who engage in them, one actor may act rightly in thwarting what another actor rightly does. To defeat this preliminary challenge to the correspondence thesis, one cannot employ the strategy of the previous section and accuse those who defend the first thesis of moral

---

[10] William K. Frankena, *Ethics*, 2d ed. (Englewood Cliffs, NJ: Prentice-Hall, 1973), 109.

[11] Phillipa Foot, "Moral Relativism," in *Relativism: Cognitive and Moral*, eds. Michael Krausz and Jack W. Meiland (Notre Dame, IN: University of Notre Dame Press, 1982), 161.

[12] Ibid., 162. As Oliver Wendell Holmes famously quipped, talk of objective values is but a reference to "a brooding omnipresence in the sky." *Southern Pacific Co. v. Jensen*, 244 U.S. 205, 222 (1917).

[13] Foot, "Moral Relativism," 155.

relativism of failing to understand the implications of their own theory. Metaethical moral relativists are not mistaken in their conviction that if they are right, the correspondence thesis is wrong. Thus, while it was unnecessary in the previous section to take up the merits of the arguments made on behalf of moral incommensurability (because, as I demonstrated, the correspondence thesis is ultimately unaffected by the truth of claims about moral incommensurability), it is absolutely necessary to take up the merits of metaethical moral relativism. In what follows, I shall outline a series of four objections to radical moral relativism, each in response to increasingly sophisticated attempts to defend it. In brief, I shall argue first that moral relativism does not lead to the conclusion that moral beliefs which are incompatible with one's own must be tolerated, and it thus does not generate the sort of principle of universal tolerance that those motivated to defend moral relativism in the name of tolerance have supposed. Second, inasmuch as moral relativism declares moral the most abhorrent cultural practices and beliefs, its claims about the content of morality appear to be simply false. Third, metaethical moral relativism is conceptually indefensible because it either violates a fundamental principle of logic – the principle of bivalence – or invokes the claims of semantic relativism and invites, thereby, both a vicious regress and a damning reductio ad absurdum. Fourth, moral conventionalism collapses into moral subjectivism, and so generates the same problems that initially motivate most moral relativists to declare subjectivism indefensible.

Tolerating Intolerance

Many declared relativists are motivated to defend the tenets of relativism because they suppose that those tenets result in a principle of tolerance requiring nonintervention in the habits, beliefs, and practices of groups other than their own. As the anthropologist Melville Herskovits declared, "in practice, the philosophy of relativism is a philosophy of tolerance."[14] It is thought that the principle of tolerance follows from the argument that, if all moral conventions are equally true, then no group is justified in imposing its values on other groups.

---

[14] Melville J. Herskovits, *Cultural Relativism: Perspectives in Cultural Pluralism* (New York: Random House, 1972), 31. Herskovits had said years earlier that relativism "is a philosophy which, in recognizing the values set up by every society to guide its own life, lays stress on the dignity inherent in every body of custom, and on the need for tolerance of conventions though they may differ from one's own." Melville J. Herskovits, *Man and His Works* (New York: A.A. Knopf, 1948), 76.

To make cross-cultural or intercommunal moral judgments is to engage in a kind of ethical imperialism. Because all moral conventions
must be said to be equally correct, all moral beliefs must be equally
deserving of respect. Thus, the truth of moral relativism, it is argued,
gives rise to a principle of tolerance that constrains our intervention
into the practices of groups whose moral beliefs differ from our own.[15]

Yet relativists who are motivated to defend moral relativism because they think it grounds a principle of tolerance are guilty of two
related mistakes. First, the principle of tolerance that they defend is
not itself relativized to a unique set of standards or beliefs. As the
principle is formulated, it imposes absolute obligations on any group
faced with moral claims that conflict with its own. Yet to advance
such a principle is clearly inconsistent with defending the moral relativism that motivates it. As Bernard Williams explains, such a relativist reaches a conclusion "about what is right and wrong in one's
dealings with other societies, which uses a *nonrelative* sense of 'right'
not allowed for [by the theory of relativism]."[16] And as Geoffrey Harrison has formulated the problem, the doctrine of moral relativism is
a metaethical theory, the truth or falsity of which is subject to empirical testing. To be a relativist is to be an outside observer of moral systems. The advocacy of tolerance, however, implies an abandonment of
any outside perspective: The advocate becomes a moral participant
whose judgments must then be considered relative to a particular
moral standpoint. Relativists are thus barred from making the moral
judgment that everyone should be tolerant of opposing views, because to make such a claim would imply that they are giving up the
external perspective that makes them relativists to begin with.[17]

---

[15]   It is somewhat difficult for us to recognize that the value which we attribute
to our civilization is due to the fact that we participate in this civilization,
and that it has been controlling all our actions since the time of our birth; but
it is certainly conceivable that there may be other civilizations, based perhaps on different traditions and on a different equilibrium of emotion and
reason, which are of no less value than ours, although it may be impossible
for us to appreciate their values without having grown up under their influence. The general theory of valuation of human activities, as taught by
anthropological research, teaches us a higher tolerance. . . .

Franz Boas, "The Mind of Primitive Man," *Journal of American Folklore* 14
(1901): 11.

[16]   Bernard A.O. Williams, *Morality: An Introduction to Ethics* (New York: Harper &
Row, 1972), 21.

[17]   Geoffrey Harrison, "Relativism and Tolerance," in *Relativism: Cognitive and
Moral,* eds. Michael Krausz and Jack W. Meiland (Notre Dame, IN: University
of Notre Dame Press, 1982), 239.

Second, and relatedly, groups who do not adopt any internal principle of tolerance must be considered by relativists to be unconstrained in the extent to which they can impose their values on others. Put differently, if a community does not consider tolerance a value, then tolerance is not a value for it; hence, that community should not (given its conventions) be tolerant of those whose conventions it rejects. Rather than enjoining the intolerant to be tolerant, moral relativism licenses intolerance in all those who do not already value it. It thus has precisely the opposite implication for tolerance from that derived by its principle advocates.[18]

Of course, advocates of moral relativism could urge its adoption because they find that it breeds tolerance in those who embrace it (however irrational that may be). But while a commitment to moral relativism may remove the motivation to be intolerant, there is nothing internal to the theory which precludes a relativist from maintaining that, since all values are equal, one is justified (by virtue of failing to endorse a principle of tolerance) in imposing one's values on others. As Max Hocutt has argued, "there is nothing to prevent a relativist from condemning a social institution or a social order simply on the grounds that it is not the sort he prefers."[19] Although a relativist may not appeal to a higher authority to condemn a moral practice, that practice may be denounced solely on the basis that it offends *his* conception of the content of morality.

While arguments that demonstrate the fallacy of deriving tolerance from moral relativism do nothing to dispute the truth of moral relativism, they go a long way toward undermining the standard motivation for defending it. Many students are quick to give up their initially spirited defense of relativism when they recognize that they cannot employ it in defense of a liberal agenda. Of course, those who adopt moral relativism as a means of defeating the correspondence thesis may plausibly claim that they were never motivated to defend moral relativism by a desire to promote tolerance at all. After all, if

---

18   Nicholas Sturgeon has further argued that, while relativism may provide "a platform from which to object to the widespread assumption in our own society that other peoples have a great deal to learn from our superior moral insights," it also implies that we have nothing to learn from the insights of others. By advocating a simple retreat to our own standards when we are faced with moral disagreement, relativism may reduce moral discussion and, with it, the opportunity to understand other viewpoints. Nicholas L. Sturgeon, "Moral Disagreement and Moral Relativism," *Social Philosophy and Policy* 11 (1994): 111–4.

19   Max Hocutt, "Must Relativists Tolerate Evil?" *The Philosophical Forum* 17 (1986): 197.

they were motivated by a commitment to tolerance, they might be inclined to embrace a thesis that precluded one actor from thwarting the justified actions of another. Hence, demonstrating that a defense of moral relativism is incompatible with a plea for universal tolerance may do little to persuade those seeking to defeat the correspondence thesis to abandon as their means the tenets of moral relativism. Let me then leave this line of argument behind in favor of one that goes, not to the motivation for relativism, but to its moral defensibility.

Making Evil Moral

It is fallacious to think that relativism generates a principle of tolerance. It remains true, however, that the relativist is committed to thinking that all moral beliefs are of equal truth so long as they cohere with the set of beliefs to which their truth is relative. In the relativist's view, the only criterion that must be met to count a moral belief as true is that the belief represents the attitudes of the community to which it is applied. Relativism thus recognizes the potential of anything to become moral. As Sanford Kadish has suggested concerning a relativist's view of due process: "If and when . . . lynching of child sex murderers ceases to offend the conscience of enough of the community, the state's sponsoring of such activity would presumably be consistent with due process of law."[20]

Because relativists cannot appeal to any absolute "external" standard of moral truth by which to criticize seemingly immoral beliefs, they are limited to what may be called "internal criticism."[21] A group's beliefs and practices can be internally criticized by showing that the beliefs rest on inconsistent, and hence, irrational conventions. Thus, a group's belief that abortion is moral may be criticized if the group is also found to believe both that abortion is the taking of a person's life and that the taking of a person's life is immoral. But what of evil beliefs and practices that are entirely consistent and internally coherent? What of a society of cannibals? – a society that believes in the torture of baby boys as a means of making them tough? – a community of slave owners? – a group that believes in ethnic cleansing? – the Ku Klux Klan? If we assume that the beliefs of these groups can

---

[20] Sanford Kadish, "Methodology and Criteria in Due Process Adjudication: A Survey and Criticism," *Yale Law Journal* 66 (1958): 345.

[21] As Joseph Bingham maintained, there exists "no external measure of the correctness or incorrectness of a particular assertion of moral rectitude or delinquency." Joseph Bingham, "The Nature of Legal Rights and Duties," *Michigan Law Review* 12 (1913): 2.

be made internally consistent (and such an assumption is plausible, because the relativist must inevitably endorse a substantively neutral, and thus weak, theory of rationality[22]), the relativist must admit that the practices in which these groups engage are beyond criticism. The relativist must thus consider moral the perpetuation of barbarism, chauvinism, racism, sadism, ethnic cleansing, religious persecution, slavery, prostitution, gang warfare, and so on.

Some moral relativists have performed surprising contortions in an attempt to deny that moral relativism necessarily makes moral what is (consistently) evil. Max Hocutt, for example, insists that relativists can condemn a society's most basic moral and legal standards, not by appealing to inconsistencies within these standards, but by employing external principles or values that themselves escape "absolutist" proportions.[23] Hocutt suggests two strategies by which relativists may succeed at "external criticism": (1) They may find the standards of another society to be contrary to the interests of those within that society; or (2) they may find the standards of another society to be "contrary to [their] personal preferences or the values of [their] hearers."[24]

To employ the first strategy, Hocutt argues, relativists must differentiate between "calling an action *right* and calling it *morally right*."[25] To ask whether an action is morally right, claims Hocutt, is merely to ask whether it is consistent with a group's conventions. To ask whether an action is right, however, is to ask "whether the agent would do well to prefer it" after taking into account "everything of relevance."[26] When the demands of convention conflict with an agent's interests, the agent is under a moral obligation to do what is contrary to reason. Because agents should never perform acts that are contrary to reason, Hocutt argues, agents should not perform moral obligations that conflict with their interests. Thus, the first strategy available to the relativist for externally criticizing a community's values is to examine whether the community's values are consistent with the interests of its members.

Hocutt supposes that this strategy provides the relativist with sufficient fodder to morally criticize or condemn the Nazi. The attack

---

[22] That is, the relativist cannot build into a theory of rationality the canon that the immoral is irrational, because to do so would constitute an abandonment of the relativist's central tenet that morality is a feature, not of rationality, but of collective conventions. Thus, the relativist cannot, without abandoning relativism, insist that Naziism could never be made consistent, because such an argument would presuppose a defense of why evil beliefs are inherently irrational.

[23] Hocutt, "Must Relativists Tolerate Evil?", 188–9.

[24] Ibid., 188.   [25] Ibid., 192.   [26] Ibid., 192.

goes as follows. Although the Nazi was morally obligated to support the party's goals, such goals were contrary to his interests and, hence, contrary to reason. The Nazi thus should not have supported the goals of Naziism. Naziism is evil, Hocutt claims, not because it is internally inconsistent, but because it is contrary to the interests of Nazi supporters, and hence is irrational.

Hocutt's first strategy, however, meets with a series of difficulties, most of which stem from his claim to provide a basis for external criticism that does not rely on objective moral premises. Yet if Hocutt has provided a source of external criticism, he has done so by smuggling in moral assumptions that are objective – a strategy that implies the abandonment of moral relativism. If, on the other hand, his thesis is construed as successfully avoiding a commitment to moral objectivity, then his thesis fails to provide relativists with a means of making *external* criticisms.

Hocutt explicitly admits that his first strategy for affording moral relativists a means of external criticism rests on the premise that persons ought to do what they would do well to prefer. Such a premise is an objective one in two respects. First, this premise is advanced as a universal maxim that is true in all circumstances for all persons, regardless of any beliefs to the contrary that some might harbor. Second, it presupposes that one can evaluate the rationality of another's ends – a presupposition that smuggles in an objectivist claim that there is some fact of the matter that determines what an agent ought to prefer. Thus, Hocutt violates his own relativism on two counts.

To eschew any reliance on objective moral claims, Hocutt must adopt the more modest thesis that the practices of a group can be criticized whenever they fail to be the most instrumentally efficacious means of accomplishing a group's goals. This strategy does not engage the relativist in an evaluation of a group's ends, only in an appraisal of its means. Yet such a thesis hardly offers an opportunity for the type of external criticism hoped for by Hocutt. It leaves relativists to evaluate whether the Nazis adopted efficient means to their ends without enabling relativists to say anything about those ends. And surely it was the Nazis' ends, and not the efficacy of their means, that demands scrutiny.[27]

---

[27] For a similar defense of relativists' ability to engage in external criticism, see Charles Sayward, "System Relatism," *Ratio* 1 (1988): 173–4. Sayward claims that moral codes may be ranked relative to the purposes with which persons adhere to moral codes. He then denies that one engages in moral judgment when saying that "relative to this or that purpose this code is better than that code."

At this point, Hocutt might resort to a defense of his second strategy for enabling relativists to engage in external criticism. Relativists, he argues, may condemn moral institutions on the grounds that such institutions are contrary to their own values or to the values of their audience. Nothing prevents the relativist, Hocutt insists, from harshly judging a principle or practice simply on the grounds that "he doesn't like it."[28] Yet such a strategy threatens a retreat to pure emotivism. It appears to be a desperate attempt to ground criticism in the highly relativistic but incorrigible world of sentiment. While this attempt preserves the externality of moral judgment, it abandons the function of criticism. To criticize a community's moral standards is not merely to respond to them emotionally; it is, rather, to provide reasoned arguments for adopting or rejecting those standards. The adoption of an emotivist thesis faces one squarely with the incommensurability of emotions: If all Nazis prefer or value or enjoy killing Jews, and all Americans find such killings repulsive, barbaric, and horrific, what help is Hocutt's second strategy in deciding whose preferences or moral sentiments should prevail? The answer is clear: None.

Hocutt thus fails in his attempt to square moral relativism with external criticism. He returns us to the objection to relativism with which we began: The most evil practices imaginable must be thought moral if consistently practiced by a community. Such an objection suggests that moral relativism is false, because when a moral theory entails that anything under the sun can be moral, it is not clear in what sense it is a viable moral theory.

The problems that follow seek to demonstrate not only that moral relativism is morally unpalatable, but that it is also conceptually indefensible. Either it implies a violation of the principle of bivalence, and so becomes incoherent, or it collapses into radical subjectivism, and so makes moral discourse meaningless.[29]

Yet, in a manner that is reminiscent of Hocutt's first strategy, this thesis either smuggles in objective moral judgments concerning the worth of the various purposes with which persons adopt moral codes or fails to provide grounds for external criticism by allowing appraisals of means but not ends.

28 Ibid., 198.
29 A third conceptual argument that is frequently made against relativism is that it results in self-contradiction. This self-contradiction is said to occur whenever relativists are asked to justify the thesis that moral truth resides in the beliefs of the current majority. If relativists claim that the thesis is true because the majority believes it to be true, they beg the question at issue. If, however, they say that it is true because it follows from other true propositions, they admit that truth is not given by the beliefs of the majority. For a similar formulation of this

Violating Bivalence

If moral relativists claim that the proposition "abortion is moral" is simultaneously true for one group but false for another, it would appear that they are committed to violating the principle of bivalence – the principle that a proposition cannot simultaneously be both true and not true. And, indeed, moral relativism would seem regularly to entail just such a contradiction. It appears that the relativist is committed to declaring each of two societies right about the morality of abortion if one society conventionally believes abortion to be moral while the other conventionally believes it to be immoral. We are reminded of the anecdote of the rabbi who was asked to adjudicate a dispute between two women. The rabbi heard the first woman and said immediately, "You're right!" He then heard the second woman and declared, "You're right!" Calling him aside, his associate whispered, "They can't both be right." And the rabbi exclaimed again, "You're right!" As this anecdote reminds us, the simultaneous assertion of both propositions p and not-p is considered definitional of incoherence. Because moral relativism appears to assert the simultaneous truth of both p and not-p, it appears to be conceptually indefensible.[30]

Not surprisingly, this criticism has been staunchly rejected by those defending relativism. In what follows, I shall take up three distinct philosophical moves that have been made by relativists to escape contradiction. The first move relativizes the semantics of moral propositions, the second relativizes the presuppositions of moral judgments, and the third relativizes the pragmatics of moral utterances.

Semantic Relativism

Semantic relativists defend against the alleged breach of bivalence by relativizing the semantics of moral predicates. They argue that

dilemma, see Steven D. Smith, "Skepticism, Tolerance, and Truth in the Theory of Free Expression," *Southern California Law Review* 60 (1987): 670–1.

This argument, however, plagues only the *cognitive* relativist. One defending *moral* relativism need not be a cognitive relativist and therefore need not justify the metaethical claim that morality is relative by making reference to the beliefs of a community. Rather, the moral relativist can maintain the realist thesis that it is a (nonrelative) fact about the world that moral truth is relative, and thereby avoid the incoherence attributed generally to relativism by the above argument.

[30] The violation of bivalence is nowhere more obvious than in the popular formulation of metaethical relativism proposed by William Frankena. According to Frankena, "in the case of basic ethical judgments, there is no objectively valid, rational way of justifying one against another; consequently, two conflicting basic judgments may be *equally valid*." Frankena, *Ethics*, 109 (emphasis added).

the very meaning of our moral predicates – "good," "bad," "right," "wrong," – is itself relative to the standards of the subject being judged.[31] Thus, when relativists say that "Abortion in society S_1 is right" and "Abortion in society S_2 is wrong," they mean that "Abortion is right-relative-to-the-standards-of-S_1" and "Abortion is wrong-relative-to-the-standards-of-S_2." Because the predicate "right-by-the-standards-of-S_1" does not contradict the predicate "wrong-by-the-standards-of-S_2," the challenge of incoherence is declared defeated. Semantic relativists thus reject the charge that they are committed to asserting that the proposition "Abortion is moral" is both true and false; rather, on their account of semantic relativism, they are asserting that the proposition "Abortion is right-relative-to-the-standards-of-S_1" is everywhere true and that the proposition "Abortion-is-wrong-relative-to-the-standards-of-S_2" is everywhere true.

It is surprising that relativists confidently assert this response as if it unproblemmatically extracts them from incoherence. On the contrary, to relativize meaning as a means of relativizing truth invites two grave conceptual problems. First, the semantic relativist's analysis of the sentence "Abortion is wrong" results in the complex sentence "Relative to standards S_1, abortion is wrong." Now the relativist needs an analysis of the meaning of the sentence fragment "abortion is wrong" within the complex sentence so created. Is this fragment also to be analyzed as "Relative to standards S_1, abortion is wrong"? If so, the relativist invites an infinite regress of prefixes to a sentence fragment whose meaning is never given.[32]

Second, the suggestion that meaning is relative to some set of stan-

---

31   Thus, as Richard Brandt says, "although the Romans and the Eskimos may use the very same words to describe a certain sort of act – and then may express conflicting ethical appraisals of it – actually in some sense they have in mind quite different things." Richard B. Brandt, *Ethical Theory: The Problems of Normative and Critical Ethics* (Englewood Cliffs, NJ: Prentice-Hall, 1959), 100. For recent attempts to relativize the meaning of moral terms as a means of rescuing moral relativism from the violation of bivalence, see James Dreier, "Internalism and Speaker Relativism," *Ethics* 101 (1990): 6–26 (arguing both that incoherence can be avoided, and that the internalist feature of moral propositions can be accounted for, by fixing the content of moral propositions by the context of their utterance); Philip Hugly and Charles Sayward, "Moral Relativism and Deontic Logic," *Synthese* 85 (1990): 139–52 (maintaining that incoherence can be avoided by appealing to the semantic metatheories of deontic logic).

32   This objection is reminiscent of G.E. Moore's famous complaint with various versions of what I have called semantic relativism. See G.E. Moore, *Ethics* (Cambridge: Cambridge University Press, 1912). See also Sayward, "System Relativism," 171, for a similar formulation of this objection.

dards invites what I shall call the reductio of semantic relativism. This reductio has four steps, each of which constitutes an independently devastating problem for semantic relativists. First, if the meaning of moral predicates is relative to a set of discrete conventions, then there exists no basis upon which conventions can be compared. While predicates such as "right-by-standards-S_1" and "wrong-by-standards-S_2" may not *conflict* on this theory, neither can they *agree.* Thus, while individuals adhering to a set of standards S_1 may assert that "Euthanasia is wrong" and individuals adhering to a set of standards S_2 may likewise assert that "Euthanasia is wrong," this does not suggest that all agree that euthanasia is wrong. The thesis of semantic relativism endorsed by relativists who are anxious to spare relativism from charges of incoherence precludes moral comparisons. The meaning of moral judgments is construed as meaning relative to some set of standards; independent of any set of standards, the notion that moral terms possess meaning lacks any sense.

Second, if predicates belonging to different standards neither conflict nor agree, how can moral standards be reached or agreed upon in any one society? After all, a moral standard or convention is an explicit or implicit agreement in the beliefs or attitudes of the members of a society. And if "right" means "right by standard S," then primitive agreements between individuals become impossible. Such agreements can be no more than syntactic coincidences of utterance. That two individuals utter the phrase "Euthanasia is immoral" merely amounts to a coincidence of oral sounds. There cannot be an identity of propositional content because there can be no standard by which either could judge that euthanasia is wrong. "Wrong" in the case of such primitive agreements – that is, agreements that establish a society's conventions – can only be a symbol without sense or reference. What else could "wrong" be, given the lack of any standard relative to which "wrong" could have meaning?

The first two steps of this reductio demonstrate that the relativist cannot account for the existence of the moral conventions to which the relativist thinks moral judgments are relative. This ought to be sufficient to prompt the metaethical relativist to give up semantic relativism. But the reductio does not stop here. In the relativized view of meaning suggested, what are we to make of the coherence of the heretofore uninteresting supposition that individuals can have belief sets – that is, intra-individual agreements? That one individual asserts p at time t_1 and p again at time t_2 cannot be construed as evidence of some agreement that she has with herself (that is, of some

belief set that she consistently possesses). Rather, the consistency of
an individual's utterances can be, at best, a syntactic (but not semantic) coincidence. If the relativist cannot rescue his theory from the reductio of semantic relativism, then he is committed to the view that
an individual's own assertions cannot be compared so as to decipher
from them a set of beliefs to which the individual can be said to subscribe. And to say this is to deny that verbal conduct (and probably
inner belief states) can ever have any real meaning at all.

Fourth and finally, vis-a-vis preagreement utterances from which
either inter- or intra-individual conventions are born, the move to
relativize meaning does not rescue moral relativism from violating
the principle of bivalence. Suppose that at time t_1 an individual asserts the proposition p, but at time t_2 that same indivdual asserts the
proposition not-p. In asserting "I believe that p," the individual is
committed to p; yet in asserting "I believe that not-p," the individual is committed to not-p. Thus for this individual both p and not-p
are true. Absent some agreement to which the truth of these moral
propositions is relative, the relativist is committed to recognizing the
simultaneous truth of both p and not-p and is thus unable to defeat
the challenge that relativism implies a violation of the principle of
bivalence.

Presuppositional Relativism
Those who recognize that moral relativism cannot escape the violation
of bivalence by relativizing the semantics of moral discourse may be
tempted to rescue relativism from incoherence by relativizing instead
the presuppositions of that discourse. On this argument, the *meaning*
of moral propositions is not given by the conventions of a society. But
in order for (meaningful) moral propositions to have a *truth-value* at
all, they must cohere with the conventions of a society. Imagine, for
example, that in society S_1 the proposition "Abortion is moral" is
unanimously believed to be true. Imagine that in society S_2 the populous neither believes that abortion is moral nor believes that it is immoral; that is, it lacks a convention about abortion. If the truth-value
of propositions is relative to societal beliefs, then, in these two societies, the presuppositional relativist is spared contradiction. According to the theory of the presuppositional relativist, because there is
only one proposition about abortion that reflects (one way or another)
a society's conventions, there is only one proposition about abortion
that has a truth-value – namely, the proposition that "Abortion is
moral." Hence, abortion is moral.

Four independent problems confound the attempt to satisfy the principle of bivalence by relativizing the presuppositions (but not the meaning) of moral propositions. First, while such a theory escapes first-order contradiction, it commits a metalevel contradiction; that is, in the above sort of case, it asserts both that "The proposition 'Abortion is moral' is true" and that "The proposition 'Abortion is moral' is neither true nor false." Since this is to assert both p and not-p (now about metapropositions concerning the truth of first-order moral propositions), presuppositional relativism appears to be as vulnerable as semantic relativism to charges of incoherence.

Second, presuppositional relativism only plausibly escapes first-order contradiction in cases in which one society has a clear convention concerning the morality of a given matter while another society has no convention at all on that matter. But what of societies that have patently conflicting conventions? If one society conventionally believes that abortion is moral while another society conventionally believes that it is immoral, then, according to the presuppositional relativist, the statements "Abortion is moral" and "Abortion is immoral" are both meaningful *and* possess a truth-value. And if their truth-value (albeit not their meaning) is given by the conventions of those who utter them, then these statements must both be deemed by the presuppositional relativist to be true.

Third, the presuppositional relativist explicitly assumes that sentences containing words lacking reference cannot possess a truth-value. Thus, in the famous debate between Bertrand Russell and Peter Strawson,[33] the presuppositional relativist would join Strawson in maintaining that the statement "The present King of France is bald" lacks a truth-value, at least so long as France lacks a king. But those persuaded by Russell will deny that meaningful propositions can lack truth-value. If France is without a King, then the proposition "The present King of France is bald" is a false one, not one that is neither true nor false, for the proposition *means* that "There is a King of France and he is bald." If those of Russell's persuasion are right, then the presuppositional relativist cannot escape incoherence by premising her argument on the claim that meaningful sentences can lack truth-value, because the truth value of the statement "Abortion is moral" is, in the second society imagined above, false. Hence, in a situation in which one society conventionally believes abortion to be

---

[33] See Bertrand Russell, "On Denoting," *Mind* New Series 14 (1905): 479–93; Peter Strawson, "On Referring," *Mind* New Series 59 (1950): 320–44.

moral and another lacks any convention at all concerning the morality of abortion, the presuppositional relativist must say that it is both true and false that "Abortion is moral."

Finally, inasmuch as the presuppositional relativist treats the statement "Abortion is moral" (when said of a society that has no convention one way or another about the morality of abortion) the same way that Strawson treats the statement "The present King of France is bald" (when said of France at a time when it has no king), the presuppositional relativist must assume that just as the latter sentence is neither true nor false because the word "King" does not refer to anyone, so the former sentence is neither true nor false because the word "moral" does not refer to anything. But this is just to say that the phrase "is moral" refers to a convention that is possessed by a society. If presuppositional relativists must fix the reference of moral terms by societal conventions, then their theory inevitably collapses into semantic relativism.

This same point can be made in a quite different way as follows. For the sake of argument, let us initially grant the presuppositional relativist the claim that sentences that lack truth-value can nevertheless be meaningful. This is the claim, of course, that allows the presuppositional relativist to dispute semantic relativism while vindicating moral relativism. Let us suppose, then, that the sentence "Abortion is moral" is meaningful, even if it lacks a truth-value because there is no society that has a convention one way or another about abortion. The presuppositional relativist is committed to claiming that such a sentence acquires a truth-value as it is repeated by the members of a society. But how does the sheer repetition of a statement make it true? On pain of thinking that stuttering can have remarkable metaphysical consequences, the only answer can be that the phrase "is moral" refers to a convention, and conventions come into existence with the repetition of moral propositions. Hence, propositions that were once neither true nor false can become true by their multiple utterance. But, of course, if this is how moral propositions acquire truth-value, then the reference of moral propositions is given by societal conventions. And inasmuch as the reference of a term (at least in part) gives the meaning of the term on any plausible theory of meaning, presuppositional relativism thus collapses into semantic relativism. Thus, not only does presuppositional relativism face problems of its own, it also faces the problems that rendered semantic relativism indefensible.

Pragmatic Relativism

Recognizing the futility of engaging in further attempts to relativize either meaning or the presuppositions of truth so as to bolster the claims of metaethical relativism, Bernard Williams and Gilbert Harman have taken a pragmatic turn. Both have constructed theories designed to demonstrate that, *as a pragmatic matter,* it is philosophically inappropriate to make moral judgments about the beliefs or practices of communities that are, in one manner or another, remote from our own. This move represents an attempt to reconcile relativism with the principle of bivalence, because it denies the legitimacy of passing judgment on the moral conventions of those who would reach moral conclusions opposite to our own, and hence it denies that one could ever appropriately say both that "Abortion is moral" and that "Abortion is immoral."

Appraisal Relativism. Bernard Williams has bred a strand of relativism that he calls both "appraisal relativism"[34] and "the relativism of distance."[35] Unlike traditional relativism, which evaluates the morality of actions relative to some set of moral conventions, Williams's appraisal relativism evaluates appraisals of moral conventions. It is thus a third-order thesis about the second-order practice of appraising moral agreements. According to Williams, the second-order practice of evaluating some set of conventions is relative to various conditions, such as the nature of one's own moral code and one's own concerns or preferences.

Appraisals of moral conventions can occur, Williams argues, only if two conditions are met: (1) there are two or more self-contained systems of belief (S1 and S2); and (2) these systems of belief are exclusive.[36] In what Williams deems the most straightforward case, S1 and S2 have conflicting consequences: When asked some yes/no question, persons holding S1 will answer "yes" while persons holding S2 will say "no." For example, two groups would be said to hold conflicting systems of beliefs if in answer to the question "Is abortion moral?" one group says "yes" while the other says "no."

When the exclusivity of two self-contained systems results in what

---

[34] Bernard A.O. Williams, "The Truth in Relativism," *Proceedings of the Aristotelian Society* 75 (1974–75): 215–28.

[35] Bernard A.O. Williams, *Ethics and the Limits of Philosophy* (London: Fontana Press/Collins, 1985): 162.

[36] Williams, "The Truth in Relativism," 175–6.

Williams calls "real confrontation," there is "a group at that time for whom each of S1 and S2 is a real option; this includes, but is not confined to, the case of a group which already holds S1 or S2, for whom the question is whether to *go over* to the other S."[37] Contrasted with real confrontation is notional confrontation, which "resembles real confrontation in that there are persons who are aware of S1 and S2, and aware of their differences" but differs from real confrontation "in that at least one of S1 and S2 do not present a real option to them."[38]

For a system of beliefs, S2, to be a "real option" for some group holding S1, two conditions must be met. First, it must be possible for members of the group to assent to S2 – to fully accept it or live within it – while still retaining "their hold on reality."[39] Second, it must be possible for the group to rationally justify adopting or going over to S2.[40]

According to Williams's pragmatic interpretation of the doctrine of moral relativism, "relativism with regard to a given type of S, is the view that for one whose S stands in purely notional confrontation with such an S, questions of appraisal do not genuinely arise."[41] The only legitimate appraisals are appraisals of real options. "[T]o stand in merely notional confrontation is to lack the relation to our concerns which alone gives any point or substance to appraisal. . . ."[42] As Williams concludes, only real options can be judged, because "the more remote a given S is from being a real option for us, the less substantial seems the question of whether it is 'true,' 'right,' etc."[43]

Williams claims to avoid the regress and reductio that semantic and presuppositional relativism invite, because he explicitly eschews any attempt to relativize the vocabulary of appraisal so as to declare options merely "true for us" or "true for them." As he says, "we must have a form of thought not relativized to our own existing S for thinking about other Ss which may be of concern to us, and to express those concerns. . . ."[44] Yet, in their stead, Williams invites three seemingly devastating problems.

The first problem derives from his conception of what constitutes a real option that is eligible for appraisal. For a system of beliefs, S2, implying consequences opposite from those of S1 to be a real option

---

[37] Ibid., 180 (emphasis in original).   [38] Ibid.

[39] Ibid., 181. See also Williams, *Ethics and the Limits of Philosophy*, 160.

[40] Williams, "The Truth in Relativism," 181. See also Williams, *Ethics and the Limits of Philosophy*, 160.

[41] Williams, "The Truth in Relativism," 183.

[42] Ibid.   [43] Ibid.   [44] Ibid., 184 (emphasis omitted).

for persons holding S1, it must be the case that persons holding S1 can "go over" to S2 without losing their "hold on reality." Williams has at last provided that long-awaited opportunity to ask in all seriousness, "What is reality?" If reality is relative to one's system of beliefs, then "going over" to a system of beliefs that implies consequences opposite to one's own must surely be the very definition of "losing one's hold on reality." If, on the other hand, reality is not relative to some system of beliefs, but is, rather, objective, then one of two sets of conflicting beliefs must not be a real option for *anyone*, because, if both were real options, this would entail that beliefs could be simultaneously true and false, right and wrong, and acceptable and unacceptable.

Williams must have in mind a notion of reality that reflects psychological rather than metaphysical commitments. He must think that at some point the adoption of wholly new beliefs – beliefs that are contradictory to those previously held – will result in an inability to cope with the world. We are thus pragmatically constrained in what we appraise as a real option: A real option must represent a system of beliefs which is sufficiently close to our own that a conversion to it does not jeopardize our ability to conduct ourselves normally. But how would we find a system of beliefs that is "close enough" to allow for nondisruptive conversion and yet so different that it renders answers to moral questions that are completely contradictory to our own?

In addition to the requirement that a real option be one which allows a group to maintain its hold on reality, Williams requires of a real option that it be a system of beliefs which a group would be rational to adopt. Once again we are entitled to ask, "What is rational?" If rationality is relative to a system of beliefs, then how could conversion to a system implying consequences opposite to those implied by one's own beliefs be rational? Alternatively, if rationality is not relative to some system of beliefs, but is something objective, then, on pain of violating the bivalence principle, this again implies that there are right answers to moral questions such that one of two groups giving conflicting answers to a moral question must be wrong. If Williams rejects this latter construction, and thereby rejects the notion that there exists some means of evaluating the rationality of ends, then he commits himself to the position that only internal criticism of a system of beliefs is possible. But if this is the case, then we could not appraise a system of beliefs as superior to our own (except to the extent that we may consider it more consistent than our own) and could not, on that basis, demonstrate that converting to it is rational. It thus appears that Williams has no clear idea of what it would mean for a conflicting system of beliefs to be a real option.

The second problem that Williams's theory engenders results from his refusal to relativize the semantics of moral discourse. It is this refusal, of course, that enables him to escape the regress and reductio that plagued the semantic and presuppositional relativists. But if the language of appraisal is not relative to a system of beliefs (such that a practice can be "right" under one system and "wrong" under another), how could there ever be two conflicting systems leading to opposite consequences that are equally real options for some group? How could the word "right" mean the same thing when applied to conflicting practices? If under S1 all answer "no" to the question "Is abortion moral?", they are committed to thinking that abortion is immoral. And if under S2 all answer "yes" to the question "Is abortion moral?", they are all committed to thinking that abortion is moral. But on any theory of semantics that ascribes the same meaning to the term "moral" in these utterances, how is it possible that the term moral could extend both to permitting abortions and to prohibiting abortions? Without relativizing the semantics of moral judgments, Williams appears committed to the view that practices can be (and indeed must be, if real confrontations are possible) both right and wrong. His theory thus appears to be in flagrant violation of the principle of bivalence.

Williams would presumably answer this charge by invoking his unique conception of ethical truth – a conception that equates ethical truth with that determinate set of ethical conclusions that "a range of investigators could rationally, reasonably, and unconstrainedly come to converge on. . . ."[45] He insists that convergence on moral truth will require the abilities that are employed "in finding our way around in a social world, . . . and this, crucially, means *in some social world or other*, since it is certain both that human beings cannot live without a culture and that there are many different cultures in which they can live, differing in their local concepts."[46] Ethical beliefs are thus true, in Williams's view, only "in the oblique sense that they [are] the beliefs that would help us to find our way around in a social world. . . ."[47] Williams would argue that this theory of moral truth enables him to reconcile his relativism with the principle of bivalence, because, according to this theory of truth, what it means to say that two persons

---

[45] Williams, *Ethics and the Limits of Philosophy*, 151.
[46] Ibid., 152.   [47] Ibid., 155.

who use the same evaluative term to describe contradictory moral practices are both right, is that a reflective group of investigators would agree that each person's moral judgment represents the best means of getting along in his or her particular society.

However, Williams cannot avail himself of this move without inviting two crucial problems. First, any set of beliefs that rational, reasonable, and unconstrained investigators would fail to converge on as demonstrative of the best means of getting around in a particular society would not be, for those investigators, a real option. But then, according to Williams's theory, those investigators would be barred from passing judgment on that set of beliefs. If Williams were to allow external investigators to evaluate or appraise a set of beliefs to determine its "truth" or "falsity" when that set of beliefs is not for them a real option, Williams would have to abandon his central claim that appraisals are inappropriate where ethical views are in notional confrontation. But if "false" beliefs are, necessarily, not real options, and are thereby insulated from evaluation, how are they to be judged false?

Second, on pain of returning to semantic relativism, Williams cannot make the argument that two individuals who employ the same evaluative term in contradictory ways may both be right if, in so doing, they reflect the best available method for living with others in their particular societies. That is, the statement of the first person would be "true-relative-to-society$_1$" while the statement of the second person would be "true-relative-to-society$_2$." This conclusion would, of course, comport with the requirements of the principle of bivalence, but it would confront Williams with the reductio of semantic relativism and so confound any attempt on his part to make sense of how individuals and groups can ever come to have shared belief sets to begin with.

The final problem that Williams's appraisal relativism invites is perhaps the most damning. By limiting ethical judgments to real options, Williams limits the scope of our evaluations of other ethical systems to those systems we could adopt. Yet it is precisely over those systems that do *not* pose a real option for us that we most feel the need for criticism. Williams's theory effectively bars our evaluation of practices when those practices become so different from our own that we could not adopt them; but this is the case whenever practices appear to us to be particularly heinous, barbaric, or unjust. Hence, just when moral disapproval looks most appropriate, Williams's theory renders it illegitimate. His theory thus allows us to appraise only what we already generally approve. We are estopped, on this theory, from condemning those practices which we consider morally outrageous precisely *because* we consider them morally outrageous. It thus appears that Williams's pragmatic theory is both conceptually and morally indefensible.

Relativism of Moral Judgments. Gilbert Harman describes his moral relativism as a "soberly logical thesis – a thesis about logical form, if you like."[48] Harman maintains that "morality arises when a group of people reach an implicit agreement or come to a tacit understanding about their relations with one another.... [M]oral judgments ... make sense only in relation to and with reference to one or another such agreement or understanding."[49] Just as it makes little sense to ask whether a dog is large independent of its relation to some class of animals or objects, so too it makes little sense to ask whether an action is wrong independent of its relation to any agreement.

According to Harman, moral judgments (defined as those that take the form "X should or should not do Y" or "X was right or wrong to have done Y") have two important characteristics: "First, they imply that the agent has reasons to do something. Second, the speaker in some sense endorses these reasons and supposes that the audience also endorses them."[50] The first characteristic that Harman assigns to moral judgments reflects a Humean theory of motivation. For reasons to motivate action, they must reflect certain subjective goals, desires, or intentions.[51] Thus, according to Harman, when we say that others ought to tell the truth, we presuppose that they have a subjective reason to tell the truth.[52]

The second characteristic that Harman assigns to moral judgments derives from his claim that moral judgments are made relative to an

---

[48] Gilbert Harman, "Moral Relativism Defended," *Philosophical Review* 84 (1975): 3.

[49] Ibid. [50] Ibid., 8.

[51] Thus, for Harman, one has a reason for action if and only if one has some motivational attitude toward doing the act. Donald Davidson provides a more comprehensive formulation of this Humean thesis. Davidson states that, "[w]henever someone does something for a reason ... he can be characterized as (a) having some sort of pro attitude toward actions of a certain kind, and (b) believing (or knowing, perceiving, noticing, remembering) that his action is of that kind." Davidson calls this set of criteria the "primary reason" for an agent's action. Donald Davidson, *Essays on Actions and Events* (Oxford: Clarendon Press, 1980), 3–4.

[52] "[A] person ought morally not to have done a particular thing only if we can assume that he had a reason not to do it." Gilbert Harman, *The Nature of Morality* (New York: Oxford University Press, 1977), 106.

agreement between the speaker and the subject of the speaker's judgment. According to Harman, agreements result from "moral bargaining." They are struck when all individuals concerned intend to adhere to a set of principles on the understanding that others will similarly constrain themselves. Harman maintains that:

> [W]hen S makes the . . . judgment that A ought to do D, S assumes that A intends to act in accordance with an agreement which S and S's audience also intend to observe. In other words, I want to argue that the source of the reasons for doing D which S ascribes to A is A's sincere intention to observe a certain agreement.[53]

When we say of others, therefore, that they ought not to lie, our judgment makes sense only if there exists some agreement about truthtelling to which we subscribe and to which we expect them to subscribe. Where others have no reason to refrain from lying because they do not share our agreement about truth-telling, our prescription that they ought to tell the truth is as empty as a warning to a blind man to watch where he is going.

Harman thus argues that it would be logically odd to say of contract killers that they ought not to murder because this incorrectly implies that they have a subjective reason not to murder. Similarly, "[i]t does not seem right to say [of cannibals] that each of them ought morally not to eat human flesh or that each of them has a moral duty or obligation not to do so."[54] And finally, it is "odd to say that Hitler should not have ordered the extermination of the Jews, that it was wrong of him to have done so."[55] By his acts, Hitler showed himself to be outside of any agreement to which we subscribe and "we therefore cannot make . . . [moral] judgments about him."[56]

Harman would declare that those who find such conclusions counterintuitive are inevitably confusing the moral "ought" with the evaluative "ought." The evaluative "ought," Harman argues, is used to describe desirable states of affairs in the world (e.g., "The Jews ought not to have been exterminated"), while the moral "ought" is reserved for judgments about the actions of agents (e.g., "Hitler ought not to have ordered the extermination of the Jews"). While we can make evaluative judgments absent anyone having subjective reasons to

53 Harman, "Moral Relativism Defended," 9–10.
54 Harman, *The Nature of Morality*, 106.
55 Harman, "Moral Relativism Defended," 7.
56 Ibid.

comply with them, we cannot sensibly make moral judgments absent a motivation on the part of those judged to act accordingly.

Because he contends that one can only morally judge those with whom one is in an agreement, Harman can insist that one will never yield simultaneously contradictory moral judgments, and hence one will never violate the principle of bivalence. For one will presumably never find oneself in simultaneous agreement with two groups who embrace contradictory moral views. One will thus never be entitled to say that one person was morally right to have an abortion while another similarly situated person was simultaneously morally wrong to have an abortion.

Yet as we have seen in the past, the cost of satisfying the bivalence principle is typically an implicit commitment to semantic relativism. And Harman, like Williams, cannot escape this toll. Harman must admit that the meaning of the terms of a moral judgment is given by the agreement that necessarily exists between the speaker and the subject. Thus, if called on to explain how one speaker might be right in saying of a woman, "She ought not to have had an abortion" while another is simultaneously right in saying of a different woman, "She ought to have had an abortion," Harman must contend that the meaning of the term "ought" varies between the agreements implicitly invoked between these two speakers and their subjects. In making this move, however, Harman invites the regress and reductio that defeated past attempts to relativize the meaning of moral language so as to escape the violation of bivalence.

In addition to succumbing to the problems of past theories, Harman fails to defend a number of premises in his argument that are, to say the least, controversial. For example, Harman leaves us with little reason to believe that one has a reason to do an action if and only if one has a motivational attitude toward an action. There is a long and reputable tradition in ethics that appeals to objective reasons for action – reasons that may not motivate us to act, but that do dictate ways in which it would be right or wrong for us to act. That such reasons for action fail to inspire motivational attitudes toward moral action in psychopaths seemingly renders them no less a proper basis for saying of such persons that they ought to act morally. Thus, even if robbers have no *inclination* to cease safecracking, they may still be thought to have a *reason* to abandon their life of crime. There appears no confusion of evaluative and moral meaning here. One is not suggesting merely that the world would be a better place if robbers did not steal; one is suggesting that robbers commit a morally bad act by stealing and *therefore* ought not to steal.

If Harman presses his distinction between the moral and the evaluative as a means of fending off the charge that he has failed to take seriously the role of objective reasons for action in moral judgments, he commits himself to defending a highly suspect bifurcation of description and prescription. That is, on his theory, we can say of the cannibal and the contract killer that they are savage and barbaric, but we cannot say of them that they ought not to eat human flesh or shoot persons in cold blood. Similarly, we can describe Hitler as evil, but we cannot say that he ought not to have murdered six million people. These claims clearly suggest that Harman considers the enterprise of identifying objective reasons for action to be descriptive, while he considers the enterprise of appealing to some agreement between the speaker and the subject as a means of evaluating the subject's actions to be prescriptive. But Harman gives us no reason to think that description is not simultaneously prescription – that the judgment that Hitler was evil is not simultaneously the judgment that he ought to have acted otherwise.[57]

These concerns suggest that Harman's thesis is not a "soberly logical" one at all. Rather, it is a pragmatic thesis about the practical uselessness of using moral terms in conversations with those who do not speak the language. As David Lyons suggests, our tendency to judge another's action according to that person's own attitudes may be accounted for "by reference to our substantive convictions about the pointlessness of advising a person when we think we cannot influence him. . . ."[58] When we know that someone has no inclination to take our advice, we may be unwise to spend our time providing it. But surely we would not want to say that the fact that our advice falls

---

[57] As Anne Wiles argues, Harman's theory inappropriately severs the ontological connection between an agent and his acts. Anne M. Wiles, "Harman and Others on Moral Relativism," *Review of Metaphysics* 42 (1989): 786–9. See also Louis P. Pojman, "Gilbert Harman's Internalist Moral Relativism," *The Modern Schoolman* 68 (1990): 27–9, 31–3 (arguing that Harman's commitment to the Humean theory of motivation conflicts with his contractual theory of morality).

[58] David Lyons, "Ethical Relativism and the Problem of Incoherence," in *Relativism: Cognitive and Moral*, eds. Michael Krausz and Jack W. Meiland (Notre Dame, IN: University of Notre Dame Press, 1982), 223–4. See also Wojciech Sadurski, "Harman's Defence of Moral Relativism," *Philosophical Investigations* 12 (1989): 35–6 (also arguing that Harman's examples appear "odd" because they are instances of rhetorical ineffectiveness, not logical incorrectness).

on deaf ears *makes* our advice false. But to admit this, of course, is to admit the objective truth of ethical statements. It is to give up the ambitious metaphysical thesis that moral truth is relative for the pedestrian empirical claim that preaching to the deaf is pointless.

Finally, just as Williams's appraisal relativism left us unable to condemn the most immoral of practices, so Harman's relativism of moral judgments bars criticism of those who most deserve it. Because, for Harman, Hitler did not share our agreement that all human life is valuable, we cannot say that he ought not to have engaged in genocide. Because the pro-life advocate does not share an agreement about abortion with the pro-choice advocate, the pro-life advocate cannot say of the pro-choice advocate that she ought not to have an abortion. Because the rape victim does not share her rapist's motivational attitude toward violent crime, she cannot say that her rapist ought not to have raped her. It seems to follow from Harman's theory that one can never say of others that they ought to do otherwise, because their very lack of motivation to do so in the first place suggests that they do not share in any agreement to which one's prescription is relative. This suggests that there is never an appropriate opportunity for prescription: If others are motivated to act as we think they ought to act, they will act without our advice; but if others are not motivated to act as we think they ought to act, they will not share our motivational attitude, and thus are not party to an agreement relative to which we can judge their conduct. Because, in Harman's view, motivation is not transitive, we cannot even prescribe action where it appears to follow deductively from other beliefs held by an individual. Harman's theory is thus reduced to a description of conditions for engaging in moral judgment where these conditions, by their very terms, preclude the possibility of moral judgment.

Collapsing into Subjectivism

We have thus far seen that relativists cannot defend their metaphysical claim that morality is relative to conventions without (1) abandoning the principle of tolerance that motivates many of them to defend relativism to begin with, (2) defending the morally counterintuitive claim that much of what we take to be evil is in fact moral, and (3) either violating the principle of bivalence or relativizing the semantics of moral discourse in ways that land them in conceptual incoherence. In this final section, let me take up one more problem for those who would defend moral relativism.

Moral relativists are typically conventionalists who would abandon their relativism if they thought it committed them to subjectivism. They recognize that if values are wholly subjective, then they are incorrigible: An individual cannot be wrong about any moral belief, and every moral belief is true by virtue of being believed.[59] Such a theory renders meaningless the practices of moral enquiry and criticism as we know them. If moral subjectivism is true, then moral discourse can be at most the attempt by individuals to persuade one another that they genuinely believe the truth of particular moral propositions because, in sincerely and consistently believing a proposition to be true, they *make* it true. And if moral propositions are made true by believing them, then to ask whether a moral statement is true is simply to ask whether another believes it.

To preserve the meaningfulness of moral discourse, most relativists have argued that values are standards shared by a community that cannot be reduced to subjective preferences.[60] An individual's moral beliefs or assertions can be criticized, claims the relativist, whenever they fail to cohere with the beliefs of those with whom the individual forms a community. Inasmuch as the truth of a judgment is measured by its coherence with a set of standards, there must exist what H. L. A. Hart called a "rule of recognition" by which to identify the standards appropriate for judging a proposition.[61] Error may result either from misapplying the rule of recognition or from misapplying the standard that such a rule recognizes.

Yet despite the claim that conventionalism preserves the possibility of error and, hence, the purpose of moral discourse, there appears to be no way in which to construe the relativist's thesis that does not either invite, once again, the regress and reductio of semantic relativism or collapse conventionalism into subjectivism. Conventionalists claim that judgments will be wrong (and thereby not purely a matter of subjective belief) whenever they fail to cohere with relevant communal standards. To make out such a claim, conventionalists

---

59 Of course, as Foot points out, even a subjectivist would agree that "a man may apply his own standards wrongly, and hence there is a possibility of 'correction' that is not simply a change of mind." Foot, "Moral Relativism," 158. Nevertheless, while individuals may fail to know their own beliefs, or may fail to act in ways that are commensurate with them, the subjectivist's claim remains that an individual's sincere and internally consistent belief in the morality of some normative proposition *makes* that proposition true (for him).

60 But see Sayward, "System Relativism," 167–9, for a relativist's admission that conventionalism must give way to subjectivism if relativism is to avoid incoherence.

61 H.L.A. Hart, *The Concept of Law* (Oxford: Clarendon Press, 1961), 92–3, 97–107.

must have a theory of coherence – a theory that fixes the conditions under which an individual's propositions comport with those deemed conventional. There are, at least in principle, two sorts of theories to which conventionalists might turn – semantic theories and syntactic ones.

Those who opt to construct a semantic theory of coherence must reject the claim that coherence can be a purely syntactic relation between sentences. Rather, the question of whether two statements cohere with one another must depend on what they mean. If this is true, then the relativist once again needs a theory of the meaning of moral predicates. As we have seen, relativists cannot adopt a semantic theory that gives moral predicates objective meaning without violating the principle of bivalence. Instead, relativists seeking a semantic theory of coherence must maintain that meaning is relative to a set of conventions or standards. But this claim invites once again the two problems that plagued semantic relativists in their attempt to relativize the meaning of moral predicates so as to escape the violation of bivalence. Not only does such a theory leave unanalyzed the meaning of the core proposition to which a community agrees or impliedly agrees (the regress problem), but it also precludes the ability to make sense of the development of agreements to begin with (the reductio of semantic relativism).

To avoid the problems that confound relativist attempts to construct a semantic theory of coherence, relativists must endorse a syntactic theory of agreement: An agreement can be said to exist whenever the utterances of individuals coincide. Thus, when two individuals both utter the proposition, "In vitro fertilization is moral," both can be said to agree that in vitro fertilization is moral. When confronted with the possibility that the propositional content may be different for each of the individuals asserting the proposition, the relativist who defends a syntactic theory of coherence must reply that all an agreement means is the utterance of the same sounds.

Yet if agreements are merely multiple-party utterances, there is nothing that prevents the extension of that kind of "agreement" to cover the multiple utterances of a single individual. Since for the relativist who propounds a syntactic theory of agreement the multiple saying of something makes it true, then the multiple saying of something by a single individual must make that saying true. And since only in the Land of Oz does the saying of something three times make it true, it must be the case that the saying of something only once by an individual is sufficient to make it true. This is, however, to affirm the truth of subjectivism. The relativist who thus attempts to escape the regress and reductio of semantic relativism by endorsing a syntactic theory of coherence invites the kind of subjectivism that his initial endorsement of conventionalism was designed to avoid.

At this point the relativist might seek to deny that terms employed in moral evaluations have reference or extension at all. Yet some argument is certainly required in support of such a maneuver. The surface grammar of the statement "Slavery is unjust" is much the same as that of the statement "Icy roads are slippery." It would perhaps be helpful here for the relativist to appeal to the familiar emotivist argument that, because we express only our own *emotions* in evaluative speech acts, we cannot be describing anything. Yet such a move would lead the relativist right back into subjectivism. It thus appears that, despite claims such as Foot's that relativists need not adopt the slogan "What he thinks is right is right,"[62] there exist no means of explaining the thesis that judgments are true by virtue of their coherence with a set of standards that does not either invite the regress and reductio of semantic relativism in a manner that threatens conceptual incoherence or collapse relativism into some form of subjectivism in a manner that renders moral discourse senseless.

The four arguments that I have directed against moral relativism in this chapter collectively speak to the indefensibility of a theory of moral relativism. If persuasive, they demonstrate that one cannot escape the choice presented by the dilemma of legal perspectivalism by employing the claims of relativism to defeat the prima facie plausibility of the correspondence thesis. In the following chapters, I shall take up the claim that, inasmuch as the law possesses the authority to trump morality in instances of conflict, the notion of justified disobedience is an empty one. If true, the dilemma of legal perspectivalism is illusory, because there are never instances in which morality requires a violation of the law, and hence there are never instances in which judges may be called on to punish the justified.

---

[62] Foot, "Moral Relativism," 160.

Chapter 3

The Indefensibility
of Practical Authority

We come now to the third presupposition of the dilemma of legal perspectivalism that I sketched in Chapter 1 – the presupposition that
the law lacks the authority to provide citizens with an overriding
reason for obedience. If the law *qua* law provides reasons for unconditional obedience, then, even though it does not perfectly mirror
morality, it nevertheless precludes justified disobedience by citizens.
We can have no cause for concern over the punishment of disobedient citizens, because the law permits no instances in which a judge
might be morally justified in refusing to punish disobedience.

In this chapter, I shall take up the dominant theory of legal authority – the theory of practical authority – which holds that the law
indeed trumps morality in instances of conflict. In Chapter 4, I shall
take up the favored alternative to this theory – the theory of influential authority – which denies that law demands blind obedience, but
holds that, in most instances, the law provides sufficiently powerful
reasons to abide by legal norms that moral conflicts do not arise. As
I shall argue, neither of these theories can sustain the claim that the
law gives persons reasons to do what morality would otherwise prohibit, and, hence, neither of these theories persuasively precludes the
kinds of conflicts between law and morals that fuel the dilemma of
legal perspectivalism.

We begin, in this chapter, with the common presumption that the
law has the power to command behavior, as opposed to merely ad-
vise or request it. Political theorists have dubbed this claim the theory of "practical authority."[1] Practical authority is thought to be the

---

[1] "Authority yields (authorities issue) commands to be obeyed or rules to be sub-
scribed to, not statements to be believed. . . . This . . . theory of authority can fairly
be said to be dominant at the present time." Richard E. Flathman, *The Practice of
Political Authority* (Chicago, IL: University of Chicago Press, 1980), 14–16. "Orders and commands are among the expressions typical of practical authority.

power not just to inspire belief in a deontic proposition, nor simply to influence conduct by providing a new reason for action; rather, it is thought to be the authority to compel action, even in the face of a plethora of good reasons to act otherwise. Because the prescriptions of this authority constitute the strongest sort possible – that of commands – they can be best understood by first examining the authority of their "weaker" cousins – that of advice and requests.

THREE MODELS OF AUTHORITY

Epistemic Authority

Those in a position to give good advice concerning how others ought to act in certain circumstances possess epistemic authority, at least over some range of deontic propositions.[2] The utterances of an epistemic authority provide reasons for belief, not reasons for action; that is, they function evidentially. When an epistemic authority makes a claim concerning right action, its utterance provides a reason to think that there are other reasons (besides the sheer fact that the authority has spoken) to act as recommended. The prescriptions of such an epistemic authority are thus heuristic guides to detecting the existence and determining the probable truth of antecedently existing reasons for action.[3] If, for example, one is advised by an epistemic authority to take one's umbrella, one has every reason to think that there are good reasons to do so, such as the fact that it is raining, that an umbrella will prevent one from getting wet, and so forth. The effect of

---

Only those who claim [practical] authority can command." Joseph Raz, *The Morality of Freedom* (Oxford: Clarendon Press, 1986), 15.

2   In Chapters 5 and 6, I shall distinguish two sorts of epistemic authority – advisory authority and theoretical authority. Advisory authority vests in persons who are well-situated to judge others' reasons for action. Theoretical authority, by contrast, vests in anything (be it advice or great literature) that better enables us to fulfill our moral obligations. While I shall thus tend to speak of advice as the product of advisory authorities, the prescriptions gleaned from theoretical authorities function in practical reasoning in a manner analogous to advice. Thus, the general attributes of epistemic authorities discussed in this section are applicable to both advisory and epistemic authorities.

3   For similar analyses of the dynamics of epistemic authority, see Flathman, *The Practice of Political Authority*, 16–17; Leslie Green, *The Authority of the State* (New York: Oxford University Press, 1988), 26–9, 108–9; H.L.A. Hart, *Essays on Bentham* (Oxford and New York: Oxford University Press, 1982), 262; Joseph Raz, *The Authority of Law: Essays on Law and Morality* (Oxford: Clarendon Press, 1979), 13–14; Raz, *The Morality of Freedom*, 29–31; Richard T. DeGeorge, "The Nature and Function of Epistemic Authority," in *Authority: A Philosophical Analysis*, ed. R. Baine Harris (University, AL: University of Alabama Press, 1976), 76.

the advice is to weight as more probable the likelihood that such other reasons exist. But it is these other reasons, not the advice itself, that serve in one's practical reasoning concerning how one ought to act.

That an epistemic authority has issued a piece of advice thus does not itself serve as a new reason for action; rather, it merely functions to make more probable the truth of antecedently existing reasons for action. The utterances of an epistemic authority thus leave untouched the balance of reasons that one antecedently has both for and against performing a certain action. Prior to another's suggesting the use of an umbrella, there exist all of the reasons that one will ever have to take an umbrella. The advice of a reliable epistemic authority concerning what one ought to do merely makes it the case that those reasons more probably pertain. The basis of epistemic authority is thus content-dependent.[4] Something is an epistemic authority concerning how others ought to act if and only if others will more often act on the balance of reasons for action if they abide by its advice than if they follow their own judgment. This can be formulated more rigorously as follows: X has epistemic authority for Y if and only if, as a result of X's stating that Y ought to do act A, Y has a reason to believe that the balance of (content-dependent) reasons dictates that Y ought to do A.[5]

If an epistemic authority fails to affect the balance of reasons for or against an action, it immediately follows that the utterances of an epistemic authority fail to obligate us. What may bind us is the antecedently existing balance of reasons that the advice of a reliably situated epistemic authority merely evidences. While it may well be irrational to disregard the evidence for that balance provided by a reliable epistemic authority, and while the dictates of rationality may well bind us, the mere issuance of advice in no way obligates us. Put another way, if we are bound to act as we have been advised to act by

---

4   The notion of a content-dependent reason referred to here is a theoretical off-spring of the notion of a content-independent reason discussed in the subsection below. Content-independent reasons were first explicated by H.L.A. Hart and later were put to more rigorous use by Joseph Raz. See Hart, *Essays on Bentham*, 254–5; Raz, *The Morality of Freedom*, 35–7; Joseph Raz, "Voluntary Obligations and Normative Powers," *Aristotelian Society Proceedings* 46 (Supp. 1972): 95–8. Content-dependent reasons made their appearance in Raz, *The Authority of Law*, 297; Raz, *The Morality of Freedom*, 41.

5   This definition captures what might be called "comprehensive epistemic authority." We can distinguish a notion of "limited epistemic authority" as follows: X has limited epistemic authority over Y if and only if as a result of Y's stating that X ought to do act A, Y has a new reason to believe that there are (content-independent) reasons to do A. The difference between limited and comprehensive epistemic authority is one of degree, not kind.

a reliable epistemic authority, our being bound is not a result of the fact that the epistemic authority has issued advice, but of the fact that rationality requires that we act on the balance of reasons of which the advice is mere evidence.

Influential Authority

Let us now turn to the intermediate case of a request. There appears a genuine and important difference between the effect of a piece of advice and the effect of a request. Unlike advice, a request often provides one with a new reason for action. One who makes a request implicitly claims to possess what I shall call "influential authority." When one requests that a friend administer aid, one intends not only to alert that friend to one's need for aid, a need that may be perfectly apparent, but to influence that friend's actions by providing her with a new reason for providing assistance, namely, that one has requested it. In addition to all of the reasons that one's friend had to provide assistance prior to one's request, such as reasons stemming from considerations of distributive justice, good samaritan obligations, principles of friendship, and so on, one's request provides her with a new reason to act. Such a reason is content-independent. It stems from the very fact that one has issued a request. As Joseph Raz explains:

> A reason is content-independent if there is no direct connection between the reason and the action for which it is a reason. The reason is in the apparently "extraneous" fact that someone . . . has said so, and within certain limits his saying so would be reason for any number of actions, including (in typical cases) for contradictory ones.[6]

Were the friend to ask why she should comply with what is asked, it would not be inappropriate to say, "Because I asked you to," and to expect that this should be added to the list of reasons that she otherwise has to render assistance.

A request thus does in fact alter the balance of reasons that one has to act. Prior to a request, one has one less reason to do the act in question. Insofar as the request functions as just one more reason to act in a particular manner, it can be overridden by other reasons to act in a contrary manner. One's friend might well conclude that, while there are reasons for providing one with aid, one of which is the fact that aid has been requested, there are nevertheless countervailing

---

[6] Raz, *The Morality of Freedom*, 35.

considerations that tip the balance of reasons for action in favor of a refusal to help. Thus, while a request is to be distinguished from a piece of good advice in that it gives one a new reason for action, not just evidence for antecedently existing reasons for action, it, like advice, does not by itself obligate. It does not by itself override reasons that we might have to refuse compliance with the request. If we are obligated to act, it is by virtue of the fact that the balance of reasons, of which the fact that there has been a request to act is but one, favors action. One can thus define the conditions of influential authority as follows: X has influential authority over Y if and only if, as a result of X's requesting Y to do act A, Y has a new (content-independent) reason to do A.

Practical Authority

Let us finally turn to the quite different case of a command. One who utters a command certainly purports to give another a new reason for action. The mother who instructs her son to take his umbrella intends her son to take the very fact that she has issued such a command as itself a reason for using an umbrella. If the mother is asked by her son why he must carry the despised object, the mother can well be expected to invoke the time-honored reason, "Because I told you to," and to anticipate that this very fact will be a reason above and beyond the ones that the child antecedently had to take his umbrella. Yet the "Because I told you to" purports to give more than just a new reason for action, because the mother does not intend the son to add her utterance to the reasons that he antecedently had to carry his umbrella, and to weigh these against what he takes to be very good reasons for abandoning the object. Rather, the mother's "Because I told you to" by itself purports to give the son a sufficient reason to take his umbrella; that is, it implicitly claims to bar action on his part in accordance with the reasons that he previously possessed not to take his umbrella. The very fact that some course of action has been commanded is thus thought to function, by itself, as a sufficient reason to act as commanded. It is thought to render impotent the reasons that one had antecedently to avoid the action commanded.[7]

---

[7] "[T]he commander characteristically intends his hearer to take the commander's will instead of his own as a guide to action and so to take it in place of any deliberation or reasoning of his own: the expression of a commander's will . . . is intended to preclude or cut off any independent deliberation by the hearer of the merits pro and con of doing the act." Hart, *Essays on Bentham*, 253. It was this theory of authority that was famously appealed to by Alfred Lord Tennyson when

One who issues a command thus purports to be a practical authority. The reasons for action provided by a practical authority are described by Joseph Raz as "protected reasons": They are both content-independent and exclusionary.[8] As a result of being commanded, one is thought to have both a new reason to act as commanded and a reason to refrain from acting on the reasons that one previously had to not act as commanded. If one had no (content-dependent) reasons to act as commanded prior to receiving the command, then the very fact that the command has been issued provides one with the only reason that one has to so act. But because the command further bars one from acting on the basis of the reasons that one has to avoid the act commanded, one is left only with this singular (content-independent) reason for action. Thus the mother's "Because I told you to" may be the sole reason that the child has to take his umbrella. It nevertheless displaces the many other reasons that he has to not take his umbrella, because it bars him from weighing those many reasons against the sole reason for action provided by the fact of the mother's command. The child is thus "forced" to comply with his mother's command. Such are the dynamics of obligation. These dynamics may be defined as follows: X has practical authority over Y if and only if, as a result of X's saying "Do act A," Y has a new and sufficient (content-independent) reason to do A.

We are now in a position to see clearly the distinctions between advice, requests, and commands. One who issues advice does not tip the balance in favor of acting as advised by adding a new reason for action or by excluding action based on countervailing reasons. One merely claims to function as an epistemic authority providing

---

he wrote: "Theirs not to reason why / Theirs but to do and die." Alfred Lord Tennyson, "The Charge of the Light Brigade," in *The Poetical Works of Tennyson,* ed. G. Robert Strange (Boston, MA: Houghton Mifflin, 1974), 226.

8   Raz, *The Morality of Freedom,* 18. While this terminology is distinctive to Raz and his followers, the notion that certain principles and rules prohibit us from giving weight to certain types of reasons for action is commonly invoked in anti-utilitarian moral philosophy. See, for example, G.E.M. Anscombe, "Modern Moral Philosophy," *Philosophy* 33 (1958): 10 (arguing that deontological prohibitions operate to preclude deliberations about their attendant consequences); Peter Geach, *God and the Soul* (New York: Schocken, 1909), 24 (maintaining that practices like lying, infanticide, and adultery are so undesirable that "men should not *think* of resorting to them"); Robert Nozick, *Anarchy, State, and Utopia* (New York: Basic Books, 1974), 28–35 (discussing rights as "side-constraints"); John Rawls, *A Theory of Justice* (Cambridge, MA: Harvard University Press, Belknap Press, 1971), 150–61 (arguing that the benefits of slavery are not to be considered in setting up a just society).

content-dependent reasons for belief concerning the existence or weight of reasons antecedently existing for or against a certain course of action. One who requests another's performance of some particular action, however, claims to possess influential authority – the power to tip the balance of reasons in favor of that action by providing a new reason to so act, but not by barring action in accordance with the genuine merits as calculated by the individual to whom the request is made. Yet one who issues a command both purports to alter another's reasons for action in favor of a particular course of action and to exclude action in accordance with the reasons against that course of action. That is, one claims to possess practical authority by giving both a content-independent reason for action and an exclusionary reason for acting in accordance with that content-independent reason, and not in accordance with the antecedently existing reasons for action.

Legal theorists have long thought that the authority of the state – of legislative institutions, regulatory agencies, and the courts – is of the practical sort.[9] Certainly it is practical authority that the law *claims* on its own behalf.[10] When one sits at a traffic light in the middle of the

---

[9]   As Richard Flathman has written:

> From anarchist opponents of authority such as William Godwin and Robert Paul Wolff through moderate supporters such as John Rawls and Joseph Raz and on to enthusiasts such as Hobbes, Hannah Arendt, and Michael Oakeshott, a considerable chorus of students have echoed the refrain that the directives that are standard and salient features of practices of authority are to be obeyed by [those over whom authority is exercised] *irrespective of [those individuals'] judgments of their merits.*

Flathman, *The Practice of Political Authority*, 90 (emphasis added). Chaim Gans makes the connection between law and practical authority a conceptual one: "The duty to obey the law is a duty to obey commands. This truth stems from the concept of law and not from those of obedience or duty." Chaim Gans, *Philosophical Anarchism and Political Disobedience* (Cambridge: Cambridge University Press, 1992), 22. For Kant's famous insistence that law demands absolute obedience, "however defective it might be," see Immanuel Kant, *Metaphysical Elements of Justice*, trans. John Ladd (Indianapolis, IN: Bobbs-Merill, 1965), 140. For a nice discussion of Kant's theory of legal authority, see Kenneth W. Westphal, "Kant on the State, Law, and Obedience to Authority in the Alleged 'Anti-Revolutionary' Writings," *Journal of Philosophical Research* 17 (1992): 383–426.
        Some contemporary legal theorists have argued that laws should be thought to articulate standards, rather than rules. Such a view rejects the common presumption that law has practical authority in favor of the claim that law possesses mere theoretical authority. See, for example, Duncan Kennedy, "Form and Substance in Private Law Adjudication," *Harvard Law Review* 89 (1976): 1685–1778. It is to this claim that Chapters 5 and 6 are devoted.
[10]   For defenses of the thesis that the law at least *claims* practical authority, see Green, *The Authority of the State*, 63–89; Flathman, *The Practice of Political Authority*, 227; Raz, *The Morality of Freedom*, 76–7. Philip Soper has recently argued,

---

night despite the blatant fact that it would be safe to cross the intersection, one is appropriately thought to take its color as both a (content-independent) reason to sit there and an (exclusionary) reason not to act on the overwhelming reasons to run the light. When one receives an adverse judgment in a court of law requiring payment of compensation to an injured plaintiff, the fact that the court has issued such a judgment is itself thought to be both a (content-independent) reason to pay compensation and an (exclusionary) reason to refrain from acting on the reasons that one presented during the trial for not paying such compensation. And when the legislature enacts a particular statutory provision barring the prosecutorial use of character evidence to prove a defendant's criminal conduct, a judge is thought to have both a new (content-independent) reason to exclude such evidence and an (exclusionary) reason to refrain from second-guessing the wisdom of the legislature and admitting such evidence on the ground that the legislature's decision is thought by the judge to be mistaken.

THE PARADOX OF PRACTICAL AUTHORITY

Despite the plausibility given by common practice to the traditional notion that governmental institutions possess practical authority, it is not at all clear that obeying traffic signals, paying compensation, and barring particular sorts of testimony are rational if done *because* a citizen or official has been so instructed. In short, it is not at all clear that the contemporary concept of legal obligation is not irresolvably paradoxical. If it is a canon of practical rationality that we act on the balance of reasons available to us, and if a government only has practical authority if it can command us to act in ways that may not comport with the balance of reasons as we see it, then obedience to law of the sort required by the exercise of practical authority violates a central principle of rationality. How could it ever be rational to act contrary to the balance of reasons as one sees it solely because one has been told to do so?[11] Such is the paradox of practical authority.[12]

however, that the data of social practice suggest that legal systems do not, in fact, make claims to practical authority of the sort commonly supposed by legal theorists. See Philip Soper, "Law's Normative Claims," in *The Autonomy of Law*, ed. R. George (Oxford: Oxford University Press, 1996).

[11] Anarchists have put this quandary in somewhat different terms. For example, according to Robert Paul Wolff's formulation, the principle of autonomy, which he took to be of supreme moral value, requires action on the basis of one's own judgment on all moral questions. Robert Paul Wolff, *In Defense of Anarchism* (New York: Harper & Row, 1970), 12–14. Because the exercise of practical

The Paradox as Illusion

Having equipped ourselves with the elementary theoretical machinery with which to understand the paradox that confronts one who posits practical authority as the foundation of legal authority, we are

authority may require action contrary to one's own judgment, it may require the forfeiture of one's moral autonomy. On Wolff's account, then, the dilemma of practical authority arises from its fundamental immorality, not, as I have cast it, from its fundamental irrationality. However, because Wolff's notion of autonomous judgment is parasitic on the principles of practical rationality herein presupposed, the dilemma confronting the defender of practical authority is ultimately better reduced to a conceptual one. For other formulations of this dilemma, see Carl Friedrich, *Tradition and Authority* (London: Pall Mall Press, 1972), 45; William Godwin, *Enquiry Concerning Political Justice*, ed. K. Codell Carter (Oxford: Clarendon Press, 1971), 90; Green, *The Authority of the State*, 23–6; Raz, *The Authority of Law*, 3; Charles W. Hendel, "An Exploration of the Nature of Authority," in *Nomos I: Authority*, ed. Carl J. Friedrich (Cambridge, MA: Harvard University Press, 1958), 4–6. For a thoughtful discussion of what he calls "autonomy-based anarchism," see Gans, *Philosophical Anarchism and Political Disobedience*, 5–41.

12 George Christie has advanced the novel argument that, if there can be no general obligation to obey the law, there can be no general moral obligations. Presumably he would insist that, if according practical authority to law is paradoxical, so is according it to the maxims of morality. Because such a conclusion is absurd, he argues, it must not be paradoxical to attribute practical authority to law. His argument proceeds from the claim that moral obligations can be as over- and underinclusive as rules of law.

> It is taken as self-evident that one is obliged to behave morally. This obligation is then interpreted to include a general obligation to keep one's promises and a general moral obligation not to lie, etc. Morality is considered as a totality and is not broken down by considering the specific moral character of particular acts. When these writers turn to the law, however, they are not content with a broad precept – such as that one has a general moral obligation to obey the law – but instead focus upon the moral obligation to obey specific legal obligations in specific circumstances. Fair enough. What I assert is that if you apply the same technique to moral obligations, not surprisingly, one arrives at the same results. People can make silly promises and even promises that it would be immoral to keep; that does not mean that it makes no sense to talk of a general moral obligation to keep one's promises.

George C. Christie, "On The Moral Obligation to Obey the Law," *Duke Law Journal* 1990 (1990): 1331–32. I do not think that moral maxims can be over- or underinclusive. If there are instances in which one should lie, then there can be no general maxim categorically and exceptionlessly prohibiting lying. Indeed, to think that moral maxims can be over- or underinclusive is to think that there are "true" obligations – call them "shmoral obligations" – relative to which our obligations can be over- or underinclusive. But to say this is to generate a vicious regress. The most that Christie can be arguing is that short, incomplete statements of our more complex moral obligations (such as is provided by the Ten Commandments) can be theoretically authoritative. The same is true of the rules of law. But, as will become clear in Chapters 5 and 6, to accord the law (or the abbreviated statements of our moral obligations) theoretical authority is not to accord it the power to obligate us.

now in a position to examine what has become perhaps the most cel-
ebrated attempt to explain both the source of and the solution to that
paradox. Joseph Raz has argued that one who thinks that the concept
of practical authority is incoherent is fundamentally confused about
the dynamics of practical reasoning.[13] His claim is that a sophisticated
view of what it is to engage in practical deliberation renders the paradox of practical authority merely apparent. Raz's appeal to a so-called
sophisticated view of practical reasoning has been hailed by many
contemporary legal theorists as the definitive means of escaping,
once and for all, the difficulties that have long been thought to plague
the traditional view of legal authority and obligation.[14] Those in the
Razian tradition agree that if what ought to be done, all things considered, were identical to what ought to be done on the balance of
first-order reasons, then the demands of a practical authority would
indeed violate the principles of rationality, because the demands of
authority would then require that we refrain from acting on precisely
those reasons which must be acted on for a particular course of action to be rationally justified.[15] Razian defenders insist that reason
never justifies abandoning one's conclusions concerning what ought
to be done, all things considered. They argue, however, that what
ought to be done, all things considered, is not identical to what ought
to be done on the balance of first-order reasons for action. Decisions
concerning what ought to be done, all things considered, involve
complex deliberations that include an appeal to both first-order and
second-order reasons for action. It is often the case that reason itself
requires that we act contrary to the balance of first-order reasons –
that we act on the basis of second-order reasons that prevent us from
considering or acting on the balance of first-order reasons.

First-order reasons for action are, on the Razian view, both those
content-dependent reasons that determine the merits of a particular
action, of which the utterances of an epistemic authority are mere

---

13 See Joseph Raz, *Practical Reason and Norms,* 2d ed. (London: Hutchinson & Sons,
    1990), 65–84.
14 As Leslie Green has said, "Joseph Raz has offered an explanation of [legal au-
    thority] which is both elegant and substantially correct. According to him, the
    dilemma of authority is an illusion created by an oversimple view of practical
    reasoning in general." Green, *The Authority of the State,* 37–8 (footnote omitted).
    See also Hart, *Essays on Bentham,* 262; Neil MacCormick, *Legal Right and Social
    Democracy* (Oxford: Clarendon Press, 1982), 232; Donald Regan, "Law's Halo,"
    in *Philosophy and Law,* eds. Jules Coleman and Ellen Frankel Paul (Oxford: Basil
    Blackwell, 1987), 15.
15 See Raz, *The Authority of Law,* 27.

evidence, and those content-independent reasons for action that are given by the performative utterances of one who possesses influential authority or practical authority (e.g., requests, commands, promises). Second-order reasons, on the other hand, are those reasons that we have either to act on the basis of certain first-order reasons or to refrain from acting on the basis of certain first-order reasons. Those in the latter category of second-order reasons were called above "exclusionary reasons." The reasons given by a practical authority – those previously called "protected reasons" – function, on the Razian view, at both the first-order and second-order levels: They function both as content-independent reasons for action, to be added to the balance of first-order reasons that bear on the wisdom of a particular action, and as exclusionary reasons which bar action based on the first-order reasons that one antecedently had not to engage in the commanded conduct.[16]

According to those within the Razian camp, one who thinks that the exercise of practical authority is inconsistent with rational choice-making wrongly assumes that there are no valid protected reasons for action – that is, that one is never justified in not doing what ought to be done on the balance of first-order reasons for action. In short, one wrongly assumes that there are no second-order exclusionary reasons for action. If there is an example that makes intelligible the manner in which one might refuse to act on the balance of first-order reasons for action, then one must admit the existence and force of second-order exclusionary reasons. And with such an admission the paradox of practical authority is rendered illusory and the traditional theory of legal obligation is vindicated.

The Paradox as Reality

Two related problems confront this account of how a complex theory of practical reasoning dissolves the paradox of practical authority. The first is that it is extremely difficult to generate an example of a case in which some principle clearly functions in a manner that is consistent with the canons of rationality as a protected reason that excludes one

---

[16] This account of the reasons provided by a practical authority captures commonly held views concerning the role of rules in practical reasoning. As G.J. Warnock states, "What the rule does, in fact, is to *exclude* from practical consideration the particular merits of particular cases, by specifying in advance what *is to be done*, whatever the circumstances of particular cases may be." G.J. Warnock, *The Object of Morality* (London: Methuen, 1971), 65 (emphases in original).

from acting on the balance of first-order reasons. The second and more significant problem provides the reason that it is difficult to construct such an example; the concept of a protected reason is conceptually incoherent, and, as such, the Razian solution to the paradox of practical authority is no solution at all.

The Problem of Examples

Consider the example that both Raz and Green employ to explicate the exclusionary feature of the protected reasons for action that laws are thought to provide.[17] Suppose that one has had a long and strenuous day and that one is both physically and psychologically exhausted. Suppose further that one is presented with a business proposition that must be considered by the end of the evening – a proposition that promises both significant benefits and a worrisome amount of risk. Suppose that one concluded that, even if one tried to compute the balance of reasons in favor of accepting the proposition, one could not be sure that one would reach an accurate conclusion. Then one would have a (second-order) reason to refrain from acting on the balance of (first-order) reasons as one sees it. That is, the fact that one is tired is a reason to turn down the business proposition – to refrain from action based on the reasons to accept such a proposition. Even if one's computation of the balance of (first-order) reasons suggests that one ought to accept the business proposition, the second-order principle dictating that one ought not to make business decisions when overly tired makes it rational, all things considered, to refuse to act on the (first-order) balance of reasons (as one now calculates it).

Despite its intuitive plausibility, this example is an unfortunate one. What the Razian theorist needs to show is that there exists a plausible case in which one has a reason not to act on what one takes to be the balance of first-order reasons. But that one is tired is not a reason to refrain from acting on the balance of first-order reasons. Indeed, it is not a reason for *action* at all. Rather, when one judges oneself incompetent to make wise decisions, one has a reason for *belief*; that is, one functions as an epistemic authority about the likely truth of one's conclusions concerning the balance of first-order reasons for and against a particular action. That one is tired is mere evidence of the fact that the premises which one is employing in one's practical

---

17 Green, *The Authority of the State*, 38; Joseph Raz, "Reasons for Action, Decisions and Norms," in *Practical Reasoning*, ed. Joseph Raz (Oxford and New York: Oxford University Press, 1978), 130.

inferences may well be false. Exhaustion gives one a reason to believe that there are *other* reasons for not engaging in the business deal that, if apparent, would show the deal to be a poor one. Insofar as exhaustion makes it probable, or at least possible, that the balance of reasons for action as one sees it is inaccurate, one has a reason to think that there are other reasons for action which are at the present elusive, but which, if added to the balance, would result in one's finding the business deal an unwise proposition. Thus, knowledge of a condition of incompetence merely makes one an epistemic authority about the truth of inferences involving complex sets of premises. And, as such, it does not purport to preclude one's deliberation about, or action on, the first-order reasons for disregarding one's incompetence. While the only rational course of conduct may well be to refrain from entering a complex contract, this course of conduct is dictated by the balance of first-order content-dependent reasons. One's condition of incompetence is but evidence of the fact that, in working out these content-dependent reasons, one may not be employing true premises.[18]

To take an example that seemingly better captures the exclusionary feature of protected reasons that can purportedly be defended with a complex theory of practical reasoning, consider the case of a promise. Let us suppose that a brother has promised his sister to look after their mother so that his sister can take a vacation. His sister has refused to leave their mother because their mother does not like to be alone, has no close friends, and is frightened of having a stranger hired to care for her. Her needs, however, are minimal. She requires only that someone write her occasional letters, do difficult maintenance work, and provide her with some company. The son, who has always disliked his mother, promises to meet these needs during his sister's absence, in the hope that in so doing he can improve his relationship with his mother. However, after a few days of shouldering this re-

---

[18] Leslie Green acknowledges this "troublesome" response: "Why then shouldn't the various incapacity cases just be treated as expressions of doubt about the validity of one's assessment of the balance of reasons? Isn't that just what it means not to trust one's own judgement?" Green, *The Authority of the State*, 53. The answer to such queries, claims Green, will fall out of analysis of how content-independent reasons can have practical force even though they are not ultimate reasons. But while Green goes on to a discussion of the validity of content-independent reasons, see ibid., 54–62, he fails to explicate just how his discussion overcomes the objection that he recognizes as so troubling to any attempt to provide an example of protected reasons by appealing to cases of incapacity.

sponsibility, he tires of the task and hires a home companion to relieve him of his duties.

In many people's view, the brother has failed to take seriously the force of his promise to his sister. As the Razian would describe it, the promise gave the brother a new, content-independent reason for assisting his mother – a reason above and beyond his desire to improve their relationship – because the very fact that he promised was itself a reason to act as promised. The promise also gave him an exclusionary reason to disregard the first-order content-dependent reasons that he would otherwise have to not render aid to his mother, such as inconvenience, frustration, anger, and so on. Thus, on promising to look after his mother, the brother was not entitled to weigh and act on the balance of antecedently existing first-order reasons affecting the provision of required assistance, even if that balance (including in it the content-independent reason given by the sheer fact that assistance was promised) weighed in favor of hiring another to take over the responsibility. In other words, the brother estopped himself from concluding that the benefits of the promise were not worth its costs, even if such a conclusion were true.[19] His promise thus made him a practical authority over his future actions, because it gave him a protected reason to render aid to his mother, however distasteful the task. Such are the dynamics of practical authority, claim those in the Razian tradition.

Of course, the problem with this example is that it fails to do the work that needs to be done. While we all tend to think that there is something especially important about promising, the example fails to show that promising is rational. The point of the example here is to illustrate how it might be rational, all things considered, to refrain from doing what the balance of first-order reasons dictates. And in the scenario with the brother, it is no more obviously rational to act against the balance of first-order reasons for action than it would be to so act in the face of a law. In their ability to give protected reasons for action, both laws and promises stand or fall together.[20] Raz and

[19] For rich discussions of the theory of promising that this formulation reflects, see P.S. Atiyah, *Promises, Morals and Law* (Oxford: Clarendon Press, 1981), 106–22; H.L.A. Hart, *The Concept of Law* (Oxford: Clarendon Press, 1961), 42–3; Rawls, *A Theory of Justice*, 344–50; Rawls, "Two Concepts of Rules," 3; Joseph Raz, "Promises and Obligations," in *Law, Morality, and Society*, eds. P.M.S. Hacker and Joseph Raz (Oxford: Clarendon Press, 1977), 210.

[20] It would thus seem to follow that, if the traditional concept of practical authority is found to be conceptually incoherent because the notion of a protected reason on which it depends (under the Razian formulation) is confused, then the

Green thus invoked the example that they did (that of the tired business person), rather than an example that appeals to promising or any other performative utterance that is thought to generate a protected reason for action, precisely because such an example appears to make more plausible the manner in which their sophisticated theory of practical reasoning makes rational what a simple theory of practical reasoning makes irrational. They thus found it necessary to appeal to an example in which reason in a sense judges itself and finds itself lacking. But, as we saw, in all such cases in which we have a reason to doubt our ability to be reasonable – to determine and balance the first-order reasons for and against action – that doubt functions only as a reason for belief concerning the validity of those reasons, not as a reason for action. It thus functions epistemically authoritatively, giving neither content-independent nor exclusionary reasons for action.

The Conceptual Problem
The difficulty that one faces in attempting to construct a persuasive example of a situation in which it is rational to refrain from acting on a balance of first-order reasons is but the tip of the philosophical iceberg. The deeper and much larger difficulty to which this problem points is the failure of those in the Razian tradition to dissolve the paradox of practical authority. The Razian "solution" depends fundamentally on one's failure to be clear about what is entailed by the concept of a protected reason for action.

Consider what one would be left with if one were in fact to have a protected reason to pursue a particular course of action. Raz claims that a protected reason for action leaves one with both a new (content-independent) reason to pursue that action and a new (exclusionary) reason not to act on the reasons for not pursuing it. But Raz explicitly slurs this formulation of the force of an exclusionary reason with a different and quite revealing account. Rather than claiming that an exclusionary reason gives one a reason not to *act* on the (first-order) reasons against the commanded course of action, Raz often claims that an exclusionary reason gives one a reason not to *consider further*

concept of promising must also be found incoherent if unpacked by reference to protected reasons. I have elsewhere argued that this conclusion is not disastrous, because the special nature of promising can be captured without invoking the troublesome components of protected reasons. See Heidi M. Hurd, "Challenging Authority," *Yale Law Journal* 100 (1991): 1661–2. See also the discussion of promising in Chapter 4.

the (first-order) reasons against the commanded action.[21] This is puzzling, because at crucial points he disavows this equation.[22]

The dissonance between these claims can be resolved by distinguishing between the respective points of view held by commanders and subjects. While a commander's order may not, from the commander's point of view, preempt a subject's own deliberation concerning the merits of the order, that order may well preempt such deliberation from the subject's point of view. Two reasons for this preemption present themselves. First, if one is barred from acting on certain reasons, it is unnecessary, at least as a pragmatic matter, to continue one's consideration of their merits.[23] Second, if one were to continue to dwell on the reasons for action that one is barred from acting on, one may be led to act contrary to the exclusionary reason provided by the practical authority. One cannot pick the reasons on which one acts; that is, one cannot make it be true that one is motivated to act for one reason rather than another.[24] Hence, to continue to consider the reasons for action excluded by a protected reason risks the possibility

---

21   "The whole point and purpose of authorities . . . is to pre-empt individual *judgment* on the merits of a case (emphasis added)." Raz, *The Morality of Freedom*, 47–8. "[T]hrough the acceptance of rules setting up authorities, people can entrust *judgment* as to what is to be done to another person or institution . . . (emphasis added)." Ibid., 58–9. Authorities "have the right to replace people's own judgment on the merits of the case." Ibid., 59. "[O]nly by allowing the authority's judgment to preempt mine altogether will I succeed in improving my performance and bringing it to the level of the authority." Ibid., 68.

22   Thus he insists that "no surrender of judgment in the sense of refraining from forming a judgment is involved, because there is no objection to people forming their own judgment on any issue they like." Raz, *The Morality of Freedom*, 40. And in reply to Hart, who formally construes authority as a power to bar deliberation, Raz maintains:

> Surely what counts, from the point of view of the person in authority, is not what the subject thinks about how he acts. I do all that the law requires of me if my actions comply with it. There is nothing wrong with my considering the merits of the law or of action in accord with it. Reflection on the merits of actions required by authority is not automatically prohibited by any authoritative directive. . . .

Ibid., 39. See also Raz, *The Authority of Law*, 26.

23   As he puts it, "One may form a view on the merits but so long as one follows the authority this is an academic exercise of no practical importance." Raz, *The Authority of Law*, 24–5. An alternative account of why these formulations are frequently conflated might rest on the claim that the mental *act* of contemplating such reasons is itself among the actions barred by the exclusionary feature of a protected reason.

24   For a defense of the thesis that persons cannot choose or control the reasons on which they act, see Michael S. Moore, "Authority, Law, and Razian Reasons," *Southern California Law Review* 62 (1989): 878–83.

that one will be led to act on the basis of one of those reasons, rather than on the basis licensed by the protected reason.

The same can be said, however, for one's consideration of the *other* first-order content-dependent reasons that one has to pursue the commanded course of action – the reasons that one had antecedent to the content-independent reason provided by the fact that the command was issued. The fact that the reasons against the commanded action are rendered impotent by the command makes it the case that one needs only a single first-order reason for acting as commanded, and this is provided by the sheer fact that the command has been issued. Upon receiving a command, one is thus left with a single reason for acting in accordance with it: the fact that the command was uttered.

The question that must be answered, then, is this: Why would it ever be rational to act solely because one has been told to do so? Is what makes such action rational the sheer fact that one has been commanded to pursue it? Or does the rationality of a commanded act depend on something further? One is curiously reminded by this question of the centuries-old puzzle that has befuddled so many Christian theologians: Is what God says right because God says it? Or does God say it because it is right? Just as this analogous inquiry appears to invite but two possible answers, so the inquiry about the rationality of action in accordance with a command invites but two possible answers.

Let us first look at the theological analogue. If the commands of God are right solely because God commands them, then any such command, however heinous it might appear (and here one should imagine a particularly egregious one), must be thought to bear the moral status of being a true deontic description of how we ought to act. Alternatively, if God issues commands because they are the right commands, then their moral pedigree comes not from God but from some "higher" authority (that is, some God-independent moral reality). Similarly, if an action is rational because one has been commanded to engage in it, then anything that can be commanded by one possessed of practical authority (and here one might think of a Gestapo's extermination orders) will have the status of being rational. On the other hand, if the rationality of an action is determined by something other than the fact that it has been commanded, then having as one's sole reason for action the fact that one has been commanded to do it is not having as one's reason for action that which is determinative of practical rationality. That is, rationality, like the moral force of God's commands, must come from a "higher" authority (some source other than the commander's authority).

Thus, practical authority appears conceptually confused. This confusion is perhaps best captured as follows:

1. If the exclusionary reason generated by a command bars action in accord with first-order reasons *against* the commanded action, then it (pragmatically) bars the consideration of those reasons.
2. If the exclusionary reason generated by a command (pragmatically) bars the consideration of those reasons, then it (pragmatically) bars the consideration of any reasons *for* the commanded action beyond that provided by the fact that the command has been issued.
3. HENCE: Upon the receipt of a command, the only reason for action that one should consider is the fact that some action has been commanded.
4. However, if an action is rational solely *because* it has been commanded, then any action that is commanded is rational. (This makes it rational to stand on one's head, quit one's job, or undertake a Kamikaze mission, if ordered).
5. If, alternatively, an action is rational *only if* it comports with other requirements, then the sheer fact that an action has been commanded cannot rationally justify the performance of the act. (This makes rationality and obligation conceptually distinct.)
6. Since the consequent of premise 4 is false, the antecedent of premise 4 must be false.
7. Since the antecedent of premise 4 must be false, then the antecedent of premise 5 must be true.[25]
8. If premise 5 is true, then to act rationally one must act for reasons other than the fact that one has been so commanded.
9. HENCE: Action pursued on the basis of an exclusionary reason is irrational.

Raz and his followers need not, at this stage of the game, roll over and admit that, in construing laws as the commands of a practical authority, they have been mistaken about the dynamics of legal authority. There is still much about the argument as I have just stated it that should stick in their collective craw. Indeed, it would appear that those anxious to defend the Razian strategy have at their disposal five arguments, each of which can be thought to demonstrate that an

---

[25] The suppressed premise in 7 is: If it is not the case that an action is rational solely *because* it has been commanded, then an action is rational only if it comports with other requirements.

exercise of practical authority does not completely curtail one's ability to engage in first-order deliberation. If any of these arguments are true, it would defeat the charge of incoherence by showing that the exclusionary feature of the protected reasons for action purportedly provided by laws is consistent with enough first-order balancing of content-dependent reasons to make legal obligation rational. The first two of these arguments are usefully seen as attempts to defeat premise 4 of the above-stated analysis, while the latter three arguments are best thought of as attempts to "soften" premise 3.

Contesting the Legitimacy and Jurisdiction of a Practical Authority. First, those of the Razian persuasion will no doubt seek to remind us that theirs is an analysis of what practical authority is if it is in fact *legitimately* possessed by anyone. Their argument does not depend on a government's actually possessing it, nor does it give us reasons to suppose that any particular government should possess it.[26] Thus, defenders of the Razian theory will argue that premise 4 in the above argument must be reformulated so as to make it conditional on an already existing, legitimate practical authority. It might thus be stated as follows:

4'. If an action is rational solely *because* it has been commanded by a *legitimate* practical authority, then any action commanded by a legitimate practical authority is rational.

By making premise 4 conditional on authoritative legitimacy, proponents of the Razian view may well think that they have carved out a considerable sphere within which rational actors are still at liberty to balance first-order reasons for action before being obligated to obey the laws enacted by a practical authority. On pain of an infinite regress, Razians readily admit that, whatever the reasons that justify the exercise of practical authority, their status must be content-dependent.[27] To suggest that the reasons that legitimate the practical authority of

---

[26] Green, *The Authority of the State*, 23; Raz, *The Morality of Freedom*, 46; Raz, *The Authority of Law*, 13, 46, 182.

[27] "[T]he validity of content-independent reasons is most plausibly explained by the fact that acting on such reasons may indirectly produce conformity with content-dependent reasons of the ordinary sort." Green, *The Authority of the State*, 56. For an explicit analysis of the dependence of content-independent reasons on content-dependent ones, see Raz's discussions of his "dependence thesis" and his "normal justification thesis." Raz, *The Morality of Freedom*, 42–57.

a governmental institution are themselves content-independent would simply send us in search of why those content-independent reasons were themselves legitimate, and this would force us to search for reasons that justify the giving of content-independent reasons. Because there must be a set of first-order content-dependent considerations that legitimates the exercise of practical authority, a rational actor is fully entitled to ask, when confronted with a claim of practical authority, whether that set of considerations in fact legitimates the claimed authority.[28] And this query enables that actor to balance the first-order content-dependent reasons for action in a manner that ultimately renders any subsequent compliance with the laws enacted by that authority rational.

Following close on the heels of this argument is a second argument which purports to modify further the above restatement of premise 4. According to this second argument, premise 4' must be made conditional on the practical authority's proper jurisdiction. It will not be rational to comply with the command of a practical authority, even if that authority is found to be legitimate, unless one has also established that the command is within the jurisdiction of that authority. As Raz says, "Most, if not all, authorities have limited powers. Mistakes which they make about factors which determine the limits of their jurisdiction render their decisions void."[29] Thus, premise 4' must be further modified as follows:

---

[28] It is on this basis that Raz reaches his piecemeal view of legal authority and obligation. As he says:

> People differ in their knowledge, skills, strength of character and understanding. Since the main argument for authority depends on such factors, it is impossible to generalize and indicate an area of government regulation which is better left to individuals. But regarding every person there are several such areas. One person has wide and reliable knowledge of cars, as well as an unimpeachable moral character. He may have no reason to acknowledge the authority of the government over him regarding the road-worthiness of his car.

Raz, *The Morality of Freedom*, 77–8. It is thus the case, according to Raz, that *legitimate* governmental authority varies from individual to individual. Because the extent to which a government is a legitimate authority for a given citizen depends on the extent to which there are content-dependent reasons to take its laws as authoritative, there is, at least initially, a need to test legitimacy by weighing first-order reasons for action. And insofar as the balance will "weigh out" differently for different citizens, a government will legitimately bind citizens differently. Hence, while there is an obligation to obey the law when it is enacted by a legitimate practical authority, there is not, as Raz admits, a general obligation to obey the law. See Raz, *The Authority of Law*, 233–49.

[29] Raz, *The Morality of Freedom*, 62.

4". If an action is rational solely *because* it has been commanded by a legitimate practical authority *acting within the limits of its jurisdiction*, then any action commanded by a legitimate practical authority acting within the limits of its jurisdiction is rational.

Razian theorists will claim that, so formulated, the consequent of premise 4" is no longer false. Once the practical authority claimed by a governmental institution is found to be legitimate, and once its laws are determined to be within its proper jurisdiction, then the rational course of action will indeed be to obey those laws, to the exclusion of contrary reasons for action. The paradox of practical authority is thus rendered delusive if the above reformulation is defensible. But is it? Can Raz and his followers in fact escape the paradox of practical authority by making premise 4 conditional on a finding of legitimacy and jurisdiction?

At the heart of the conviction that premise 4" is true, and perhaps trivially true, is the assumption that once one has established the legitimacy and jurisdiction of a practical authority it will then be rational to take that authority's commands as singularly sufficient reasons for action.[30] In other words, once one has modified premise 4 so as to make it conditional on there being a legitimate practical authority whose commands are within the limits of its proper power, premise 6 will be false, because it will in fact be the case that it is rational to comply with its commands.

Such a view rests squarely on the further assumption that practical reasoning in the presence of a legitimate practical authority is a hierarchical process. The rational course of action in such circumstances is first to establish the legitimacy and jurisdiction of the authority, and then to abide by that authority's directives without further examining one's reasons for thinking the exercise of that authority either legitimate or within its proper jurisdiction.[31] That is,

---

[30]   "One can be very watchful that it shall not overstep its authority and be sensitive to the presence of non-excluded considerations. But barring these possibilities, one is to follow that authority regardless of one's view of the merits of the case (that is, blindly)." Raz, *The Authority of Law*, 24.

[31]   As Richard Friedman states:

[An individual cannot] make his obedience *conditional* on his ... personal ... examination of the thing he is being asked to do. Rather, he accepts as a sufficient reason for following a prescription the fact that it is prescribed by someone acknowledged by him as entitled to rule. The man who accepts authority ... surrender[s] his ... individual judgment ...

one must surrender one's judgment of the content-dependent reasons for and against action and act solely on the basis of the content-independent reason for action provided by the fact that the authority (which one antecedently found to be legitimately acting within its jurisdiction) has issued some directive.[32] It is the commitment to a tiered process of practical reasoning that justifies this surrender of judgment; and it is this justification for the surrender of judgment that allows those who defend a Razian theory of practical authority to dispute the truth of premise 6 upon the modification of premise 4, and so to "solve" the above paradox. Yet the adoption of a hierarchical theory of practical deliberation itself generates difficulties of such dimensions that it cannot provide the foundation for a solution to the paradox of practical authority.

What could possibly make one's surrender of judgment practically rational? How could it be rational to comply with the laws of a legitimate practical authority *solely because* those laws have been enacted and are in keeping with the jurisdictional limits of that authority? Raz's own answer has two parts, corresponding to the two theses that must be made out in order to defend both the legitimacy and the jurisdiction of a practical authority. First, once one has established the legitimacy of a practical authority, one's "blind" obedience to the will of that authority will in general allow one to better achieve action that is consistent with the balance of content-dependent first-order reasons

---

[in that] he does not insist that reasons be given that he can grasp and that satisfy him, as a condition of his obedience.

Richard Friedman, "On the Concept of Authority in Political Philosophy," in *Concepts in Social and Political Philosophy,* ed. Richard E. Flathman (New York: Macmillan Co., 1973), 129. The effect of an authoritative rule is that, "in the cases in which it applies, it is specified in advance what is to be done; that question is removed from the sphere of judgment on the particular merits of each case." Warnock, *The Object of Morality,* 65 (emphasis omitted).

32 "There has been a remarkable coalescence of opinion around the proposition that authority and authority relations involve some species of 'surrender of judgment' on the part of those who accept, submit or subscribe to the authority of persons or a set of rules. . . ." Flathman, *The Practice of Political Authority,* 90. See, for example, Hannah Arendt, "What Was Authority?," in *Nomos I: Authority,* ed. Carl J. Friedrich (Cambridge, MA: Harvard University Press, 1958), 82 ("Authority . . . is incompatible with persuasion. . . .Where arguments are used, authority is left in abeyance."); Thomas Hobbes, *Leviathan,* ed. Michael Oakeshott (Oxford: Basil Blackwell, 1946), 166 ("COMMAND is, where a man saith, *do this, or do not this,* without expecting other reason than the will of him that says it."); John Locke, *The Second Treatise of Government,* ed. J.W. Gough (Oxford: Basil Blackwell, 1976), 44 ("All private judgment of every particular member being excluded, the community comes to be umpire. . . .").

for action than one would achieve if one acted directly on one's judgment of that balance (Raz's "normal justification thesis"[33]). Second, once one has established that the laws of a practical authority are within the jurisdiction of that authority, one can be relatively confident that one's "blind" obedience to those laws in general comports with the reasons that would have antecedently applied to one's conduct (Raz's "dependence thesis"[34]). Judgment thus requires its own surrender. Because in the long run our actions will better comport with the right reasons for action if we cease to balance those reasons and act instead on the commands of a legitimate authority that do not exceed that authority's jurisdiction, practical rationality itself requires that we cease to balance the reasons for action. Practical reason thus requires that we abandon its methods in the short run to assure behavior that best accords with those methods in the long run.

However, as those in the Razian tradition readily admit, this justification for the surrender of judgment pursuant to a finding of authoritative legitimacy and jurisdiction implies that a legitimate practical authority may indeed pass undesirable and morally objectionable laws from time to time.[35] Raz writes: "Even so, it may be that regarding each individual, he is less likely successfully to follow right reasons which apply to him anyway if left to himself than if he always obeys the directives of a just government including those which are morally reprehensible."[36] Still, as Raz says, some directives may be so immoral – so grossly in violation of the balance of reasons for action under the circumstances – that no government may be thought legitimate that issues them.[37] And herein lies the crux of the trouble.

---

[33] Raz, *The Morality of Freedom*, 53–7.

[34] Ibid., 47–53. Raz's dependence thesis is a moral thesis about how authorities *ought* to act; they *ought* to issue directives that in general reflect the balance of reasons for action available to the subjects of those directives. Yet insofar as a rational actor would assess the likelihood that an authority would comply with the dependence thesis at the point of determining the legitimacy of an authority (via the normal justification thesis), the actor's determination of legitimacy gives her reason, thereafter, to take the authority's commands as dependent, and therefore rational.

[35] "Remember that sometimes immoral or unjust laws may be authoritatively binding. . . . Governments may be acting within their authority when they act unjustly or immorally." Ibid., 78, 79. "Under the best conditions, there is no guarantee that all laws will be consistent with morality." William N. Nelson, *On Justifying Democracy* (London and Boston: Routledge & Kegan Paul, 1980), 131.

[36] Raz, *The Morality of Freedom*, 79.

[37] Ibid. Thus, as Green recognizes, "Content-independence must be construed so as to be compatible with the substantive truth that grossly immoral [laws] do not bind." Green, *The Authority of the State*, 47.

If it is rational to abide by the laws enacted by a practical authority only if that authority is *legitimate* (premise 4"), and if an authority is legitimate only if its laws better cohere with the balance of content-dependent reasons for action than do the judgments of those for whom it is an authority (the normal justification thesis), then it must be the case that, to judge whether indeed an authority is acting legitimately, one must balance for oneself the reasons for action in each case in which a law applies so as to police the ability of the claimed authority to order action in conformity with that balance. The ability of a claimed authority to achieve action that in the long run better accords with the balance of reasons can only be measured if, at each decision, one judges for oneself the reasons for action and compares one's judgment with that reached by the authority. Without engaging in such long-term comparisons, one has no basis for thinking the claimed authority legitimate, and hence one has no rational foundation for abiding by that authority's will. In short, one lacks any foundation for thinking that Raz's normal justification thesis applies. Yet, because the attribution of practical authority to governmental institutions bars one from engaging in just the sort of comparisons upon which practical rationality depends, that attribution cannot be rationally defended.

Raz purports to defeat this objection when he denies that "the legitimate power of authorities is generally limited by the condition that it is defeated by significant mistakes which are not clear."[38] As Raz maintains, there is a substantial difference between great mistakes and clear mistakes. While authoritative legitimacy is defeated by the making of a clear mistake, it is not defeated by the making of a mistake that would be laborious to discover, however great such a mistake may be. And because "[e]stablishing that something is clearly wrong does not require going through the underlying reasoning,"[39] the admission that clear mistakes defeat legitimacy is not an admission that individuals must balance the content-dependent reasons for action in each case in which an authority commands action in order to establish the legitimacy of that authority.

Yet the analogy on which this argument rests is its undoing. Raz asks us to consider the addition of thirty numbers. Such an addition may be only slightly but quite clearly mistaken, as when the sum is an integer while only one of the added numbers is a decimal fraction. But it may be grossly but quite undetectably mistaken, as when the

---

[38] Raz, *The Morality of Freedom*, 62.
[39] Ibid.

sum is off by several thousand for a reason that can only be discovered by laborious recalculation. The point of this example is to provide us with the intuition that when a calculator makes the clear but small mistake, we may consider it "illegitimate"; but when it makes the gross but undetectable mistake, we may nevertheless be entitled to take its figure as definitive of the sum, if, in general, it provides us with correct figures.

But, of course, a calculator might systematically miscalculate only when the going gets tough (when the figures get large and the computations get lengthy). That is to say, it might never make a clear mistake while constantly making obscure ones. We thus need some means of determining whether, in general, such a calculator provides us with the right results. Surely Raz would not think it rational to judge a calculator's accuracy on difficult calculations solely by its accuracy on simple ones. Similarly, Raz could not think it rational to judge a government's authoritative legitimacy by its failure to make clear mistakes. Just as a calculator that systematically but obscurely miscalculates is not much of a calculator, so a government that enacts laws which systematically but obscurely fail to reflect the right reasons for action is not a legitimate authority (on Raz's own view). And because such systematic error can only be discovered by recalculating (or otherwise evaluating) a calculator's computations and by "rebalancing" the reasons for the laws enacted by a government, it must be admitted that legitimacy indeed requires just the sort of first-order deliberation that a practical authority purportedly bars.

Thus, if (1) the rationality of abiding by a practical authority depends on the legitimacy of that authority, and (2) the legitimacy of a practical authority can be established only by balancing the first-order content-dependent reasons for action, and (3) practical authority bars one from balancing those first-order content-dependent reasons, then practical authority cannot be rational. Such is the difficulty that is inevitably invited by an attempt to piggyback the rationality of practical authority on the concept of legitimacy.

A parallel argument can be mustered against the jurisdictional condition. If it is rational to abide by the laws of a practical authority only if those laws are within the proper *jurisdiction* of that authority (premise 4"), and if an authority acts within its proper jurisdiction only when its laws are based on the reasons for action that apply to one prior to the promulgation of those laws (the dependence thesis), then it must be the case that, to judge whether the laws enacted by a government are within the jurisdiction of its practical authority, one must balance the antecedently existing reasons for action in each case in which those laws apply, so as to ensure that in extending its authority to that case the government has not exceeded the bounds of its jurisdiction. The propensity of a claimed authority to issue commands in keeping with its jurisdiction can only be measured if, at each decision, one judges for oneself the antecedently existing reasons for action, and then determines whether the commands of the authority in fact reflect that balance. Without engaging in such a balancing process, one has no basis for thinking that the commands of the claimed authority are in keeping with its appropriate jurisdiction, and hence no rational foundation for thinking that Raz's dependence thesis applies. Yet again, because the attribution of practical authority bars one from engaging in just this sort of first-order deliberation, that attribution cannot be rationally defended.

Thus, if (1) the rationality of abiding by a practical authority depends on the extent to which that authority acts within its jurisdiction, and (2) the jurisdiction of a practical authority can be determined only by balancing the first-order content-dependent reasons for action, and (3) practical authority bars one from balancing those first-order content-dependent reasons, then practical authority cannot be rational. Such is the further difficulty that is inevitably engendered by an attempt to make the rationality of practical authority conditional on a jurisdictional limitation.

The difficulties that attend attempts to supplement premise 4 with the conditions of legitimacy and jurisdiction cannot be avoided by claiming that one's investigation of these conditions must be temporally limited. That is, it cannot be the case that a practical authority need only undergo a probation period. One cannot test a government's authority for some trial period and conclude at the end of that period that, because the laws enacted by that government in fact better achieved action in accord with the balance of reasons than would one's own decisions, one's rational course of conduct is to surrender one's judgment to that government and obey its laws without question in the future. So long as rationality depends on an authority's legitimacy or jurisdiction – so long as premise 4" remains true – it will only be rational to comply with the will of an authority if that will comports with the balance of reasons for action, and this can only be determined by comparing one's own judgments concerning that balance to those of the authority throughout the duration of that authority's claim to legitimacy or jurisdiction. The process of comparison in which one must engage to establish the legitimacy or jurisdiction of a government's claim to practical authority must thus last as long as does the claim.

The upshot of this argument, then, is that, even if we were to replace premise 4 with premise 4", the concept of practical authority would remain confused; because the consequent of premise 4" is no more true than was the consequent of premise 4, premise 6 remains true. If the Razian theory is to make practical authority conceptually coherent, it must do so by contesting some premise other than premise 4.

Let us now turn to an alternative set of arguments with which those persuaded by the Razian approach might avail themselves – that set which purports to soften the force of premise 3. As a means of motivating these arguments, it will be useful to recall the lemma of which premise 3 is the conclusion. That lemma runs as follows:

1. If the exclusionary reason generated by a command bars action in accordance with first-order reasons *against* the commanded action, then it (pragmatically) bars the consideration of those reasons.
2. If the exclusionary reason generated by a command (pragmatically) bars the consideration of those reasons, then it pragmatically bars the consideration of any reasons *for* the commanded action beyond that provided by the fact that the command has been issued.
3. HENCE: Upon the receipt of a command, the only reason for action that one should consider is the fact that some action has been commanded.

If premise 3 can be softened – if it can be shown that a command does not exclude one's consideration of *all* first-order reasons for action except the content-independent one provided by the sheer fact that the command has been issued – then the paradox of practical authority is solved.

Contesting the Unstated Exceptions to a Practical Authority's Laws. One means of contesting premise 3 is by claiming that, while the commands of a legitimate practical authority indeed give sufficient reasons for action, those to whom they are addressed must nevertheless interpret just what actions those commands in fact require. Commands that apparently function as general orders may in fact carry unstated exceptions, in the same way that promises, as Rawls has argued, carry unstated exceptions.[40] One who makes a promise does not mean that it shall be fulfilled come hell or high water. And similarly, one who issues an order is not likely to intend that it be carried out if it becomes apparent that its execution will lead to unforeseen disaster. That is, insofar as unstated exceptions are indeed unstated, one who receives a general order must consider more than the fact that such an order was issued (contrary to what is claimed by premise 3). One must consider whether one's circumstances are those within which one is excepted from action. And presumably this will require that one balance the content-dependent reasons for action as a means of determining the likelihood that one's circumstances are among those that give rise to an unstated exception. Premise 3, according to such an argument, is overstated, because it fails to allow for a substantial amount of deliberation concerning the content-dependent reasons to think that an unstated exception is implicit in the command.

Yet this means of allowing content-dependent reasons for action to enter into one's practical deliberations concerning what one ought to do in the face of a law is surely doomed as a means of blunting the force of premise 3. If there were an unstated exception to the generality of a law in *every* case in which there existed a conflict between the action commanded by that law and the action licensed by the balance of first-order content-dependent reasons, then laws would lack the sort of normative power that those of the Razian persuasion attribute to them. By never requiring anything other than what is antecedently required by the balance of first-order content-dependent reasons for action, laws would fail to change our reasons for action, and so fail to possess practical authority as it is analyzed along Razian lines. On pain of giving up the very concept that they are seeking to defend, Raz and his followers thus cannot allow all conflicts between the commands of law and first-order reasons for action to be a result of unstated exceptions within the commands.

However, if only some laws carry unstated exceptions, one is returned to the paradox as it is stated above. Defenders of the Razian theory must provide an account of how one is to distinguish between those instances in which the laws of a legitimate practical authority

40 See Rawls, "Two Concepts of Rules," 17. See also Flathman, *The Practice of Political Authority,* 115 (defending the view that rules and commands possess unstated conditions that are analogous to those possessed by statements of intentions and statements of right).

bear unstated exceptions that exempt one's compliance and those instances in which they do not. To determine whether a law is accompanied by an unstated exception, one will be forced to balance the content-dependent reasons for action, concluding, presumably, that if the reasons against the commanded action overwhelmingly outweigh the reasons for that action, one is likely excepted from acting as commanded by some unstated proviso. This is, however, just the sort of full-scale first-order deliberation that one is barred from engaging in by the exclusionary reason that a law provides under the Razian analysis. And thus the paradox: If (1) the laws enacted by a practical authority carry, in some instances, unstated exceptions, and if (2) one must balance the content-dependent reasons for and against a law in *each* set of circumstances in which that law applies to determine whether the law excepts action in those circumstances, and if (3) one is barred by the exclusionary nature of the laws of a practical authority from balancing these content-dependent reasons for action in each set of circumstances to which a law applies, then (4) a practical authority requires what it simultaneously prevents, and is thus incoherent. Insofar as the argument concerning unstated exceptions attempts to enable one to consider more than the sheer fact of a practical authority's command, it is in conflict with a central tenet concerning the nature of practical authority, namely, that the exclusionary aspect of protected reasons bars one from considering the content-dependent reasons for action each time one is called on to act for those protected reasons. Premise 3 thus cannot be softened via an appeal to unstated exceptions without jettisoning the central concept of practical authority defended by Raz and his followers.

Contesting the Scope of a Practical Authority's Laws. Premise 3 might be attacked, however, on a somewhat different basis. Those defending a Razian theory of practical authority are likely to claim that the conclusion reached in premise 3 fails to reflect the fact that exclusionary reasons tend to be restricted in scope.[41] While the protected reasons

---

[41]   Leslie Green has written:

> It is not, of course, presumed that political authority must claim or enjoy maximal *exclusionary scope*, ruling out of court all reasons but those which the law sanctions. The authority of the state may well be, and had better be, limited. Within those limits, however, it functions to control the commitments of its subjects (emphasis added).

Green, *The Authority of the State*, 61.

for action that are provided by the commands of law indeed exclude one's further deliberation about some first-order reasons for action, they do not exclude one's deliberation about all such reasons. The limited exclusionary scope of a command thus entitles one to consider more than the sheer fact that a certain action has been commanded. If in fact there are reasons for action that lie beyond the scope of an authoritative directive, one is at liberty to weigh these against the content-independent reason for action that the authority's command otherwise makes sufficient for action.[42] Thus, for example, the mother's command to her son to take his umbrella might well exclude him from further considering some reasons for not taking his umbrella, such as the fact that he *wants* to get wet, that he *wants* to ruin his new pants, and that he feels silly carrying an umbrella, while not excluding him from considering other reasons for not taking his umbrella, for example, that the umbrella is not in fact his own or that the umbrella is broken and so will not keep him dry. Premise 3 may thus be softened by admitting the limited scope of authoritative directives. And once softened, premise 3 fails to give rise to the paradox of practical authority as it is played out in premises 4 through 9.

Yet just what determines the scope of a practical authority's legitimate commands? It is clear that commands themselves do not specify their own exclusionary scope. The mother's command to take an umbrella does not specify the fact that her son's embarrassment is excluded as a reason for not taking the umbrella while the true ownership of the umbrella is not excluded as a reason for not taking the umbrella. Instead, the exclusionary scope of a command must be derived from the content-dependent reasons for action that exist antecedent to the command. In keeping with the Razian normal justification thesis, the enactment of a law must be thought to exclude those reasons for action that, if included, would cause one to act less often on the right reasons for action than one would if those reasons for action were in fact excluded. A law must not be thought to exclude those reasons for action that, if included, would result in action that

---

[42]   As Raz writes:

> [T]o maintain that orders are both first-order and exclusionary reasons is not tantamount to maintaining that they are absolute reasons. They may not exclude certain conflicting reasons, and when this is the case one must decide what to do on the balance of the non-excluded first-order reasons, including the order itself as one prima facie reason for the performance of the ordered action.

Raz, *The Authority of Law,* 22.

better conformed with the right reasons than would action that was not based on those reasons.

Once again, this test of a law's exclusionary scope requires us to engage in just the sort of first-order deliberation that is purportedly barred by the exercise of practical authority. On receiving a command, we must first determine the content-dependent reasons for action, and then judge which of those reasons would be best excluded from our deliberations and which would be best included. Those reasons that are best excluded can then be thought to determine the exclusionary scope of the command. This degree of first-order deliberation already exceeds that which is thought consistent with the decrees of a practical authority, but it does not stop here. To know which reasons would be best included in our deliberations and which would be best excluded, we would have to have some notion of which reasons, if included in our deliberations, would enable us to act, in the long run, in a manner that comports with the right balance of reasons for action, and vice versa. The problem thus becomes analogous to the problem encountered when attempting to determine the legitimacy of a practical authority. The extent to which one's actions in the long run better accord with the balance of reasons if certain reasons are excluded from one's deliberations can only be measured if, at each decision over the course of the long run, one judges whether one's action in the face of excluded reasons better comports with the balance of right reasons for action than would one's action if those excluded reasons were included. But this process requires far more first-order deliberation than does the mere balancing of (all of) the content-dependent reasons for action, because we are now forced to balance our balances! To determine whether embarrassment functions as a reason for action that should in general be either included or excluded, we must balance all of the times in which including embarrassment as a reason for action produced the right balance against all of the times in which excluding it resulted in a more accurate balance. And we must compute all of our balances over again and weigh them against each other in each case in which we are called on to determine the scope of a command – because they will change with each new instance that contributes to those balances a reason either to include or exclude a particular content-dependent reason.

The Razian is thus caught in the same old bind. If he attempts to soften premise 3 by allowing individuals to limit the exclusionary scope of a law, he is forced to admit that premise 3 will license all manner of first-order deliberation. Because this deliberation is precisely what is meant to be excluded by the protected reasons for action that the commands of law uniquely give, this strategy will defeat the concept of practical authority that the Razian seeks to defend. Those who seek a means of preserving the Razian theory of practical authority are thus still stuck with premise 3 as it is stated above, and, as such, they remain unable to resolve the paradox to which the Razian theory gives rise.

Contesting the Force of a Practical Authority's Laws. A final strategy remains, however. Those persuaded that the difficulties encountered above are overwhelming may indeed decide that it is high time to dispose of the Razian notion of a protected reason. They thus may be inclined to join Stephen Perry in thinking that the concept of an exclusionary reason as it is formulated by Raz and many of his followers must be modified. The modification proposed by Perry involves taking exclusionary reasons as reasons to change the weight of antecedently existing reasons for action, rather than as reasons to exclude those content-dependent considerations altogether.[43] In Perry's view, a protected reason excludes the antecedently existing *force* of certain content-dependent reasons, but it does not bar the consideration of those reasons altogether. Once their force is diminished, however, it is not surprising that these reasons fail to compete with the content-independent one that is provided by the fact that one has been commanded to pursue a particular course of action.

Does this reevaluation of the dynamics of a protected reason help to defeat the paradox of practical authority? Perry might well think that it does, because once one is not excluded by a law from considering the content-dependent reasons for action, premise 3 appears false and, hence, the paradox appears defunct. Yet the same questions can be asked about the diminishment of a reason for action as were asked about its exclusion. How could the sheer fact that a law has been passed reduce the importance of antecedently existing reasons for action? What would possibly be rational about reducing the weight of certain content-dependent reasons for action solely on the basis that a command has been issued? Something analogous to the normal justification thesis is called for here. But just as the normal justification thesis fails to provide an escape from the paradox of practical authority because it depends on what it prevents – namely, the

---

43 See Stephen Perry, "Judicial Obligation, Precedent and the Common Law," *Oxford Journal of Legal Studies* 7 (1987): 215.

long-term balancing of all first-order reasons for action – so an analogous thesis will fail here. All of the arguments that demonstrated the dependence of the normal justification thesis on our ability to balance first-order reasons for action will be available to demonstrate the dependence of an analogous thesis on our long-term ability to calculate the correct weight of those first-order reasons. Thus, diminishing the weight of certain first-order reasons will turn out to be as irrational as excluding those first-order reasons altogether.

It thus appears that the paradox of practical authority has proved itself to be of a particularly resilient strain. The Razian solution to the paradox is no solution at all. Raz and his followers have failed to show that what ought to be done, all things considered, is not tantamount to what ought to be done on the balance of first-order reasons. And as Raz himself has admitted, if what ought to be done, all things considered, is identical to what ought to be done on the balance of first-order reasons, then the demands of practical authority violate the principles of rationality. By virtue of first reducing one's (first-order) reasons for action to the singular, content-independent reason provided by the fact that a law has been passed, and then requiring action in accordance with that reason, practical authority entails the conceptual divorce of obligation and rationality. Because commands do not make all commanded actions rational, even when they are issued by a legitimate practical authority that is acting within its jurisdiction, and despite their possessing unstated exceptions and limited scope, it must be conceded that what is rational to do is conceptually distinct from what one may be commanded to do. While what is commanded may well correlate with the balance of first-order (content-dependent and content-independent) reasons as computed in accordance with the demands of practical rationality, it need not do so. But then, to act rationally, one must compute that balance of reasons – that is, one must engage in just the sort of practical deliberation that the exclusionary aspect of a protected reason bars – and then act on that balance. Protected reasons are thus conceptually incoherent. They require what reason prohibits. And because the concept of practical authority requires the giving of protected reasons, it too cannot be sustained.

Chapter 4

The Failure of Influential Authority

If the traditional concept of legal authority is indefensible, then we are compelled to conclude that the source of legal obligations must lie elsewhere. Those who have sought to construct an alternative theory of legal obligation that captures commonplace convictions about the binding power of law have turned to what I call the notion of "influential authority." According to a theory of influential authority, the law does not possess the power to compel blind obedience – that is, it does not provide exclusionary reasons for action. But it does provide new (content-independent) reasons for action – reasons that are typically sufficiently weighty to require one to act "as if" the law possessed practical authority.

If, by virtue of possessing influential authority, the law gives persons reasons for obedience in all but the most exceptional circumstances, then the dilemma of legal perspectivalism may rightly fail to inspire serious concern. While citizens in exceptional circumstances may find themselves morally justified in breaking the law, and judges in such cases may find themselves torn between the demands of the correspondence thesis and the systemic values that make sense of their role as judges, one could hardly characterize this as a cause for jurisprudential crisis.

In this chapter, I shall explore the claim that law possesses influential authority of a sort that precludes disobedience in virtually all instances. In Chapters 5 and 6, I shall distinguish two theories that construe the authority of law as epistemic rather than moral. As I shall argue, only the second of these provides us with a conceptually cogent and normatively attractive theory of the kind of obedience that the law can rightly claim. While that theory will return us squarely to the dilemma of legal perspectivalism, it will escape the fundamental problems that confront those who advance alternative, more traditional theories of authority.

THE NATURE OF INFLUENTIAL AUTHORITY

Those who attribute to law influential authority claim to provide compelling reasons for legal obedience without inviting the paradox of practical authority. They maintain both that, in assessing whether to obey the law, persons are entitled to consider (and act on) those reasons that would define the limits of the law's legitimacy, jurisdiction, and scope, *and* that, once these factors are considered, persons will still have persuasive reasons to abide by the law, even in most instances in which they may deem its provisions morally illegitimate.

To motivate this theory, imagine that, in response to his mother's command to take his umbrella, a son argues that the sheer fact that she has issued an order is not a reason for him to act in a manner that is contrary to the many reasons that he has not to take his umbrella. In short, he denies the coherence of her claim to practical authority. The mother might reply that there exists an alternative account of why her son should take an umbrella. Such an account is two-pronged. First, the son must admit that her utterance is at least entitled to the weight of a request: It gives him a new content-independent reason for taking his umbrella, although this reason is merely to be added to the other (first-order content-dependent) reasons that he might have for so doing and weighed against the reasons that he has to leave the device behind. Second, the mother might insist that, while her utterance gives him but another first-order reason for action, there are a number of other (content-independent) considerations which make that reason a particularly weighty one. For example, children owe their parents a considerable debt of gratitude, and honoring parental requests (whatever their content) is a particularly good way of repaying, to some measure, this debt. On this alternative account of the mother's authority, the son is compelled to take his umbrella because, as a result of the weight that must be assigned to his duty of gratitude and, hence, to his mother's request, the balance of reasons favors this action. And indeed, because any request on her part is entitled to great weight for similar reasons, her son will always be compelled to act "as if" his mother were a practical authority.

The mother, in effect, invokes just the sort of claims to which one would have to appeal to make compliance with the demands of a practical authority rational; that is, she claims to ground the rationality of her son's action on something other than the issuance of a command. There are, she claims, normative considerations that make the very fact that she has prescribed a certain act a particularly compelling first-order reason for performing that act. Instead of claiming that such a new first-order reason is also a protected reason, however, she only claims that it is a first-order reason of great weight. Insofar as this reason will generally possess sufficient weight to trump countervailing ones, her son will generally act in the manner that would be required if her reasons were of a protected sort; that is, he will act "as if" she were a practical authority.

Inasmuch as a theory of influential authority makes possible the weighing and balancing of all reasons for and against action, it does not give rise to the lemma that triggers the paradox of practical authority. By providing a new content-independent reason for action, an influential authority does not exclude our consideration of countervailing reasons for action (and thus premise 1 of the lemma is avoided). An influential authority does not render superfluous our consideration of the reasons for action that support the content-independent reasons provided by its utterances (and thus premise 2 of the lemma is avoided). It is not the case, then, that when one receives a request, the only reason for action that one need consider is the fact that the request has been made (the conclusion reached in premise 3 of the lemma). And once this is clear, no question arises concerning the rationality of one's subsequent action; that is determined by the accuracy of one's assessment of the balance of the first-order reasons for action, including both the content-dependent and the content-independent reasons that are available.

If, in fact, the laws of the state provide new content-independent reasons for action, and if there are persuasive normative arguments to be made for why such reasons are particularly weighty, then we have at hand a plausible account of why it *appears* that the prescriptions of the state require a surrender of judgment on the part of citizens. If the reasons for action provided by legislative enactments in general possess substantial weight, then it is no surprise that citizens act, and must continue to act, as though they thought the law possessed practical authority. In what follows, I shall take up, and ultimately dispute, a set of normative arguments that purport to explain why the state should be thought to generate new content-independent reasons for action that are of a particularly compelling weight.

SOURCES OF INFLUENTIAL AUTHORITY

As a means of approaching the types of arguments that must be made to establish that the state ought to be thought to give content-independent reasons for action, consider the types of arguments needed to show why it is that we ought to take another's request as a new reason for action. Let us begin by supposing that we have received a request for a loan that we think lacks merit. The individual who has made the request is not in need of money, is fully capable of earning money on her own, and will spend the money poorly if it is given. Are there reasons, however, to give the individual money solely because she has requested it? Those who would answer in the negative should recall the many occasions on which they have given money to local beggars and street people solely because they have been unable to avoid their requests. If there are indeed reasons to take requests as new reasons for action, those reasons must be of a special type. They must justify why a request that lacks merit nevertheless functions as a reason for action of some weight.

One who thinks that a nonmeritorious request is itself a reason for action cannot claim that it is such a reason only because, and to the extent that, it comports with the balance of first-order content-dependent reasons for action because, *ex hypothesi*, the nonmeritorious request does not. What one must argue is that there exists a *further* (first-order content-independent) consideration that justifies one in taking a nonmeritorious request as a content-independent first-order reason for action. Such a further reason must function in a manner which is distinct from the content-dependent reasons that comprise the balance of reasons which determines the morality of the action in question, but must not, on pain of inviting the paradox of practical authority, exclude one's consideration of that first-order balance. The reasons that must be given in support of the authority of a request must thus meet two conditions. First, such reasons must be based on considerations that are independent of the merits of the request (the independence condition). Their status thus cannot be that of purely evidential reasons for *belief* about the content-dependent merits of what is requested, because they would then fail to make out why requests provide new content-independent reasons for action. Second, such reasons cannot be of an exclusionary sort, because otherwise the theory of influential authority will invite the same paradox as does a theory of practical authority (the nonexclusionary condition).

The same conditions will apply to the reasons that might be given for why the laws of a state ought to be considered influentially authoritative. Any account of why one should take the fact that the state has enacted a law as itself a weighty reason for obeying that law must (1) avoid an appeal to the merits of acting as directed (the independence condition), and (2) allow for the consideration of countervailing reasons for not acting as directed (the nonexclusionary condition).

To test the extent to which the laws of a state give new content-independent reasons for action, it will be useful to postulate a scenario that is similar to the one assumed in the discussion of requests; that is, we must suppose that we are faced with a government that periodically issues nonmeritorious laws. We must then determine whether there are any grounds to think that the sheer fact that such laws have been passed is itself a reason to act as directed. What we need is thus a plausible example of a government that would give us content-independent reasons to act in accordance with its laws even when those laws are wrong on the balance of the content-dependent reasons for action.

It has long been assumed that democratic governments provide us with this example. Few have doubted that the fact that a government is democratic is itself a uniquely compelling reason to take its laws as particularly weighty reasons for action.[1] When asked why it is that one should abide by the majority's will when what is willed fails to comport with one's own accurate judgment of the merits, it is tempting to appeal to the substantive principle that the majority has a right to have its way. No one is entitled to run red lights, withhold taxes, drive without insurance, ship toxic chemicals without the required identification, or engage in public displays of nudity without taking very seriously the sheer fact that a majority of her fellow citizens have manifested their disapproval of such conduct through democratic legislation.

I propose to take up what appears to be the most convincing argument for thinking that a government can function as a particularly compelling influential authority: the argument from democracy.[2] If laws enacted by democratic institutions provide weighty content-independent reasons for action, then at least some sorts of government have the potential to claim an influential authority that is sufficient

---

[1] But see Michael J. Perry, *Morality, Politics and Law* (New York: Oxford University Press, 1988), 110 ("[N]o argument from democracy can support the claim that . . . there is a presumptive obligation to obey all laws.").

[2] There is, in fact, no single argument from democracy – there are only democratic theories. See Robert A. Dahl, *Preface to Democratic Theory* (Chicago, IL: University of Chicago Press, 1956), 52–3. Indeed, as the rich literature on the topic suggests, there is no single concept of what democracy *is*. I do not propose to spend time on this definitional question. Instead, I will follow those who insist that the proper definition of democracy will fall out of the proper justification of majoritarian decision making. See ibid., 2–6.

to prompt citizens to act "as if" they were bound by a practical authority. On the other hand, if we lack reasons to accord democracies influential authority, then it seems that *a fortiori* we are forced to conclude that no government should be taken to function as an "as if" practical authority. If democracies fail to give (content-independent) reasons for obedience when their directives are mistaken, it is reasonable to suppose that the same will be true of other systems of government, such as dictatorships and aristocracies, for which we have less compelling normative arguments. Thus, the extent to which we can appeal to a theory of influential authority as a means of preserving a rich notion of legal obligation will seemingly turn on the extent to which we can defend the principle of democracy as a reason to take the laws of a state as giving particularly weighty content-independent reasons for action.

Our inquiry can now be cast as follows. Suppose that we are faced with a choice between a dictatorship and a direct majoritarian democracy – a democracy in which all citizens vote on proposed pieces of legislation, and those pieces voted for by the majority are enacted into law.[3] Suppose further that the content of the laws enacted and enforced under each of these systems is identical. Suppose finally that these laws lack merit. Just as in the case of the request above, the content-dependent reasons for acting in accordance with the laws are outweighed by the content-dependent reasons for acting in a con-

---

[3] I have picked this form of government over its unanimous or representative competitors because it best provides us with a means of testing the majoritarian principle. Were we instead to adopt a model of unanimous direct democracy, we would encounter the same difficulty as that quite willingly faced by the anarchist Robert Paul Wolff. On Wolff's account, only a unanimous direct democracy can be justified, because only under such a regime is it the case that the state's authority does not jeopardize moral autonomy. Robert Paul Wolff, *In Defense of Anarchism* (New York: Harper & Row, 1970), 120–8. But as Jeffrey Reiman has pointed out, "A person who 'obeys' a command *because* it coincides with his autonomous decision is not obeying authority." Jeffrey H. Reiman, *In Defense of Political Philosophy* (New York: Harper, 1972), 11. To test the persistent intuition that a legal authority binds citizens even when they disagree with its laws – even when the content-dependent reasons that bear on the legislated action conflict with the content-independent reason for action provided by a law – we must adopt a model of democratic government that allows for conflicts between what we would choose (prior to the enactment of the law) and what is required under that law. A *majoritarian* democracy provides us with such a model. And because nothing except complexity is added by supposing that democracy to be representative, we shall suppose for the sake of argument that the government in question is a direct one. For an exhaustive discussion of the various models of democracy, see Dahl, *Preface to Democratic Theory*, and Alf Ross, *Why Democracy?* (Cambridge, MA: Harvard University Press, 1952), 202–43.

trary manner. The issue is this: Are there reasons to obey the laws enacted by a direct majoritarian democracy that are not applicable within a dictatorship? Does the very fact that those laws were enacted by a majority of citizens give us a special reason to comply with them that we do not have in the case of their enactment by a single individual? In short, does the majority have a right to be wrong? If these questions are answered affirmatively, then at least the dictates of democratic institutions give content-independent reasons for action and so possess influential authority of a sort that may be sufficiently weighty to bind citizens "as if" those directives possessed practical authority. We might then rightly conclude that the dilemma of legal perspectivalism does not pose a significant threat to our most basic moral and systemic values, because only in the most exceptional circumstances will citizens be justified in disobeying the law, and in such cases whatever judges decide will have little bearing on the systemic integrity of our judicial system.

There are two types of theories that might be thought to give special reasons for why rules enacted by a majority give new content-independent reasons for action while the identical rules enacted by a minority (a dictator or an aristocracy, for example) do not. The first sort of theory can be characterized as *act*-based: Theories of this sort generate content-independent reasons to comply with democratically enacted laws from the performance of certain voluntary actions. The second sort of theory can be characterized as *duty*-based: Theories of this sort generate content-independent reasons to abide by democratically enacted laws from moral requirements that apply irrespective of any acts performed by citizens. In what follows, I propose to outline three act-based theories and one duty-based theory, each of which is designed to give a special reason for taking the rules enacted by a majority as giving new reasons to behave in a manner consistent with those rules, even when one thinks those rules wrong.[4] In each case I will argue that the theory fails to give us a reason to grant influential

---

[4] This taxonomy of the reasons to attribute influential authority to democratic states is motivated by the similar categorization of the reasons for political obedience in general that is provided by John Simmons. See A. John Simmons, *Moral Principles and Political Obligations* (Princeton, NJ: Princeton University Press, 1979), 11–16. For helpful discussions of these arguments as they function in that more general context, see Chaim Gans, *Philosophical Anarchism and Political Disobedience* (Cambridge: Cambridge University Press, 1992), 42–93; Kent Greenawalt, "Promise, Benefit and Need: Ties That Bind Us to the Law," *Georgia Law Review* 18 (1984): 727–70; R. George Wright, "Legal Obligation and the Natural Law," *Georgia Law Review* 23 (1989): 997–1020.

authority (of any weight) to democratically enacted laws because it either violates the independence condition (and so collapses into an account of why democratic laws possess theoretical authority) or violates the nonexclusionary condition (and so invites the paradox that defeated the theory of practical authority).

Act-Based Theories of Influential Authority

Many have thought that one's performance of particular acts within a democracy gives rise to special obligations to take the rules enacted by that democracy as giving content-independent reasons for compliance, even when one objects to the content of those rules – that is, even when one is in a political minority. In other words, certain acts are thought to generate an obligation to treat democratically enacted laws as having influential authority. H.L.A. Hart has defined the sort of special obligation generated by act-based theories of obedience in terms of four conditions: (1) it is generated by the performance of some voluntary act (or omission); (2) it is owed by a specific person (the "obligor") to a specific person or persons (the "obligee[s]"); (3) it generates a correlative right on the part of those to whom it is owed (the obligees); and (4) it is the nature of the transaction or relationship into which the obligee and obligor enter, not the nature of the required act, that renders the act obligatory.[5] The theories examined in this section each purport to establish an obligation to take rules enacted by a political majority as sources of new reasons for action on the basis of voluntary acts performed by those who may find themselves in a political minority. These acts are thought to create special relationships between those in a minority and those in the majority, and so are thought to provide content-independent reasons for a minority to abide by the majority's will (that is, reasons that satisfy the independence condition) – even when the minority takes the majority to be wrong about the balance of content-dependent reasons for action.

The Theory of Reciprocity

Both H.L.A. Hart and the early John Rawls maintained that an important source of the special obligation to abide by the rules enacted by one's government is the principle of reciprocity or fair play.[6] The

---

5 H.L.A. Hart, "Are There Any Natural Rights?", *The Philosophical Review* 64 (1955): 179–80.
6 Ibid., 108–14; John Rawls, "Justice as Fairness," *The Philosophical Review* 67 (1958): 179–83. Peter Singer has advanced an argument that rests on a principle very like reciprocity. In his view, democratic procedures serve as fair means of achieving

principle of reciprocity prohibits the unjust enrichment of those who would enjoy the advantages of others' cooperation without themselves cooperating. According to this principle, individuals who enjoy the benefits that accrue from others' adherence to rules have an obligation to follow those rules also, and those who have followed the rules have a right to demand cooperation by those who have reaped the benefits of their compliance.

In this section, I propose to examine whether this principle can be thought to function as a reason to take the fact that rules have been enacted by a democratic government as an additional content-independent reason to comply with those rules. To test whether the principle functions as a reason to confer influential authority on majoritarian democracies, it must be reformulated. On the necessary reformulation, the principle claims that individuals who enjoy the benefits that accrue from the willingness of others to attribute influential authority to democratically enacted rules have a reciprocal obligation to treat such rules as having influential authority, and so to take such rules as giving new content-independent reasons for action.

According to Rawls, obligations of reciprocity arise in situations that satisfy the following three conditions: (1) there is a mutually beneficial and just scheme of social cooperation that yields advantages only if everyone, or nearly everyone, cooperates; (2) cooperation requires a certain sacrifice from each individual, or at least involves a certain restriction of liberty; and (3) the benefits produced by cooperation within this scheme are, to a certain extent, free – that is, if any one person knows that others will continue to do their part, she will be able to share in the gains even if she does not do her part.[7] But mere benefaction from a cooperative scheme is insufficient to generate an obligation of reciprocity. In the language of our current discussion, mere benefaction fails to give one a reason to take the rules of a cooperative scheme as giving new reasons for action. While obligations of reciprocity need not be deliberately or knowingly incurred, a voluntary action of some sort is required: One who is obligated under

---

a compromise in situations of disagreement by which force is avoided. "To disobey when there already is a fair compromise in operation is necessarily to deprive others of the say they have under such a compromise. To do so is to leave the others with no remedy but the use of force in their turn." Peter Singer, *Democracy and Disobedience* (Oxford: Clarendon Press, 1973), 36. Because Singer's theory gives way to the same objections raised in this section to the theory of reciprocity, I will not further distinguish it here. For a full defense of the theory, however, see ibid., 30–45.

7   Rawls, "Justice as Fairness," 179–83.

this theory must have made some effort to obtain the benefit in question, or to have taken the benefit willingly and knowingly.[8] It is this voluntary action that both gives those responsible for the benefits rights to require reciprocal rule-following by those benefitted, and gives those benefitted a duty to so reciprocate.

As a theory of the influential authority of majoritarian democracies, the theory of reciprocity demands that we take the fact that a majority has enacted particular laws as a (content-independent) reason to adhere to those laws because we have accepted the benefits of others doing likewise. As members of a political majority, we benefit from the minority's willingness to add to the balance of reasons for action the fact that we in the majority prefer a particular course of action. The theory of reciprocity thus requires that when we find ourselves in a political minority, we reciprocally fulfill our obligation to take the laws enacted by the majority as a source of new reasons for action.

This account of why we should attribute influential authority to democratically enacted laws appears to meet the three conditions specified by Rawls for the generation of an obligation of reciprocity. First, the benefit that one receives from the democratic process is the opportunity to legislate one's will for oneself and others; but this benefit is only available if, in general, most individuals take the fact that the majority wills some course of action as itself a new reason to act as willed. One accepts this benefit whenever one participates in a political scheme that, at least some of the time, realizes (or at least has the potential to realize) this opportunity. Second, the sacrifice that one must make to assure this benefit amounts to taking the fact that a majority prefers some course of conduct as a new reason for action. One gives up the liberty of acting solely on the balance of the content-dependent reasons for action as one calculates it. Finally, the benefits of cooperation are to a certain extent free: If most individuals take the

---

[8] "He who accepts the procedures, the ideology, and the benefits of a legal system is obligated to submit to the enacted laws, even though he denies their wisdom or even their justice." Paul Weiss, "The Right to Disobey," in *Law and Philosophy*, ed. Sydney Hook (New York: New York University Press, 1964), 98. It is the condition of acceptance that prompts Robert Nozick to argue that the theory of reciprocity collapses into the theory of consent. Robert Nozick, *Anarchy, State, and Utopia* (New York: Basic Books, 1974), 90–5. For a helpful discussion of the theory of reciprocity and Nozick's criticism of it, see Simmons, *Moral Principles and Political Obligations*, 101–42. As a means of determining when one has "accepted" the benefits of a political system, see the analogous discussion of what is required to be thought a "participant" in a political process in Singer, *Democracy and Disobedience*, 45–59.

fact that a majority prefers a certain course of action as itself a reason to act in accordance with that preference, then one in the majority may enjoy the fact that the minority takes her preference as a reason for action without similarly doing so when she finds herself in the minority.

Yet despite the fact that the principle of reciprocity appears to be a reason to take democratically enacted laws as giving new content-independent reasons for action, this account of how democracies could be thought to possess influential authority rests on a host of unacceptable assumptions. First, to provide a reason to think that *all* citizens within a democratic state are obligated to treat democratic enactments as having influential authority, those who hold this theory must convincingly establish that all such citizens *participate* in the political processes of such a state, and so *accept* the benefits that they receive when a political minority reciprocally takes the majority's expression of will as itself a reason for action. Yet as has long been recognized, a great many citizens of democratic states fail to engage in activities that stand a chance of realizing the opportunity to constitute a political majority (the will of which the minority must then take to be a new reason for action according to the principle of reciprocity).[9] It must thus be admitted that this large class of citizens does not accept the benefits that may come from the willingness of others to add to the balance of reasons for action the fact that a majority has expressed a preference for a particular course of conduct, and so such a group cannot be thought to be obligated to reciprocate those benefits by following laws it deems unjustified.

Second, and more significant, the account construes the proper aim of citizens who *do* participate in democratic processes to be the imposition of their will on others, rather than the collective pursuit of optimal ways in which to organize and regulate social relationships. "Having one's way" is construed on this account to be the benefit of a majoritarian democracy and the sole basis for taking the laws enacted by a majority as giving new content-independent reasons for action. The theory of reciprocity thus licenses moral logrolling

---

[9] For similar arguments that might be employed against the theory of reciprocity, see the second section of this chapter concerning the theory of consent. As John Ladd notes, the theory of reciprocity differs from the theory of consent only insofar as it "provides us with a model of consent through participation rather than through contract." John Ladd, "Legal and Moral Obligation," in *Nomos XII: Political and Legal Obligation*, eds. J. Roland Pennock and John W. Chapman (New York: Atherton Press, 1970), 21.

in the interests of achieving the imposition of our preferences on others.[10]

But why should one treat "having one's way" as a benefit, unless one were to take "one's way" to be reflective of how society ought best to be organized and regulated? Having one's way appears to be of value only if one's way is in fact the *right* way of doing things – that is, only if one's way comports with the balance of content-dependent reasons for action. If the rules that one prefers are in fact the wrong rules – because they are unjust or inefficient (i.e., because they fail to reflect the balance of reasons for action) – then one should not want them to be enacted, and so one does not benefit from others' taking their enactment as a new content-independent reason for action.[11] But if one admits that "having one's way" counts only because one takes it to be reflective of how best to design rules to govern social transactions, then one must admit that having one's way is not, by itself, a value.[12] Similarly, if one believes that the only reason to grant the majority its way is because the will of the majority is likely to be reflective of how best to structure political arrangements, then one must

---

[10] As Henry David Thoreau said of the sort of compromise upon which the theory of reciprocity seems to rest:

> All voting is a sort of gaming, like checkers or backgammon, with a slight moral tinge to it, a playing with right and wrong, with moral questions; and betting naturally accompanies it. The character of the voters is not staked. I cast my vote, perchance, as I think right; but I am not vitally concerned that that right should prevail. I am willing to leave it to the majority. Its obligation, therefore, never exceeds that of expediency.

Henry David Thoreau, "Civil Disobedience," in *Civil Disobedience: Theory and Practice,* ed. Hugo Bedau (New York: Pegasus, 1969), 28.

[11] This argument clearly depends on an objective theory of preferences. What in fact is of benefit may not be what one thinks is of benefit; that is, one is benefitted by living in a just society – not necessarily by living in a society one thinks is just. This objective thesis, however, is implicit in people's subjective preferences. One may prefer that one's organs be donated at one's death. And one may think that death is synonymous with heart failure. But one's theory of death may turn out to be wrong (that is, death may be synonymous not with spontaneous heart and lung failure but with the cessation of brain activity). In that case, one does not want one's organs donated at the point of heart failure, but at the point of "real" death (whatever our best theory holds that to be). Anything short of this objective account of the content of preferences presupposes a shallow view of preferences, because it fails to take seriously the counterfactual thought experiment that so clearly characterizes what most persons in fact prefer: If one knew what would *in fact* benefit one, one would prefer it to one's own (mistaken) view of what would be of benefit.

[12] Such a conclusion reflects Thomas Nagel's claim that desire-satisfaction is not, by itself, a reason for action. See Thomas Nagel, *The View from Nowhere* (New York: Oxford University Press, 1986), 151.

admit that the fact that the majority has willed a particular rule is not, *by itself,* a reason to obey such a rule. And if one admits this, then one admits that there is no content-independent reason to abide by the rules enacted by the majority.

If individuals should comply with rules enacted by the majority only because such rules are more likely to be better than those preferred by the minority, is there any room left for considerations of reciprocity? One might think that there is. Reciprocity might function, for example, as an epistemic rule of thumb. In cases in which we are uncertain as to which of two rules might be optimal, the fact that others have deferred to our judgment in the past in cases in which we have been confident may give us a reason to defer to their confidently held judgments in cases in which we are uncertain. But the sort of reciprocity that this strategy represents is certainly not the sort that political theorists have invoked to ground a general obligation to obey democratic laws. Reciprocity on this account is simply the result of taking others' confidence in cases of uncertainty as a heuristic guide to determining which rules are optimal, because in cases in which we are confident we take own our confidence to be a heuristic guide to the rules to enact and so take our confidence to be a good basis for others to opt for the same rules. Reciprocity, on this account, does not generate a content-independent reason to adhere to the will of the majority. Rather, it functions as an epistemic strategy for detecting the content-*dependent* reasons for and against the enactment of proposed rules. If the principle of reciprocity merely functions as an epistemic rule of thumb, it fails to give us a reason to attribute influential authority to democratic governments: In failing to provide a foundation for taking democratically enacted laws as new reasons for action, it violates the independence condition.

It thus appears that the theory of reciprocity does not provide us with a reason to think that the laws enacted by a political majority give content-independent reasons for action. In other words, it does not support a claim that the fact that a majority has willed a particular set of rules is *itself* a reason to adhere to such rules. The principle of reciprocity thus fails to function as a reason to attribute influential authority to democratic enactments.

The Theory of Gratitude
In an attempt to solve the first of the two problems I raised against the theory of reciprocity, one might appeal to an alternative source of influential authority, one that does not rely on the requirement that

individuals *accept* the benefits received from cooperative schemes to be bound by their rules. This alternative account, the traditional version of which was first propounded by Socrates in Plato's *Crito*,[13] bases the obligation to attribute influential authority to a majority on the moral requirement of gratitude for the benefits received from the enactments of that majority (although such benefits may never have been accepted). In this theory, even the vast number of individuals who do not and who may never participate in democratic processes are obligated to factor in, as a new reason for action, the fact that a particular law has been preferred by the majority, because they owe a debt of gratitude for the benefits they have received as a result of others' taking majority preferences as new reasons for action. Such a debt functions as a "special case of the general obligation to help persons who benefit us."[14]

To think that those who do not participate in democratic processes nevertheless benefit from others' willingness to attribute influential authority to majoritarian laws, one must be able to give an account of just what these benefits are. One might think, for example, that the *potential* to become a participant who is capable of constituting a political majority (the preferences of which all citizens must then take as new reasons for action) is itself a benefit that is sufficient to give rise to an obligation of gratitude requiring those who never realize this potential (and thereby never accept the benefits of a majoritarian democracy) nevertheless to attribute influential authority to the majority's laws. However, such an argument would surely stretch the notion of a benefit to an extreme.

---

[13]   Plato, *Crito*, in *The Collected Dialogues of Plato*, eds. Edith Hamilton and Huntington Cairns, trans. Hugh Tredennick (Princeton, NJ: Princeton University Press, 1961), 27.

[14]   John Plamenatz, *Consent, Freedom and Political Obligation*, 2d ed. (London and New York: Oxford University Press, 1968), 24. For a defense of the view that gratitude can ground a general obligation to obey the law, see A.D.M. Walker, "Political Obligation and the Argument from Gratitude," *Philosophy and Public Affairs* 17 (1988):191–211; A.D.M. Walker, "Obligations of Gratitude and Political Obligation," *Philosophy and Public Affairs* 18 (1989): 359–64. For a critique of Walker's thesis, see George Klosko, "Political Obligation and Gratitude," *Philosophy and Public Affairs* 18 (1989): 352–9. Ronald Dworkin might also be thought to have a gratitude-based theory of obligation because, as he argues, in a "true community" citizens have an obligation to obey the law that derives from their having received the benefits of the community. See Ronald Dworkin, *Law's Empire* (Cambridge, MA: Harvard University Press, 1986), 167–216. For general discussions of the significance of gratitude to political obligation, see Greenawalt, "Promise, Benefit and Need," 754; Wright, "Legal Obligation and the Natural Law," 1000.

Alternatively, one might suggest that the outcomes of democratic decision making are more likely to be substantively beneficial than are the outcomes of dictatorial decision making. Democratic decision making, in such an argument, might best produce legislation that accords with the balance of content-dependent reasons for action and so might achieve greater equality, distributive justice, and individual liberty. One owes a debt of gratitude to those who take the laws that result from democratic processes as new reasons for action, because one reaps greater substantive rewards from those laws than one would from the laws of any other system.

Two responses to such an argument are in order. First, such an argument bucks our original hypothetical. We began by assuming that we are faced with two regimes, one a majoritarian democracy and one a tyranny, both of which produce *identical* substantive outcomes by enacting *identical* laws. The question we set out to answer was whether we have any special reason to take the laws enacted by a majority as giving us new reasons for action that we do not have when the same laws are enacted by a dictator. To suggest that our reasons for attributing content-independent status to the reasons for action generated by the majoritarian enactment of laws is that such rules produce different (and better) substantive outcomes is thus question-begging. If we owe obligations of gratitude to those who treat the laws enacted by a majority as having influential authority, because by so doing they produce for us a just distribution of substantive benefits, then we must owe the same obligations of gratitude to those who take the laws passed by a dictator as having influential authority, because by so doing they produce the same just distribution of benefits.

Second, even if we were to set aside our own hypothetical for the moment and endorse the supposition that, in general, the results produced by attributing influential authority to the laws enacted by majorities are substantively more just than are the results produced by attributing influential authority to the laws enacted under dictatorships, the reason for complying with democratically enacted laws to which this supposition gives rise is not a content-independent one that requires for its justification something like the theory of gratitude. If the conduct preferred by the majority is more likely to be the right conduct – that is, if it is more likely to accord with the balance of the content-dependent reasons for action (and so be the most just, the most efficient, etc.) – then one indeed has a reason to comply with the majority's will. But one's reason for compliance is not a content-independent one; rather, the majority's enactments provide a reason to believe that there are *other*, antecedently existing, content-*dependent* reasons for compliance. One's reason for obeying laws enacted by the majority is thus epistemic. By obeying such laws, one is more likely than not to act in accordance with the balance of content-dependent reasons for action. The will of the majority thus becomes a heuristic guide to just those content-dependent reasons that make the rules which the majority endorses the right rules. The attempt to justify the influential authority of a democratic government by claiming that the government achieves substantively better laws thus violates the independence condition.

Defenders of the theory of gratitude might argue that while we indeed have content-dependent reasons to comply with democratically enacted laws, the obligation of gratitude nevertheless provides us with an *additional* content-independent reason to comply with such laws, because the additional increment of substantive justice that is supposed to result from democratic processes is only made possible if most citizens in fact take such laws as the source of new reasons for action. One owes an obligation of gratitude to those citizens who do take democratically enacted laws as giving content-independent reasons for action, because their doing so makes possible the continued existence of a scheme that produces greater substantive justice than any alternative scheme.

Two problems, however, defeat this argument. First, it is not at all clear that we *do* owe obligations of gratitude to those who confer content-independent status on the reasons generated by the rules of a democracy, even when their doing so confers on us unique benefits. As John Simmons has argued, there appear to be at least five necessary conditions for the generation of an obligation of gratitude.[15] First, the benefit must have been conferred on us as a result of some special effort or sacrifice made on our behalf. If others benefit us merely in the course of pursuing their own affairs, we do not feel that any special debt is owed them. Second, the benefit must not have been conferred on us for disqualifying reasons (such as self-interest, duress, a desire to hurt another, etc.) Third, the benefit must not have been forced on us against our will. Fourth, we must have wanted the benefit (or it must be the case that we would have wanted the benefit had our judgment been unimpaired). And finally, we must not have wanted the benefit *not* to be provided by those who made sacrifices on our behalf.

---

[15] Simmons, *Moral Principles and Political Obligations*, 170–9.

It is not at all clear that those who might be thought to attribute influential authority to the laws produced by democratic processes do so for reasons that give rise to obligations of gratitude on the part of those who are benefitted by such an attribution. Those who factor into their reasons for action the fact that certain laws have been democratically enacted are unlikely to do so as a special effort to aid individuals who do not participate in the democratic process and who are not inclined to give similar status to the fact that that process has produced particular rules. More plausibly, any benefits that one receives as a result of others' willingness to take the directives produced by a democratic process as having influential authority are conferred on one unintentionally. It would thus appear that the first condition for the generation of an obligation of gratitude is unsatisfied, and the second condition is rendered moot. And because a large number of citizens do not make their will known through political participation, it is difficult to know whether such individuals indeed want (or would want) the additional benefits that may accrue from others' attribution of influential authority to majoritarian rules. It is thus difficult to know whether the very individuals whom the theory of gratitude is supposed to bind (those who fail to engage in any political activities) indeed satisfy the final three conditions that must be met before they can be thought to have an obligation of gratitude that requires them to confer influential authority on democratic results.

This brings us to the second problem that faces the theorist who claims that we owe a debt of gratitude to those who confer the unique benefits of democracy on us by weighting the balance of reasons for action with the fact that the majority has preferred a particular course of action. This problem arises from the fact that, in most cases, there appear to be many ways of discharging debts of gratitude; taking the rules enacted by the majority as giving new reasons for action appears to be just one of several methods by which we might discharge our supposed debt to those who have benefitted us by doing likewise.

One might claim in response that, while debts of gratitude may be discharged in many ways, the continued existence of a majoritarian democracy depends on the willingness of most citizens to take the will of the majority as an additional reason to act as willed. The salient means of repaying others for doing this is by doing so similarly. Taking the laws enacted by the majority as giving new content-independent reasons for action is thus the means by which this particular debt must be discharged.[16] Yet from the fact that a benefactor has a particular need, it does not follow that a debt of gratitude must be discharged in a manner that helps to meet that need. Indeed, one might reflect on the common practice of deliberately choosing "thank you" gifts for others that, in the face of their many needs, meet only some of their most trivial wants. Even if a debt of gratitude requires that one meet the needs of one's benefactor, however, this could be accomplished in the political case by often, but not always, taking the laws of the majority to give new reasons for action. The theory of gratitude thus fails to provide a general account of why individuals should attribute content-independent status to the reasons for action that are given by the majoritarian enactment of rules. It thus fails to give us a reason to think that laws enacted under majoritarian democracies possess influential authority of any weight, let alone a weight sufficient to enable such democracies to function as "as if" practical authorities.

The Theory of Consent

The final act-based account of why one should attribute influential authority to laws enacted by majorities has perhaps the most influential legacy. On this account, we have an obligation to treat democratically enacted rules as giving new content-independent reasons for action because we have, in some manner or another, consented to do so. Our obligation to attribute influential authority to democratic governments functions, on this theory, as a special case of the obligation to keep promises. Two strands of consent theory can be distinguished. The first grounds the obligation to confer influential authority on democratically enacted laws in each citizen's *personal consent* to do so. The second grounds this obligation on a notion of *historical consent*, maintaining that a historical group's initial consent to attrib-

---

[16] This argument is the basis of Philip Soper's theory of legal obligation. As Soper concludes, the obligation to obey the law derives from the obligation to show respect for political leaders who perform their public duties in good faith. Subjects should respect the good faith efforts of those with authority, and a crucial way to show this respect is by obeying their directions. Philip Soper, *A Theory of Law* (Cambridge, MA: Harvard University Press, 1984), 80–84; Philip Soper "The Moral Value of Law," *Michigan Law Review* 84 (1985): 63. For a discussion of Soper's unique version of the gratitude-based theory of obligation, see Kent Greenawalt, "Comment," in *Issues in Contemporary Legal Philosophy*, ed. Ruth Gavison (Oxford: Oxford University Press, 1987), 157. See also Nannerl O. Henry, "Political Obligation and Collective Goods," in *Nomos XII: Political and Legal Obligation*, eds. J. Roland Pennock and John W. Chapman (New York: Atherton Press, 1970), 263.

ute influential authority to a majoritarian democracy binds all subsequent generations.[17] Because this second version is highly implausible, for only when an individual has been authorized to give consent
can his consent bind another, I shall deal here only with the merits of
the first version.

Central to the consent theorist's account is the assumption that
performative acts such as promise-making and consent-giving change
the normative universe. Individuals, on the theory of consent, are
"naturally free."[18] Only by a voluntary act, performed with a clear
understanding of its moral significance, may an individual leave this
"natural state of freedom" in which no individual or institution can
obligate him, and shoulder duties to others. When an individual
promises to perform an act or consents to another's exercise of influential authority, this act itself provides the individual with a content-
independent reason to keep the promise or abide by the will of the
designated authority. That is, the individual's voluntary act generates a reason over and above those he might already have to engage
in the promised conduct or comply with the will of the authority.

As an account of our political obligations, the theory of consent has
been thought to possess substantial intuitive plausibility. It appears
reasonable to claim, for example, that under a *direct, unanimous* democracy, citizens are obligated to take the fact that they have voted for a

---

[17] As the medieval political philosopher Richard Hooker claimed:

> [T]o be commanded we do consent, when that society whereof we are
> part hath at any time before consented. . . . Wherefore as any man's deed
> past is good so long as himself continueth; so the act of a public society
> of men done five hundred years sithence standeth as theirs who
> presently are the same societies, because corporations are immortal; we
> were then alive in our predecessors, and they in their successors do live
> still.

Richard Hooker, *On the Laws of Ecclesiastical Polity* vol. 1, ch. 10, 8, quoted in J.W.
Gough, *John Locke's Political Philosophy* 2d ed. (Oxford: Clarendon Press, 1972), 56.
This notion of historical consent was severely criticized by Hume and Kant. *See*
David Hume, "Of the Original Contract," in *Social Contract: Essays By Locke, Hume
and Rousseau,* ed. Sir Ernest Barker (Westport, CT.: Greenwood Press, 1980),
147–66; Immanuel Kant, *The Metaphysics of Morals,* ed. Mary Gregor (Cambridge:
Cambridge University Press, 1991), 125. See also Margaret Macdonald, "The
Language of Political Theory," in *Essays on Logic and Language,* ed. 1st series
Antony G.N. Flew (Oxford: Basil Blackwell, 1952), 167.

[18] See Thomas Hobbes, *Leviathan,* ed. Michael Oakeshott (Oxford: Basil Blackwell,
1946), pt. II, ch. 14, 128; Kant, *The Metaphysics of Morals,* 125; John Locke, *The
Second Treatise on Government,* ed. J.W. Gough (Oxford: Basil Blackwell, 1976), 4;
Jean-Jacques Rousseau, *The Social Contract,* trans. Maurice Cranston (Baltimore,
MD: Penguin Books, 1968), 1; Hart, "Are There Any Natural Rights?," 175–6.

particular law as itself a reason to abide by it; that is, their vote is appropriately taken as a clear signal of their willingness to change their normative environment by adding to the reasons for a particular course of action the fact that they consented to such action. Similarly, it is plausible to think that citizens who participate in direct, majoritarian democracies consent to take the majority's will as a reason for action, even when they find themselves in a minority. Finally, the account can seemingly be generalized to *representative* democracies, because citizens who participate within such systems may be said to consent to the attribution of influential authority to laws enacted by a majority of their representatives.

Despite the intuitive virtue this theory may be supposed to possess, there are a set of reasons for rejecting it as an adequate account of why laws enacted by political democracies command influential authority. The first reason to find the theory unacceptable is a version of a reason long touted by political theorists for rejecting any consent theory of political obligation. It seems virtually impossible to determine when and how citizens living under democratic institutions consented to the attribution of influential authority to the laws enacted by such institutions.[19] Consent theorists have historically recognized this problem. Yet they have maintained that, while few have indeed been faced with a situation in which *express* consent has ever been possible or appropriate, "signs of contract [may be] either 'express' or by 'inference.'"[20] They have argued that what is important is that individuals manifestly accord to the majority a special right to influence behavior in areas within which the individuals would otherwise be free to act – a right that generates on the part of those individuals a

---

[19]   This rejoinder to the consent theory is old hat. As John Mackie says: "An alleged contractual duty to obey the law is the basis of one of the main Socratic arguments [in support of an obligation to obey the law]. But . . . there is nothing in the lives of most ordinary citizens in a modern state that could constitute even a tacit or an implied agreement to obey." John Mackie, "Obligations to Obey the Law," *Virginia Law Review* 67 (1981): 145. The argument from consent "is incredible," agrees David Lyons, "because few of us have ever been parties to such an agreement. . . . This argument does not work, because its conclusion rests on false premises." David Lyons, *Ethics and the Rule of Law* (Cambridge and New York: Cambridge University Press, 1984), 211. See also Richard E. Flathman, *Political Obligation* (New York: Athenaeum Press, 1972), 209; Simmons, *Moral Principles and Political Obligations,* 79; A. John Simmons, "Consent, Free Choice, and Democratic Government," *Georgia Law Review* 18 (1984): 819; Singer, *Democracy and Disobedience* 22–6; M.B.E. Smith, "Is There a Prima Facie Obligation to Obey the Law?," *Yale Law Journal* 82 (1973): 960–4; Wright, "Legal Obligation and the Natural Law," 1000.

[20]   Hobbes, *Leviathan,* pt. II, ch. 14, 128.

special obligation not to thwart the majority's will. Consent theorists have argued that this can be done *tacitly,* and indeed *is* done tacitly, by all individuals living under democratic regimes.

There has been considerable disagreement concerning the sort of conduct that might be said to constitute tacit consent to a majority's exercise of authority. Locke maintained that the receipt of the benefits of democracy through residence sufficed to constitute tacit consent.[21] Others have followed Locke by maintaining that voting in elections, running for political office, and applying for a passport are all acts that constitute the tacit acceptance of legal obligations within democratic systems.[22]

Yet such claims slur a distinction that is crucial to the theory of consent. This distinction is between "signals of consent" and "signs of consent."[23] An act constitutes a signal of consent if, in the context in which it is performed, the act conventionally counts as an expression of an actor's intention to consent. Thus, all express acts of consent are signals of consent. But in saying that an act is a sign of consent or "implies" consent, we mean neither that the actor intended to consent

---

[21]   Locke wrote:

> [E]very man that hath any possessions, or enjoyment of any part of the dominions of any government, doth thereby give his *tacit consent,* and is as far forth obliged to obedience to the laws of that government, during such enjoyment, as anyone under it; whether this his possession be of land to him and his heirs for ever, or a lodging only for a week; or whether it be barely travelling freely on the highway. . . .

Locke, *Second Treatise on Government,* 61 (emphasis added) (editor's footnote omitted).

[22]   See Alexander Meiklejohn, *Free Speech and its Relation to Self-Government* (New York: Harper, 1948), 11–14; Plamenatz, *Consent, Freedom, and Political Obligation,* 168, 170–1; Singer, *Democracy and Disobedience,* 50–1; Alan Gewirth, "Political Justice," in *Social Justice,* ed. Richard B. Brandt (Englewood cliffs, NJ: Prentice-Hall, 1972), 137–8. T.H. Green even went so far as to say that no despot, however arbitrary, ever really governs simply by force alone, or against the general will. T.H. Green, "The Principles of Political Obligation," in *The Political Theory of T.H. Green,* ed. John R. Rodman (New York: Appleton-Century-Crofts. 1964), 117.

[23]   I have developed this distinction in greater detail in Heidi M. Hurd, "Sovereignty in Silence," *Yale Law Journal* 99 (1990): 953–4. In the specific context of political consent theory, John Plamenatz makes a similar distinction between "direct consent" and "indirect consent." See John Plamenatz, *Man and Society,* vol. 1 (London: Longmans, Green and Co., 1963), 239–41. Peter Singer captures this dichotomy by distinguishing between "real consent" (which includes tacit consent) and "quasi-consent." See Singer, *Democracy and Disobedience,* 47. And John Simmons talks of this distinction as one between "signs of consent" and "acts which 'imply consent.'" See Simmons, *Moral Principles and Political Obligations,* 88.

nor that the act would normally be taken as an attempt to consent. There appear to be at least three ways in which an act might be said to function as a sign of consent.[24] First, an act may be such that it leads us to conclude that the actor was in an appropriate frame of mind to consent had she been called on to do so. Second, an act may be such that it commits the actor to consent on pain of irrationality. And third, an act may be such that it binds the actor morally to the same performance to which she would be bound if she had in fact consented.

The acts that Locke and many other consent theorists have taken to constitute tacit consent to a majority's exercise of (influential) authority are acts that at best function only as signs of consent; they are not signals of consent.[25] And acts that are merely signs of consent cannot consistently be appealed to by consent theorists as a basis for attributing influential authority to democratic enactments, because such acts do not constitute deliberate undertakings of obligations intentionally incurred with a clear understanding of their morally binding significance. For one to have genuinely, if only tacitly, consented to take the laws enacted by a political majority as giving new reasons for action, one must have performed an act that functions as a signal of consent.[26] But if this is the case, then it would seem that we are forced to conclude that tacit consent meets the same fate as does express consent: Very few individuals have so consented to take the rules enacted under majoritarian or representative democracies as possessing influential authority.[27] And since few citizens, then, can

---

[24] See Simmons, *Moral Principles and Political Obligations,* 89.

[25] But see Plamenatz, *Consent, Freedom and Political Obligation,* 7 (attempting to refute the view that Locke confused tacit consent with acts implying consent).

[26] For a detailed discussion of the *mens rea* and *actus reus* requirements of consent, as well as the background conditions that must be present for such *prima facie* elements to have moral and legal force, see Heidi M. Hurd, "The Moral Magic of Consent," *Legal Theory* 2 (1996): 121–46.

[27] Leslie Green has advanced an interesting variation on the Lockean attempt to ground political obligation in tacit consent. Green argues that political obligations can be assumed by voluntarily entering into the *role* of citizenship. The assumption of this role "will rarely be a single act of commitment." Leslie Green, "Law, Legitimacy, and Consent," *Southern California Law Review* 62 (1989): 823. Just as one voluntarily becomes a lawyer (and so voluntarily assumes a set of duties that are not themselves subject to individual alteration) without performing any *one* act that at a given moment makes one a lawyer, so one can voluntarily assume the role of citizen (with its accompanying nonvoluntary duties) through a successive set of choices. Ibid., 823–4. To the extent that many voluntarily assume the *role* of citizen, they assume the duties of obedience that (nonvoluntarily) attach to that role. In the language of this discussion, the incremental adoption of the role of citizen brings with it the obligation to treat majoritarian laws as a source of new reasons for action.

be thought to have consented to the attribution of influential authority to the directives of most democratic political systems, few can be thought to have an obligation to take democratic enactments as new reasons to act as directed.[28]

Yet this argument against the consent theory may be guilty of the same sort of "hypo-bucking" of which I accused past defenses of influential authority. Recall that we began by assuming that we were concerned solely with a *direct*, majoritarian democracy. Under such a regime, all citizens participate in the enactment process. If this sort of political participation entails tacit consent to the attribution of influential authority to majoritarian results, then the above objection would fail to defeat the consent theory of influential authority, at least as it applies to direct, majoritarian democracies.

One might at this point plausibly retreat to the realities of modern democracies, which do not enjoy the sort of universal political involvement that is characteristic of direct, majoritarian models. There remains, however, a more interesting and subtle problem with the theory of consent (even as applied to direct, majoritarian democracies) – a problem that stems from its fundamental assumption that acts of consent provide content-independent reasons for action. To motivate this problem, let us suppose that everyone in the democratic regime

> There is much to be admired in Green's new take on this old theme. And perhaps Green is right in thinking that if political obligations are role-relative obligations, they, like parental obligations, can be construed as consensually assumed even in the absence of any single act of consent. But Green still faces two problems. First, he must make plausible just how political citizenship constitutes a discrete role, like being a lawyer, a parent, or a judge. To speak of citizenship as a voluntarily adopted role, as opposed to a nonvoluntary status, appears metaphorical. Second, to the extent that a role functions like a promise, Green's argument invites the problem that I shall turn to next concerning the theory of consent as a source of influential authority.

[28] For a useful critique of consent theories of obligation in general, and of theories that depend on explicit consent in particular, see Edward A. Harris, "From Social Contract to Hypothetical Agreement: Consent and the Obligation to Obey the Law," *Columbia Law Review* 92 (Note 1992): 651–83.

> Steven Smith has argued that political authority can be predicated on the notion of consent, even when that notion is a purely fictional one. As he maintains, "the fiction should permit citizens to believe 'as if' the necessary conditions for legal authority had been satisfied, even though at another level they know that this belief is not 'really true.'" Steven D. Smith, "Radically Subversive Speech and the Authority of Law," *Michigan Law Review* 94 (1995): 395–6. Of course, as Smith admits, the "obtuse and boorish" critic (as he would call someone like me), who is interested less in the question of whether we have reasons to pretend that the law has authority than in the question of whether the law in fact has authority, has little use for fictions.

with which we are concerned has indeed done all that it takes to consent (either expressly or tacitly) to the rules of the system. Why would we take these acts of consent as providing citizens with content-independent reasons for action? The answer has always been that such acts constitute a form of promising, and promises function to give content-independent reasons for action. But do they?

One can sensibly maintain that promises function not as new reasons for action, but as expressions of intentions to act. The unique moral significance that they appear to possess is not a result of the fact that they *change* the normative universe, but rather a result of the fact that they *map* it. As predictions of behavior, they inevitably provide a basis for others' reliance. When others in fact rely on one's predictions to such an extent that they would be harmed if one failed to act as predicted, their reliance generates a new reason to act as one predicted one would. But this new reason is a content-*dependent* one. The right thing to do, given the weight of their reliance, may well be to act as one said one would, even if, absent their reliance, one has ceased to have enough reasons to act as predicted to make that course of action rational.[29]

If what I have said about promise-keeping is plausible, the same can be said of acts of consent to the exercise of influential authority. Were we in fact to consent expressly or tacitly to take the majority's expression of will as a new reason for action, our consent would merely provide others with a reason to think that we have other reasons for abiding by the will of the majority, even when we find ourselves part

---

[29] My position on this point comes close, in part, to that held by William Godwin. As Godwin recognized, "Previously to my entering into a promise, there is something which I ought to promise, and something which I ought not." William Godwin, *Enquiry Concerning Political Justice,* ed. K. Codell Carter (Oxford: Clarendon Press, 1971), 218. Thus, when we promise, we either have adequate reasons for promising or we do not. If we do not, then our promise cannot provide them. As Godwin goes on to argue, if one does have sufficient reasons for promising, then the promise functions as an "additional inducement" to do what ought otherwise to be done. But to the extent that we act on the basis of this inducement, he says, we act for a wrong reason. Because morality requires that we act for the right reasons, "promises are, absolutely considered, an evil." Ibid.

My thesis does not require that we think of promises as evil. On the contrary, because predictions of future events are in many cases extremely helpful, promises, to the extent that they are generally reliable predictions of future behavior, will be helpful. And insofar as they are helpful – insofar as people develop reliance interests as a result of them – they will stand proxy for content-dependent reasons for actions (reasons that reflect those reliance interests) that are in fact right reasons for action.

of a minority. Others may well rely on our consent, and so abide by the dictates of the majority when they are in the minority because they anticipate that we will do the same. And their reliance on our consent may indeed give us a new reason to abide by the laws enacted by the majority. But such a reason is not a content-independent one. The reliance of others is not a reason that is independent of the content of the reasons that we already have to comply with democratically enacted laws; rather, it becomes part of those reasons. If the reasons against complying with the laws enacted by a political majority outweigh the reasons that we have to prevent harm to those who have relied on our predicted compliance with those laws, then, on the balance of content-dependent reasons, we should refuse to comply with those laws. In other words, we lack any content-*independent* reason for complying with the will of the majority when what that majority wills is, on the balance of content-dependent reasons for action, wrong. The theory of consent thus appears to violate the independence condition, and so appears to fail as a basis for treating democracies as influential authorities.

In brief, then, the theory of consent fails to give us a special reason to comply with laws enacted by political majorities both because few of us have indeed consented (by any theory of consent) to take the laws of a majority as giving new, content-independent reasons for action, and because such consent, even if procured, would not *by itself* constitute a reason for compliance. These problems are reminiscent of those that we encountered when considering the theories of reciprocity and gratitude. In each case, we failed to discover how individuals could be thought to have voluntarily acted so as to shoulder obligations of obedience – either by accepting benefits, receiving benefits, or consenting to the rules that provide those benefits. And in each case, we failed to discover how such acts, even if performed, would in fact constitute content-*independent* reasons to comply with the will of a political majority. Because a majority can function as an influential authority only if there are content-independent reasons to abide by it, the failure of the three act-based theories to establish any content-independent reasons for complying with the will of the majority represents a failure to establish any basis upon which democratically enacted laws could possess influential or "as if" practical authority. And because this failure appears endemic to act-based accounts of why we should attribute influential authority to democratically enacted laws, it would appear that one cannot avoid the dilemma of legal perspectivalism by arguing that the role of a citizen involves the performance of voluntary actions that entail obligations to abide by democratic laws whenever those laws depart from morality.

A Duty-Based Theory of Influential Authority: The Theory of a Natural Duty of Justice

If no other act-based accounts of our political bonds can be given beyond those provided by the three theories discussed above, then either we must accept the supposedly counterintuitive conclusion that individuals are not morally bound to take the laws favored by a majority as giving new reasons for action, or we must try to find a duty-based account of these bonds. One such duty-based account was advanced by John Rawls after he disavowed his theory of reciprocity, and it is to this account that this section is devoted.[30]

Recall that Hart defined act-based obligations as moral requirements generated not by virtue of the nature of the obligation itself, but by virtue of the nature of the relationship that exists between the specific person bound and those to whom she is bound. Duty-based obligations, in contrast, are independent of any institutional setting or special relationship: They apply to all individuals, irrespective of their status or the acts they perform. As Rawls explicitly claims, "Obligations can be accounted for by the natural duty of justice ... [for] [i]t suffices to construe the requisite voluntary acts as acts by which our natural duties are freely extended."[31]

According to Rawls, each member of a political community is bound by a natural duty of justice to support and further the just political institutions of her community. This duty is two-pronged: "First, we are to comply with and do our share in just institutions when they exist and apply to us; and second, we are to assist in the establishment of just arrangements when they do not exist, at least when this can be done with little cost to ourselves."[32] This theory purports to provide a perfectly general account of political duty, in that all citizens of societies governed by institutions that are just are bound equally under them, "irrespective of [their] voluntary acts, performative or otherwise."[33] The natural duty of justice further purports to satisfy the independence condition that must be met by any account of how institutions possess influential authority, because this duty is con-

---

[30] John Rawls, *A Theory of Justice* (Cambridge, MA: Harvard University Press, Belknap Press, 1971), 114–17, 333–42.
[31] Ibid., 343.   [32] Ibid., 334.   [33] Ibid.

ceived of as a reason to obey the rules enacted by an institution above and beyond the reasons to think the rules just.

In order for Rawls' theory to give us a special reason to attribute influential authority to the rules enacted by a majority that we do not have if those same rules are enacted by a dictator, we would have to have some account of why democratic institutions are just and tyrannical ones are not. Two sorts of accounts present themselves. The first sort is motivated by a substantive theory of justice. On this account, democratic processes of legislation are just because they are more likely to produce substantively just outcomes than are dictatorial systems of legislation – that is, they are more likely to produce results that accord with the antecedently existing content-dependent balance of reasons for action. But while this may indeed be true, such an account faces the same problems that earlier confronted the theory that we owe gratitude to those who attribute influential authority to the rules governing democratic processes, because in so doing those individuals preserve a system that produces greater benefits for us than do other systems. The first common problem is that this argument fails to take seriously the hypothetical that tests the moral uniqueness of democracies. If a dictatorial government were to pass laws identical to those passed by a majority, and if such laws produced identical results in both the dictatorship and the democracy, then it would appear that, under a substantive theory of justice, both regimes would be equally just. Rawls' natural duty of justice would thus require that we attribute influential authority to both the democracy and the dictatorship. It thus appears that Rawls' natural duty of justice, if filled out by a substantive theory of justice, fails to give us a special reason for taking democratically enacted laws as giving new reasons for action.

The second common problem that faces both the gratitude theorist and the theorist defending a natural duty of justice is that their theories violate the independence condition. While one certainly has a reason to comply with the directives of the majority if those directives accord with the balance of content-dependent reasons for action, one's reason to do so is not content-independent. The preferences of the majority in such a case merely function as heuristic guides to the antecedently existing content-dependent reasons for action, and so function only epistemically. They thus give no new reasons for action; they merely evidence already existing reasons for action.

Notice further that if we were to suppose that democracies in general produced greater substantive justice than alternative sorts of political systems, Rawls' natural duty of justice would not require that we comply with democratically enacted laws that are not substantively just. If our duty is to achieve substantive justice, then it cannot be the case that this very same duty demands our attribution of influential authority to substantively unjust laws. Rawls' natural duty of justice, if conceived of under a substantive theory of justice, thus fails to give an account of why a political minority is obligated to take the laws enacted by the majority as a source of new reasons for action when those laws are rightly deemed wrong on their merits. That is, it fails to give a content-independent reason for complying with the will of the majority, and thus it fails to give an account of why democratically enacted laws possess influential authority.

An alternative theory of why democracies are uniquely just might stem from a procedural conception of justice. On such a theory, democracies are just because the procedures that produce their results are themselves fair, while tyrannies are unjust because they lack fair procedures.[34] To defend such a view, one has to think that political participation is itself a value: The process of political decision making is more just if all of the individuals who are to be bound by its outcomes have a say in that process. But the same challenge that was issued to the theorist defending a duty of reciprocity can be raised here. Why value our own participation in the process of political decision making unless that participation produces for us and others substantively better results? The answer given by the famous anarchist, Robert Paul Wolff, is that participation maximizes our ability to be self-legislating because it allows for the autonomous exercise of choice, and this is of greater value than accomplishing substantively beneficial arrangements. But the fully rational and autonomous agent would seemingly be considerably less rational if he valued the imposition of his will solely for its own sake, and so preferred to participate in the political process despite the fact that his participation produced substantively inferior results for himself and others. A fully rational person should seemingly value political participation only if he thinks that his participation will accomplish better results (results that better accord

---

34 While Peter Singer has advanced what may best be thought of as a theory of reciprocity, he often makes reference to the intrinsic procedural fairness of democracy as a source of special duties of obedience to democratically enacted laws. As he maintains: "There are strong reasons for playing one's part in supporting and preserving a decision procedure which represents a fair compromise." Peter Singer, *Democracy and Disobedience* (Oxford: Clarendon Press, 1973), 36. For three interpretations of Peter Singer's theory, see Gans, *Philosophical Anarchism and Political Obedience*, 109–16.

with the balance of content-dependent reasons for action) than will his nonparticipation.

But if participation is only a value if it produces greater benefits to those who participate than does nonparticipation, then we must conclude that the procedural theory of justice collapses into the substantive theory of justice. Like the act-based theories of influential authority, Rawls' defense of the natural duty of justice as a source of political obligation founders on the independence condition. In failing to give us a content-independent reason for complying with laws enacted by a majority, it seems that Rawls' natural duty of justice does not provide an account of why such laws possess influential authority.

In light of the failure of both act-based and duty-based accounts to provide us with a special, content-independent reason to comply with laws enacted by a democratic majority, we must seemingly conclude that persons are not morally bound by the will of the majority. Put differently, we have no reason to confer even influential authority on democratically enacted laws, because the fact that such laws have been democratically enacted itself possesses no special *moral* status. And if the laws enacted under democracies lack influential authority, then it seems likely that the laws enacted under other regimes will fare no better. Because democratically enacted directives appear to require reciprocal compliance, to be the product of civic consent, and to be born of procedures that seem maximally just, they stand a better chance of satisfying the conditions that give rise to content-independent reasons for action than do directives enacted nondemocratically. That democratically enacted laws fail to possess influential authority is thus a reliable indication that laws enacted under systems that are less likely to meet these conditions will similarly lack influential authority.

So where does this leave us? The answer is, seemingly worse off than before. First, the failure of the theories of practical and influential authority leaves us face to face with the dilemma of legal perspectivalism. If citizens do not have compelling reasons to abide by the law when the law conflicts with morality, then there seemingly will be numerous circumstances in which the right thing for citizens to do is to violate the law. Judges will then be confronted with the unhappy prospect of having either to punish the justified (in violation of the correspondence thesis and its theoretical cousin, the principle of weak retributivism) or to acquit the disobedient in ways that deeply offend the rule of law, democracy, and the separation of powers.

The failure of the traditional theories of legal authority would appear to leave us on the edge of anarchy. Are we then to suppose that there is no such thing as legal obligations as they have long been conceived? The answer seems quite clear: Yes. But while there may be nothing that obligates us legally, there may be much that obligates us morally. And inasmuch as our ability to fulfill our moral obligations may be aided by crafting certain epistemic obligations to abide by legal directives, there remains an authoritative role for legal institutions. It is to this role, and the concepts of authority compatible with it, that I shall turn in the next two chapters. On constructing, in Chapter 6, an alternative theory of legal authority to the standard ones discussed above, we will be in a position to determine whether the dilemma of legal perspectivalism survives to force our choice between its equally compelling jurisprudential principles.

Chapter 5

The Limits of Advisory Authority

I have argued thus far that, to account for the persisting intuition that we are bound by the law, it is necessary to seek a source of legal authority that does not suggest that the law subjects us by imposing obligations unique from those already imposed by morality. Two final theories of legal authority fit this bill, each construing the power of law as epistemic rather than moral. The first theory, which I shall explore in this chapter, I shall call the theory of advisory authority. The second one, which I shall defend in Chapter 6, I shall call the theory of theoretical authority.

Both of these theories provide accounts of how law can be characterized as a heuristic guide to the moral obligations and permissions that I have argued alone comprise the reasons for action that determine how citizens and officials ought to act. Both construe legal authority as a form of epistemic authority. The first accords *lawmakers* epistemic authority, construing the laws they pass as the advice of those possessed of moral expertise. The second theory locates the authority of law not in the expertise of its authors, but in the law itself. According to this second theory, laws are authoritative if, regardless of the beliefs or intentions that motivated them, they enable persons to act morally more often than would otherwise be possible. As I shall argue, while there surely are persons who possess advisory authority, we have compelling reasons to think that the authority of the law is better construed as theoretical, rather than advisory.

THE NATURE OF ADVISORY AUTHORITY

Recall from Chapter 3 that an epistemic authority about action functions to give reasons for belief in certain deontic propositions. That is, the authoritative utterances of epistemic authorities give reasons to *believe* that we ought to do what is prescribed – but they do not themselves give reasons to *do* what is prescribed. Unlike the directives of a practical or influential authority, the utterances of an epistemic authority do not affect the balance of reasons for action; they simply provide information about that balance as it exists independently of those utterances. The directives of an epistemic authority are thus wholly evidential. They provide counsel, but they do not command or request.

Consider, for example, a case in which a legislature bans smoking in all public buildings. If the legislature were to function as a practical or influential authority, then the fact that the legislature issued such a decree would itself provide a reason not to smoke in public buildings. But if the legislature functions as an epistemic authority, then its decree constitutes only evidence that there are other, content-dependent reasons for refraining from smoking in public buildings (such as the irritation and health risks posed to others by secondary smoke).

An advisory authority is a secondary source of information: It "sums up" other reasons for belief. To borrow from Donald Regan, an advisory authority about moral matters issues "indicator rules." When we receive advice about what to do from such an authority, we are given a second-order epistemic reason to believe that that advice reflects the balance of first-order reasons for belief that are available from sources other than the advice. The advice itself is an "indication" or summary of those first-order reasons for belief.[1]

Inasmuch as an exercise of advisory authority involves summing and weighing evidence, and inasmuch as such a process is a rational endeavor, it follows that only persons can exercise advisory authority.[2] Only persons can say "Do A" as a result of evaluating the reasons

---

[1]   See Donald H. Regan, "Authority and Value: Reflections on Raz's *The Morality of Freedom,*" *Southern California Law Review* 62 (1989), 995–1095. If another's advice accurately reflects some sorts of reasons for action, but not others, then those who defend an advisory theory of authority should say that it possesses limited epistemic authority. See the first section in Chapter 3. It does not give one an indication of what the balance of reasons requires, because it does not sum up all of the relevant reasons for action. It simply serves as a summary of a set of reasons that one must add to the other reasons for action that make up the balance determining what one ought to do. Thus, one might consult an economist for a cost-benefit analysis of a particular course of action, because in the absence of deontological side-constraints, the moral thing to do is typically the cost-efficient thing to do. But one should recognize that such an analysis may fail to reveal agent-relative obligations that bind one without regard to their costs and benefits. Hence, the advice of the economist might best be accorded limited, but not comprehensive, epistemic authority.

[2]   Richard Flathman clearly invokes a theory of advisory authority when he argues that authority is an attribute of persons (as opposed to a creation of rules or of-

for and against doing act A. When an advisory authority issues advice, her words should presumably be treated as heuristics to the observations and inferences in which her epistemic authority primarily resides. In the event that we distrust the heuristic value of her words (because they are vague, ambiguous, or apparent misstatements), we should seek directly the beliefs and intentions with which she uttered such words, because it is ultimately in these beliefs and intentions that her advisory authority resides.

PROBLEMS WITH A THEORY OF ADVISORY AUTHORITY

There appear to be four distinct problems with employing a theory of advisory authority to capture the kind of authority that the law can claim. While some of these problems prove surmountable, others provide good reasons to reject an application of advisory authority to law. First, the theory of advisory authority articulated above threatens to revive the same sort of paradox that defeated the coherence of the theory of practical authority. As such, it may suffer from the same sort of conceptual problems that confound attempts to defend the notion of practical authority. Second, for the theory of advisory authority to be meaningful, a person who is not an advisory authority must be able to identify and evaluate those who are. Because it seemingly takes one to know one, it would appear that those who most need reliable advice are least able to obtain it. Third, as applied to law, a theory of advisory authority requires one to conceive of lawmakers as particularly astute moral observers whose motivations and powers of moral reasoning make them better able than most individual citizens to amass, evaluate, and draw inferences about the moral considerations relevant to determining, all things considered, how citizens ought to act. If contemporary cynicism concerning the degree to which politicians function as well-motivated moral experts is justified, then the theory of advisory authority proves a poor basis for vindicating the attention that many feel compelled to pay to legal rules. Finally, a theory of advisory authority commits one to an intentionalist theory of interpretation. Inasmuch as such a theory is difficult to apply in the context of common law interpretation, and seemingly impossible to

fices), and that it is impossible to understand authority without understanding the substance and purpose of the statements that it provides. Richard E. Flathman, *The Practice of Political Authority* (Chicago, IL: Chicago University Press, 1980), 14–16.

implement in the context of statutory and constitutional interpretation, we have good grounds for rejecting any theory of authority that is hostage to its methodology.

The Return of Paradox

A number of theorists have argued that an advisory authority affects our reasons for belief in a manner that is symmetrical to the way in which a practical authority affects our reasons for action.[3] If this is the case, then we should worry that a theory of advisory authority generates a paradox that is analogous to the paradox of practical authority. The concern that advisory authority is paradoxical is made acute under Regan's analysis. As he maintains, insofar as advice simply reflects the balance of all first-order reasons, it does not exclude independent beliefs about that balance, and, as such, it does not provide protected reasons for belief of the Razian sort. But because advice sums up the balance of all first-order reasons for belief, it cannot, on pain of double-counting, be added to those reasons. As such, when and if considered, advice indeed preempts those other reasons for belief. It excludes our ability to consider *both* the indicator rule that is provided by the advice and the antecedently existing reasons for belief that that advice purports to sum up. Thus, when an attorney advises a client that the client's will should be signed by two witnesses, the attorney issues an indicator rule that the client can substitute for, but not add to, all of the reasons that the client could independently accumulate from other sources (such as law books, law school classes, the experience of friends, etc.) for the belief that wills should be signed by two witnesses. If the client takes to heart the attorney's advice, she is excluded from further considering the reasons for belief summed up by that advice.

If one cannot add the statements of an advisory authority to the balance of reasons for belief, then it would indeed appear that the theory of advisory authority generates a paradox that is similar to the paradox of practical authority. That paradox would run as follows:

1. If advice provides a summary of the reasons for belief concerning what ought to be done, then in formulating one's belief about what

---

[3] See, for example, Flathman, *The Practice of Political Authority*, 18–19, 92–100, 247; Joseph Raz, *The Morality of Freedom* (Oxford: Clarendon Press, 1986), 67–9. But also see Leslie Green, *The Authority of the State* (New York: Oxford University Press, 1988), 27; Kent Greenawalt, *Conflicts of Law and Morality* (New York and Oxford: Oxford University Press, 1987), 59.

one ought to do, one is barred (on pain of double-counting) from considering other reasons for belief that either support or dispute the reason for belief provided by a particular piece of advice.

2. Upon the receipt of advice, therefore, the only reason that one should consider for believing that a certain action should be performed is the fact that that action has been advised.

3. But, if a belief is rational *because* it is the product of advice, then any advice gives one a reason for belief. (Thus, the advice that one should prepare for snow in Hawaii gives one a reason to believe that one should.)

4. If, alternatively, a belief is rational only if it comports with the balance of all (reasonably available) reasons for belief, then the sheer fact that a belief is a product of advice does not (necessarily) make that belief rational.

5. Because the consequent of premise 3 is false, the antecedent of it also must be false.

6. Because the antecedent of premise 3 must be false, then the antecedent of premise 4 must be true.[4]

7. If premise 4 is true, then to hold rational beliefs one must form one's beliefs on the basis of reasons other than the fact that one has been given advice.

8. HENCE: Beliefs formed on the basis of advice are irrational.

Common sense clearly rebels against this conclusion. But to vindicate the ordinary conviction that it is perfectly rational to take another's advice, we must either give up the theory of advisory authority or revise its terms. Because it seems plausible to maintain that advisory authority can reside in the intentional statements of other persons (by virtue of the fact that other persons may be motivated to discover the truth, or they may be in possession of greater information, or they may possess superior inference-drawing abilities), we would do well to seek a modified version of the theory of advisory authority before abandoning it altogether.

Crucial to Regan's conclusion that advice has preemptive force is a distinction between summary evidence (of which advice is a sort) and primary evidence. Ultimately, this is a distinction that cannot be maintained. Because the paradox engendered by Regan's version of

---

[4] The suppressed premise in 6 is: If it is not the case that a belief is rational *because* it is the product of advice, then a belief is rational only if it comports with the balance of all (reasonably available) reasons for belief.

the theory of advisory authority is triggered by this distinction, to abandon the distinction is to escape the paradox.

Regan's claim that the utterances of an advisory authority function as preemptive summaries of other, more primary evidence might be motivated by a desire to draw a distinction between what I called in the previous chapter "signals" and "signs."[5] As intentional communications of deliberative judgments, the utterances of an advisory authority constitute "signals." To be contrasted with (intentional) signals are pieces of evidence that, simply by virtue of being causally related to, or symptomatic of, certain natural phenomena, function as "signs" of those phenomena.[6] Thus, storm clouds are signs of snow; the weatherperson's forecast of snow is a signal of snow. Similarly, the defendant's fingerprints on the murder weapon are signs of guilt; the defendant's confession is a signal of guilt. According to Regan's analysis, signals sum up signs, and hence, on pain of double-counting, they cannot be considered together with those signs.

Yet while there is a genuine distinction between signs and signals, this distinction does not track the supposed distinction between summary evidence and primary evidence upon which Regan relies. Signals do not sum up or function as indicators of signs. Rather, signs and signals are two categories of evidence, each causally related to the phenomena of which they are evidence. To see that one cannot maintain the distinction between summary evidence and primary evidence that the sign/signal distinction might misleadingly suggest, consider the following. If one would be guilty of double-counting evidence of an impending snowstorm if one were to add the weatherperson's forecast to one's observation of advancing storm clouds, would one not be guilty of double-counting evidence were one to add the thermometer's reading to the coldness of the day, because the thermometer sums up that coldness? And would one not also be

---

[5] See also David Lewis, *Convention: A Philosophical Study* (Cambridge, MA: Harvard University Press, 1969), 122–59; H.P. Grice, "Meaning," in *Readings in the Philosophy of Language*, eds. Jay F. Rosenberg and Charles Travis (Englewood Cliffs, NJ: Prentice-Hall, 1971), 437.

[6] Signs possess what H.P. Grice termed "natural" meaning. Grice, "Meaning," 437. Thus we can say, "Her sneeze *means* that she has allergies"; "The clatter of dishes *means* that dinner will soon be served." In contrast, signals (utterances intended to convey messages to others) have what Grice called "nonnatural" meaning, or "meaning$_{NN}$." Ibid. According to Grice, signaling successfully occurs when a speaker, seeking to signal others, uses conventional actions (verbal or otherwise) because he reasonably believes that such actions will be taken by the audience in the manner intended, and the audience so takes them.

guilty of double-counting evidence if one added the ice on the lake to that coldness, because the ice also sums up that coldness? Indeed, would one not be guilty of double-counting evidence if one added the coldness to the atmospheric conditions that cause it, because those atmospheric conditions sum up that coldness? To answer these questions in the affirmative is to put oneself in a position in which one must conclude that one cannot, on pain of irrationality, consider the forecast, the thermometer's temperature reading, the ice that has formed on the lake, and the atmospheric conditions of the day as evidence that it is cold.

Yet surely this conclusion offends our understanding of what constitutes evidence. That pieces of evidence are causally related does not render each a summary of the others. On the contrary, their causal connectedness is what allows us to consider each of them evidence of a single phenomenon. To the extent that advice (that is, an intentional communicative signal) is good advice, it is indeed causally related to the phenomenon that is its subject. That is, there is something about the thing advised that makes a reliable advisor say of it what he does. Thus, advice will function as evidence of the matter advised for the same reasons that natural manifestations of that matter also serve as evidence. Thus, just as the fact that a thermometer reads thirty-two degrees is causally connected to the temperature which it reports, so the fact that a well-trained, well-informed meteorologist asserts that it is thirty-two degrees is causally connected to the fact that it is thirty-two degrees. And just as the thermometer reading can be added to other evidence (such as the freezing of the lake, the chill of the wind, and so forth) in determining the truth of a proposition about the weather, so the weatherperson's statements about the weather can be added to the thermometer reading by virtue of being causally related to the weather in a manner that is ultimately no different (although it is often considerably more complex) than the thermometer itself. As such, the advice of a weatherperson no more preempts consideration of other reasons for belief than any other evidence preempts other reasons for belief to which that evidence is causally akin.

While it will be useful to continue to think of the statements of advisory authorities as summaries of the balance of reasons for action, it is important to be clear that, in providing a summary of reasons for action, an advisory authority provides a new reason to think that one should act as advised, but she does not provide a preemptive reason for such a judgment. One is thus entitled to add her advice to the other evidence that one has concerning the balance of reasons for action – that is, to treat it as another first-order reason to believe that the reasons for action are as advised.

The Appearance of Circularity

While the theory of advisory authority can be defended against charges of conceptual incoherence, its conceptual vindication may have a hollow ring, because a practical problem remains. Under this theory, epistemic authority concerning deontic propositions is assigned to persons by virtue of their having observational, informational, and inferential skills that make them particularly adept at summarizing others' reasons for action. But for advisory authorities to be of meaningful assistance to those who do not possess their expertise, it must be the case that one has a means of identifying them without oneself becoming one. Just as it would seem that one would need to know the spelling of a word before one could look it up in a dictionary to determine its spelling, so it would seem that one would need to be an advisory authority to determine whether another is better situated than oneself to be an advisory authority. While our personal experience of the trial and error method with which we in fact employ dictionaries vitiates the temptation to declare the very notion of using a dictionary viciously circular, it takes a bit of explaining to render the practical employment of an advisory authority similarly noncircular. And the theory of advisory authority will only be a meaningful one if we can in fact provide such an explanation and so make out the conditions on which the theory is applicable. How is this to be accomplished?

The answer derives from our ability to specify the motivational and capacity conditions that must be met by an individual to think that individual better situated than ourselves to judge the merits of particular courses of action. And such conditions can indeed be specified without in fact judging the merits of these courses of action. As I shall spell out in more detail in the following section, to be better situated to evaluate reasons for action, one must be properly motivated to judge those reasons, and one must be in possession of resources with which to judge them that exceed those of the persons advised. The first condition – that of determining proper motivation – is initially a psychological question, although there may be institutional grounds for thinking that self-interested individuals in particular settings will function "as though" they are morally motivated. The second condition – that of establishing superior epistemic capacities – involves determining the characteristics and resources of a good moral observer.

Such an observer, for instance, must have extensive fact-finding facilities, sufficient time for deliberation and debate, the ability to determine the implications of any given decision for other decisions, and so forth. Just as we can specify the conditions under which scientific research optimally proceeds without in fact possessing the ability to conduct that research, so we can specify the conditions under which moral deliberation optimally occurs without in fact possessing the ability to engage in that deliberation. We can thus specify the conditions under which someone might be deemed an advisory authority without ourselves possessing such authority.

Construing Lawmakers as Moral Experts

While the theory of advisory authority can thus be made both coherent and noncircular, its application to law requires a theory of why lawmakers are, or can be, good at what advisory authorities are supposed to be good at, *viz.*, deciphering the reasons for action that citizens possess better than citizens can themselves. Why would lawmakers function as reliable observers of those moral facts that themselves generate reasons for action? Why should citizens look to the legislature or to the courts for moral expertise, rather than to religious leaders, philanthropists, moral philosophers, or the living examples of heroic citizens? While (appointed) judges may enjoy a special moral vantage point by virtue of both their relative inability to use their positions for personal gain and their insulation from political pressures, the degree to which politicians can be thought to possess moral expertise is notoriously suspect. In assessing the viability of applying the theory of advisory authority to law, it is thus useful to take the hardest test case. We should ask whether legislators, by virtue of special observational, informational, and inferential abilities, can be plausibly construed as reliable epistemic authorities about the conditions of morally right action.

As was outlined in the previous section, there are two assumptions that must be defended to make out why a democratically elected legislature may function as an advisory authority about the antecedently existing obligations of its citizens. The first is a motivational assumption, namely, that enough legislators try to organize society in an optimal way that there is substantial chance that they will succeed over others who might be thought to pursue the same goal. The second is a capacity assumption, namely, that legislators *can* accurately describe citizens' moral obligations toward one another if they are motivated to do so. If legislators can be made out to be both more motivated to promote the general good and more able to do so than individual citizens and other groups, then the legislature may genuinely function as an advisory authority about the nature of that good which all citizens antecedently have reasons to promote.

The motivational question is usually treated as a question of psychological fact about individual legislators, and that is indeed where those defending the attribution of advisory authority to law should start. The conventional position on this question of individual psychology suggests that legislators may well function as advisory authorities. As Dwight Lee explains, "Most academics (including most economists) whose work concerns government policy and practice tend to assume, if only implicitly, that political decision makers are motivated by the desire to promote the interest of the general community."[7] There is, however, an extensive literature that eschews the "public interest model" of legislative motivations in favor of a very different motivational assumption. For example, public choice theorists assume that individual legislators are narrowly self-interested when they vote on legislation; hence, the last thing that we should expect from them is legislation that actually promotes public interests.[8] Traditional defenders of democratic theory have responded by claiming that not only are the public choice theorists' motivational assumptions pernicious, they are also *just* assumptions.[9] Public choice theory pro-

---

[7] Dwight Lee, "Politics, Ideology, and the Power of Public Choice," *Virginia Law Review* 72 (1988): 191.

[8] For classic defenses of the tenets of public choice theory, see James M. Buchanan, "Politics Without Romance: A Sketch of Positive Public Choice Theory and Its Normative Implications," in *The Theory of Public Choice II*, eds. James M. Buchanan and Robert D. Tollison (Ann Arbor, MI: University of Michigan press, 1984), 11 (arguing that public choice theory replaces romantic ideals with realistic appraisals of human motivation); Gordon Tullock, "Problems of Majority Voting," *Journal of Political Economy* 67 (1959): 571 (articulating the theory of log-rolling or vote-trading to explain why democratic structures will exhibit overly expansive public spending); James M. Buchanan and Gordon Tullock, *The Calculus of Consent: Logical Foundations of Constitutional Democracy* (Ann Arbor, MI: University of Michigan, 1962) (outlining a series of private interest strategies in democratic representation); William H. Riker, *The Theory of Political Coalitions* (New Haven, CT: Yale University Press, 1962) (defending his now-famous minimum winning coalition principle); George J. Stigler, "The Theory of Economic Regulation," *Bell Journal of Economics and Management Science* 2 (1971): 3–21 (formalizing interest-group or capture theory of regulation).

[9] For useful surveys of the arguments made against the public choice model and in support of a public interest conception of legislation, see Jon Elster, *Ulysses and the Sirens: Studies in Rationality and Irrationality* (New York: Cambridge University Press, 1979); Steven Kelman, *Making Public Policy: A Hopeful View of American Government* (New York: Basic Books, 1987); Mark Kelman, "On Democracy-

ceeds *from* the assumption that legislators do not aim to promote the public good; it does not use its methods to sustain this empirical assumption.

Absent an ability to resolve this psychological question with any confidence, those predicating the epistemic authority of law on claims of legislative expertise might point to institutional features of the legislative process that temper the expression of self-interested motivations. After all, institutional design can counteract the effects of undesirable individual motivations. Such is the assumption at the core of the adversarial system in which the search for truth is pursued in courtrooms staffed with advocates who are motivated by anything but a disinterested desire that the truth emerge.

Lon Fuller did much to describe the form that we should demand of legislation before honoring it as law.[10] As Fuller argued, legislation should be prospective, public, general, clear in meaning, free of contradiction, stable over time, judicially imposed, and within the realm of the possible. Fuller called these requirements the "inner morality" of the law, and he maintained that when applied procedurally, these requirements produce substantively better legislation than would be produced without them. He based this conviction on his faith in the maxim that "substantive aims should be achieved procedurally, on the principle that if men are compelled to act in the right way, they will generally do the right things."[11] More specifically, Fuller thought that substantively good results are likely to be produced by both legislatures and common law courts, even if these institutions are staffed by imperfectly motivated individuals, so long as they adhere to the dictates of procedural fairness. "[C]oherence and goodness have more affinity than coherence and evil. . . . [W]hen men are compelled to explain and justify their decisions, the effect will generally be to pull those decisions toward goodness, by whatever standards of ultimate goodness there are."[12]

Fuller's faith that fair processes lead to substantive justice has met with a good deal of criticism. As H.L.A. Hart and the legal positivists

---

Bashing: A Skeptical Look at the Theoretical and 'Empirical' Practice of the Public Choice Movement," *Virginia Law Review* 74 (1988): 199; Mark Kelman, "'Public Choice' and Public Spirit," *Public Interest* 87 (1987): 80.

[10] See Lon L. Fuller, *The Morality of Law*, rev. ed. (New Haven, CT: Yale University Press, 1969), 33–94.

[11] Lon L. Fuller, "Positivism and Fidelity to Law – A Reply to Professor Hart," *Harvard Law Review* 71 (1958): 643.

[12] Ibid., 636.

pointed out, surely pernicious regimes *could* operate through Fuller's forms of fair legislation.[13] Or, as Grant Gilmore pithily put it: "In Heaven there will be no law, and the lion will lie down with the lamb. . . . In Hell there will be nothing but law, and due process will be meticulously observed."[14]

Yet the truth of Fuller's claim lies in the motivations that legislators have to comply with the inner morality of fair legislating. John Finnis puts Fuller's point nicely:

> Individuals can only be *selves* – i.e., have the "dignity" of being "responsible agents" – if they are not made to live their lives for the convenience of others but are allowed and assisted to create a subsisting identity across a "lifetime." This is the primary value of the predictability which the law seeks to establish through [Fuller's eight desiderata]. . . . A tyranny devoted to pernicious ends has no self-sufficient *reason* to submit itself to the discipline of operating consistently through the demanding processes of law, granted that the rational point of such self-discipline is the very value of reciprocity, fairness, and respect for persons which the tyrant, *ex hypothesi*, holds in contempt.[15]

Legislators forced to operate within a system justified by and operating on public interest assumptions may well find that such assumptions "rub off" on their substantive aims when legislating.

Aside from the eight features of the inner morality of legislation, there exists a second formal feature of lawmaking that may more directly blunt the expression of non–public-interest motivations by individual legislators. One need not be a utilitarian to recognize that, when tabulating interests relevant to particular legislative options, each is to count for one and only one. As a private citizen, no one gives equal

---

13   H.L.A. Hart, *The Concept of Law* (Oxford: Clarendon Press, 1961), 202; Marshall Cohen, "Law, Morality and Purpose," *Villanova Law Review* 10 (1965): 640; Ronald M. Dworkin, "The Elusive Morality of Law," *Villanova Law Review* 10 (1965): 631; H.L.A. Hart, "Book Review," *Harvard Law Review* 78 (1965): 1281 [Reviewing Lon L. Fuller, *The Morality of Law* (New Haven, CT: Yale University Press, 1964)].

14   Grant Gilmore, *Three Ages of American Law* (New Haven, CT: Yale University Press, 1977), 111.

15   John Finnis, *Natural Law and Natural Rights* (Oxford: Clarendon Press, 1980), 272–3. Lest public choice theorists think that the word "tyrant" does not apply to their self-interested legislator, Finnis is explicit that "[t]he sort of regime we are considering tends to be . . . exploitative, in that the rulers are out simply for their own interests regardless of the interests of the rest of the community. . . ." Ibid., 274.

consideration to all other persons. Spouses, children, parents, and friends each have a prior claim to our time, interest, affection, and aid. Yet the legislative point of view is to put these personal interests aside and to give each citizen "equal concern and respect."[16] Not surprisingly, this is also very much the moral point of view.[17] Thus, legislators, no matter how self-interested they may be, must put their justifications for legislation in terms of interests that are proper to the legislative/moral point of view. This is not just the point that hypocrisy is the compliment that vice pays to virtue. Rather, it is the point that a piece of legislation motivated by pure self-interest is likely to run into difficulties at the stage of public justification as well as at the stage of enactment.

The final feature of legislation that can be thought to moderate the institutional expression of individual self-interest is the interpretive stance taken by courts toward legislation. Much of what a statute becomes is in the hands of the courts when they interpret and apply statutory language. And courts do not interpret or review statutes by seeking to advance the self-interested political motivations of their particular sponsors. Rather, purposive interpretation aims to find a legitimate public goal for a statute and to interpret its language in light of that goal. Courts that interpret statutes in this way force a public interest conception onto the legislature, no matter what the motivations of individual legislators may have been. By so doing, courts force (possibly self-interested) legislation toward a conception of the good and so make it at least plausible to regard such legislation (as interpreted) as epistemically authoritative concerning the content of the good.

Notice that insofar as these three arguments on behalf of the motivational integrity of lawmaking give us a reason to think that legislation, and not legislators, are epistemically authoritative, it better supports the attribution of theoretical authority to law than the assignment of advisory authority to legislators. Inasmuch as those who defend an advisory theory of authority locate the authority of law primarily in lawmakers and only derivatively in the laws they produce, these arguments in fact undermine their thesis. They permit an attribution of epistemic authority to law in the face of contempt for the

---

[16] See Ronald M. Dworkin, *Taking Rights Seriously* (Cambridge, MA: Harvard University Press, 1978), 180–3, 272–8.
[17] See Kurt Baier, *The Moral Point of View* (Ithaca, NY: Cornell University Press, 1958), 187–213.

insights and motivations of those who author it. And in so doing, they reverse the priority of expertise.[18]

Let us turn now to the second assumption that must be made for legislators to be construed as advisory authorities – what I have called the capacity assumption. To make out this assumption, it must be possible to construe legislators as what moral philosophers call "ideal moral observers." An ideal observer in moral theory is not only one who possesses the motivation to determine what is genuinely in the common good, but also one who is well-situated to decipher the moral facts that determine that good. Being well-situated to judge moral matters is in part a matter of individual capacity: The observer must possess sound practical reasoning skills, a good deal of experience with matters of the sort to be decided, a willingness to admit error in the past, a willingness to entertain opposing points of view, an ability to empathize with those points of view, a willingness to restrain premature or preconceived opinions from dominating subsequent deliberations, an ability to reconcile the present decision with others in the past, an imagination that is capable of hypothesizing other situations arguably affected by the decision before her, and the humility to think that there is much to learn from the unique experiences of others. Being well-situated to make moral judgments is also, in a part, a function of the information available to the observer: It must be complete enough without being numbing in its detail, and it must be organized in a manner that vividly presents the moral issues to be decided.

One who would defend the advisory authority of law must be able to make out the claim that legislators have the cognitive and empathetic skills, and the information-gathering capacities, that collectively make them moral observers of a more ideal sort than most. In an effort to avoid the guffaws with which such a claim is likely to be met, advisory theorists are likely to be tempted to hold up those institutional features of courts and legislatures that may make them, as institutions, the kind of "reliable observers" that merit assignments of expertise. According to Fuller, both legislatures and courts are engaged in what he called the "collaborative articulation of shared purposes."[19] Fuller maintained that, "by pooling their intellectual resources," in-

---

18 I shall make further use of these arguments in the next chapter where they more clearly belong – to make out why law (as distinct from lawmakers) might credibly be thought to serve as a heuristic guide to our moral obligations. See the third section in Chapter 6.
19 Lon L. Fuller, "Human Purpose and Natural Law," *Journal of Philosophy* 53 (1956): 702; reprinted in *Natural Law Forum* 3 (1958), 73.

dividuals can "come to understand better what their true purposes are. . . ."[20] We all recognize the power of such collaboration in daily life because "we all know from personal experience that in moments of crisis consultation with a friend will often help us to understand what we really want."[21] Fuller extended this observation of personal moral decision making to the law. In Fuller's view, common law cases "show that communication among men, and a consideration by them of different situations of fact, can enable them to see more truly what they were trying to do from the beginning."[22] More generally, he claimed, "the process of moral discovery is a social one. . . ."[23]

These thoughts go some way toward supporting those seeking to assign advisory authority to lawmakers. For example, legislatures are comprised of a large number of individuals who (if the above arguments are right) are at least institutionally pressured to articulate optimal states of affairs. These individuals have extensive fact-finding capacities at their disposal. They are representative of many points of view. They have strong institutional incentives to reach agreement, but not in a way that produces checkerboard results.[24] All of these features combine to make plausible the claim that legislators collectively possess many of the necessary capacities to function as advisory authorities concerning the content of moral obligations when they are motivated to do so.

Two points are in order, however. First, these arguments once again do more to support the theoretical authority of law than the advisory authority of lawmakers. They make it clear why intellectually limited, short-sighted, self-interested, uninformed, and unsympathetic individuals might collectively produce results that are, so to speak, greater than the sum of their parts. If laws collectively reflect moral insights that individual lawmakers never had, then we would do well to invest laws with epistemic authority while remaining skeptical of any claims to authority made by their authors. Second, however heroic the efforts to make out advisory authority on the part of lawmakers, they are unlikely to impress those who harbor a deep-seated cynicism about the moral merits of legislative outputs. Because our contemporary political climate is one of such cynicism, a theory that

---

[20] Ibid., 703–4; reprinted in *Natural Law Forum* 3 (1958): 74.
[21] Ibid., 702; reprinted in *Natural Law Forum* 3 (1958): 73.
[22] Lon L. Fuller, "A Rejoinder to Professor Nagel," *Natural Law Forum* 3 (1958): 98.
[23] Ibid., 84.
[24] See Ronald M. Dworkin, *Law's Empire* (Cambridge, MA: Harvard University Press, 1986), 217–8.

characterizes the authority of law as advisory seemingly fails to explain why average citizens feel bound to follow the law. If our theory of legal authority must, in significant measure, square with our rule-following practices, a theory that fails to explain our practices also fails to provide an adequate account of the authority of law. Thus, inasmuch as the theory of advisory authority depends on characterizing lawmakers as moral experts, and inasmuch as most citizens do not so characterize their lawmakers, the theory fails to capture the nature of the authority that citizens implicitly invest in the law.[25]

The Commitment to Intentionalist Interpretation

Despite its attempted exorcism, legal interpretation has been haunted by intentionalism. This has puzzled those who have considered themselves successful in demonstrating the conceptual and normative indefensibility of intentionalist interpretation. But the persistent specter of intentionalism should come as no surprise to legal theorists whose battles with intentionalist theories of interpretation have been fought in the shadow of one of the theories of legal authority that I have thus far explicated. Inasmuch as the theories of practical authority, influential authority, and advisory authority all ultimately locate the authority of law in the beliefs of lawmakers, they necessarily demand, at one point or another, that one seek the intentions of lawmakers in interpreting laws. Because there are good reasons to think that intentionalist interpretation of collective legal utterances such as statutory enactments and constitutional provisions is deeply problematic, and that intentionalist interpretation of judicial utterances is in many cases practically impossible, any theory of authority that commits us to an intentionalist methodology appears to be fundamentally flawed.

We will begin by examining the scope and legitimacy of the commitment to intentionalism that is characteristic of a theory of advisory authority. We will then be in a position to consider whether any

---

[25] Joseph Raz has further argued that the attribution of advisory authority to lawmakers generates the following puzzle:

> To assume that expertise gives lawmakers timeless authority is to assume either or both that no advance in knowledge in the relevant area nor an advance in its spread are likely. Such advances would negate the expertise of the old lawmaker relative to new experts (new advances in knowledge) or relative to the population at large (the spread of knowledge).

Joseph Raz, "Authority and Interpretation in Constitutional Law: Some Preliminaries," in *Objectivity in Constitutional Law,* ed. Larry Alexander (Cambridge: Cambridge University Press, forthcoming).

of the previous theories of authority can be revised so as to avoid the problems that beset the theory of advisory authority as a result of its reliance on intentionalist interpretation. As I shall argue, because neither the theory of practical authority nor the theory of influential authority can be extricated from the grip of intentionalism, those seeking a viable theory of authority have good grounds for preferring a revised theory of epistemic authority to any attempt to resurrect one of the theories that we previously examined.

If the law functions as an advisory authority about moral obligations, then it must be by virtue of lawmakers reliably amassing and evaluating the relevant evidence concerning those obligations. In the event that we are in doubt about the moral lesson to be learned from the law, we should thus seek the beliefs of the lawmakers, because it is in these mental states – and not in their legal expression – that genuine advisory authority resides. Since what lawmakers believed at the time of legislation is probably best evidenced by what they meant by their utterances, and by what effects they meant to achieve in the world by those utterances, it will be important to seek two sorts of intentions. First, one would do well to decipher the lawmakers' "semantic intentions" – the intentions that capture what they meant by their words. Semantic intentions reflect what a speaker means, given her theory of interpretation. Second, one should determine lawmakers' "linguistic motivations" – those further intentions with which they issued their utterances. Linguistic motivations reflect the effects in the world that a speaker seeks to achieve. Thus, in the event that one finds the enactment "No vehicles in the park" ambiguous, one does best to detect the background moral beliefs of the lawmaker by asking into the lawmaker's understanding of the reference of the term "vehicles" (e.g., whether the lawmaker's understanding of the term included motorcycles, ambulances, bicycles, and so forth) and (if helpful) by seeking the further purpose with which the lawmaker sought to prohibit such things from the park (e.g., reduction of emission pollution, reduction of noise, protection of pedestrian safety, and so on). One who would defend the application of advisory authority to law thus appears committed to an intentionalist theory of interpretation as the best means of detecting the beliefs of lawmakers in which the law's authority ultimately resides.

If intentionalist interpretation is indefensible – because, for example, it is empirically impossible to detect intentions or normatively undesirable to conform our behavior to them – then theories of authority that necessitate it are indefensible. Few, however, would issue the blanket claim that intentionalism as a whole is indefensible. While the ability to read minds is a rare skill, most of us are fairly confident of our ability to detect the intentions of our family members, colleagues, friends, and foes. Moreover, many of us plainly attribute advisory authority to at least some of these persons, implying thereby that we consider it morally appropriate, at least on some occasions, to be guided by their intentions. General skepticism about intentionalist interpretation thus appears unwarranted.

Skepticism about intentionalism in interpreting the utterances of groups of individuals (such as statutory enactments and constitutional provisions) stands in better stead.[26] As one critic has put it: "The folly of any attempt to conjure up a legislative intent has been asserted so often that many respectable scholars refuse to recognize the concept."[27] As another has said, an intentionalist theory of interpretation as applied to legislation requires one to search for a "psychic transference of the thought of an artificial body [that] must stagger the most advanced of ghost hunters."[28]

Legal theorists have performed some astonishing contortions to vindicate, conceptually and empirically, the search for legislative intentions. Some – call them "pure realists" – have been so bold as to declare that groups can possess intentions in precisely the same manner as individuals.[29] Presumably these theorists would also argue that

---

26 In what follows, I shall focus on the hardest case: that of vindicating the conceptual integrity of intentionalism in the context of statutory interpretation. If intentionalist interpretation of statutes is conceptually defensible, then presumably intentionalist interpretation of constitutional provisions and common law opinions can be conceptually defended. There may remain problems with intentionalism, some of which may be unique to constitutional or common law interpretation. But such problems are likely to be of an empirical sort only, not of a conceptual sort. Thus, while it may not be possible to detect the intentions of constitutional drafters two centuries after they wrote their constitutional text, or the intentions of judges about whom little is known except the opinions they authored that demand interpretation, such empirical obstacles may collectively serve less as an indictment of intentionalist interpretation than as a reminder of its limits and, hence, the limits of attributions of advisory authority.

27 Reed Dickerson, *The Interpretation and Application of Statutes* (Boston, MA: Little, Brown, 1975), 68. See, for example, Fuller, *The Morality of Law*, 86; Robert E. Keeton, *Venturing to Do Justice: Reforming Private Law* (Cambridge, MA: Harvard University Press, 1969), 81; J.A. Corry, "Administrative Law and the Interpretation of Statutes," *University of Toronto Law Journal* 1 (1936): 290; Michael S. Moore, "A Natural Law Theory of Interpretation," *Southern California Law Review* 58 (1985): 345–52.

28 John Chipman Gray, *The Nature and Sources of the Law*, 2d ed. (Boston, MA: Beacon Press, 1963), 170.

29 These theorists have based their claims on the work of a small school of psy-

groups *qua* groups can experience moods, emotions, sensations, and memories that are not reducible to those of the individuals that comprise them. To make out these remarkable claims, however, pure realists would have to make out how groups can have minds that are distinct from those of their individual members. And they could seemingly do this only if they could plausibly maintain that individuals in groups function in a manner analogous to neurons in a brain.

Those who are skeptical about the ontology of group minds have had to premiss their legislative intentionalism on the intentions of individual legislators. Their task has been to make sense of the notion of a singular "legislative intent" in the face of their admission that the legislature, as such, lacks any intentions at all. Majoritarians have pursued this task by arguing that the legislative intent behind any particular statute is constituted by the intention shared by the majority of legislators at the time of enactment.[30] But the business of tabulating individual intentions is a messy, if not hopelessly confused, one. First, whose intentions should count? Should one tally only the intentions of those who voted *for* the bill? Or should the intentions of those who voted *against* it be computed, so as to determine the possible limits of the intent with which the statute was passed? What should be done in the face of multiple intentions, none of which commands a majority? And what of those legislators who had no intention one way or another concerning the enactment of a statute? Second, how should one count "overlapping" intentions? Are the lesser included intentions of some legislators to be counted the same as, or different from, the more general intentions of other legislators within which they are included (as when one legislator intends to exclude hotrods from the park while another intends to exclude automobiles)? Third, what should one do when legislators share the same linguistic motivations but diverge from one another in their semantic intentions (as when all intend to prohibit vehicles in the park as a means of increasing pedestrian safety, but only some intend the word "vehicles" to include skateboards)? And finally, what should one do when legislators share the same semantic intentions but diverge from one

chologists who maintain that masses do in fact manifest unique, nonreducible, psychological experiences. See Helen Silving, "A Plea for a Law of Interpretation," *Pennsylvania Law Review* 98 (1950), 510.

30 Raz appears to have a majoritarian theory of legislative intent in mind when he urges that "[e]very attribution of an intention to the law is based on an attribution of a real intention to a real person in authority or exerting influence over authority." Joseph Raz, "Authority, Law and Morality," *Monist* 68 (1985): 318.

another in their linguistic motivations (because, for example, they each possess a different ordering of the effects in the park that they seek to achieve by banning vehicles from it)?[31]

In the face of the counting and combination problems that confront majoritarians, some theorists have sought to anthropomorphize the legislature so as to treat its enactments *as if* they were issued by a singular author.[32] They have argued that the diverse and sometimes conflicting intentions of legislators should be treated *as if* they were evidence of a coherent set of intentions possessed by a single individual. One should reconstruct from such "evidence" a unified account that represents what a rational person possessed of such intentions would intend. The problem, of course, is that one can hardly treat something as evidence when one knows that it does not evidence anything. Because there is literally nothing that the "evidence" (the individual intentions of the legislators) evidences, the process of reconstruction is really just a process of creation. Anthropomorphic intentionalism thus stands to intentionalism as hypothetical consent stands to actual consent. Just as a trespasser could hardly defend himself by claiming that the offended landowner gave hypothetical consent to his invasion, so a judge could hardly claim an allegiance to legislative intent if she resolved conflicts between the particular intentions of legislators by assigning them new ones.

An alternative means of reducing, if not escaping, the counting and combination problems that plague majoritarian intentionalists is advanced by theorists who defend what has been dubbed a "delegation model" of legislative intent.[33] According to this theory, the legislature's intent is constituted by the intentions shared by the small group of persons who actually drafted the statute. Other legislators are to be taken to have delegated to this small group the authority to speak (and intend) on their behalf. Yet two problems befuddle such a theory. First, as a matter of psychology, it would appear that few, if any, leg-

---

31 For more extensive discussions of these sorts of counting and combination problems, see Ronald Dworkin, *A Matter of Principle* (Cambridge, MA: Harvard University Press, 1985), 38–55; Frank H. Easterbrook, "Statutes' Domains," *University of Chicago Law Review* 50 (1983): 547–8; Hurd, "Sovereignty in Silence," 971–3; Michael S. Moore, "The Semantics of Judging," *Southern California Law Review* 54 (1981): 266–70; Joseph Raz, "Dworkin: A New Link in the Chain," *California Law Review* 74 (1986): 1103–19 [Reviewing Ronald Dworkin, *A Matter of Principle* (Cambridge MA: Harvard University Press, 1985)].

32 See Scott Bice, "Rationality Analysis in Constitutional Law," *Minnesota Law Review* 65 (1980): 26–33.

33 See Gerald MacCallum, "Legislative Intent," *Yale Law Journal* 75 (1966): 754.

islators have a second-order intention of the delegatory sort, namely, the intention that their intention should be taken to be whatever intention the drafters of the statutory language had in mind. Second, even if a majority of legislators had such delegatory intentions, the *legislature* itself would not have the requisite intentions. When a legislator delegates to draftspersons the power to intend something without knowing or intending what it will be, the legislator is not intending what they intend – they are. When a legislator receives the bill from the draftspersons and transmits it by an affirmative vote without knowing what the draftspersons intended, the legislator is also not intending what they intended. By hypothesis, someone intends something (the draftspersons), but the delegation theory has no way of transforming that fact into the desired conclusion that the legislature *qua* legislature acts with a specific intention.

I have here canvassed only a smattering of the problems that confront those who attempt to defend intentionalism. Inasmuch as many of these obstacles are not just empirical but conceptual, they pose serious theoretical challenges to those who would attribute to law a kind of authority that necessitates intentionalist interpretation. I have elsewhere identified further problems with the intentionalist's presupposition that laws must be construed as communications that satisfy the complex conditions for communication famously articulated by Paul Grice.[34] In light of the serious problems that confront any attempt to defend the conceptual coherence and empirical viability of appealing to authorial intentions in the course of interpreting laws, one has to wonder why theorists have been so reluctant to abandon the endeavor. The hypothesis that I advanced at the beginning of this section is that they implicitly attribute to law an authority that demands intentionalist interpretation. Despite their nagging doubts about its conceptual and empirical viability, legal theorists feel persistent pressure to vindicate (or at least accommodate) intentionalism. Hence, the contortions.

---

[34] Hurd, "Sovereignty in Silence," 953–89. Others have since advanced alternative arguments against conceiving of laws as intentional communications. See Jeremy Waldron, "Legislators' Intentions and Unintentional Legislation," in *Law and Interpretation*, ed. Andrei Marmor (Oxford: Oxford University Press, Clarendon Press, 1995), 329–56. For defenses of the intentionalist's assumption that statutes function as communications which employ a Gricean analysis of communication, see Geoffrey P. Miller, "Pragmatics and the Maxims of Interpretation," *Wisconsin Law Review* (1990): 1179–1225; M.B.W. Sinclair, "Law and Language: The Role of Pragmatics in Statutory Interpretation," *University of Pittsburgh Law Review* 46 (1985): 373–420.

To understand why legal theorists feel pressure to make room for intentionalism in legal interpretation, it is important to recognize that one cannot escape the problems attendant on such a methodology by giving up a theory of advisory authority in favor of a return to one of the previous theories of legal authority. In one manner or another, each of the previous theories also located the source of legal authority in the mental states of lawmakers. Because these theories have dominated conceptions of legal authority, most theorists have at least implicitly presupposed one of them, and have thereby been compelled to accommodate intentionalism in the face of finding it irresolvably problematic. In the remainder of this chapter, let me make it clear just why the previous theories of authority are necessarily committed to intentionalist interpretation. We will then be in a position to appreciate fully the fact that we must forge a new theory of legal authority to escape both the unique problems that beset the previous theories of authority and the problems of intentionalist interpretation that make pointless any further attempt to defend the application of advisory authority to law.

A Brief Return to Practical Authority
Recall that Raz defends the traditional attribution of practical authority to law when, and to the extent that, law complies with the what he calls the "normal justification thesis." According to this thesis, persons or institutions have practical authority when their commands enable us to act on the balance of reasons for action more often than do our own judgments. If one's own judgment is more fallible than that of the authority, one will do the right thing less often by second-guessing the directives of the authority than by following them "blindly." Upon establishing another's practical authority, therefore, one will act most morally if one acts "because I was told to."

Andrei Marmor has advanced an argument against Raz akin to the one I advanced above to show that the theory of advisory authority is wedded to an intentionalist theory of interpretation. As Marmor argues, those, like Raz, who advance an epistemic justification for the law's practical authority are likely to find a happy marriage with those who defend intentionalist interpretation.

> When one's reasons for acknowledging the authority of another are based on the assumption that the authority is more likely to have a better access to the right reasons bearing on the pertinent issue, it would

typically be most sensible to take the authority's intentions into account when his directives require interpretation.[35]

If a legislature functions as a practical authority by virtue of being a better "moral observer" than are citizens and individual officials, then citizens and officials would do well to abide by its enactments. And when those enactments are vague or ambiguous, citizens and officials should repair to the moral observations that motivated lawmakers to author them. They should seek the mental states possessed by the individual legislators at the time of enactment, because the expertise that makes their legislative enactments practically authoritative resides in the beliefs and intentions that prompted individual legislators to act.[36]

Yet unlike the marriage between intentionalism and advisory authority, the union of practical authority with intentionalism is not always a happy one. Consider the case of *United States v. Kirby*,[37] in which a county sheriff was prosecuted under a federal statute that made it a crime "to obstruct or retard the passage of the mail, or of any driver or carrier,"[38] after he carried out a warrant to arrest an on-duty federal mail carrier suspected of murder. By the plain meaning of the statute the sheriff committed a crime, because his execution of the warrant certainly delayed the delivery of the mail. But let us suppose, quite plausibly, that we have good evidence that (whatever else they intended) the legislators who enacted the statute did not intend for the mail to be delivered on time at any cost – including the cost of letting a murderer go free. Let us suppose that they did not intend for a sheriff to be arrested for obstructing the mail upon executing a lawful warrant against a murderous mail carrier. Rather, they intended for courts to recognize exceptions to the statute that would exculpate persons when they obstructed the passage of the mail for a higher

---

[35] Andrei Marmor, *Interpretation and Legal Theory* (Oxford: Clarendon Press, 1992), 178.

[36] Marmor is quick to warn that legal directives may have authority because they solve coordination problems and dissolve prisoners' dilemmas. Insofar as there are no right answers to coordination problems (there are merely salient solutions), those who have authored coordinating directives have little claim to any special moral expertise. There thus appears to be little reason to seek their intentions when their directives are ambiguous. One should simply seek less ambiguous, and hence more salient, coordinating rules. Marmor, *Interpretation and Legal Theory*, 176–84.

[37] 74 U.S. (7 Wall. 482 (1968)).

[38] 74 U.S. at 483 (quoting 4 Stat. 104 (1825)).

purpose (for example, self-defense, defense of others, law enforcement, necessity). Because the latter intention is presumably more authoritative than its imperfect expression in the federal mail obstruction statute, a court should ignore the language of the statute in favor of the legislative intent to exculpate those like Sheriff Kirby.

The problem with this solution is that it appears self-defeating, because it thwarts the purpose of ascribing practical authority to the law. While the exercise of practical authority may ultimately be justified on epistemic grounds, it functions to preempt individual judgment, to exclude moral enquiry, and to usurp the role of private practical reasoning. Its point is to allow persons to act solely because they have been told to. Insofar as the directives of a practical authority bar one from second-guessing their wisdom, they seemingly cannot permit one to penetrate their plain meaning. Hence, when the commands of a practical authority possess a plain meaning, one is seemingly estopped from seeking their authorial intentions, because to do so implies that one is second-guessing their wisdom. And inasmuch as they are not to be second-guessed precisely because in second-guessing them one will do worse than if one follows them blindly, the search for authorial intentions appears inconsistent with abiding by the commands of a practical authority when those commands possess a plain meaning.[39]

Only when the commands of a practical authority are vague, ambiguous, or open-textured do they demand intentionalist interpreta-

---

[39] Marmor goes so far as to insist that what it *means* to follow a rule laid down by a practical authority (as opposed to set it aside) is to abide by its plain meaning. Were one to set the plain meaning of the rule aside in favor of purposive interpretation (or, presumably, an intentionalist interpretation) one would "confuse the question of what *following a rule consists in* . . . with that of *whether a rule should be applied in the circumstances.*" Marmor, *Interpretation and Legal Theory*, 136 (emphasis in the original). Such a claim echoes the sentiments of Hart and Sacks when they wrote:

> . . . [Courts] cannot permit the legislative process, and all other processes which depend upon the integrity of language, to be subverted by the misuse of words. . . . [T]hese policies of clear statement may on occasion operate to defeat the actual, consciously held intention of particular legislators, or of the members of the legislature generally. . . . [T]hey constitute conditions of the effectual exercise of legislative power.

Henry Hart and Albert Sacks, *The Legal Process: Basic Problems in the Making and Application of Law*, eds. William N. Eskridge and Philip P. Frickey (Westbury, NY: Foundation Press, 1994), 1194–5. The analytic derivation of the plain meaning theory of interpretation from the concept of a practically authoritative rule is not altogether convincing. I find it more plausible to claim that the normative function of a practical authority is best preserved by interpreting its utterances according to their plain meaning.

tion without apparent self-contradiction. In such cases, one cannot simply do as one has been told, because what one has been told to do admits of several possible interpretations. To identify correctly which of the various interpretations reflects the moral insight of the commander, one must apparently seek the content of that insight. And to do so, one must presumably employ an intentionalist theory of interpretation, because the beliefs that motivated the practical authority to issue the command are probably best reflected in the semantic intentions and linguistic motivations with which she spoke.

Given the point of declaring lawmakers practical authorities, it would thus seem that intentionalism must play second fiddle to a plain meaning theory of legal interpretation. Such a conclusion is puzzling, however, in just those cases in which the plain meaning of a legal text departs from the intentions of its author. In such cases, the rule departs from its rationale. One should do as one is plainly told (because all other reasons for action are preempted), but the reason for doing as one is plainly told (the fact that the authority knows better what one should do) speaks against so doing.

It should come as no surprise, however, that practical authority generates an interpretive puzzle. As I argued in Chapter 3, practical authority is itself inherently paradoxical. Its point is to bar one from considering reasons for and against actions that determine the morality of those actions. Inasmuch as (1) the morality of an action is determined by the balance of reasons for and against that action, all reasons considered, and (2) practical reason must therefore consist in weighing all of the available reasons for and against an action, and (3) practical authority bars one from considering all available reasons for and against an action save the fact that one has been told to do it, obeying a practical authority appears irrational. The most promising means of rescuing practical authority from the charge of incoherence is to insist, with Raz, that practical authority is properly possessed only by those with greater practical expertise than our own. But not only does this move fail to resolve the paradox of practical authority, it also generates the puzzle of interpretation described above. The epistemic defense of practical authority purportedly makes it rational to do as one is told by a practical authority; but what one is told to do may depart from what the authority intended. And because the expertise that justifies the exercise of practical authority resides in the authority's beliefs and intentions, one fails to act rationally when one acts on the authority's words rather than on the authority's intentions.

The interpretive puzzle that is generated by a theory of practical authority may say more about the problems with practical authority than it does about the problems with intentionalism. However that may be, it is clear that, so long as legal language may be vague, ambiguous, or open-textured, a theory that accords law practical authority will demand intentionalist interpretation as a backup to plain meaning interpretation. Hence, one cannot hope to escape the problems of intentionalist interpretation outlined above by further attempting to shore up the conceptual viability of a theory of practical authority. Moreover, inasmuch as a theory of practical authority embodies a cardinal preference for abiding by the plain meaning of a text over its authorial intent, it threatens to catapult one out of the frying pan and into the fire. Any theory that allows a Sheriff Kirby to be convicted, or that bars toddlers from riding tricycles in the park, has problems that survive the vindication of its conceptual coherence.[40]

A Brief Return to Influential Authority

While one who defends a theory of practical authority must invoke intentionalist interpretation only secondarily, one who advances a theory of influential authority must defend intentionalism as the primary interpretive methodology. This is because granting influential authority to persons or groups is a function of the moral importance of honoring their will. We accord influential authority to friends and family members because the moral significance of such relationships compels us to treat their express desires as new reasons for action. On the theory of influential authority explored in Chapter 4, we should grant influential authority to democratically enacted laws, because there are particularly compelling moral reasons to abide by the will of a majority (e.g., reciprocity, gratitude, consent, the duty to support just institutions).

If it is the moral importance of attending to another's will that drives us to accord that person influential authority, then one must seemingly employ an intentionalist theory of interpretation to detect that will. That is, one must penetrate the plain meaning of the authority's words to determine whether those words accurately capture

---

[40] These further problems were famously articulated by Lon Fuller in his critique of Hart's theory of interpretation – a theory that Fuller characterized as advocating a plain meaning methodology. See Fuller, *The Morality of Law*, 224–32; Lon L. Fuller, "Positivism and Fidelity to Law – A Reply to Professor Hart," *Harvard Law Review* 71 (1958): 630–72.

the authority's will. In the event that the authority has misspoken (uttering the word "and" when it means "or"[41]), or has used words in ways that are not conventionally identical to the authority's semantic intentions (uttering the phrase "Gleeg! Gleeg!" to convey the belief that it is snowing in Tibet[42]), one must seemingly disregard the plain meaning of their words in favor of their semantic intentions (as informed, when helpful, by their linguistic motivations). After all, to give a friend what he asks for, as opposed to what he wants (and intends to ask for), is a cruel elevation of form over friendship.[43]

Those who accord the law influential authority must thus necessarily seek the intentions of lawmakers. If the views of the city council are representative of the views of the majority in a manner that entitles its enactments to be characterized as democratic, and if the city council intends the word "vehicles" to include skateboards, then a judge has a reason to prohibit skateboards in the park (whether or not the word "vehicles" conventionally connotes skateboards), because only by so doing does the judge honor the will of the majority. If a judge is better able to determine the council's semantic intentions by attending to its linguistic motivations, then a judge has good reason to inquire whether the council sought to prohibit vehicles in the park

[41] In 1982, the California electorate, motivated by the decision in the Hinkley trial, passed an initiative explicitly requiring a return to the early M'Naghten test of legal insanity. The drafters of the initiative recapitulated what they apparently took to be that early test, requiring a jury to find a defendant not guilty by reason of insanity if the accused "proves by a preponderance of the evidence that he or she was incapable of knowing or understanding the nature and quality of his or her act *and* of distinguishing right from wrong at the time of the commission of the offense." Cal. Penal Code, sec. 25, subd. (b). Since the early M'Naghten rule contained a disjunctive requirement, not a conjunctive one, the California Supreme Court concluded that in passing the initiative the electorate had misspoken, and thus concluded that, as a matter of law, the initiative should be read to require juries to find *either* that a defendant did not know the nature and quality of his action, *or* did not know that the action was wrong. *People v. Skinner*, 39 Cal. 3rd 765, 217 Cal. Rptr. 685, 704 P.2d 752 (1985). In so doing, the Court implicitly penetrated the plain meaning of the initiative so as to act in accordance with what it took to be of primary importance – namely, the actual will of the California electorate.

[42] For this famous example of how a speaker's meaning can depart from the meaning of a sentence, see Paul Ziff, "On H.P. Grice's Account of Meaning," in *Readings in the Philosophy of Language*, eds. Jay F. Rosenberg and Charles Travis (Englewood Clifs, NJ: Prentice-Hall, 1971), 447–8.

[43] As Oliver Wendell Holmes said, it would be puzzling to think that the separation of powers required a court to respond to a legislature's unclear or misstated enactments by saying: "We see what you are driving at, but you have not said it, and therefore we shall go on as before." Quoted in Learned Hand, *The Bill of Rights* (Cambridge, MA: Harvard University Press, 1958), 18.

as a means of enhancing pedestrian safety, reducing fuel emissions, or redressing complaints of noise pollution.

In the end, then, those who attribute to law either practical or influential authority commit themselves to claiming that laws should be interpreted in accordance with the intentions of their authors. One cannot revise such theories to escape intentionalism without giving up such theories of authority altogether. Inasmuch as these theories thus suffer from the problems of intentionalism that beset the theory of advisory authority, and inasmuch as these theories also have serious problems of their own, we have reason to seek a fourth theory that both accurately describes the law's apparent power over us and does so in a manner that is conceptually, empirically, and normatively defensible.

Chapter 6

A Defense of Theoretical Authority

The preceding chapters revealed a set of errors that, if made, defeat either the conceptual integrity or normative defensibility of a theory of legal authority. The challenge, then, is to advance a theory of the law's authority that is modest enough to claim only epistemic force and bold enough to depart from the standard conviction that, whatever the nature of legal authority, it fundamentally resides in lawmakers rather than law.

In this chapter, I shall defend a view that locates the authority of law in legal texts, not legal authors, and that conceives of that authority as purely theoretical. Such a theory must answer to two masters. First, it must demonstrate that it indeed escapes the problems that motivate its defense. That is, it must avoid the difficulties that plagued theories of practical and influential authority by explaining the bindingness of law without invoking claims about the ability of law to generate unique obligations through new or exclusionary reasons for action. And it must surmount the obstacles that confronted the theory of advisory authority by eschewing attributions of moral expertise to lawmakers and by manifesting independence from any commitment to intentionalist interpretation. Second, such a theory will have to account for the ability of law to perform essential *legal* functions, such as solving coordination problems, defusing prisoner's dilemmas, administering sanctions, and so forth, when many of these functions initially appear possible only if the law possesses something more than epistemic authority.

THE NATURE OF THEORETICAL AUTHORITY

Like advisory authority, theoretical authority is a breed of epistemic authority.[1] A theoretical authority about moral matters gives reasons

---

[1]   For a more extensive reminder of the dynamics of epistemic authority, see the first section in Chapter 3.

for belief in the truth (or falsity) of deontic propositions, but it does not give reasons for action. The directives of a theoretical authority are thus wholly evidential. When they concern themselves with normative matters, they do not affect the balance of reasons on the main issue of what a person ought to do; rather, they affect the balance of reasons on the subsidiary issue of the evidence available concerning the main issue. Theoretically authoritative utterances give us reasons to believe in antecedently existing reasons for action generated by antecedently existing moral facts, and are thus entirely content-dependent.

Unlike advisory authority, which derives from the expertise with which an intentional agent is able to assess and issue judgments about other content-dependent reasons for action, theoretical authority resides in the sheer ability of something (be it a natural sign or an intentional signal) to assist us in acting on the balance of antecedently existing reasons for action. It matters not why a theoretical authority has the ability to function heuristically, nor whether we can give an account of the source of its epistemic potency. What matters is whether its succeeds, and nothing succeeds like success.

To get a grip on the essential nature of theoretical authority, it is useful to distinguish discovery procedures from justification procedures. One seeking to do the right thing may well find that its discovery is aided by any number of mental or physical pursuits. One may find it useful to socialize with friends, to meditate, to sing in the shower, to read great literature, to hike in the mountains, or to eat ice cream. Any one of these pursuits might function as a useful discovery procedure; that is, any one of them might cause one to do the right thing. But if asked to justify one's subsequent conduct, it will not do to say, "I was justified in doing what I did because I sang in the shower; or because I ate ice cream; or because it came to me while reading Twain." One must, rather, point to the available reasons for action and demonstrate that, on balance, these reasons favored doing what one did. And presumably, singing in the shower, eating ice cream, and reading Twain are not among any set of reasons for action, even if they are causes of action.

If there are practical or influential authorities, then among the reasons for action that one might be entitled to point to as a means of morally justifying one's conduct is the sheer fact that one was told or requested to do the act in question. Recall that such authorities give reasons for action – reasons that are justificatory, and not just explanatory (that is, causal). As we saw, however, we have good grounds for rejecting the claim that there are *any* practical authorities, and good grounds for refusing to conceive of lawmakers as influential authorities, even if there are others who can plausibly claim such status. We must conclude, therefore, that conduct can be neither morally justified by demonstrating its compliance with law nor morally condemned by showing its departure from law.

If there are advisory authorities, then among the reasons for belief that one may be entitled to point to as a means of justifying one's evaluation that one's action accorded with the balance of the reasons for action is the fact that one was advised to do the act in question. One cannot justify one's *action* by invoking the advice of an advisory authority, but one can justify one's *beliefs* concerning the rightness of one's action by pointing to such advice. In effect, then, one cannot appeal to advice to defeat claims of wrongdoing, but one can employ it to defeat claims of culpability.[2] On the theory of advisory authority, epistemic reliance can be justified only by establishing the moral expertise of the advisor. One must thus show that the advisor possesses superior knowledge of the balance of reasons for action (or some subset thereof) to show that one was epistemically justified in abiding by the conclusion reached by that advisor concerning what one ought to do. Because the last chapter established both that it is implausible to credit lawmakers with moral expertise and frequently impossible to detect the intentions of lawmakers even if they possess such expertise, it left us without a means of explaining how law can properly affect conduct – either morally or epistemically.

Like an advisory authority, a theoretical authority offers a source of discovery, not justification. It can aid one in acting morally, but it cannot make one's actions moral. One can thus fend off claims of culpability by pointing to the epistemic justification of relying on the authority in instances of moral uncertainty, but one cannot defeat accusations of wrongdoing if, despite one's reasonable reliance on the authority, one acted contrary to the balance of reasons.

---

[2]   For an extensive discussion of the distinction between wrongdoing and culpability, see Heidi M. Hurd, "What in the World is Wrong?," *Journal of Contemporary Legal Issues* 5 (1994), 157–216. In a nutshell, one does wrong when one's action fails to comport with the balance of objective reasons for action, all reasons considered. One acts culpably when one is epistemically situated to know that one's actions are likely to be wrong (that is, when one intends to do wrong, believes that one will do wrong, is consciously aware of a substantial and unjustifiable risk that one will do wrong, or has information as a result of which one should be consciously aware of a substantial and unjustifiable risk that one will do wrong).

An argument for theoretical authority is not dependent on any specific account of the basis on which a heuristic can be epistemically useful. It contents itself with the sheer success of the heuristic. Thus, unlike an attribution of advisory authority, one need not justify an attribution of theoretical authority by showing the authority to be possessed of greater moral wisdom. While there may be plenty to be said about why something might function as a heuristic (including the fact that it possesses moral expertise), one is epistemically justified in according it theoretical authority if, in abiding by its prescriptions, one is caused to act morally more often than one otherwise would if one relied solely on one's own judgment.

Inasmuch as a theoretical authority merely constitutes an effective decision procedure, and inasmuch as anything can potentially provide an effective decision procedure (from reading literature to consulting one's horoscope), potentially anything can function as a source of theoretical authority; that is, one need not locate theoretical authority in persons. This is the crucial difference between a theory of advisory authority and a theory of theoretical authority. One is free, then, to invest the law, as distinct from its authors, with theoretical authority *if* and to the extent that attention to the law assists one in acting morally more often than one otherwise would.

In the sections that follow, I seek to test the viability of a theory that characterizes law as a theoretical authority about our antecedently existing moral obligations. Our inquiry can be usefully organized around two questions. First, is this theory subject to any of the problems that caused us to reject the previous theories of authority? That is, does this theory avoid the conceptual and normative objections leveled against the theories of practical, influential, and advisory authority, including the charge that all three are hostage to an indefensible theory of intentionalist interpretation? Second, to the extent that this theory avoids the problems of the previous theories, is it robust enough to explain how law can fulfill the functions that we assign it?

ESCAPING THE PROBLEMS OF PAST THEORIES

The Conceptual and Normative Viability of the Theory

We need not belabor the problems that inspired the successive construction of the previous theories of authority. We need only content ourselves that a theory of theoretical authority neither explicitly nor implicitly invites their return. If it did, there would be as much reason to renovate one of the previous theories as to further construct this new one.

The theory of theoretical authority certainly does not invite a return of the paradox of practical authority (or the analogous paradox of epistemic authority explored in the previous chapter), because it does not suggest that theoretical authorities provide reasons for action or belief that are preemptive of those reasons that must be open to the consideration of rational agents. It also does not suffer from the normative problems that beleaguered the theory of influential authority. One need give no compelling moral reasons (akin to the arguments for reciprocity, gratitude, and the like) to accord a person or institution theoretical authority. One need only conclude that, by following the prescriptions of such a source, one will better fulfill one's already existing moral obligations.

This is, in the end, an empirical rather than a moral claim. If challenged, one would need to map patterns of conduct that demonstrate the heuristic reliability of abiding by the authority's prescriptions. A thorough defense of the theoretical authority of law would thus require empirical proof that attention to the law inspires an increase in moral conduct over attempts to determine moral obligations without such consultation. I do not propose in this chapter to speculate about the likely results of such an ambitious empirical inquiry. Rather, I seek to defend the conceptual and normative integrity of the theory of theoretical authority, and to advance some reasons to think that in certain circumstances the law is unique in its ability to provide us with information that is necessary to moral action. If these latter claims are plausible, we have good grounds to think that, as an empirical matter, individuals will effectively fulfill their moral obligations only if they attend to the epistemic ones generated by the law's unique abilities to reflect the content of morality.

Finally, for reasons that I will explore in more detail in the next subsection, we need not fear that, in attributing theoretical authority to law, we are naively presupposing that politicians possess an enviable moral expertise. Under this theory, our attention to law can and should be justified independently of our faith in the moral motivations and insights of lawmakers. Thus, those who find the attribution of advisory authority to judges and legislators preposterous may still find the attribution of theoretical authority to law plausible. And if they do not, they have cause to be true anarchists, because, if the law cannot even claim to be a helpful heuristic guide to determining our moral obligations, it cannot claim to give us new or exclusionary reasons for action that compel our blind, or at least constant, obedience.[3]

A Compatible Theory of Legal Interpretation

Under the Copernican reversal required by the theory of theoretical authority, instead of locating the authority of law primarily in the mental states of lawmakers, and only derivatively in the texts they produce, we should locate it primarily in the texts produced by lawmakers, and only derivatively (if at all) in the intentions with which they produced them. This theory invests the law – and not (necessarily) its authors – with theoretical authority. It treats legal texts as moral guides when complying with their language reliably assists us in satisfying our moral obligations. To the extent that detecting the intentions possessed by those who drafted the law would assist us in fixing the law with a determinate content, we have reason to look to their authorial intentions. But their intentions are, on this theory, mere heuristics to what is itself only a heuristic. That is, they are heuristic guides to determining the content of the law, which is itself a heuristic guide to determining the content of morality. In the end, only morality obligates. All "secondary principles" by which to determine the maxims of morality, and all interpretive techniques by which to fix the content of such secondary principles, should thus be judged by their ability to conform our conduct to the demands of morality. In the event that the law is ambiguous, we may do well to fix its content by reference to the intentions of its drafters. But in the event that these intentions are undiscoverable or unreliable,[4] they lose their heuristic value, and we would do well to fix the content of the law by other means, or to seek altogether an alternative guide to moral action.

There is nothing, then, in a theory that accords law theoretical au-

---

[3] As Kent Greenawalt has argued in response to my earlier development of the thesis that law may be thought to possess theoretical authority, "in light of all the compromise and logrolling in legislatures, viewing legislation as a description of optimal legal arrangements seems severely strained." Kent Greenawalt, *Law and Objectivity* (New York and Oxford: Oxford University Press, 1992), 246 n.25. Of course, if this is the case, then crediting law with any greater authority seems all the more strained. Greenawalt's criticism, however, is blunted once one distinguishes advisory from theoretical authority and premises the law's ability to guide action on something other than claims about the moral expertise of law makers.

[4] "There is no more reason why a person who uses a word correctly should be able to tell what it means than there is why a planet which is moving correctly should know Kepler's laws." Bertrand Russell, *My Philosophical Development* (New York: Simon & Schuster, 1959), 147 (quoting from Bertrand Russell, *The Analysis of Mind* [New York: MacMillan, 1921]).

thority that commits one to an intentionalist theory of interpretation. In the face of undecipherable, conflicted, contradictory, or overlapping intentions, one need not embark on further philosophical contortions in an effort to make sense of "the framers' intent" or "the intent of the legislature." One is free, rather, to fix the meaning of legal language via other methodologies. Thus, one might invoke a plain meaning theory that fixes the content of a legal text by reference to the conventional use of its terms;[5] or a theory that invokes the "spirit of the law," fixing the meaning of its terms by the purpose (i.e., function) the law might best be thought to serve;[6] or a paradigm case theory, which extends the reference of the terms of the text to actions that are analogous to those that would be paradigmatically prohibited or permitted by the plain meaning of the text;[7] or a natural law theory, which would define the meaning of legal terms by the true nature of the things to which they refer.[8]

By liberating the law from the grip of intentionalism, however, one openly invites a set of objections that are collectively designed to show that one is not left with anything that one can meaningfully think of as *law*. Let us take up each of these objections, because by exploring their claims we will better understand the nature of the authority claimed in this chapter on behalf of law.

First, the objection will be made that on the theory I have advanced, laws are just like sea gull tracks in the sand. Without an understanding of their author's intentions, they are mere marks on paper. To recall the idiom of Lewis Carroll's "Humpty Dumpty," one cannot know what a word means until one knows what the speaker meant by using it; therefore, legal utterances must derive their meaning from the intentions of their speakers to be meaningful at all. How else could legal utterances be interpreted when one could not even know, in the absence of authorial intentions, what language we should read them

5   See, for example, Frederick Schauer, "Easy Cases," *Southern California Law Review* 58 (1985): 399–440; Frederick Schauer, "Statutory Construction and the Coordinating Function of Plain Meaning," *The Supreme Court Review* 7 (1990): 231–56; Frederick Schauer, "The Practice and Problems with Plain Meaning: A Response to Aleinikoff and Shaw," *Vanderbilt Law Review* 45 (1992): 715–41. Lon Fuller characterized H.L.A. Hart as a plain meaning theorist in Lon L. Fuller, "Positivism and Fidelity to Law: A Reply to Professor Hart," *Harvard Law Review* 71 (1958): 630–72.

6   See, for example, Fuller, "Positivism and Fidelity to Law," 661–9.

7   See, for example, H.L.A. Hart, "Positivism and the Separation of Law and Morals," *Harvard Law Review* 71 (1958): 606–15.

8   See, for example, Michael S. Moore, "A Natural Law Theory of Interpretation," *Southern California Law Review* 58 (1985): 277–398.

in? And absent a desire to seek their author's intentions, why would one want to interpret them, given that we do not typically seek to interpret sea gull tracks in the sand? Do we not need to assume that laws are communications to make sense of paying attention to them at all?

The answer to this challenge is straightforward. If the marks laid down on paper by lawmakers assist us in determining the content of morality when we invest them with meaning, then they should be thought theoretically authoritative. The same goes for sea gull tracks in the sand and the oracular whistling of wind through rock walls. So long as the authorial intentions with which they were laid down do not give us reasons for action, we are not bound to determine the content of those intentions as a means of fulfilling our moral obligations. That is, we are free to invest such marks with a meaning that is distinct from that contemplated by their authors if so doing better enables us to act on the balance of reasons for action. Of course, knowing what their authors intended might assist us in fixing the marks with a meaning that is maximally instructive. In that event, we have reason to seek such intentions. But if such intentions are nonexistent (because the sea gull lacked any to begin with) or unavailable (because we lack any readily available evidence of them) or conflicted (because we confront counting and combination problems that confound any attempt to detect them), we would do well to fix the meaning of the marks in other ways.

The next objection to my claim that the content of law should be thought distinct from the intentions of lawmakers follows close on the heels of this first objection. According to this objection, to interpret sea gull tracks in the sand so as to achieve moral insight is not to *interpret* anything, and certainly not anything that can be called a "text." One who "reads" and reasons from sea gull tracks is simply engaged in the sort of moral reasoning that one engages in when short on sea gull tracks. One's moral conclusions are phrased in the "symbols" of the sea gull, but they are not derived from those "symbols." Similarly, to interpret marks on paper in the same manner as one interprets sea gull tracks is not to *interpret* anything. One who reads and reasons from such marks is simply engaged in the sort of moral reasoning that one could engage in without such marks. One's conclusions might be expressed in terms of the marks on the paper, but their genesis lies elsewhere.[9]

---

[9] One could put this objection in the words of Bishop Hoadly: "Whoever hath an *absolute authority* to *interpret* any . . . laws, it is *he* who is truly the Law-giver . . .

Joseph Raz voiced this objection to the value-oriented interpretive theories defended by Ronald Dworkin and Michael Moore.[10] Whatever be the responses available to Dworkin and Moore, mine is and must be epistemic. We are constrained in our interpretation of sea gull tracks by whatever sea gull semantics maximize our moral insight. Suppose that Jonathan Livingston Sea Gull smartly runs a pattern of the following shape: "Duties of beneficence are not owed to all persons equally, but only to those near and dear." In answer to the first objection, it matters not at all that Jonathan is an Italian sea gull; we will do better to interpret these marks with English semantics. (This is, after all, pretty lousy Italian.) In answer to the second objection, we might better figure out to whom we owe duties of beneficence if we respect the normal English meaning of words like "near" and "dear" than if we try to reason our duties out *ab initio.*

Now why might this be true? The answer is that, for many people, moral insight is more easily achieved if they reason under the guise of interpreting an authoritative text than if they reason with Sartrean self-awareness that everything is up for grabs at once.[11] This I take to explain the staying power of the world's popular religions. Despite their bizarre metaphysics, these religions give their believers theoretically authoritative moral texts the interpretation of which yields greater moral insight than believers are likely to achieve on their own.[12]

and not the person who first wrote . . . them." Quoted in John Chipman Gray, *The Nature and Sources of the Law* 2d ed. (Boston, MA: Beacon Press, 1963), 172 (emphasis in original). According to the good Bishop, if we are to avoid giving ourselves our own individual laws, we must interpret laws as they were intended to be interpreted, because only by so doing do we preserve the role of the lawmaker as "Law-giver."

10 Raz, "Dworkin: A New Link in the Chain," 1103–19. Larry Alexander revisits this objection when evaluating the interpretive theories of Dworkin and Moore. See Larry Alexander, "All or Nothing At All?," in *Law and Interpretation,* ed. Andrei Marmor (Oxford: Clarendon Press, 1995), 361–2. See also Charles Fried, "Sonnet LXV and the 'Black Ink' of the Framers' Intention," *Harvard Law Review* 100 (1987), 751–60.

11 As Richard Posner has put it: "When a court reads the Eighth Amendment, it is (or at least should be) looking for authoritative guidance, and it would get none if it felt free to give 'cruel and unusual punishments' any meaning that the words wrenched free of their historical context might yield." Richard A. Posner, *Law and Literature: A Misunderstood Relation* (Cambridge, MA: Harvard University Press, 1988), 227.

12 For a creative explication of this thesis by one less cynical, if not less skeptical, about the metaphysics of religions than myself, see Howard Lesnick, *Listening for God: Religion and Moral Discernment* (New York: Fordham University Press, 1998).

Consider, as another example, how we should frame jury instructions when we wish a jury to make a moral determination. Let us suppose that the Royal Commission on Capital Punishment was right in advancing its 1954 recommendation: In criminal cases in which the insanity defense is raised, the jury should ultimately determine whether the defendant is so mentally diseased as to be irresponsible. One might nonetheless refuse to instruct a jury in these terms, because to do so would leave its members "at sea."[13] Instead, one might require it to focus on archaic questions like, "Did the defendant know the difference between right and wrong?"; or literally meaningless questions like, "Was he irresistibly impelled to do what he did?"; or vague questions employing psycho-babble like, "Did he lack a substantial capacity to conform his conduct to the requirements of law?" It may well be true that, if jurors are asked to answer these curious questions, they will separate responsible from irresponsible defendants more accurately than if they are asked directly to determine defendants' responsibility.

The heuristic justification for paying attention to a text at all also gives us a reason to respect certain interpretive restraints, such as the ordinary semantics of English, when the text in question is a constitution, statute, or judicial opinion. One might think that the meaning of words in a statute should be given by their definitions, or by their paradigmatic exemplars, or by the nature of the things they denote, or by their conventional use amongst native speakers, or even by the intentions of their authors (if one could ever figure out how to overcome the counting and combination problems that prevent their detection in constitutional and legislative contexts). One might be an eclectic about such semantic matters, employing different semantic constraints in different circumstances.[14] The point is that, like all heuristics, the only test of the value of interpretive restraints is their ability to generate insight. And, once more, nothing succeeds like success.

The next major source of criticism will probably originate from those who remain convinced that epistemic authority must derive from advisory authority. Those of this persuasion will argue that the reason that legal texts function as heuristic guides to moral action,

---

[13] This argument was made in Abraham Goldstein, *The Insanity Defense* (New Haven, CT: Yale University Press, 1967), 81–2.

[14] For a defense of such an eclectic approach, see William N. Eskridge, "Dynamic Statutory Interpretation," *University of Pennsylvania Law Review* (1987): 1479, 1483.

while sea gull tracks do not, is that the authors who draft them possess a certain moral expertise. They pick the marks they do because they know that we will invest them with conventional meaning; and if we do, we will be lead to act on the balance of reasons for action.[15] We do well to look to law, as opposed to sea gull tracks, the sounds of the whistling wind, great works of literature, or our horoscopes, because lawmakers are better equipped to make moral judgments than are the authors of these works. Only the moral expertise of lawmakers can account for the comprehensive epistemic authority that the law enjoys[16] – an epistemic authority that, in contrast to every other epistemic authority, informs one's decisions about virtually every aspect of life. And if the law's comprehensive epistemic authority *is* a product of the moral expertise of lawmakers, then surely we should seek to discover the beliefs and intentions that motivated its enactment when its terms leave us in doubt about how to act.

Those persuaded by this rejoinder are unlikely to be impressed by the insistence that it matters not *why* the law is epistemically authoritative; it matters only that it *is,* or that it can be made to be by any number of interpretive techniques other than intentionalist ones. Such critics will maintain that, unless an account can be given of why legal texts compete more favorably than other sources for our epistemic adherence, we have no reason to attend to them over other possible moral heuristics. Much of the answer to this question is provided in Section IV, which both revisits the arguments concerning how the procedural features of lawmaking conspire to produce moral results through often immorally motivated or morally ignorant actors and argues that, if law is accorded theoretical authority, it can more readily solve coordination problems, dissolve prisoners' dilemmas, and serve the classic functions that have long defined its special province than can any other institution.

Those unwilling to wait for this answer, however, might do well to consider Jeremy Waldron's thesis that legislation can plausibly claim greater validity than can be claimed on behalf of the beliefs of the legislators who enacted it.[17] Waldron quite cleverly argues that

---

15 See Anthony D'Amato, "Can Legislatures Constrain Judicial Interpretation of Statutes?," *Virginia Law Review* (1989): 561–603 (arguing that a legislature manipulates the interpretation of its enactments by employing its audience's theory of interpretation to give meaning to its statutory terms).

16 Recall the distinction between comprehensive and limited epistemic authority spelled out in Chapter 3.

17 See Jeremy Waldron, "Legislators' Intentions and Unintentional Legislation,"

democratic decision procedures yield results that are morally superior to those generated by the individual judgments of legislators. He advances three reasons for this claim. First, it is likely that democratic decision procedures aggregate individual preferences in the manner required by the applicable social welfare function. Second, democratic decision procedures plausibly yield results that comport with the Condorcet Theorem – namely, the probability that they are correct is greater than the probability that any one of the views tabulated is correct. Finally, democratic decision procedures are likely to forge a "deliberative synthesis" that is superior in content to any view that even the wisest of individuals could come to hold on her own.

As Waldron concludes, these arguments do not just give us reasons to think that theoretically authoritative results could be generated by a "democracy machine" of the sort that Richard Wollheim famously hypothesized[18] – a machine that generates results which "cannot be conceived as . . . something produced 'by an intentional being, . . . situated in some enterprise in relation to which he has a purpose or point of view.'"[19] More radically, insofar as these arguments give us a reason to accord epistemic authority to democratic enactments, they also give us "a reason for discounting the authority of the views or intentions of particular legislators considered on their own."[20] That is, they give us a reason to think that, while democratic legislation may itself possess a certain moral expertise, individual legislators do not. If Waldron is right, one need not, and should not, concede that the only reason to think that legislation is epistemically authoritative is that legislators possess moral beliefs that are superior to those of citizens or officials that entitle them to be thought of as advisory authorities. One should rather maintain that legislation is theoretically authoritative inasmuch as its terms (interpreted without recourse to any legislators' intentions) can enable one to act morally more often than one otherwise would.

Let me now turn to two objections to the theory of theoretical authority that take their leave from particular metaethical theories. The

---

in *Law and Interpretation,* ed. Andrei Marmor (Oxford: Clarendon Press, 1995), 329–56.

[18] Richard Wollheim, "A Paradox in the Theory of Democracy," in *Philosophy, Politics and Society,* eds. Peter Laslett and W.G. Runciman, 2d series (Oxford: Basil Blackwell, 1969), 75–6.

[19] Waldron, "Legislators' Intentions and Unintentional Legislation," 335 [quoting Stanley Fish, *Doing What Comes Naturally: Change, Rhetoric and the Practice of Theory in Literary and Legal Studies* (Durham: Duke University Press, 1989), 99–100.].

[20] Ibid., 349.

first derives from a defense of nonnatural realism. Nonnatural realists maintain that, while moral facts exist, they are not natural facts. To know them, one must possess a "sixth sense" – a special faculty of perception that G.E. Moore called "moral intuition."[21] Only persons can possess moral intuition, and hence only persons can possess theoretical authority about moral matters. To say that the law – as distinct from its authors – can be theoretically authoritative about morality is thus absurd.

Even if nonnatural realism were defensible,[22] this argument would fail. While moral insight might require the exercise of moral intuition, one might find that one can assist one's moral intuition by experiencing phenomena that do not themselves originate from moral intuition. When particular phenomena reliably induce useful moral insights, they can be taken to give reasons to believe that one has reasons for action. That is, they can rightly be thought to possess theoretical authority. Thus, while legal texts may not reflect, or be interpreted in light of, moral intuitions possessed by lawmakers, they may serve to trigger useful moral insights on the part of readers who possess moral intuition.

The second metaethically based challenge to my claim that the law's theoretical authority should not be thought to reside primarily in its authors derives from the tenets of moral conventionalism. As we explored in Chapter 2, conventionalists maintain that moral truths are natural facts, but they equate them with sociological facts about the beliefs of the community. Such a view gives rise to the claim that beliefs of persons are the only source of evidence about what one should do. While the beliefs of individuals might depart from the beliefs of the community as a whole, they offer the only source of theoretical authority concerning the content of conventional morality. Hence, only persons can possess theoretical authority.

This argument invites the same response as did the last one. Even if conventionalism were defensible,[23] it would not give us a reason to think that only persons possessed of the beliefs that constitute the content of morality could serve as theoretical authorities about those beliefs. On the contrary, for precisely the sorts of reasons that Waldron outlines, a democracy machine might better capture the beliefs

---

[21]   G.E. Moore, *Principia Ethica* (Cambridge: Cambridge University Press, 1903), 1–36.
[22]   I have elsewhere argued that it is not. See Hurd, "Sovereignty in Silence," 1000–6.
[23]   Recall the arguments in Chapter 2 to the effect that it is not.

of the majority.[24] Alternatively, examining what most people *do*, as opposed to what most people *say*, might better guide one's judgment about what most people believe. And if most people follow the letter of the law, and not its authors' intentions (assuming that there are such things), then the plain meaning of the law, and not the authorial intentions behind it, will better serve to capture the beliefs of the majority.

A final challenge may be made by those who fear that, in advancing the thesis that law should be thought distinct from the intentions of lawmakers, I have unwittingly fallen in with the rebel forces who champion a poststructuralist revolution in jurisprudence. As Richard Posner has noted, "[t]he thread that connects the various schools of poststructuralism is their determination to reverse the traditional primacy of author over reader in the interpretation of texts."[25] By rejecting intentionalist interpretation and denying legal texts anything more than theoretical authority, have I not really made the reader the sole and only source of meaning and moral authority? Have I not joined the ranks of those who wave the banners of "deconstructionism," "postmodernism," and "critical legal studies" in protest against any and all who would defend the objectivity of law? And are not my conclusions therefore subject to the same criticisms that have been directed against the claims of the Academic Left?

I have addressed above a number of criticisms that echo those directed at poststructuralist theories of law. In the course of so doing, I have sought to make it clear that law can be accorded an authority that is distinct from that possessed by either its authors or its readers. Such a thesis is not motivated by, nor does it threaten, the metaethical subjectivism that makes one an apostle of poststructuralism. Legal poststructuralists use arguments against the authority of law and the relevance of lawmakers' intentions as means of undermining claims about the objectivity of the rules by which we are governed. Most radically, they claim that the meaning of legal texts rests not in its author, but in its reader. When judges claim to derive meaning from legal texts, they disguise what they are really doing: imposing their own (economically, racially, and sexually privileged) biases on

---

24 For just such an argument, see Robert W. Bennett, "Mere Rationality in Constitutional Law: Judicial Review and Democratic Theory," *California Law Review* (1979): 1095–7.

25 Posner, *Law and Interpretation: A Misunderstood Relation*, 216. See, for example, Jonathan Culler, *On Deconstruction: Theory and Criticism After Structuralism* (Ithaca, NY: Cornell University Press, 1982), 227–80.

those who lack their power. On this theory, there are no objective moral maxims that bind us. And there are no institutionally created laws or principles that operate (even epistemically) to constrain us. We are hostage only to the exercise of power at the hands of the powerful. And in many cases we ought to recognize that we are operating as the captors, and not the hostages.

As Chapter 2 made clear, one of the central premises of this book is that there are objective moral maxims that bind us. We cannot invest legal texts with any meaning whatsoever without running the risk that they will mislead us about our moral obligations. If legal texts are to assist us in acquiring subjective moral beliefs that better cohere with objective moral maxims, we cannot interpret legal texts so that they simply mirror our own subjective moral beliefs. We must instead employ semantic restraints that generate a proverbial market place of ideas. We must adopt interpretive techniques that yield moral conclusions that are distinct from our own moral beliefs, because only by so doing are we able to test our own beliefs in contrast. Institutionally created laws and principles should thus be thought to have an autonomy all their own. And when they provide reliable insights into the content of the moral maxims that bind us, they indeed constrain us. They give us reasons for belief that as practical reasoners we are epistemically bound to consider. One cannot derive from the theory of theoretical authority articulated in this chapter, as one can from the claims of poststructuralism, the conclusion that law is only a ruse for power and politics. It is, rather, a source of education about antecedently existing moral obligations, which, like any good educator, derives its authority from its ability to inspire insight into genuine truths.[26]

There remain a number of viable concerns about a theory that makes law significant if and only if our interpretation of it assists us in doing what we already have reason to do. Many of these concerns involve the claim that law cannot do the action-guiding tasks it is called on to do if it is thought to possess only theoretical authority.[27]

---

[26] This thesis thus subscribes far more to what Posner has described as "New Criticism" than to the poststructuralist challenge that he calls "reader response criticism." As he describes them, "Intentionalism assigns primacy in the creation of the meaning of the work . . . to the author, reader-response criticism to the critic or other reader, New Criticism to the work itself." Ibid., 221.

[27] As one critic has maintained, "The legislature cannot adequately discharge its responsibility of shaping the future unless the integrity of the accepted communication process is maintained." Reed Dickerson, *The Interpretation and Application of Statutes* (Boston, MA: Little, Brown, 1975), 11.

If legitimate, these concerns would be enough to motivate a return to one of the previous theories of legal authority, with its concomitant commitment to intentionalist interpretation. As I shall argue in the next section, however, we need make no such retreat, for the law can fulfill its action-guiding functions even if it commands only theoretical authority. We thus have persuasive reasons to prefer such a theory of legal authority to one that would return us to the problems that beset the previous theories.

AN ACCOUNT OF LEGAL FUNCTIONS

That law might possess theoretical authority without inviting conceptual and normative objections does not yet give us a reason to attribute such authority to it. We acquire such a reason only if we establish that law is in fact a reliable moral guide. As I mentioned at the start, we can ultimately prove this fact only by doing the sort of empirical research required to establish that, if persons attend to the law, they will act morally more often than if they keep their own counsel. Because I do not pretend to have done such research, I cannot vindicate with complete confidence the theoretical authority of law.

Nevertheless, there are certain functions that the law alone has classically been thought to serve – functions that enable persons to act morally when they would otherwise be unable or unwilling to do so. For example, law has classically been thought to provide persons with uniquely salient solutions to coordination problems. Inasmuch as coordination is, in many instances, morally optimal, and inasmuch as the law uniquely serves to make coordination possible, one must seemingly attend to the law to fulfill one's moral obligations. If the law can fulfill its traditional functions when invested only with theoretical authority, then insofar as these functions make moral action possible on the part of citizens when it would otherwise be impossible (or very difficult), we have sound reasons for thinking that the armchair attribution of theoretical authority to law is empirically plausible. It is to this task, then, that the rest of this chapter is devoted.

Joseph Raz has claimed that a theory of theoretical authority leads to what he calls "the no-difference thesis" – a thesis that defeats any account that credits law solely with epistemic authority. To construe law as only theoretically authoritative is to commit oneself to the thesis that legal authority does not (and should not) change people's reasons for action. As Raz puts the claim of the no-difference thesis: "There is nothing which those subject to [legislative] authority ought to do as a result of the exercise of [legal] authority which they did not have to do independently of that exercise, they merely have new reasons for believing that certain acts were prohibited or obligatory all along."[28] To endorse the no-difference thesis is to accept that "the exercise of authority should make no difference to what its subjects ought to do, for it ought to direct them to do what they ought to do in any event."[29]

According to Raz, the following three problems result from endorsing the no-difference thesis concerning legal authority: (1) One cannot account for how law solves coordination problems; (2) one cannot account for how law defuses prisoners' dilemmas; and (3) one cannot account for why persons have duties to act (rather than just reasons for action).[30] Let us add to this list a fourth apparent problem with a commitment to the no-difference thesis, namely, that one cannot account for what Leslie Green has called "the omnipresence and importance of sanctions in real legal systems."[31] These objections collectively challenge not the coherence or normative validity of the concept of theoretical authority, but rather the viability of its application to law.

Solving Coordination Problems

Raz argues first that a conception of the law as a theoretical authority prevents one from explaining how law can play a role in the solution of coordination problems. Coordination problems arise when members of a group share an interest in coordinating their conduct but lack a salient means of choosing from a set of possible actions a single one that will unite their efforts.[32] As John Finnis points out,

---

28 Joseph Raz, *The Morality of Freedom* (Oxford: Clarendon Press, 1986), 30.
29 Ibid., 48 (emphasis omitted).
30 Ibid., 30–31, 48–51.
31 Leslie Green, "Law, Co-ordination, and the Common Good," *Oxford Journal of Legal Studies* 3 (1983): 315.
32 David Lewis explains the search for a coordination solution as follows:

> Two or more agents must each choose one of several alternative actions. ... The outcomes the agents want to produce or prevent are determined jointly by the actions of all the agents. So the outcome of any action an agent might choose depends on the actions of the other agents. That is why ... each must choose what to do according to his expectations about what the others will do.
>
> Some combinations of the agents' chosen actions are *equilibria:* combinations in which each agent has done as well as he can given the actions of the other agents. In an equilibrium combination, no one agent could have produced an outcome more to his liking by acting differently, unless some of the others' actions also had been different.

David Lewis, *Convention: A Philosophical Study* (Cambridge, MA: Harvard University Press, 1969), 8.

coordination problems arise not only when coordination is advantageous, but also when it is obligatory. Thus, for example, we must achieve coordination equilibria when determining how children should be educated, how natural resources should be managed, and how traffic patterns should be determined. "[F]or most though not all of these coordination problems there are, in each case, two or more available, reasonable, and appropriate solutions, none of which, however, would amount to a solution unless adopted to the exclusion of the other solutions available, reasonable, and appropriate for that problem."[33]

As Raz insists, the problem of how to coordinate our actions when we have a mutual interest or obligation to do so can be easily solved if law, as a general matter, functions as a practical authority. A practical authority can command the performance of one of many equally efficacious options, and, because its command provides persons with a new, content-independent and exclusionary reason for action, it will resolve their coordination problem by *making* the commanded action the only right action available.[34] But, according to Raz, such a reso-

---

[33] John Finnis, *Natural Law and Natural Rights* (Oxford: Clarendon Press, 1980), 232.

[34] Raz's argument for how a practical authority solves a coordination problem is actually ambiguous between two interpretations. In the interpretation advanced above, a practical authority *makes right* one of the antecedently equally good means of coordination. In the alternative interpretation, a practical authority merely uses the *perception* that it is making right one means of coordination. But, in fact, its prescription in the context of equally acceptable coordination solutions leaves untouched the actual balance of reasons for action. The latter interpretation is supported by Raz's exchange with Finnis over the question of whether the solution to a coordination problem achieved by according the law practical authority itself possesses moral authority. As Raz suggests in that exchange, even if the law solves a coordination problem by being generally taken to function as a practical authority, the morally relevant reasons for complying with the scheme of coordination in fact derive entirely from the practice of coordination. The morality of coordination is the same, whether coordination derives from legal pronouncements, legal sanctions, public education, or custom. This is a puzzling interpretation for Raz, because even if one has sufficient reasons to coordinate one's conduct around, say, a particular set of customs, inasmuch as law gives new reasons for action, it seemingly gives one a new (albeit sometimes unnecessary) reason when it fixes a course of conduct as a means of coordinating multiple actions.

Finnis, in replying to Raz, maintains that there is a set of features that are characteristic only of law that make it a fair method of solving coordination problems when there are disputes about the relative merits of admittedly possible solutions. These features give one *moral* reasons to employ the law to coordinative ends. That is, they make a legal solution to a coordination problem morally authoritative in a way that other solutions cannot be. See Joseph Raz,

lution is not available if the law functions only as a theoretical authority about antecedently existing moral facts. This is because there exists no (moral) fact of the matter that determines a single right answer to the question of how persons ought to behave in a situation requiring coordination. For example, when legislation picks out one course of action from among a set of equally moral options (for example, when it specifies that persons ought to drive on the right side of the road, rather than on the left), it describes just one of at least two antecedently existing solutions to the coordination problem. If such legislation has only theoretical authority, its description gives us only an evidentiary reason to believe that the solution described is among a set of acceptable means of resolving the problem of coordination. It does not, according to Raz, give us a reason to act as is legislatively described, because, in the absence of giving any reasons for action at all, the legislation does not give us any reason to believe that others will conform their behavior in the manner described.[35] "Since solving coordination problems is one of the important tasks of political and many other . . . authorities, and as their relative success in it can only be explained by regarding authoritative utterances as reasons for action, one must reject the recognitional [theoretical] account of . . . authority."[36]

Raz's conclusion that theoretical authorities inevitably fail to provide solutions to coordination problems is, however, overstated. All that is required to achieve the sort of coordination equilibrium that solves a coordination problem is some salient reason for each person to expect that others will behave in one manner rather than another.[37]

The Authority of Law: Essays on Law and Morality (Oxford and New York: Oxford University Press, 1979), 248–9; John M. Finnis, "Law as Co-ordination," *Ratio Juris* 2 (1989): 101–2.

[35] "A wise man can tell me which options belong to that set, but he cannot tell me which of the options to choose before it is known what others will do." Raz, *The Morality of Freedom*, 30.

[36] Ibid., 31.

[37] As Gerald Postema explains:

Solutions to coordination problems are based on each party's exploiting mutually concordant expectations. . . . Since what I do depends on what you will do, in the ideal case I attempt to replicate your practical reasoning to determine what you will do. And since I know that what you want to do depends on what I do, I must, in replicating your reasoning, determine what you expect *me* to do. And since you are engaged in the same process with regard to me, to replicate your reasoning I must replicate your attempts to replicate mine, and so forth. Given this framework for the nesting of expectations, all that is needed to break the deadlock of a coordination problem is some fact about one of the equilibria which

Consider, for example, the problem posed by individuals preparing for a picnic. Each has a reason to believe that others will not attend the picnic if there is a threat of rain. What is needed on the day of the picnic, then, is some salient reason for each person to think that others will share a fixed expectation about the weather. It would hardly be surprising if the weatherperson's report provided such a salient reason to expect a common perception about the likely weather, because it is customary for people to consult this report before engaging in outdoor activities. The coordination problem would thus be solved in this case by the weatherperson's description of the weather – a description that has only *theoretical* authority.

The solution in this case reflects what game theorists have called a coordination norm or convention.[38] In matters requiring public coordination, a salient reason for a particular behavior would be provided if people, as a matter of convention, conformed their behavior to law. The fact that they do, of course, gives us a reason to think that they will. But lest such an answer appears to beg the question by refusing to give an account of the genesis of the law's conventional salience that is compatible with a theory of theoretical authority, it is important to speculate about how law could come to displace other sources of coordination when, *ex hypothesi*, it fails to give new reasons for action and fails to reflect a greater expertise on the part of its individual authors than can be claimed by those seeking coordination.

While several possible accounts of how law might become a salient source of coordination when functioning only as a theoretical authority are at hand, only some of these escape charges of circularity. In large part conceding Raz's argument, Larry Alexander, for example, has argued that the law cannot in fact accomplish the task of solving coordination problems if citizens come to appreciate its lack of practical or influential authority. As he argues, "because individuals would know that the institutionalized decisionmaking process, how-

isolates it from the others and which is obvious to both of us and known by us both to be obvious to the other. Thus, successful coordination requires the parties to locate some *salient* fact about one of the equilibria that makes it stand out, that is, to read the same message in the common situation, and with that message converge on a solution.

Gerald J. Postema, "Coordination and Convention at the Foundations of Law," *Journal of Legal Studies* 11 (1982): 174 (emphasis in original).

38 For useful accounts of when a regularity in behavior in recurrent situations can be considered a coordination norm or convention, see Lewis, *Convention,* 42; Green, "Law, Co-ordination and the Common Good," 301–2; Postema, "Coordination and Convention at the Foundations of Law," 176.

ever well-designed, was fallible, they would occasionally disagree with the institution's decisions and fail to act in accordance with them."[39] Inasmuch as the law would fail to guide action as a matter of course, it would fail to function as a reliable source of coordination by persons who were unsure that others would look to it in the face of its recognizable fallibility. Thus, claims Alexander, notwithstanding the fact that the law cannot possess anything more than theoretical authority, we have grounds for demanding that it act as if it had practical authority, and grounds for telling others that it in fact *has* such authority. Moreover, "[w]e as subjects of legal directives may have reason to have those directives applied coercively even when the balance of first-order reasons is against compliance. . . ."[40] Alexander's argument suggests that, while law cannot provide new reasons for action, our interest in regular coordination gives us a reason to encourage citizens and officials to treat law as though it can provide such reasons. And further, it gives us a reason to have law treat us as though it is a practical authority for us, even when we know that it is not, and even when we think that it is mistaken.

The problem with this argument is that it fails to answer the call that motivates it. It fails to spell out why we would invest law, as opposed to sea gull tracks or the edicts of the Roman Catholic Church, with false authority to begin with. It merely makes clear that *if* we do, we will better be able to coordinate our conduct because we will then (erroneously) take law to give new reasons for action that weight certain otherwise equally acceptable alternatives more heavily than the rest.

We might revise Alexander's argument as follows. People have historically credited law with practical or influential authority, because the law has long claimed to exercise that authority. This has enabled it to trump all other sources of social coordination when a salient course of conduct is required. That the law should never have claimed such authority, and that people should never have believed its claims, is neither here nor there. What matters is that our irrational rule-mongering has put us in the now fortunate position of having a salient source of social coordination.

The problem with this revised argument is that it simply pushes us back to asking why law would ever have claimed practical or influential authority to begin with absent some feature about it that

---

[39] Larry Alexander, "Law and Exclusionary Reasons," *Philosophical Topics* 18 (1990), 9–10.
[40] Ibid., 17.

made it, already, either a practical or influential authority or a salient source of coordination. Joseph Raz has answered such a challenge by arguing that such Napoleonic claims are inherent in the very concept of law. What it means for something to be law at all is for it to *claim* practical authority.[41] If this were true, however, defending the theoretical authority of law would be like defending the claim that, when we are not looking, tables move. One would have to argue that even though what it means for law to be law is for it to claim greater authority, and even though virtually everyone takes it to have greater authority, and even though law only effects social coordination by virtue of the fact that people believe it to have greater authority, the law in fact has only theoretical authority. Since we need not advance this unhappy argument unless law can solve coordination problems only by boasting to be more than it is, we would do well to examine alternative explanations of the genesis of law's salience.

The most plausible account, consistent with the theory of theoretical authority, of the ability of law to coordinate action appeals to the features of lawmaking that explain why the law would be theoretically authoritative in answering moral questions that do not invite multiple, equally acceptable responses. If we can account for the theoretical authority of law concerning moral questions that have but singular right answers, it becomes plausible to surmise that persons would begin to conventionally seek its guidance when such questions arise. In situations where there are several equally right answers concerning how best to bring about a desirable state of affairs, this convention of looking to law would provide persons with a reason to think that others would conform their behavior to the solution prescribed by law. And this convention would thus provide a reason for so conforming one's own behavior to the law. We could expect, therefore, that even when the law specifies just one of a set of equally good actions, the habitual appeal to legislative prescriptions to guide action would result in near unanimous conformity with the law's coordinative prescriptions. Coordination problems would be solved on this account not by authoritative commands, but by the salience of charting behavior in a situation allowing for several courses of action by the same guide as is used in a situation requiring a single course of action.[42] And once a coordination problem is solved, a (moral) fact of

[41] Raz, *The Morality of Freedom*, 23–8.
[42] As Finnis says, a commander is not necessary for there to be an authoritative solution to coordination problems. "Rather, the required state of facts is this:

the matter exists that makes right those actions that preserve the solution – a fact about which the law that accomplished the solution is then theoretically authoritative.

What institutional features of lawmaking might make law theoretically authoritative about our moral obligations and permissions? The answer, in brief, includes that set of procedural constraints invoked in the previous chapter to explain how the often petty dealings of self-interested politicians lead to publicly justifiable maxims for action. Recall that those defending a theory of law's advisory theory could not, in the end, use these features of democratic government to justify their attribution of moral expertise to lawmakers because, ultimately, these features give us reasons to think that laws, but not lawmakers, possess epistemic authority. It is thus open to us at this point to employ the arguments concerning the structural integrity of legislative results that the advisory authority theorist was forced to abandon.[43]

A revised version of these arguments can be summarized here as follows. First, lawmakers must conform their enactments to Fuller's eight features of the inner morality of law in order for their enactments to be action-guiding at all. This requires that laws be prospective, public, general, clear, noncontradictory, stable over time, and so forth. If these unique features of law force law in the direction of morality, then law may be a better source of moral knowledge than sources that need not comply with such constraints. Second, because the results of lawmaking must be publicly justifiable, lawmakers are forced to assume "the moral point of view" – to treat each citizen as one and only one when assessing the impact of any rule that affects the distribution of benefits and burdens across society. Thus, as Finnis puts it, the law's "forms and its modes of application and enforcement, too, tend to ensure that its solutions will be relatively dis-

---

that in the circumstances the say-so of this person or body or configuration of persons probably will be, by and large, complied with and acted upon, to the exclusion of any rival say-so. . . ." Finnis, *Natural Law and Natural Rights*, 249.

[43] For a fuller exploration of these arguments, see the second section in Chapter 5. Waldron's arguments concerning the moral superiority of legislative outputs to legislative inputs discussed in the previous section of this chapter are also applicable here. These arguments give us further reasons to think that citizens would conventionally come to trust the law for moral guidance, even as they increasingly distrusted their lawmakers. See Waldron, "Legislators' Intentions and Unintentional Legislation," 329–56. For further arguments concerning why law, as opposed to propaganda, exhortation, or custom, possesses a special claim to authority about moral matters, including coordination solutions, see Finnis, "Law as Co-ordination," 101–2.

criminating but non-discriminatory. . . ."[44] Third, because the meaning of a law ultimately resides in the interpretation that it is given by the courts, and because courts tend to construe laws in accordance with legitimate purposes (rather than the illegitimate ones that might have motivated their enactment), bad laws are often construed as good indications of what is in the public's best interests. Finally, lawmakers possess unprecedented fact-finding capacities and are compelled by their institutional roles to use them to achieve solutions that are acceptable to (or at least not unduly burdensome for) diverse constituencies. The upshot of these features of lawmaking is that laws are likely to command an epistemic authority about moral matters that no other institution can boast.

If we can make sense of the law's legitimate claim to theoretical authority concerning moral questions for which there are (singular) right answers, then, as I previously outlined, it is not difficult to explain why the law would become a source of coordination in circumstances in which there are several, equally right answers concerning how individuals ought to coordinate their conduct. That is, attention to law in the first circumstance would make salient one's attention to it in the second. Thus the law need not function as anything more than a theoretical authority to enjoy the salience required to solve the sorts of coordination problems that we classically look to law to solve.

Dissolving Prisoners' Dilemmas

Raz argues that prisoners' dilemmas constitute a second class of cases in which practical authorities can make a difference while theoretical authorities cannot. In prisoners' dilemmas, persons have reasons to act in ways that fail fully to maximize their interests; they also have reasons to change their situations so that they can in fact maximize these interests, but they have no means of changing the situations by themselves.[45] Raz claims that prisoners' dilemmas are like coordina-

---

[44] Finnis, "Law as Co-ordination," 102.

[45] Edna Ullmann-Margalit defines the dynamics of a prisoner's dilemma involving two or more persons, each of whom repeatedly faces the decision of whether to do A or non-A as follows:

> (i) If, in any occurrence of the dilemma among them, most of them do A, the outcome is (and is known to them to be) mutually harmful;
> (ii) If, in any occurrence of the dilemma among them, most of them do non-A, the outcome is (and is known to them to be) mutually beneficial – or at any rate better than the outcome produced when most of them do A;
> (iii) Each of the persons involved obtains, at least in some occurrences of

tion problems inasmuch as the commands of a practical authority can give the persons involved content-independent reasons for behaving in a manner that maximizes everyone's interests.[46] Raz, however, appears to understate the size of the problem posed by prisoners' dilemmas by making them analogous to coordination problems. As he argues, it is the sheer inability of the individual to effect change that makes the prisoners' dilemma, like the need for coordination, a problem.

In fact, however, what makes the prisoners' dilemma situation special and distinct from the situation posed by a coordination problem is that each individual involved has an interest in effecting change on the part of *others* but *not* on her own part. All of us, for example, have an interest in devising a means of keeping others from treading on public lawns while continuing to do so ourselves. We would, of course, prefer to give up our shortcuts if this were the only means of prompting others to give up theirs, because the worst possible state of affairs is one in which the lawns are ruined by the criss-crossing of multiple paths. But absent some incentive that makes us confident that others will give up their shortcuts if we give up ours, it will remain rational for us to encourage others to keep off the grass while refusing to do so ourselves. And in our duplicity, we will collectively ruin the grass.

Raz's notion is that a practical authority can provide the much-needed incentive to cooperate by providing new, content-independent reasons to abide by directives that promote collectively optimal solutions to prisoners' dilemmas. This new reason for action alters the payoffs at stake in choice situations and so defuses prisoners' dilemmas. Absent such reasons for choosing cooperation over non-cooperation, individuals will lack sufficient reasons to cooperate. Since theoretical authorities fail to give new content-independent reasons for action, they will fail, in Raz's view, to give persons reasons to cooperate, and hence they will fail to solve prisoners' dilemmas.

the dilemma among them, the highest possible payoff in the situation when he himself does A while most of the others do non-A;
(iv) If, in any occurrence of the dilemma among them, some do A, the outcome to the non-A doers is less beneficial than it would have been had everyone done non-A.

Edna Ullmann-Margalit, *The Emergence of Norms* (Oxford: Clarendon Press, 1977), 25–6.

[46] Finnis quite explicitly treats many prisoners' dilemmas as a breed of coordination problems, because he construes coordination problems as "all problems constituted by the collision of one person's interests or desires with another's." Finnis, "Law as Co-ordination," 100.

Yet as those steeped in the Humean tradition of ethics have long argued, the maxims of morality themselves function to give sufficient reasons for cooperation. According to David Gauthier, for example, when faced with a prisoners' dilemma, a moral person is one who chooses to cooperate on the assumption that others will make the same choice, and who does not deviate from his choice even if he is certain that his deviance will go undetected or unpunished.[47] If morality itself provides a means of defusing prisoners' dilemmas, then we must assume that the reason such situations recur is that persons either lack a complete understanding of the maxims of morality or are not motivated by them.[48]

To the extent that the first reason explains the recurrence of prisoners' dilemmas, the law could effectively defuse such situations simply by functioning as a reliable source of information concerning the content of morality. That is, the law could solve prisoners' dilemmas in just the manner that I have suggested it solve other problems generated by moral uncertainty – by prescribing conduct consistent with the antecedently existing balance of reasons for action defining how citizens ought to act.

To the extent that the second reason explains the prevalence of prisoners' dilemmas, nothing precludes the law from attaching sanctions to noncooperative acts so as to alter the appreciable payoffs involved in the choice situations in a manner that favors cooperation. As I shall argue below, the imposition of sanctions is entirely consistent with a view that law is, at most, theoretically authoritative. Where cooperation is morally superior to noncooperation,[49] so too may be the punishment of those who fail to choose it. Inasmuch as the law can prescribe cooperation, it can prescribe the punishment of defectors. If such prescriptions are theoretically authoritative, then officials have reasons to believe that the reasons for action favor the imposition of

---

[47] David P. Gauthier, *Morals By Agreement* (Oxford and New York: Oxford University Press, 1986), 8–10.

[48] For a discussion of the difference between moral internalists (who account for all immoral conduct on grounds of ignorance) and moral externalists (who explain some immoral conduct on grounds of weakness of will), see Heidi M. Hurd, "The Levitation of Liberalism," *Yale Law Journal* 105 (1995): 809–16 [Reviewing John Rawls, *Political Liberalism* (New York: Columbia University Press, 1993)].

[49] It is important to note that prisoners' dilemmas can function positively in situations where we think cooperation dangerous. For a discussion of the advantages of noncooperation in the area of anti-trust law, see Ullmann-Margalit, *The Emergence of Norms*, 44–45.

sanctions on persons who defect from optimal cooperative strategies. The likelihood of judicially imposed sanctions, the knowledge of which is enhanced by legal prescriptions, can thus blunt the temptation to opt for noncooperation and so defeat prisoners' dilemmas.

Providing Duties to Act

Raz's third argument against a theory that assigns only theoretical authority to law rests on his contention that "[a]uthoritative directives make a difference in their ability to turn 'oughts' into duties."[50] Raz claims that we often have reasons to act, but these reasons are not obligation-creating unless and until the legislature passes a statute, or a common law court issues an opinion, that generates from these reasons a duty to act. Put simply, Raz's point is that laws turn reasons for action into obligations, and a theory that attributes to laws only theoretical authority cannot capture this fact.

Yet the category of "oughts," which in Raz's view do not obligate without enactment into law, is an altogether mysterious one. Surely Raz would not want to suggest that, while one ought not to murder, one is not obliged to forgo the activity until the legislature enacts a penal code prohibiting unjustified homicide. The obligation not to murder must be thought to exist antecedent to its legal declaration and to be in no way *transformed* by that declaration. Perhaps, however, Raz believes that some behavior is not obligatory until it is required as a means of solving coordination problems or defusing prisoners' dilemmas. One ought, for example, to drive on the same side of the road as others and to pay taxes to support one's government, but one is not obligated to drive on the right or to send annual checks to the government unless and until such behavior is legally required.

There are at least two responses to this form of the argument. First, it is redundant. To argue that the legislature transforms reasons into obligations only when those reasons are reasons to coordinate or to cooperate is only to reiterate the claim that ran through the previous two sections. If Raz's criticism of the theory of theoretical authority is to be a third and separate criticism, it cannot rely on the supposed inability of a theoretical authority to solve coordination problems and prisoners' dilemmas by "creating" obligations. Second, the obligations that are derived from the need for coordination and cooperation are not *created* or *transformed* from mere "oughts" by the enactment of law. We have an antecedent obligation to avoid risking harm

---

[50] Raz, *The Morality of Freedom*, 60.

to others (akin to the obligation not to murder), and if this obligation cannot be met without conforming to the conventions of the road, then we have an obligation to conform to those conventions that is independent of any declaration by the state. Similarly, we have an antecedent obligation to pay for the benefits we enjoy when failing to do so would be unjustly enriching. If this obligation can only feasibly be met through a series of financial contributions to governmental institutions, then we have an obligation to pay taxes that exists antecedent to its legal declaration and independent of others' failure to live up to a similar duty. The most that law does, in such cases, is define clearly the antecedently existing obligations that have always bound us. That the law often makes clear for the first time the existence of such obligations gives law the *appearance* of *creating* duties to act. But, contrary to Raz's assumption, an appearance need only be explained away, not explained.

Imposing Sanctions

According to Leslie Green, "[o]ne need not take Kelsen's extreme view that sanctions are part of the concept of law in order to see that a legal theory which could not account for the omnipresence and importance of sanctions in real legal systems would not count as a very good theory of law."[51] An account of the justification of imposing sanctions may seem problematic for one defending the view that the law can, at most, claim theoretical authority, because if law is merely a heuristic guide to moral action, how can one be punished for ignoring its prescriptions?

There are two worries concerning the compatibility of the law's theoretical authority with the law's administration of sanctions. The first worry goes to the means by which a theoretical authority could impose sanctions. The second goes to the justification with which one could be punished for disobeying a theoretical authority.

It is important to recognize that sanctions do indeed change the balance of reasons for action. They give persons new reasons to do what is required. But legal sanctions must not be confused with the law itself. To say that the law can change reasons for action by administering sanctions is not to say that the law *qua* law changes reasons for action. There is thus nothing conceptually confused about claiming both that the law does not give new reasons for action and that it can effect the administration of sanctions that do.

---

[51] Green, "Law, Co-ordination and the Common Good," 315.

It is tempting to suggest, however, that in denying law practical authority while according law the power to sanction disobedience, one takes away with one hand what one gives back with the other. But notice that I am not suggesting that the law can command the application of sanctions while serving only as a theoretical authority. To say this would be to say that the law possesses practical authority for officials, even if it possesses only theoretical authority for citizens. Rather, I am saying that the law, *qua* theoretical authority, can prescribe official conduct in the same manner that it prescribes the conduct of citizens. That is, just as conduct rules may be theoretically authoritative for citizens, so decision rules may be theoretically authoritative for officials. If they are, then judges have reasons to believe that the balance of reasons for judicial action favors the administration of punishment in circumstances in which the legislature has prescribed such punishment as a response to a citizen's failure to fulfill the obligations reflected in legislatively described conduct rules.[52]

Let us now turn to the second worry – the worry that even if theoretical authorities have the means to punish, they do not have a justification to do so. According to the traditional command theory, the law (conceived of as that set of "oughts" that obligates) is simply comprised of the orders of a sovereign. To violate any one of these orders is to violate the law (that is, it is to breach an obligation). Hence, sanctions are justified whenever one fails to comply with the commands of a sovereign, because whenever one fails to comply with the commands of a sovereign one has broken the law (i.e., violated an obligation).

Such a justification is not available under a theory that accords law theoretical authority, because the enactments of legislatures and the opinions of courts do not comprise that set of obligations that bind us. Rather, they give us, at best, better reasons than we would otherwise have to believe that we have certain already existing obligations. But how can persons be justifiably punished for failing to take into

---

[52]   The remainder of this book is devoted to determining whether the content of decision rules can be at odds with the content of conduct rules. Nothing I say here is meant to address the relationship between the balance of reasons that determines right action for citizens and the balance of reasons that determines right action for officials. At this point, the claim is only that, whatever the reasons for action applicable to citizens and officials (whether different or the same), the law might accurately reflect those reasons. And if among the actions it recommends is the punishment of citizens who have violated obligations reflected in law, then officials may have good reasons to believe that they should punish such citizens.

account available evidence? Is not the punishment of one who fails to take seriously the epistemic import of another's statements really a punishment for (irrational) thoughts, not for deeds? And is it not indefensible to punish for thoughts alone?

The answer to this charge is that a theoretical authority would not be justified in punishing persons for failing to appreciate the epistemic worth of its prescriptions. It would be justified in punishing persons only for failing to fulfill moral obligations of which the authority's utterances were evidence. Thus, for example, a person who defects from an optimal coordinative strategy in a prisoners' dilemma situation might be legitimately punished, *not* because the legislature prescribed cooperation, but because cooperation was indeed morally required in the circumstance in question and the citizen had reason to realize this by virtue of having been given legislative notice.

This answer returns us, at long last, to the dilemma of legal perspectivalism. If, when citizens violate the law, they cannot be punished *because* they have done so, then judges must seemingly penetrate the conduct rules specified by law to determine whether those rules comport with the demands of morality. But if judges are entitled (or worse, compelled) to substitute the demands of morality for the demands of law, then what will become of the rule of law? A society seemingly has no *law* at all when it lacks binding rules that are prospective, public, general, clear, noncontradictory, predictable, stable over time, and so forth. And if, when judges ignore the law by refusing to punish disobedient citizens, they cannot be disciplined *because* they did so, then system designers must seemingly penetrate the decision rules laid down by law to determine whether those rules demand judicial action that is inconsistent with the demands of morality. But if system designers are entitled (or worse, compelled) to permit judges to substitute their own individual moral judgments for those of a democratic legislature when their judgments are more accurate, then what becomes of democracy and the separation of powers? The majority does not rule itself and the powers are not kept separate if judges are entitled to substitute their own opinions for the judgments of the legislature (however more accurate their opinions).

Inasmuch as many of the remaining concerns about a theory of theoretical authority are likely to have as much to do with the terms of the dilemma of perspectivalism and the possible solutions to it than with further difficulties concerning the ability of a theoretical authority to perform traditional action-guiding functions, I propose to turn our attention to the merits of the choices posed by that dilemma. If the arguments advanced in the chapters of this part have done their job, then it should be clear by now that we cannot avoid choosing between the jurisprudential axioms that the dilemma pits against one another.

Part III

The Moral Case
for Legal Perspectivalism

In the previous parts I argued both that law departs in content from the provisions of morality and that law possesses only theoretical authority. That is, law cannot itself obligate; it can only shed light on what does obligate – namely, morality. Collectively, these arguments make possible the moral justifiability of significant acts of civil disobedience. The battered woman who fears for her life and the lives of her children may be wise to take the counsel of the law and await imminent peril before employing deadly force against her abusive husband. After all, persons cannot, as a general matter, predict the future with any confidence, and thus they should not resort to deadly force unless and until peril is imminent and the need for such force is thereby made certain. Yet there are clearly cases in which the force necessary to prevent peril can only be meaningfully wielded when peril is not imminent. A battered woman may rightly conclude that to abide by the prohibition against deadly force absent imminent peril will guarantee her inability to defend herself and her children when peril is imminent. She may be able to predict with confidence both that her husband will kill her and her children and that, when he makes his move, his ability to overpower her and to cut off all avenues of rescue will defeat any attempts at self-defense on her part. She may also be right in believing that any attempt to escape his control will only result in her pursuit and punishment. The only means of effectively defending herself and her children is thus to use deadly force in advance of peril.

This is not a special case. Indeed, because it is virtually a truism that every law is over- or underinclusive relative to the values that it can be said to serve (or, in my terms, the moral obligations about which it is theoretically authoritative), we can readily construct cases that illustrate how every law can be rightly violated. But if this is the case, then we are in a philosophical pickle. We seemingly cannot hold fast to those principles that have functioned as the philosophical foundations of our legal system. We seemingly cannot assert both that innocent persons ought not to be punished and that legal officials must protect democracy, the separation of powers, and the rule of law by obeying the law even when they disagree with its requirements. To punish the battered woman who preemptively kills her husband is to punish the innocent; to acquit her is to violate the law in a manner that jeopardizes our systemic commitments to the rule of law, not individual fiat, and to the self-government of majorities, not minorities claiming the wisdom of philosopher kings. We are returned, then, to the dilemma of legal perspectivalism. The roles that we must assign to legal officials to achieve the virtues of the rule of law, and the constraints that we must impose on legal officials to accomplish democratic self-government, appear to require actions that could not be justified outside of those roles and cannot be avoided within those roles.

The previous parts established that the dilemma of legal perspectivalism cannot be defeated by rejecting any of its fundamental presuppositions. We must choose between the two options that the dilemma uncompromisingly presents. Either we must give up the principle of weak retributivism and punish those who justifiably break the law, or we must give up our traditional understandings of the rule of law, democracy, and the separation of powers and admit that judges and system designers should break laws when they rightly deem them to be, all things considered, in error.

Those who have squarely confronted the dilemma of legal perspectivalism have felt compelled to seize its first horn and abandon the principle of weak retributivism. As Larry Alexander has maintained, "There is an always-possible gap between what we have reason to do, all things considered, and what we have reason to have our . . . officials . . . require us to do."[1] Recognition of this gap, according to Alexander, necessitates that we give up the principle of weak retributivism and punish those who do the right thing in breaking the law. "[I]n one role we occupy, that of authority, we should impose sanctions on ourselves for actions that are correct in another role we occupy, that of subjects of rules. It may be morally good that we punish ourselves for breaking morally good rules for morally good reasons."[2] Frederick Schauer has similarly argued that authority is

---

[1] Larry Alexander, "The Gap," *Harvard Journal of Law and Public Policy* 14 (1991): 695.
[2] Ibid., 696.

asymmetrical. "[T]he lack of a (good moral) reason for obeying authority does not entail the lack of a (good moral) reason for imposing it, . . . *a fortiori*, the practice of imposing authority and of enforcing compliance with rules *qua* rules, can be seen as sometimes justified. . . ."[3]

Implicit in the willingness to reject the principle of weak retributivism is a commitment to role-relative morality or perspectivalism. The "always-possible gap" that Alexander identifies is a product of the view that public roles provide officials with reasons for action that are different from the reasons for action possessed by those who do not occupy such roles. Hence, a single act may be moral when judged from the perspective of a citizen but immoral when judged from the perspective of a judge. Alternatively, it may be moral when judged from the perspective of a judge but immoral when judged from the perspective of a system designer. I will ultimately argue that role-relative morality is misconceived, and hence that we need not and should not embrace the paradoxical conclusion that morality justifies the punishment of the morally justified. But it is important to appreciate the power of the claim that the dilemma of legal perspectivalism is an inescapable one, and that our theoretical commitments suffer least by forfeiting the principle of weak retributivism.

There are two potential sources of role-relative morality. First, role-relative morality is thought to follow from the need to prevent the moral errors that are the inevitable product of human fallibility. Theorists who consider error to be the sole source of role-relative morality provide what I take to be a pragmatic defense of the need to punish the justified. Such a defense furnishes a weak theory of perspectivalism because, in the absence of moral error, there would be no basis for espousing role-relative morality, and hence there would be no basis for abandoning the correspondence thesis. But role-relative morality is also thought by some to be a product of institutional concerns that would survive the (admittedly unlikely) perfection of our practical reasoning. Theorists who take these institutional concerns to be the source of role-relative morality provide a principled defense of perspectivalism that serves as a substantially stronger reason for sacrificing the principle of weak retributivism.[4] If such theorists are

---

[3] Frederick F. Schauer, *Playing by the Rules: A Philosophical Examination of Rule-Based Decision-Making in Law and in Life* (Oxford: Clarendon Press, 1991), 129–30.
[4] I discuss this distinction between pragmatic and principled defenses of role-relative morality more thoroughly at the end of Chapter 7.

successful in advancing a principled defense of role-relative morality, then we must conclude that morality is inherently paradoxical. It
requires us to do what it requires others to prevent or punish.

In Chapter 7, I shall explore the pragmatic defense of perspectivalism provided by concerns about human fallibility. In the subsequent chapters of this part, I shall take up the principled defenses of
judicial perspectivalism and constitutional perspectivalism, respectively.

Chapter 7

Practical Errors: Pragmatic Foundations for Legal Perspectivalism

Those who seek to derive role-relative morality from considerations of human fallibility must be prepared to explain how such considerations give rise to differential reasons for action for citizens, officials, and institution designers. At least three accounts appear to be available.

THE ARGUMENT FROM PERSONAL ERROR

Larry Alexander has maintained that the reason for the gap between justified disobedience and justified punishment is that, "we as the subjects of rules are fallible, and we are more likely to produce those consequences demanded by our moral principles if we are governed not directly by those principles but by blunt (over- and underinclusive) rules that are relatively easy to follow and monitor."[1] This insistence on rule-governed conduct is reminiscent of John Stuart Mill's conviction that, "whatever we adopt as the fundamental principle of morality, we require subordinate principles to apply it by. . . ."[2] Insofar as the law provides just such a set of subordinate principles for action, this thesis suggests that compliance with the law will accomplish results that are morally superior to those achieved by attempts to comply with the dictates of morality. This claim, by itself, fails to

---

[1] Larry Alexander, "The Gap," *Harvard Journal of law and Public Policy* 14 (1991): 696. See Frederick F. Schauer, *Playing by the Rules: A Philosophical Examination of Rule-Based Decision-Making in Law and in Life* (Oxford: Clarendon Press, 1991), 149–55.

[2] John Stuart Mill, *Utilitarianism,* in *Selected Writings of John Stuart Mill,* ed. Maurice Cowling (New York: New American Library, 1968), 266. Such a conviction was born of the recognition that "there is not time, previous to action, for calculating and weighing the effects of any line of conduct on the general happiness." Ibid., 264. Absent such time, individuals are bound to make mistakes that lead to wrong action. For a similar defense of the argument from personal error, see John Rawls, "Two Concepts of Rules," *The Philosophical Review* 67 (1958): 23.

provide us with a defense of role-relative morality. It merely suggests that, by virtue of our inevitable fallibility, all of us, citizens, judges, and institution designers alike, have a reason to defer to the law if the law prescribes conduct that accords with the relevant moral principles more often than does our own calculation of those principles. Those who contemplate disobedience (of either decision rules or conduct rules) must factor into their calculations the possibility that they are in error in thinking that the relevant rules are over- or underinclusive. If this calculation is itself likely to be erroneous, then concern for personal moral error may provide a good reason for general deference to the law. But such a reason appears to be equally applicable to citizens, judges, and institution designers.

To generate differential reasons for action, those who appeal to the potential for personal error must provide some account of why the fear of personal moral error should lead judges to comply with decision rules in instances in which the fear of personal moral error should not lead citizens to comply with conduct rules. Such an account would be available if judges were prone to greater error than citizens. Under such circumstances, a judge would have a more weighty reason to abide by the decision rule requiring punishment of a battered wife than the battered wife would have in deciding whether to violate the conduct rule prohibiting homicide in the absence of imminent peril. But because there are grounds for thinking that judges and other officials are at least as well situated as citizens, if not better situated, to assess the balance of reasons for action,[3] the simple argument from personal error fails to provide a compelling reason to embrace role-relative morality.

THE ARGUMENT FROM EXAMPLE

A more sophisticated version of the error thesis is more persuasive. Alexander has sketched its foundations as follows:

> Rules are formulated by finite, fallible human beings whose ability to foresee and consider possible applications of rules is limited. The rules they promulgate will therefore be imperfect. Suppose that an agent correctly sees that the rule that commands him to do not-A in situation X would be improved were it to command him to do A in X instead.

---

[3] Recall the discussions in Chapters 5 and 6 concerning the institutional features that account for the theoretical authority of democratic enactments.

Suppose that he then disobeys the rule and does A. This argument assumes that A will necessarily have better consequences than not-A because a better rule would command A and not not-A. But . . . [s]ome agents will mistakenly believe that departures from rules are warranted when in fact no exception is called for, and the negative effects of these mistaken exceptions may outweigh the positive effects of justified exceptions.[4]

This more sophisticated argument appeals not to the possibility that the actor's decision to break the law will itself be erroneous, but to the possibility that an actor's otherwise correct decision will cause erroneous decisions by others.[5] Its claim is that, because morality requires action based on the balance of reasons, all things considered, and one of the reasons against breaking the law that one must seemingly consider is the possibility that one's (otherwise justified) disobedience will serve as a poor example to others, then morality compels the assessment of the precedential value of one's justified acts. Where that precedential value is great, an otherwise justified act of disobedience may be unjustified.

This more sophisticated claim, like its simpler counterpart, fails, by itself, to provide citizens and officials with differential reasons for action. It merely suggests that all actors who debate the merits of abiding by the law must discount the reasons for disobedience by the probability that such disobedience will encourage a disproportionate amount of unjustified disobedience by others. In order for this claim to provide a basis for role-relative morality, it must be supplemented with an account of why a judge might have a reason to punish a citizen who has *correctly* calculated that her (otherwise justified) disobedience will not encourage a disproportionately greater amount of unjustified disobedience.

The necessary corollary to the sophisticated error thesis is the quite plausible claim that the precedential effect of a citizen's (otherwise justified) disobedience is a less weighty reason for the citizen to comply with the law than is the precedential effect of a judge's (otherwise justified) disobedience. Because public officers occupy highly visible positions, and because their conduct within these positions is often taken, by citizens and other officials alike, to define the extent of

---

4   Larry Alexander, "Pursuing the Good – Indirectly," *Ethics* 95 (1985): 322.
5   See Fred Feldman, *Introductory Ethics* (Englewood Cliffs, NJ: Prentice-Hall, 1978), 97, for the thesis that setting an example constitutes a consideration that should enter into the balance of reasons for action.

obedience required, their disobedience provides a more powerful incentive for (unjustified) disobedience by others than does that of most private citizens.[6] Insofar as judicial disobedience is more likely than private disobedience to encourage moral mistakes by other citizens and officials, the sophisticated argument from error purportedly provides a more weighty reason for judges to abide by decision rules than for citizens to abide by conduct rules. It provides a basis for thinking that a judge might be morally compelled to punish a battered wife who was morally justified in breaking the law of homicide.

There is a tempting rejoinder to the argument from example. This rejoinder draws on the intuition that we should each be entitled to do the right thing, even if it causes others to do the wrong thing. One way of unpacking this intuition is by invoking an argument that limits the consequences that serve as reasons for and against an action to those that are the proximate result of that action. When another mistakenly employs our justified disobedience as precedent for an unjustified act of disobedience, that individual's violation is the sort of voluntary intervening act that breaks the causal chain between our conduct and any subsequent unjustified consequences. While all of the proximate consequences of our actions serve as reasons for and against those actions, consequences that are not proximate do not

---

6   [E]veryone, judges and citizens alike, has an obligation to support just institutions. This obligation to support just laws does not give rise to a general obligation to obey the laws on the part of *citizens*, . . . because 'it is a melodramatic exaggeration to suppose that every breach of law' by a citizen sets such a bad example that it will endanger the just system of laws everyone has an obligation to support. . . . [I]t is not nearly such an exaggeration to claim that judges cannot disregard the laws as they exercise their offices without demotivating by their example a large number of their fellow citizens to comply themselves. For citizens might well think that if even judges can be lawless in their official behavior, what reason is there for ordinary citizens to be law-abiding? If that is so, then judges have a special obligation to obey the laws as they judge . . . .

Michael S. Moore, "Authority, Law, and Razian Reasons," *Southern California Law Review* 62 (1989): 836, quoting Joseph Raz, *The Morality of Freedom* (Oxford: Clarendon Press, 1986), 102 (footnotes omitted). See also Chaim Gans, *Philosophical Anarchism and Political Disobedience* (Cambridge: Cambridge University Press, 1992), 7. This argument should be supplemented with the observation that, insofar as a court's precedent formally influences future judges, a court's disobedience would appear to formally encourage future disobedience on the part of other courts. See Joseph Raz, *The Authority of Law: Essays on Law and Morality* (Oxford: Clarendon Press, 1979), 105–11. Insofar as courts will erroneously misconstrue examples of judicial disobedience, precedential disobedience may encourage more unjustifiably disobedient adjudication than justifiably disobedient adjudication.

enter into the balance of reasons that determines right action. In short, while our error is of our concern, others' error is not, because the error of others is a proximate consequence of their voluntary acts, not ours.

As I will argue in Chapter 10, the attempt to invoke proximate cause limitations to curtail the consequences for which one is causally responsible is metaphysically untenable. But even if this rejoinder could be rendered metaphysically plausible, it would only provide us with a reason to think that those who set examples do not *cause* the unjustified conduct of those who take such examples to heart. This would be morally significant only if morality required us to refrain from causing harm but did not require us to affirmatively act to prevent harm when we are capable of so doing. While considerations of individual liberty may justify us in thinking that the law ought not to require good samaritanism, those considerations are unlikely to be of a type that will convince us that morality does not require it. Liberty interests may be sufficiently hefty to outweigh reasons for affirmatively acting to rescue others from peril, but it would take a particularly virile strain of libertarianism to exclude reasons for aid altogether from the balance of reasons that justifies action.[7]

There thus seems no means of denying that practical rationality requires individuals to consider the likelihood that they will induce, by example, unjustified conduct on the part of others. Insofar as judges are more likely than citizens to encourage unjustified disobedience by their justified disobedience, it would appear that judges have a more weighty reason to abide by legal rules than do citizens. As such, the argument from example appears to provide a promising basis for vindicating the sort of role-relative morality that would justify the punishment of justified offenders. The judge ought to punish the battered wife for justifiably killing her husband, because if she does not, other citizens will resort to deadly force in unjustified circumstances, and other judges will unjustifiably acquit those citizens.

---

[7] Many libertarians are libertarians in part because they consider charity, generosity, and kindness to be praiseworthy only if uncoerced. To preserve opportunities for moral action, they insist that the state must not legislate all acts that would be praiseworthy. They thus recognize moral duties of good samaritanism, but insist that such duties cannot be meaningfully fulfilled if coerced. See, for example, Robert Nozick, *Anarchy, State and Utopia* (New York: Basic Books, 1974), 167–73; Tibor Machan, *Individuals and Their Rights* (La Salle, IL: Open Court Publishers, 1989), 162–3; Richard A. Epstein, "A Theory of Strict Liability," *Journal of Legal Studies* 2 (1973): 200, 203–4.

THE ARGUMENT FROM OPPORTUNITY

The third version of the error thesis is a sophisticated hybrid of the first two versions. It takes its start from the claim that one who can affirmatively act to prevent or reduce morally bad consequences has a reason to do so. This claim is less controversial than it may first appear. Moral and political theorists of virtually all stripes are likely to sign onto it once they recognize its limitations, because the claim as made is a moral one, not a political one, and hence it need not concern libertarians and liberals who object to the legislation of good samaritan obligations. Moreover, the principle holds that the opportunity for good samaritanship is but *a* reason for action, and hence the principle is perfectly compatible with the supposition that in many circumstances it will be overridden by other reasons for action, for example, reasons given by the fact that aid to others will substantially jeopardize the life, liberty, or property of the would-be good samaritan. In the face of these limitations, the principle simply affirms the moral value of charity – a value that few would deny, and hence a value that in certain circumstances (i.e., those that pose the opportunity for aid to others) is plausibly thought to function as one, among many, reasons for action.

To generate a defense of role-relative morality, however, the claim that one has a reason to prevent bad consequences when provided with an opportunity to do so must be combined with some account of how officials have opportunities that are unavailable to citizens to prevent moral harm through their adherence to the law. This account is plausibly grounded in the following three-step argument. First, citizens are compelled by the demands of practical reason to act on the balance of reasons for action available to them.[8] Whenever citizens conclude that the law conflicts with the balance of reasons for action, including in that balance the reasons for obedience provided by the arguments from personal error and example, citizens should break the law.[9]

---

[8] Insofar as right action constitutes action based on the balance of *all* reasons for action (see Chapter 1 and the much more lengthy discussion in Chapter 10), and insofar as actors may lack the time, talent, resources, or foresight to determine *all* of the reasons for action that are applicable to a given decision, the most that practical rationality can require is that actors act on the balance of reasons for action that are reasonably available to them. For a more extensive discussion of this conclusion, see Chapter 10.

[9] This is the conclusion of Chapter 3, to which all theorists who accord law less than practical authority are committed.

But citizens are fallible. They often lack the ability to assess accurately the balance of reasons for action.[10] And, what is worse, they lack the ability to assess when they lack the ability to assess the balance of reasons for action.[11] As a result, citizens would abide by the correct balance of reasons for action more often if they could escape the demands of practical reason and simply follow the law on every occasion, including those occasions on which the law both is and appears to them to be patently wrong or even gravely immoral.[12]

Thus, citizens face a predicament. Practical rationality dictates that

---

[10] As Holly Smith has argued, actors often suffer from both motivational and cognitive handicaps.

> There are . . . at least four cognitive handicaps that could prevent human agents from utilizing a variety of moral principles in actual decision-making: incapacity to comprehend the principle, lack of sufficient information to apply it, erroneous empirical beliefs, and limited ability to make the requisite calculations.

Holly M. Smith, "Two-Tier Moral Codes," in *Foundations of Moral and Political Philosophy,* eds. Ellen Frankel Paul, Fred D. Miller, and Jeffrey Paul (Oxford and Cambridge, MA: Basil Blackwell, 1990), 115.

[11] "If we do not trust a decision-maker to determine x, then we can hardly trust that decision-maker to determine that this is a case in which the reasons for disabling that decision-maker from determining x either do not apply or are outweighed." Schauer, *Playing by the Rules,* 98.

[12] "Formal rules, because they refer to a few, easily identified factual circumstances and require no great ability in abstract reasoning or empirical knowledge for their application, enable ordinary, fallible human beings to come closer to realizing their abstract political/moral principles than would direct application of those principles." Larry Alexander, "Painting Without the Numbers: Noninterpretive Judicial Review," *University of Dayton Law Review* 8 (1983): 460. But, as Raz has argued, to maximally reduce moral error, such formal rules must be given the sort of preemptive weight that is denied to them under theories of influential, advisory, and theoretical authority. Unless individuals surrender their own judgment, they will not prevent as many errors as rule-following will prevent in a regime in which the rules reflect the balance of reasons for action more often than do individual judgments.

> Suppose I can identify a range of cases in which I am wrong more than the putative authority. Suppose I decide because of this to tilt the balance in all those cases in favor of its solution. . . . This procedure will reverse my independent judgment in a certain proportion of the cases. . . . If, we are assuming, there is no other relevant information available, then we can expect that in the cases in which I endorse the authority's judgment my rate of mistakes declines and equals that of the authority. In the cases in which even now I contradict the authority's judgment, the rate of my mistakes remains unchanged, i.e., greater than that of the authority. This shows that only by allowing the authority's judgment to pre-empt mine altogether will I succeed in improving my performance and bringing it to the level of the authority.

Raz, *The Morality of Freedom,* 68.

they act on the balance of reasons for action available to them, and thus that they break the law when they judge the balance of reasons to so dictate. But citizens are sufficiently prone to error in assessing that balance (as well as in assessing the degree to which they should discount their judgments about that balance by the likelihood of their own error) that they would do better to follow the law blindly.

Finally, those who occupy institutional roles have an opportunity to rescue citizens from this predicament. That is, they have the power to act affirmatively so as to prevent or reduce moral error. One source of this power stems from their unique ability to influence by example. But as we saw in Chapter 6, even if the law possesses only theoretical authority, judges also have the power to levy sanctions on citizens who break the law, and a threat of sanctions gives citizens a new and often weighty reason for obedience. In most instances, such a reason will be sufficient to tip the balance of reasons for action in favor of compliance. Punishment thus provides a judicial vehicle for reducing moral error. Insofar as one has a reason to act whenever one has an ability to prevent immoral consequences, and insofar as the power of punishment provides judges with a unique ability to prevent such consequences, judges have a reason to abide by the law (and thus to punish all law-breakers) that is not a reason for citizens to abide by the law.[13]

This argument is different from the previous two versions of the error thesis because it focuses not on the worry that disobedience will either constitute moral error (on one's own part) or cause moral error (on the part of others), but on the worry that disobedience will constitute a failure to prevent moral error. If citizens would do better to follow the law even in circumstances in which practical rationality would dictate that they disobey it, and if judges have at their disposal a means of providing citizens with a reason for obedience that is so weighty that in most circumstances it will be sufficient to prompt citizens to obey the law, then judges should employ that power to rescue citizens from moral peril. Similarly, if judges would do better to

---

[13] Schauer has advanced an argument of this sort in Frederick Schauer, "Judicial Self-Understanding and the Internalization of Constitutional Rules," *University of Colorado Law Review* 61 (1990): 749–71. See also Frederick Schauer, "Formalism," *Yale Law Journal* 97 (1988): 509–48. For a discussion of Schauer's argument and a general examination of the degree to which the rule of law constitutes a role-relative reason for judges to resist "mak[ing] up provisions superior to the ones they are called upon to apply," see Kent Greenawalt, "The Perceived Authority of Law in Judging Constitutional Cases," *University of Colorado Law Review* 61 (1990): 783–93.

blindly follow entrenched decision rules, but if they are constrained in so doing by the demands of practical reason, then institution designers should use their powers of discipline to supplement the balance of judicial reasons for action with the subjective reason for obedience that derives from the threat of punishment. Hence, judges and institution designers have reasons for punishment that those who are punished do not have when deciding to disobey the law.

EVALUATING THE ERROR THESIS

The error thesis, in either or both of its two more plausible forms, constitutes a basis for role-relative morality only if it is in fact the case that citizens do not have, as a reason for obedience, the fact that judges are likely to induce error or fail to prevent error if they are forced to adjudicate cases involving civil disobedience. This is an inquiry to which I shall return in Parts IV and V of this book.

At this point it is useful to appreciate both the implications and limitations of the error thesis. First, the error thesis explicitly encourages the use of legal institutions as tools of deceit. Its claim is that citizens will achieve morally superior results if they are caused to believe the false proposition that they ought never to break the law.[14] But the

---

[14]   As Alexander maintains, the error thesis provides a compelling moral reason to create institutions "that demand that we act *as if* their decisions were morally preemptive of all other first-order moral reasons. . . . [even though] their decisions cannot in fact be morally preemptive." Alexander, "The Gap," 10. Moreover, it may provide a compelling moral reason "not only to establish institutions that make such demands, but also to teach that their demands are morally preemptive (though they are not)." Ibid., 11. See also Larry Alexander and Emily Sherwin, "The Deceptive Nature of Rules," *University of Pennsylvania Law Review* 142 (1994): 1191–1225 (arguing that rule-makers can and should lie about the bindingness of the rules they make); Steven D. Smith, "Radically Subversive Speech and Authority of Law," *Michigan Law Review* 94 (1995): 348–70 (arguing for "the construction of fictional authority" as a means of achieving social coordination).

Meir Dan-Cohen has argued that the natural acoustic separation that exists between citizens and officials makes it both possible and desirable to enact conduct rules that depart from decision rules. Meir Dan-Cohen, "Decision Rules and Conduct Rules: On Acoustic Separation in Criminal Law," *Harvard Law Review* 97 (1984): 625–42. Citizens can be given conduct rules that do not contain any exceptions which might be misconstrued or exploited. Officials can be provided with decision rules that call on them to acquit citizens in exceptional circumstances. Such a combination both maximizes rule-following and allows for fairness. To the extent that conduct rules diverge from decision rules, however, they function as lies to the public. Contrary to what the public is told, ignorance of the law may excuse, the use of deadly force will be allowed in

inculcation of this belief comes at the price of sacrificing the morally right result in instances in which that result cannot be achieved without undermining false faith in the law's ability to achieve moral results or without failing to exploit an opportunity to strengthen that faith.

There are a number of reasons, which have been extensively explored and articulated by others, to doubt that morality is ever best accomplished through deceit. It might be argued, for example, that deceiving others is intrinsically immoral, and thus that it cannot be justified. Yet as Holly Smith has argued, one typically thinks deceit immoral because it causes false beliefs, and false beliefs cause wrong acts.[15] But the deceit that is accomplished by punishing the justified purportedly causes individuals to hold more true beliefs (about what they ought to do) than they would otherwise hold, and hence to act morally more often than they would otherwise act. Thus, to base an argument against deceit on some claim that deceit produces harmful beliefs, one would have to argue that true beliefs about the principles that in fact justify actions are more important than are true beliefs about how one should in fact act.

Alternatively, one could claim that deceit is inherently immoral because it deprives an agent of his or her autonomy.[16] But the background thesis would have to be that autonomy is a function of choices based on true beliefs about justificatory principles of action rather than on true beliefs about how one should in fact act. One who thinks that autonomy requires moral action will be unpersuaded by the claim that a system which produces more moral action than its alternatives jeopardizes autonomy.

Bernard Williams has argued that, even if deceit can be morally innocuous, its use by the state will inevitably result in governmental manipulation of the populous that is anti-democratic, and *this* result is not morally innocuous.[17] Members of the state (e.g., judges) will be

special circumstances, and duress can exonerate. The public is deceived because it is encouraged by the conduct rules to believe otherwise.

　　See also Scott C. Idleman, "A Prudential Theory of Judicial Candor," *Texas Law Review* 73 (1995): 1307–1417 (arguing against a general obligation of candor on the part of judges).

15　Smith, "Two-Tier Moral Codes," 125–6.
16　See Barbara Herman, "The Practice of Moral Judgment," *The Journal of Philosophy* 82 (1985): 431.
17　Williams, "A Critique of Utilitarianism," in *Utilitarianism: For and Against*, eds. J.J.C. Smart and Bernard Williams (New York: Cambridge University Press, 1973), 138–9. See Smith, *Moral Codes*, 121–2.

called on by citizens (e.g., through the legislative enactment of particular decision rules) to act on rules that they know are in some instances either over- or underinclusive. In those instances, they will be compelled by the true moral rules to be unresponsive to majority will, and hence will be undemocratic in their methods of governance. John Rawls has alternatively suggested that any attempt to inculcate false moral beliefs (however benign the background intention) will violate what he calls "the publicity condition" – a formal constraint that invalidates moral principles that are undermined by their public articulation.[18] Rawls takes such a condition to be axiomatic to a public conception of justice, and so concludes that, because it could not be rejected within the original position, it cannot be rejected outside of it.

All of these arguments, to the extent that they point to genuine problems with the use of deceit, suffer from the same problem. Unless they bear some exclusionary status, these arguments can at most serve as reasons for judges and institution designers to refuse to sacrifice moral results as a means of preserving a moral myth. As such, they must be weighed against the reasons to think that myth a valuable one to preserve. Thus, such reasons, while important to explore and weigh, provide no basis for thinking that the error thesis could not serve as a source of role-relative reasons for action.

Holly Smith has advanced a second reason to think that the error thesis provides a questionable foundation for a defense of role-relative morality.[19] Implicit in the error thesis is the presupposition that law allows individuals to act morally more often than does morality itself, because individuals can know and correctly apply the law in instances in which they cannot be sure of and cannot easily apply the general principles of morality. Yet for the law to approximate morality more often than does individual practical reason, the law must be laid down by individuals who (1) themselves understand and can apply the general principles of morality, (2) understand how individuals can be confused about the content or application of those general principles

[18] John Rawls, *A Theory of Justice* (Cambridge, MA: Harvard University Press, Belknap Press, 1971), 133.

[19] This is a variation of the argument advanced by Holly Smith against two-tiered moral codes that replace the complex principles of morality with simple moral rules – rules that collectively comprise what Henry Sidgwick called an "esoteric morality." See Smith, "Two-Tier Moral Codes," 128–32; Henry Sidgwick, *The Methods of Ethics* 7th ed. (Indianapolis, IN: Hackett Publishing Co., 1981), 475–95.

of morality in particular circumstances, and (3) recognize how to overcome this confusion by translating the general principles of morality into particular prescriptions or prohibitions that will be understood and applied in a manner that (more often than not) produces actions that are identical to those that the general principles of morality would require. Individuals who are capable of substituting a list of particular prescriptions and prohibitions for the general principles of morality would also be capable of identifying instances in which those prescriptions and prohibitions are over- or underinclusive (because one could not understand how a rule could approximate the outcome prescribed by its background principles without understanding the circumstances in which the rule does not apply). But individuals possessed of this sort of knowledge would seemingly be capable of remedying the moral error of others by educating them to be equally sophisticated moral reasoners, rather than by manipulating them through deception. To put it bluntly, if lawmakers know enough to manipulate citizens to act morally, they must know enough to educate citizens so that they need not manipulate them.

Smith's argument appears predicated on the assumption that law constitutes a guide to moral action if and only if lawmakers possess advisory authority. If this were indeed our best account of the source of the law's authority, it is plausible to think that deception could be replaced by education, because, if lawmakers know enough to give reliable advice, they must know enough to teach citizens how to manage without their assistance. If the arguments advanced in Chapter 6 are correct, however, there are reasons to think that law may possess theoretical authority without lawmakers possessing moral expertise. Under such a conception of legal authority, law may be capable of guiding action without lawmakers being capable of explaining to citizens how law so functions. Smith's argument would then fail to give us a reason to think that public education could displace public deception, and hence it would fail to give us a reason to reject the error thesis as a source of role-relative morality.

Yet even if lawmakers lack moral expertise, and so lack the power to educate citizens to act morally, Smith's argument may be salvageable. If the reason that the law, as distinct from lawmakers, possesses theoretical authority about moral obligations is that it derives from a particularly reliable deliberative procedure (one that requires, for example, results that reflect Lon Fuller's eight desiderata of law and demands that persons publicly justify their judgments from "the moral point of view"),[20] then inasmuch as citizens can be taught to emulate this procedure, they can be taught to reason morally in ways that defy the need for deceptive manipulation.

There may remain reasons to think that deception is preferable to education. Considerations of economy might suggest that only an elite few should master the general principles of morality. The rest should act on the rules that are produced by the moral elite, even when doing so produces moral errors, because the costs of those errors are not as great as the costs that would accompany the universal mastery of the principles that would reveal the exceptions to those rules.

But to recognize that legal deception can practically be replaced by moral education is to recognize that a theory of role-relative morality, if premised on the error thesis, can be of pragmatic interest only. It functions as a strategic prescription rather than a metaphysical claim concerning the content of morality. It holds that, for practical reasons, not for theoretical reasons, judges ought to punish the justified. Just as one must recognize that one cannot aim directly at a target when shooting an arrow in a high wind, so judges must recognize that they cannot acquit the justified when adjudicating cases in a system in which those cases are erroneously construed as examples to the unjustified. But just as a high wind does not *alter* the location of the target one is aiming at, but merely changes the way in which one aims at it, so too error does not *change* the content of the principles of morality; it simply alters the practical manner with which those principles are best realized. In the absence of error the correspondence thesis applies, because the reasons for and against a citizen's actions would exhaust the reasons for and against judicial action. If one's concern is with the content of morality, and not with the strategic methods necessary for its realization, one will find the thesis of role-relative morality to be beside the point – at least if that thesis is premised solely on the fact that actors make errors.

While error theorists may be content to make their modest pragmatic claim because of their (quite plausible) confidence in human fallibility, it strikes me that there is a considerably more interesting and theoretically powerful claim to be made on behalf of role-relative morality. Even if we were all infallible moral reasoners, such that we

---

[20] Recall the institutional features of democratic decision making discussed in Chapters 5 and 6 that explain why lawmakers who lack moral expertise might nevertheless enact laws that possess it.

never misconstrued others' examples of disobedience or otherwise miscalculated the balance of reasons for action, there might still be principled grounds for thinking that institutional roles create, and are in part defined by, reasons for action that are not applicable to individuals who do not occupy such roles. If this is the case, then even if citizens never made mistakes about when morality required their disobedience of the law, judges might still have moral reasons to punish them for their justified disobedience. And even if judges never made mistakes about when morality required the acquittal of justifiably disobedient citizens, institution designers might still have moral reasons to punish them for their justified failure to punish justified offenders. That is, if principled perspectivalism is defensible, then morality is inherently paradoxical, because morality in principle calls for the punishment of those who act morally. The abandonment of the principle of weak retributivism will not constitute a "second-best" solution to the problems of human imperfection; it will follow from the content of an ideal morality.

Chapter 8

The Rule of Law Values:
Principled Foundations
for Judicial Perspectivalism

According to Lon Fuller, a legal system can accomplish the rule of law only if its enactments are general, public, prospective, clear, logically consistent, practically possible, relatively constant, and predictably applied.[1] With the exception of the first (which simply states a formal condition for there to be a system of rules at all), these requirements speak to the importance of three values: the promotion of individual liberty, the protection of reliance interests, and the preservation of equality.

It has been commonly claimed that these rule of law values "generally define the job of judging."[2] They "justif[y] the judiciary having a limited role in a democracy such as ours. . . . [by] mandat[ing] that judges should not dispense justice on some ad hoc, case-by-case basis."[3] Implicit in this claim is the view that rule of law values are reasons for action that are unique to adjudicators.[4] They enter into the

---

[1] Lon Fuller, *The Morality of Law,* rev. ed. (New Haven: CT: Yale University Press, 1969), 33–94. Recall the discussion in Chapters 5 and 6 about why law, by virtue of possessing such characteristics, might well be accorded theoretical authority about normative matters.

[2] Michael S. Moore, "A Natural Law Theory of Interpretation," *Southern California Law Review* 58 (1985): 314. For a defense of the claim that judges in the United States have consistently solved the dilemma that I have described by favoring the rule of law, see Matthew Lippman, "Liberating the Law: The Jurisprudence of Civil Disobedience and Resistance," *San Diego Justice Journal* 2 (1994): 317–94.

[3] Moore, "A Natural Law Theory of Interpretation," 313. "[I]n a constitutional democracy where there is a commitment to adjudicating disputes rather than having them decided by judicial fiat, the rule of law requires that the institutional role and responsibility of the judge be that of applying the law rather than making it." Rolf E. Sartorius, *Individual Conduct and Social Norms* (Encino, CA: Dickenson Publishing Co., 1975), 179.

[4] As Chaim Gans has put it:

   [T]he authorities' duty to obey . . . constitutes part of the value of the rule of law. . . .

   The authorities, unlike the citizens, owe more to the rule of law than mere obedience. . . . To fulfill their task in creating the rule of law, the

balance of reasons that justifies judicial action, but not into the balance of reasons that justifies private conduct.[5] As such, the rule of law values serve as a source of role-relative morality that might well justify the punishment of justified offenders.

In this chapter, I shall articulate the nature of these values and the reasons to think them role-relative.[6] While these values are well known in the jurisprudential literature, their ability to provide principled foundations for role-relative morality is variable, and hence their separate treatment is necessary. Throughout this discussion it is important to assume that error is not a concern. This assumption will allow us to isolate whether there are any role-relative reasons for action that are principled rather than pragmatic. Our task is to determine whether morality is in principle paradoxical – whether it issues different reasons for action to different actors so that the same action might be right for one actor and wrong for another (that is, justified, given the reasons for action applicable to one actor, and justifiably punished,

judiciary, for instance, must be equally accessible to all, keep the rules of natural justice, explain their decisions, etc.

Chaim Gans, *Philosophical Anarchism and Political Disobedience* (Cambridge: Cambridge University Press, 1992), 6. And as Steven Burton has written:

The rule of law is a political ideal. . . . [T]he ideal is the part of a modern political theory that sets forth certain conditions for legitimate action by government officials. It is the basis in political theory for specific demands that the law constrain judges and other officials. The rule of law supposes that legal constraints on official action are necessary to support a government of limited power, a separation of powers among its parts, and a citizenry that realizes a high degree of liberty.

Steven J. Burton, "Particularism, Discretion, and the Rule of Law," in *Nomos XXXVI: The Rule of Law,* ed. Ian Shapiro (New York and London: New York University Press, 1994), 179–80.

5   For a defense of the claim that rule of law values give lawyers "a special obligation to exercise special caution before engaging in civil disobedience," see Judith A. McMorrow, "Civil Disobedience and the Lawyer's Obligation to the Law," *Washington and Lee Law Review* 48 (1991): 139–63. But see also Martha A. Minnow, "Breaking the Law: Lawyers and Clients in Struggles for Social Change," *University of Pittsburgh Law Review* 52 (1991): 723–51 (arguing that it is good lawyering both to represent those who are civilly disobedient and to engage in civil disobedience when necessary to advance the worthy causes of civilly disobedient clients). See also the comments on Minnow's thesis in the symposium on her article, all of which are sympathetic to the call for lawyerly disobedience. Symposium, *University of Pittsburgh Law Review* 52 (1991).

6   The rule of law values are not the only ones that have been thought to define the job of judging, although they are the only ones that I shall address in this chapter. Philip Soper has interestingly argued, for example, that the role of legal officials requires them to view legal positivism as false. See Philip Soper, "Legal Theory and the Claim of Authority," *Philosophy and Public Affairs* 18 (1989): 209–37.

given the reasons for action applicable to another). If the rule of law values depend for their normative force on the need for judges to prevent erroneous decision making on the part of citizens (or other judges), then they will not serve as role-relative reasons for action that are distinct from those considered in the previous chapter. That is, they will not serve as reasons to think that morality might in principle demand the punishment of the justified.

THE PROTECTION OF INDIVIDUAL LIBERTY

The first value that is thought to be served by the rule of law is that of personal liberty. Liberty is enhanced when individuals are able to predict the consequences of their actions. To the extent that those consequences are variable (so as to make their prediction impossible), or are kept secret (so as to preclude their discovery), or are vague (so as to prevent their accurate assessment), individuals are handicapped in their ability to make plans or chart future conduct. Insofar as this handicap chills industry, it chills liberty.

Because judges alone wield the power of punishment, judges appear uniquely situated to affect the consequences of individual actions. For this reason, the value of liberty appears of concern to judges in a manner in which it is not of concern to private individuals. While individuals can affect the liberty of others by responding to their actions in unpredictable ways, they are seldom capable of affecting as many individuals in as substantial a manner as are judges who impose punishment in unforeseeable circumstances. Thus, while the citizen who contemplates the violation of the law must factor into her deliberations the likelihood that her illegal conduct will be unpredictable to others, and hence liberty-limiting, this reason for obedience appears unlikely to weigh as heavily in her calculations as it weighs in the calculations of a judge who contemplates the violation of the law for purposes of acquitting a justified offender. As Fuller maintained, because the law, unlike any other institution, affects the conduct of *all* citizens, liberty interests are uniquely jeopardized when the consequences of the law become unknown, unclear, variable, or contradictory.[7] If law is to protect and enhance liberty, its mandates must be clear and its penalties obvious.

If judges can make penalties obvious only by applying them to all offenders, both unjustified and justified alike, then judges have a

---

[7] Fuller, *The Morality of Law*, 38–41.

role-relative reason to punish the justified. We need not, however, pursue this defense of role-relative morality at any great length, because its success clearly depends on the assumption that citizens are prone to error. Its implicit presupposition is that citizens are often unlikely to see exceptions for what they are, and are thus likely to believe erroneously that a rule has been altogether altered when it is only the case that an exception to that rule has been made. They are thus likely to change their course of conduct, or abandon it altogether, when their predictions are confused by the erroneous belief that the standards that apply to that conduct have been changed. They will attempt to conform their behavior to the example set by the justified offender in instances in which that behavior is unjustified. When penalized for violating what they mistakenly thought was an old rule, they are likely to be confused into paralysis. To prevent this paralysis, rules must be promulgated without the exceptions that are likely to be erroneously construed as contradictions. Insofar as the acquittal of justified offenders conveys contradictions to those prone to error, justified offenders should be punished.[8]

If individuals were free from error, however, they would not mistake the acquittal of justified offenders for an indication that the rules to which they should conform their conduct have been altered. They would recognize that they would be entitled to violate the law in circumstances relevantly similar to those in which the justified offender violated it, but in no others. That is, the punishment of the justified would not serve as a necessary means of preserving the clarity of the law or the predictability of the penalties that attend its unjustified violation.

Because the protection of liberty might justify the punishment of the justified only in a world in which individuals are likely to misconstrue the significance of acquittals, a defense of role-relative morality that relies on the value of liberty collapses into an error argument. Its claim is that the liberty of citizens who are prone to error is protected only if they are not led to err (by the judicial recognition of exceptions that they will erroneously take to be rules) and then confused into inaction by being punished for that error. While judges seemingly have a reason to

---

[8] This error argument is a version of the argument from the example discussed in Chapter 7. Its claim is that the judicial acquittal of a justifiably disobedient citizen will be erroneously believed to constitute a message that the law making the citizen's conduct an offense has been changed. Other citizens will thus engage in such conduct indiscriminately, thus violating the still-existing law more often than is justifiable.

punish the justified if doing so prevents liberty-limiting errors by others, this reason should be classed among those that provide pragmatic rather than principled foundations for role-relative morality.

Moreover, if construed as a version of the error thesis, the argument from liberty may very well fail to establish a convincing case for role-relative morality. While our society highly prizes the protection of liberty through the rule of law, it has nevertheless adopted penal codes that embody a general balance of evils defense to what would otherwise constitute criminal violations.[9] In Chapter 1, I charted three sorts of cases in which justified offenders are unable to avail themselves of this legal defense. But there remain a considerable number of cases in which offenders may escape punishment because the harm done by their offenses is less than the harm averted by those offenses. Insofar as we give legal recognition to the moral justification for such offenses, we clearly do not think that citizens are so prone to error as to construe all acquittals as acts that repeal rules against killing, stealing, destroying property, and so on. At most, such acquittals leave citizens in doubt about whether particular killings or particular acts of theft would be justified on their part under the balance of evils defense. And we rightly regard this doubt as insufficiently liberty-limiting to warrant the wholesale punishment of justified offenders.

THE PROTECTION OF RELIANCE INTERESTS

The second rule of law value to which those who seek a principled foundation for role-relative morality might appeal is the value of protecting reliance. At least three arguments can be distinguished for the importance of preserving reliance interests. The first is an argument from fairness. When individuals *justifiably* rely on another's actions or statements and change their positions accordingly, fairness dictates that they should not be surprised by having their expectations thwarted and their positions changed for the worse. The second is an argument from industry. Even when individuals *unjustifiably* rely on the statements or actions of another, their reliance should be protected as a means of ensuring that their efforts are not wasted. The third is an argument from the value of coordination. Where reliance is necessary for the solution of coordination problems and prisoners' dilemmas, that reliance should be protected as a means of achieving the collective goods that coordination makes possible.

---

[9]   See, for example, American Law Institute, *Model Penal Code* sec. 3.02.

The Argument from Fairness

Fairness demands that if one encourages others to alter their positions, one should not leave those individuals worse off by failing to fulfill their expectations.[10] If it is unfair to thwart the expectations of those who justifiably alter their positions in reliance on one's words or deeds, then, other things being equal, neither citizens nor officials should act contrary to the way in which they have encouraged others to expect them to act. Thus the argument from fairness appears to provide both citizens and judges with a reason to act in accordance with the justified expectations of others. Insofar as citizens justifiably rely on one another to abide by the law, citizens have reasons (and in some instances, very weighty reasons) to obey laws that in the absence of any reliance interests would be justifiably disobeyed. Similarly, insofar as citizens and other officials justifiably rely on judges to abide by the law, judges have reasons (and perhaps, very weighty ones) to reach decisions that in the absence of such reliance interests might not be required.[11]

The argument from fairness will give rise to differential reasons for obedience only if the justified expectations concerning citizens' conduct differ from the justified expectations concerning judges' decisions. In particular, the argument from fairness would justify the punishment of a justified offender only if there existed legitimate expectations of the offender's punishment that differed from the legitimate expectations of the offender's obedience. For example, a justified offender is one who rightly calculates that the reasons for obedience provided by the justified expectations of others are outweighed by the reasons for disobedience. For a judge to be justified in punishing such an offender on grounds of fairness to others, it would have to be the case that the judge's failure to punish would cause sufficient unfair surprise to tip the balance of reasons for judicial action in favor of punishing an individual for whom unfair sur-

---

10 "[I]t is confessedly unjust to *break faith* with anyone – to violate an engagement, either express or implied, or disappoint expectations raised by our own conduct, at least if we have raised those expectations knowingly and voluntarily." John Stuart Mill, "Utilitarianism," in *Selected Writings of John Stuart Mill*, ed. Maurice Cowling (New York: New American Library, 1968), 285.

11 The argument from fairness constitutes the basis of what Fuller called "the bond of reciprocity" between the citizen and the state. "Government says to the citizen, in effect, 'These are the rules we expect you to follow. If you follow them, you have our assurance that they are the rules that will be applied to your conduct." Fuller, *The Morality of Law*, 39–40. See also Sartorius, *Individual Conduct and Social Norms*, 166.

prise did not tip the balance of reasons for private action in favor of obedience.

Four conditions appear necessary to a claim of unfair surprise: (1) One must in fact believe that another will do a certain action; (2) one's belief must be reasonable, that is, it must be epistemically justified; (3) one must change one's position as a result of that belief in a manner that is potentially costly or detrimental to oneself; and (4) one's change of position must not itself be morally reprehensible. In order for justified reliance to provide a judge with a reason to punish a justified offender, it must be the case that some class of persons meets the above four conditions. But who might *justifiably* rely on the punishment of the justified? Whose efforts or expectations would be *unjustifiably* thwarted by the acquittal of someone who has done the right thing? Three categories of persons come to mind: the offender herself, those who prosecute the offender (either criminal prosecutors or private litigants), and members of the public at large. To assess whether any of these might justifiably rely on the punishment of a justified offender, it is necessary to work through the reasons to think that one or more of them might meet the four conditions specified above.

Grounds for Justified Belief in the Punishment of Justified Offenders
Offenders, prosecutors, and members of the public at large might all be justified in believing that offenders will be punished even when their offenses are morally justified. Most straightforwardly, these individuals might in fact believe that justified offenders will be punished, and they might be justified in so believing because, as we explored in Chapter 1, the criminal law and civil law so provide. There might, of course, be other sources of such a belief – old Perry Mason television shows, advice from one's family lawyer, self-help books, and so forth. But to appeal to such alternative sources would demand the development of more than an intuitive understanding of the conditions for a justified belief – and this I shall here forgo.

Adverse Acts of Reliance
In addition to establishing that citizens might reasonably believe that justified offenders will be punished, those who would appeal to justified reliance as a role-relative reason for judicial action must demonstrate that at least some citizens in fact alter their positions in potentially adverse manners as a result of that belief. Who might alter her position for the worse as a result of justifiably believing that justified offenders will be punished?

Adverse Acts by Offenders. In cases of civil disobedience in which offenders seek punishment as a means of calling public attention to an immoral law, offenders might be thought to alter their positions in a potentially adverse manner. Consider the case of a war protester who avoids the draft just because his expected punishment is likely to cause public outrage and resentment over the war. If his disobedience is judged to be justified and he is acquitted, he will no doubt have cause to complain that he is worse off than he would have been if he had directed his activist energies toward other projects. If the fourth criterion is met, the reliance interests of such a civilly disobedient citizen will provide a judge with a reason to punish that citizen.[12]

Such cases are relatively rare. Typically, while a justified offender might be surprised at her acquittal, she will not be unfairly surprised, any more than will an unjustified offender be unfairly surprised by mercy. Unfair surprises are unfair precisely because they make persons worse off. Because acquittals typically make offenders better off, they typically come as a pleasant surprise. Hence, in most cases, the offender herself will not have altered her position in a manner that will make her worse off if she is not punished.

Adverse Acts by Prosecutors and Plaintiffs. Insofar as criminal prosecutors and civil plaintiffs justifiably believe that a justified offender will be punished or civilly sanctioned, their prosecution of such an offender will leave them worse off if the offender is not punished. While surprising public prosecutors may seem less unfair than inefficient, surprising private litigants smacks of substantial unfairness. If the law promises to sanction justifiably disobedient defendants, and if private litigants spend substantial amounts of time and money to bring suit against such defendants as a result of that promise, they will surely find themselves substantially worse off if that promise is breached by judges. Hence, if the fourth criterion is met, the reliance interests of plaintiffs and, to a lesser degree, of criminal prosecutors might provide judges with a reason to civilly sanction or criminally punish justified offenders.

Adverse Acts by the Public. Members of the public who reasonably believe that justified offenders will be punished may rightly suppose that

---

[12] The conditions under which it would be moral to consent to one's own (unjustified) punishment are discussed in the first section of Chapter 11, as well as in the next section of this chapter.

such punishment will deter the justified from disobeying the law. As such, they may fail to take precautions that they would otherwise take if they anticipated justified disobedience. That is, they might coast through green lights without looking for drivers who might be justified in running opposing red lights – because they might rightly suppose that such drivers will be deterred from doing what they would be justified in doing.

Does this argument provide a reason for judges to think that members of the public might have changed their positions for the worse as a result of the expectation that justified offenders will be punished? If it does, it would seemingly also provide a reason for would-be offenders to obey the law. That is, if members of the public expect that others will obey the law because they will be punished even if they disobey it justifiably, then those who contemplate disobedience must factor in this expectation as a reason to obey the law. If they do so accurately, and if the balance of reasons for action still favors disobedience, then it would seem that judges should not punish such offenders for thwarting public expectations, because the citizen's calculation of public reliance will exhaust a judge's calculation of that reliance. Were one to resist this by arguing that acquittals will reduce the degree to which justified offenders will take seriously the public's expectation that they will obey the law out of fear of punishment, one would smuggle in assumptions about error. One would suppose that justified offenders will come to make errors – but if they did, they would cease to be justified. Hence, while civilly disobedient offenders and public and private prosecutors may entertain reliance interests that are of unique concern to judges, members of the public probably do not.

The Morality of Relying on the Punishment of the Justified
Even if offenders and prosecutors alter their positions to their potential detriment on the basis of a justified belief that judges will punish justified offenders, their reliance will not be justified unless it is itself morally legitimate. For individuals are unfairly surprised when their expectations are thwarted only if their expectations are not morally reprehensible. Thus, for example, one is not justified in relying on another's performance of an immoral promise (to kill one's enemy, for example), even if one has every reason to believe that that promise will be kept, and even if one alters one's position substantially as a result of that promise. Insofar as the act relied on is immoral, one's own reliance on that act is morally unjustified. Hence, one cannot

complain of an unfair surprise when the would-be killer reneges on his promise.

Consider, as a second example, the reliance claim at stake in the famous case of *MacPherson v. Buick Motor Co.*[13] Buick in fact believed that it would not be held liable for injuries caused to consumers as a result of defects in the manufacturing of its automobiles. It justifiably believed this because the law had upheld privity of contract in product liability cases, thus allowing auto manufacturers to be sued only by distributors (who were rarely injured by defects in the cars that they sold to consumers). Buick priced its cars on the assumption that it would not be held liable to remote purchasers, and so changed its position to its potential detriment. But Buick's use of the privity doctrine to escape responsibility to those injured by its negligence was morally reprehensible. Buick, after all, had both a moral and a legal duty to build safe automobiles, and the privity limitation on which it relied to escape liability was only a limitation on the legal remedies available to consumers to redress breaches of Buick's duty. Hence, Buick was not *unfairly* surprised when Justice Cardozo concluded that privity would not bar a suit by a remote purchaser.

Just as reliance on the performance of a promise will not constitute *justified* reliance if the promise is an immoral one, so reliance on the punishment of the justified will not constitute *justified* reliance if such punishment is itself unjustified. But whether it is justifiable to punish the justified is precisely the question to which reliance was supposed to provide an answer. Those who have supposed that there are role-relative reasons to punish the justified cannot, without circularity, maintain that justified reliance is one of them – at least until they have found others that vindicate the morality of punishing the justified, so that reliance on that punishment is in fact morally justified.

It might seem, then, that we have come a long way for nothing. There are two reasons to think that this is not so – two reasons that I hope justify the detail with which I have infused the discussion. First, an appeal to justified reliance is virtually a knee-jerk reaction for many lawyers and legal theorists who are called on to advance a reason to think that judges should follow the rules. It is crucial to see that this reaction should be tempered by recognition of the facts that justified reliance may be difficult to make out and justified reliance depends on arguments other than reliance to make it justified. Second, if there are arguments other than reliance that justify the punishment of the

---

[13]   217 N.Y. 382, 111 N.E. 1050 (1916).

justified, then reliance on that punishment will itself be justified (so long as the other conditions for such reliance are satisfied). Thus, one need not despair that justified reliance does not provide a reason to punish the justified – because it does provide such a reason if there are (also) other reasons to punish the justified.

The Argument from Industry

I have argued that individuals who rely on the punishment of the justified are not justified in so doing unless there are other reasons (besides their reliance) to consider that punishment justified. Hence, on pain of circularity, their surprise is not necessarily unjust. Yet those who favor role-relative morality might circumvent the charge of circularity by arguing that, even if individuals *unjustly* rely on the punishment of justified offenders, that reliance nevertheless provides a reason (although not one of fairness) for judges to administer such punishment, because unjustified reliance produces efforts that in some circumstances ought not to be wasted.

Consider a case that does not involve the issue of punishing the justified, but that clearly demonstrates the moral force of the argument from industry. In *Tennessee Valley Authority v. Hill*,[14] the Tennessee Valley Authority (TVA) received millions of dollars from the House Appropriations Committee to build the Tellicoe Dam. Upon discovering that the dam would render extinct a species of three-inch fish known as "snail darters," the TVA consulted with the House Appropriations Committee to determine whether the project was barred by the Endangered Species Act. Having received assurances from the Committee that the Act did not prevent construction of the dam, the TVA completed the project. In subsequent litigation, this reliance by the TVA on the Committee's statutory interpretation was deemed unjustified, because the Committee was neither a court charged with statutory construction nor a legislative body capable of modifying the terms of the Endangered Species Act. Nevertheless, it was thought that the industry and expense that such reliance engendered should not be casually wasted. Thus, the Supreme Court came in for heavy criticism when it subsequently enjoined the operation of the dam, because it was thought that the Court failed to attribute sufficient weight to the multi-million dollar waste that would occur as a result of such a decision.

In the context of the present discussion, the argument from industry

14   437 U.S. 153 (1978).

213

would appear to provide a role-relative reason for punishing the justified in circumstances in which individuals rely on that punishment (however unjustifiably) and invest resources that will go to waste in the event that such punishment is not administered. Recall the case discussed in Chapter 5 of *United States v. Kirby*,[15] in which a county sheriff was prosecuted under a federal statute that made it a crime to "obstruct or retard the passage of the mail, or any driver or carrier"[16] after he carried out a warrant to arrest an on-duty federal mail carrier suspected of murder. The federal prosector in this case unjustifiably relied on the court to enforce the letter of the law over its spirit, and thus invested prosecutorial resources in the expectation that a justified offender would be punished. He was not.

Because those who would seek a source of role-relative morality need only establish that there are some reasons for action unique to judges, it might be enough to point to the waste of resources that accompany instances of unjustified reliance and argue that such a waste, while not a weighty reason for punishing the justified, is nevertheless some reason for punishing them. While such an argument will lead to the seemingly absurd conclusion that, other things being equal, a judge should decide in favor of the litigant who spent the most resources to litigate the case before the court, this conclusion may be one that those supporting role-relative morality would embrace. I do not propose to dwell on this line of argument any further. But if unjustified reliance is the sole source of role-relative morality, role-relative morality is sufficiently weak as to cause us little concern. Even if unjustified reliance constitutes a role-relative reason for action, it is unlikely to justify the punishment of the justified, for it is unlikely to weigh more heavily than the value of acquitting those who do the right thing.

The Argument from Coordination

The protection of reliance interests is often thought important on grounds other than fairness or efficiency. Insofar as coordination solutions require individual reliance on the cooperation of others, the collective goods that such solutions produce may be thought to depend on the protection of such reliance interests. That is, if the advantages of coordination can be achieved only if citizens comply with coordinating conventions (like the rules of the road) and do not default on cooperative solutions to prisoners' dilemmas (such as those

---

[15]   74 U.S. (7 Wall.) 482 (1869).   [16]   Ibid., 483.

established by tax laws, environmental protection laws, and criminal laws), and if citizens will comply with such conventions only if they can rely on the fact that others will comply with such conventions, then judges have a reason to punish those who break laws that serve coordinating functions as a means of protecting important reliance interests.

But does this reason for punishment differ from any of those reasons that a citizen has to comply with the law in the first place? If not, then the punishment of the justified cannot be justified by the argument from coordination because, *eo ipso*, the justified offender has accurately assessed the importance of preserving the relevant coordination solutions and the degree to which her disobedience will affect the salience of those solutions. Her decision to break the law is justified *because* she has given due weight to the value of others' reliance on her obedience and correctly calculated that that value is outweighed by the values accomplished by disobedience. For the judge to justifiably punish the justified offender, the value of the reliance interests involved, or the importance of the coordinative schemes protected, must be greater for the judge than for the citizen.

There are tempting reasons to suppose that calculations concerning reliance interests do vary between citizens and judges. A citizen calculates the reliance of others on *his* obedience while a judge calculates the reliance of others on *her* obedience. Because the latter seems likely to be greater than the former, the argument from coordination seems to provide a plausible source of differential reasons for action.

Prisoners' Dilemmas

Consider first the reliance interests at stake in cases involving prisoners' dilemmas. Recall from Chapter 6 that prisoners' dilemmas arise in circumstances in which individuals would be best off if they could default from cooperative ventures without causing others to do the same. Thus, for instance, an individual would be best off if he alone could avoid paying taxes, union dues, and cable television pledges, because he would then be able to enjoy the public goods made possible through others' contributions without himself contributing to their support. Because all individuals are similarly inclined, collective goods are fragile accomplishments. They can be sustained only if each individual can rely on (almost) all other individuals not to freeride on his or her cooperative efforts or contributions.

Those who defend role-relative morality point to the fact that, in many instances, individuals are fully justified in freeriding on the co-operative efforts of others, notwithstanding the fact that such efforts depend on the absence of such freeriding. That is, citizens appear justified in refusing to cooperate when they rightly believe that their refusal will not substantially affect the cooperative efforts of others or the collective goods accomplished by such efforts.[17] This will be the case when the effect of an individual's contribution to a cooperative scheme is small, the impact of her default is negligible, and the gain from such a default is great. When union dues would be better spent on individual acts of charity, cable television pledges would be better spent on food and clothing for one's children, and the time devoted to voting would be better spent on virtually anything, individuals are justified in failing to pay fees or vote, so long as they rightly calculate that their individual failures will not substantially contribute to the dissolution of the union, the bankruptcy of the cable company, or the collapse of democracy.[18]

As we saw in Chapter 6, many believe that the primary purpose of law is to provide cooperative strategies by which to achieve collective goods and, when necessary, to induce compliance with those strategies by means of sanctions. Such sanctions accomplish two ends. First, the threat of punishment provides individuals with a new reason for action that is typically sufficiently weighty to tip the balance of reasons for action in favor of cooperation.[19] Second, sanctions enable the individual to rely on the fact that she will not be one of the sole contributors to a scheme predominately enjoyed by freeriders. The abil-

---

[17]   But see the third section in Chapter 6 for a discussion of the claim that morality itself precludes noncooperation when cooperation is collectively required to preserve a collective good.

[18]   [I]t is a melodramatic exaggeration to suppose that every breach of the law endangers, by however small a degree, the survival of the government, or of law and order. Many acts of trespass, breaches of contract, violations of copyright, and so on, regrettable as some of them may be on other grounds, have no implications one way or another for the stability of the government and the law.

Joseph Raz, *The Morality of Freedom* (Oxford: Clarendon Press, 1986), 102.

[19]   Raz, *The Morality of Freedom*, 50–1; Peter Singer, *The Expanding Circle: Ethics and Sociobiology* (Oxford: Clarendon press, 1981), 46; Heidi M. Hurd, "Sovereignty in Silence," *Yale Law Journal* 99 (1990): 1019–21.

There is a large and well-known literature devoted to vindicating the claim that morality itself provides sufficient reasons for cooperation in prisoner's dilemma situations. See, for example, David P. Gauthier, *Morals by Agreement* (Oxford: Oxford University Press, 1986), 8–10, 113–56; Singer, *The Expanding Circle*, 47. Chapters 10 and 11 contribute a limited argument to this literature.

ity to rely on the cooperation of others thus makes the individual's own cooperation rational.

Were judges to refuse to punish justified offenders, they would destroy the incentives that make collective goods possible. Individuals would cease to calculate the pain of punishment among the reasons for compliance and, absent that factor, the rational course of conduct might well be a noncooperative one. Hence, judges have weighty reasons to punish those who, absent punishment, would have weighty reasons to refuse to follow the law in situations that comprise prisoners' dilemmas. That is, the argument from coordination justifies the punishment of justified offenders in cases in which that punishment is required to solve a prisoners' dilemma.

Coordination Problems

Now consider the reliance interests at stake in cases involving coordination problems rather than prisoners' dilemmas. It will be recalled that coordination problems arise when individuals seek to cooperate (rather than to freeride on the cooperation of others) but are unable to settle on a means of so doing. Classic examples include instances in which individuals have a mutual desire to avoid a collision but lack a convention that will coordinate their actions so as to eliminate the risk of that collision. Coordination problems are not necessarily the product of human error. Even individuals who possess superb practical rationality may find themselves in circumstances that demand coordination with others, but which provide no salient means by which to so coordinate. Coordination problems are thought by most to be the product of a plurality of *equally* moral and *equally* practicable coordinative solutions.[20] Only if one were prepared to defend a rigorous right-answer thesis – a thesis that held that morality provided a right answer to every normative question (including whether persons should drive on the right or the left, shake hands with their right or their left, place their forks on the right or the left, etc.) – could one maintain that coordination problems are the product of persons

---

[20] As Aristotle put it, a natural rule of justice is one "which everywhere has the same force and does not exist by people's thinking this or that. . . ." A conventional rule is a rule "which is originally indifferent, but when it has been laid down is not indifferent. . . ." Aristotle, "Nicomachean Ethics," in *The Complete Works of Aristotle*, vol. 2, ed. Jonathan Barnes, trans. David Ross, rev'd by J.O. Urmson (Princeton, NJ: Princeton University Press, 1984), 1790–91 (V.7.1134b 18–21).

erroneously failing to see the singularly right course of conduct that morality prescribes in those circumstances.

The solution to a coordination problem depends on widespread recognition of a single, salient cooperative strategy. While the law provides such salient coordination strategies in many circumstances that demand coordination, the salience of those strategies may well depend in large part on their judicial enforcement. This is true for two reasons. First, as the argument in Chapter 6 suggested, we have good grounds to think that judges function as a salient source of information about the law. Hence, citizens who seek to coordinate their efforts with others will look to judges for information concerning the coordination solutions that have been provided by law, because they justifiably expect that others will do likewise. Second, inasmuch as the law will provide a solution to a particular coordination problem only if people in fact abide by the law (as opposed to some other coordinating convention), and people are more likely to abide by the law if they believe that those who break the law are punished for noncompliance, citizens will look to judges for evidence that they are punishing noncompliance, because this fact makes it more likely that the law is serving as the dominant or salient coordination convention.

Of course, citizens can themselves affect the salience of a particular coordinative strategy. Their failure to comply with a particular coordination solution will make that solution less salient, because it will make it the case that others cannot as readily rely on the solution, and so it will provide an impetus to seek other bases of coordination. But there are two reasons to suspect that individual departures from legally established coordination conventions will not affect the salience of those conventions as dramatically as will the judicial refusal to enforce those conventions. First, individual departures are unlikely to achieve widespread recognition, and hence they are unlikely to shake the faith of the majority in the salience of a particular coordinative strategy. Second, coordination solutions, unlike solutions to prisoners' dilemmas, do not provide incentives to default. If most people drive on the right side of the road, it is in the individual's (self-) interest to do so as well. Knowledge of the fact that coordination solutions are in everyone's best interests provides individuals with a reason to interpret others' noncooperation as a product of ignorance, irrationality, or emergency. Unless they have a reason to suspect that a substantial number of others will alter their course of conduct by virtue of the (ignorant, irrational, or imperiled) individual's noncompliance, they have no reason to think that that individual's noncooperation makes a widely recognized cooperative strategy less salient.

There thus appear reasons to suppose that the reliance interests at stake in situations that pose coordination problems vary between citizens and judges. A citizen may rightly calculate that running a red light in the middle of the night will not substantially affect the practice of stopping for red lights, but a judge may rightly calculate that her acquittal of that citizen will quite substantially affect that practice. Insofar as citizens look to the judicial enforcement of the rules of the road as evidence that others will abide by those rules, an acquittal may cause citizens to think that others will alter their behavior. And this by itself will make it rational for them to alter their behavior accordingly. An acquittal may thus have a domino effect that forces citizens to look beyond the law for alternative coordination schemes by which to reduce traffic injuries at intersections. Insofar as the failure of a judge to punish an offender is likely to affect the salience of a coordination solution on which others depend, while the failure of the citizen to abide by such a solution is not, a judge will have a more weighty reason to abide by the decision rule requiring the punishment of a disobedient citizen than that citizen will have to abide by the conduct rule that assures coordination. The argument from coordination thus appears to support role-relative morality.

We should however be hesitant about this conclusion, because the argument from coordination threatens to collapse into the argument from example by smuggling in assumptions about the propensity for error on the part of citizens. That is, the argument seems to suggest that a judge should punish justified offenders as a means of affirming the salience of a convention for those who might mistakenly take an acquittal to be grounds for thinking that a particular convention should no longer be trusted. Morally perfect reasoners, on the other hand, could be expected to see an exception to a conventional rule for what it is, namely, an exception. Such an exception ought not to shake their faith in the salience of a particular coordination rule, so long as they have no reason to suspect that that exception will become the rule. Hence, in a world devoid of error, judges could afford to recognize such exceptions by acquitting justified offenders without fear that they would promote unjustified departures from genuinely salient coordination solutions.

But herein lies the rub. The recognition of exceptions to coordination solutions only creates new coordination problems that demand solutions. Even if citizens, by virtue of being capable moral reasoners, were not induced to abandon coordinative strategies by virtue of the judicial recognition of justified departures from those strategies, they would nevertheless be forced to seek means by which to coordinate with justified offenders. And if there were second-order conventions that would allow citizens to coordinate their conduct with justified offenders of first-order conventions, judges would be called on to recognize exceptions to those second-order conventions in cases in which individuals justifiably departed from those second-order conventions. Such exceptions would create, once again, coordination problems for those seeking to coordinate their conduct with second-order justified offenders, thus creating the need for third-order conventions. The potential for regress looms large.

To appreciate the regress, consider the following. Traffic lights currently provide first-order coordination solutions for drivers who meet one another at intersections. There are, however, recognized instances in which individuals are justified in violating traffic signals. Ambulance drivers, police officers, and firefighters often have reasons to run red lights that exceed the reasons to stop at them. Recognizing this fact, and recognizing that such a fact creates a new coordination problem for those who seek to coordinate their actions with the justified violations of such officials, a second-order coordination solution has been created by the use of flashing lights and sirens. Such devices signal a violation of the first-order convention, and hence solve the second-order coordination problem that the recognition of such potential violations creates.

Now imagine the following case. An ambulance transporting an individual who is injured but in stable condition approaches an intersection with lights flashing and sirens blaring. An unmarked private car transporting an individual who is near death approaches the same intersection at the same speed. Both drivers confront red lights. If they simultaneously run their red lights, they will collide with each other. And because the private car is unmarked, it may well be hit by those who are seeking to comply with the second-order convention that requires them to yield to the ambulance. (This admittedly takes a complex intersection, so we should suppose that this takes place in New Jersey.) The driver of the car rightly supposes that he has reason to violate the first-order convention that requires him to stop at the red light. He also rightly guesses that it is more important for him to get his patient to the hospital before the ambulance driver gets her patient to the hospital. He thus rightly supposes that he has reason to violate the second-order convention that requires him to yield to the ambulance. He takes seriously the fact that there is no convention that governs this situation, and that neither the ambulance driver nor other private drivers will recognize the justifiability of this violation so as to yield to it. He nevertheless rightly calculates that the life at stake justifies the risk of a collision.

Were a judge to acquit the driver of the car and thereby carve out an explicit exception to the second-order convention that now governs the justified violation of first-order traffic conventions, the judge would create the need for a third-order convention that would enable ambulance drivers and other citizens to yield to individuals who justifiably violate both the first-order and second-order conventions. And this convention would plainly have its justified violations, which, if judicially recognized, would lead to the need for a fourth-order convention, and so on, ad infinitum.

Those who defend role-relative morality would be justified, prima facie, in supposing that this regress could be curbed (albeit not wholly eliminated) by the punishment of justified offenders, because the punishment of justified offenders would provide such offenders with a new and weighty reason to comply with recognized first-order (or, in rare cases, second-order) conventions. And knowledge of this fact by others would return their confidence in the general salience of the first-order conventions that make coordination possible.

If the acquittal of justified offenders generates a regress that defeats coordination altogether, then judges seemingly have a reason to punish justified offenders: Coordination is necessary to achieve certain collective goods, and such coordination can only be accomplished if judicial decrees provide salient courses of conduct. If judicial decrees are susceptible to a recursive set of exceptions, they will not provide salient courses of conduct. Hence, the judicial promulgation of a coordination strategy must be exceptionless for it to do its task. And it is exceptionless only if justified offenders are punished.

THE PROTECTION OF EQUALITY

The third and final rule of law value to which those seeking a principled foundation of role-relative morality might turn is the value of equality. Equality requires the similar treatment of those who are identical in morally relevant respects. Conversely, it permits (and perhaps requires) the differential treatment of those who are not identical in morally relevant respects.

There exists a long-standing controversy over the question of whether equality functions as an independent value at all,[21] and I do not propose to add footnote fodder to that debate. Suffice it to say that if equality does function as a genuine value, then it provides a reason to treat present and future cases like past cases, even when those past cases were dealt with unjustly or erroneously. Similarly, it provides a reason to treat present cases like future cases if one can predict the treatment that will be administered in those future cases, even if that treatment is now, and will be then, unjust or ill-conceived.

To the extent that equality is a value at all, it does not seem to be a value that is of exclusive concern to those occupying judicial roles. If parents let their son drive the family car on his sixteenth birthday, the value of equality speaks in favor of allowing their daughter to drive the car when she turns sixteen (even if it has become apparent, in the interim, that the decision in the son's case was an unwise one). Moreover, the value of protecting equality may properly enter into a citizen's practical deliberations concerning whether to break the law. If a bartender knows that other bartenders will follow the law that prohibits them from serving alcohol after 2:00 A.M., then the value of equality speaks in favor of refusing to serve alcohol after that hour, because to do so would give an unequal benefit to that bartender's small set of patrons.

---

[21]   Some have argued that the principle of equality is, or can be, grossly unjust. See William K. Frankena, "The Concept of Social Justice," in *Social Justice*, ed. Richard Brandt (Englewood Cliffs, NJ: Prentice-Hall, 1962), 17; Phillip Montague, "Comparative and Noncomparative Justice," *The Philosophical Quarterly* 30 (1980): 133. Others have argued that it is merely empty. Its requirements "possess both more truth and less content than is sometimes supposed: more truth because they not only happen to be true but are necessarily true; less content because, being necessarily true, they add nothing to what we already know." Peter Westen, *Speaking of Equality* (Princeton, NJ: Princeton University Press, 1990), 186. See Wolfgang Von Leyden, *Aristotle on Equality and Justice: His Political Argument* (Houndsmills, Basingstoke: Macmillan, 1985), 5; Kenneth Cauthen, *The Passion for Equality* (New Jersey: Rowman & Littlefield Pub., 1987), 5; Hans Kelsen, *General Theory of Law and State* (Cambridge, MA: Harvard University Press, 1945), 439; Peter Westen, "The Empty Idea of Equality," *Harvard Law Review* 95 (1982): 537; Larry Alexander, "Constrained by Precedent," *Southern California Law Review* 63 (1989): 5–13; Larry Alexander and Ken Kress, "Against Legal Principles," in *Law and Interpretation*, ed. Andrei Marmor (Oxford: Clarendon Press, 1995): 301–6.
   Fred Schauer has convincingly advanced the surprising argument that if equality is a value, it is jeopardized rather than protected by rule-based decision making. "When rule-based decision-making prevails, what increases is the incidence of cases in which relevantly different cases are treated similarly, and not the incidence of cases in which like cases are treated alike." Frederick F. Schauer, *Playing by the Rules: A Philosophical Examination of Rule-Based Decision-Making in Law and in Life* (Oxford: Clarendon Press, 1991), 137.

Notwithstanding the fact that equality concerns may enter into the balance of reasons that determines what is right for a citizen to do, many suppose that their weight is greater when they enter into the balance of reasons that determines what is right for a judge to do. Thus, for example, many find intuitive the claim that a judge should seek comparative rather than substantive proportionality in sentencing.[22] Thus, if first-time shoplifters have been sentenced in the past to eight months of jail time, a judge has a weighty reason to sentence a convicted first-time shoplifter to eight months, even if the judge considers the severity of this punishment to be substantively disproportionate to the severity of the offense.

The demand for comparative proportionality, or numerically equal punishment in like cases, creates a complex coordination problem for judges. If it is more important to give the same sentence that is given by others than to give a sentence considered substantively proportional, then judges need a means of coordinating their sentencing decisions. Both common law precedents and legislatively enacted decision rules fit the bill, because they provide judges with salient means of ensuring the equal treatment of litigants. Insofar as judges can be confident that other judges follow the law, they can be confident that the law provides them with accurate information about how cases

---

[22] I follow both Plato and Aristotle in defining substantive proportionality as punishment proportional to desert; and comparative proportionality as numerically identical punishment. Plato, "Laws," in *The Collected Dialogues of Plato*, eds. Edith Hamilton and Huntington Cairns, trans. A.E. Taylor (Princeton, NJ: Princeton University Press, 1961), 1337 (VI.757–58); Aristotle, "Politics," in *The Complete Works of Aristotle*, vol. 2, ed. Jonathan Barnes, trans. Benjamin Jowett (Princeton, NJ: Princeton University Press, 1984), 2067 (V.1.1301b30–1302a15); Aristotle, "Eudemian Ethics," in *The Complete Works of Aristotle*, vol. 2, ed. Jonathan Barnes, trans. J. Solomon (Princeton, NJ: Princeton University Press, 1984), 1967–8 (VII.9.1241b33–40). While Plato insisted that substantive proportionality "'[t]is the very award of Zeus," ibid., insofar as it is necessarily just, while comparative proportionality is only contingently just, Aristotle insisted that rectificatory justice is constituted by comparative proportionality. Aristotle, *Nicomachean Ethics*, in *The Complete Works of Aristotle*, ed. Jonathan Barnes, trans. David Ross, rev'd by J.O. Urmson (Princeton, NJ: Princeton University Press, 1984), 1785 (V.3.1131a29–1131b24).

Modern sympathy for Aristotle's position often derives from the recognition that substantive proportionality is, at best, difficult to assess, and, at worst, arbitrary. Does mail fraud merit three years of imprisonment? Seven years? Nine years? Is two weeks of jail time proportional to the offense of indecent exposure, or two years? Perhaps the most that judges should aspire to is comparative proportionality, at least in cases in which the punishment that is comparative does not depart from the seemingly wide range of possible proportionately just punishments.

similar to their own were adjudicated in the past and how they will be adjudicated in the future. It thus provides them with a reason to think that their own obedience will ensure the equal treatment of like cases.

If the value of protecting equality provides a weighty reason for judges to achieve comparative proportionality in punishment, and if comparative proportionality can be accomplished only by faithful adherence to the law, then judges have a reason to abide by the law that citizens do not. But does this fact provide a role-relative reason to punish the justified? After all, insofar as justified offenders are not morally culpable, they are morally dissimilar to unjustified offenders. Hence, concerns for equality would appear to favor dissimilar treatment.

Yet if justified offenders were not treated differently in the past than were unjustified offenders, or if justified offenders are not likely to be treated differently in the future than are unjustified offenders, a judge has a reason to impose comparable punishments on justified and unjustified offenders alike. Insofar as judges recognize that they can collectively accomplish comparative proportionality only if they coordinate their individual actions through obedience to the law, and insofar as the law instructs them to punish *all* offenders who satisfy the conditions of *legal* culpability and who are not justified or excused on *legally recognized* grounds, judges have evidence both that other judges probably punished justified and unjustified offenders comparably in the past and that other judges will probably punish justified and unjustified offenders comparably in the future. The value of equality will thus provide a role-relative moral reason for a judge to punish justified offenders.

It is important to recognize that this argument does not smuggle in presuppositions about the need to protect against errors, and hence it functions, at least prima facie, as a principled argument for role-relative morality. It rests on the claim that, even if judges were perfect reasoners, they would still require a salient source of coordination, because morality makes equal punishment more important than substantively correct punishment. Once one judge expects others to follow the law as a means of accomplishing the equal treatment of like cases, and thus employs the law as a means of determining the appropriate punishment in a particular case, all other judges have a reason to do likewise. While the law's failure to distinguish the punishment due to justified and unjustified offenders may itself be in error, the first judge's compliance with that law may not be erroneous if the law provides the *only* salient source of coordination and if coordination is indeed more important than substantive justice. Thereafter, the justifiability of punishing the justified increases as the number of cases in which justified offenders are punished multiplies.

Let us now pause to take stock of the argument thus far. Our task in this part has been to determine whether there are at least prima facie reasons to embrace perspectivalism and abandon the correspondence thesis. If there are, then we have reason to think that the dilemma with which we began is solved, because morality will itself demand that we punish the justified to honor morally valuable systemic commitments.

We began our analysis in Chapter 7 by canvassing the bases upon which concerns about moral error might provide both judges with reasons to punish justified private offenses and institution designers with reasons to punish justified judicial offenses. We saw that error might provide a pragmatic reason to punish the justified, but that it cannot provide a principled reason to do so. We then turned to the question of whether there are principled reasons for punishing the justified that are uniquely applicable to those within judicial roles. We saw that there are *prima facie* reasons to think that the protection of reliance interests (of the sort required to generate solutions to co-ordination problems and prisoners' dilemmas) and the preservation of equality are more weighty concerns for judges than they are for citizens and, hence, that in some circumstances, the balance of reasons for judicial action might justify the punishment of a citizen for whom the balance of reasons justified disobedience. We now turn to the question of whether there are principled reasons for punishing the justified that are uniquely applicable to those who design and preserve legal institutions (such as the role of the judiciary). If there are such reasons, then even if judges are justified in refusing to punish justifiably disobedient citizens, institution designers may be justified in punishing judges for such refusals.

Chapter 9

The Values of Democracy
and the Separation of Powers:
Principled Foundations for
Constitutional Perspectivalism

Frederick Schauer has maintained that the standpoint of the designer of a decision-making environment is quite different from the standpoint of a decision maker within that environment.[1] If this is the case, then we must distinguish judicial perspectivalism from what I shall call "constitutional perspectivalism." Constitutional perspectivalism is the thesis that those who design and protect the decision-making institutions of the state – including judicial institutions – occupy a role that is characterized by reasons for action that are inapplicable to those in other roles.[2]

The constitutional role is a nebulous one because, unlike the judicial role, it no longer has a distinct set of occupants. In the absence of the framers of the Constitution, the task has fallen to those who periodically step out of their other roles for the purposes of creating, evaluating, or policing decision-making systems that are essentially self-executing. Thus, the constitutional perspective is sometimes occupied

---

[1] Frederick Schauer, "Rules and the Rule of Law," *Harvard Journal of Law and Public Policy* 14 (1991): 691. See also Frederick F. Schauer, *Playing by the Rules: A Philosophical Examination of Rule-Based Decision-Making in Law and in Life* (Oxford: Clarendon Press, 1991), 130–3 (discussing the "asymmetry of authority" that exists between those who have adopted the perspective of one charged with designing a system of rules and those who have assumed the perspective of one expected to conform to those rules).

[2] As Chaim Gans has argued:

> [S]ome of the considerations supporting the authorities' obedience are completely irrelevant to the question of the subjects' obedience. These have to do with the separation of powers. Were the authorities entrusted with the roles of bringing to trial, judging and carrying out the courts' rulings, to disobey the law, or in other words to enforce it or fail to punish its violators, it would be in place to ask just who determines society's conduct – these authorities or the government and the legislature.

Chaim Gans, *Philosophical Anarchism and Political Disobedience* (Cambridge: Cambridge University Press, 1992), 7.

by the legislature (most obviously, for example, the Senate when it votes on the appointment or impeachment of a judge); sometimes by appellate court judges and justices (when they evaluate the decisions of lower court judges); sometimes by political activists; sometimes by lawyers, legal scholars, and philosophers; and quite often by journalists and political pundits. Anyone who judges the manner in which judges execute their responsibilities, for example, takes on the constitutional role. If such a role is perspectival – that is, if it generates reasons to criticize, discipline, or impeach individuals who do the right thing from a different perspective – then it raises the dilemma with which we began. If the content of morality is perspectival, then morality is inherently paradoxical: It makes moral the punishment of the moral.

The task of this chapter is to explore the viability of constitutional perspectivalism. We shall seek *prima facie* reasons to think that those who do or could assume the constitutional perspective might be justified in disciplining or impeaching judges who are justified in acquitting justified offenders.

THE CLASSIC ARGUMENTS FOR DEMOCRACY AND THE SEPARATION OF POWERS

The discussion in Part II and the arguments advanced in the previous two chapters of this part combine to suggest that, while there are important values that may be served by judicial obedience to the law, there may nevertheless be circumstances in which judges should set aside the law and act in accordance with their own best judgments. The recognition that judges may be compelled by the demands of practical reason to substitute their own judgments for those of the legislature flies in the face of our understanding of the principle of democracy and its concomitant demand for the separation of powers. That principle has traditionally been thought to prohibit judges from setting aside legislatively enacted rules in the name of background moral considerations. Government by the people gives way to dictatorship by an elite if unelected judges can rewrite democratic legislation.

There is a vast literature devoted to defending structural pluralism. For our purposes, it is useful to think of this literature as embodying two alternative theories of the importance of democracy.[3] In

---

[3] I follow John Arthur's taxonomy of "instrumental" and "internal" theories of democracy. John Arthur, ed., *Democracy Theory and Practice* (Belmont, CA: Wadsworth Pub. Co., 1992), xi.

one theory, democratic decision making constitutes our most reliable means of achieving right results. As between competing sources of rules, democratic institutions are more likely to achieve rules that square with the balance of reasons for governmental action than are other institutions. As such, democratic institutions should be accorded the power to make rules while other institutions should be restricted to the lesser tasks of interpreting, implementing, and enforcing those rules. I shall call this first sort of theory an "instrumentalist" one, because its claim is that we should value democracy only to the extent that it achieves right results. In the event that democratic results fail to cohere with the balance of reasons for action, they lack any value at all. In this theory, we value democracy only because we value truth, and we take democratic results to possess reliable theoretical authority.

In the second sort of theory, democratic decision making is intrinsically good. While it may fail to accomplish results that accord with the balance of reasons for action (absent the reasons provided by the intrinsic goodness of democracy itself), it nonetheless instantiates certain values that other decision-making procedures do not. Insofar as it is morally preferable to live by wrong rules that reflect these values than to live by right rules that do not, democracy is valuable even when its results are inaccurate. Hence, undemocratic institutions (like the judiciary) ought not to set aside the decisions of democratic institutions, even when it is apparent that these decisions fail to reflect the balance of reasons for legislative action, because to do so is to thwart values that are more important than truth. I shall call this sort of theory an "internalist theory," because its claim is that democratic decision making is internally or inherently valuable.

In what follows, I shall canvass some of the classic instrumentalist and internalist arguments that have been made on behalf of democracy and the separation of powers. I shall demonstrate that each of these arguments provides a reason to punish disobedient judges only insofar as it provides a reason to think that judges who depart from legislatively enacted rules also depart from the balance of reasons for judicial action. That is, I shall show that each argument furnishes a basis for supposing that disobedient judges are *unjustified* offenders who in fact deserve punishment. If I am right, these classic theories of democracy and the separation of powers cannot, themselves, justify the punishment of judges who are genuinely *justified* in violating the law. But they might well provide reasons to think that the argument from error considered in Chapter 7 is applicable. Recall that the argument from error justifies the punishment of the justified in instances in which that punishment is a necessary means of deterring unjustified conduct by others. If the classic arguments for democracy and the separation of powers provide reasons to think that judicial disobedience is more often in error than not, then they provide grounds for thinking that the acquittal of justified judicial offenders may trigger more unjustified judicial disobedience than justified judicial disobedience. As such, these arguments might ground an argument from error that would provide those who assume the constitutional perspective with a role-relative reason to punish judges who are justified in acquitting justifiably disobedient citizens. But, as has already been argued, such a reason would constitute only a pragmatic basis for punishing justified judicial offenders. It will remain to be established, at the end of this chapter, whether there are any remaining principled reasons to think that system designers might be justified in punishing justifiably disobedient judges.

Instrumentalist Theories of Democracy

According to the instrumentalist, the reasons for judicial action are exhausted by the reasons for legislative action. That is, the fact that the legislature reached a particular decision is not itself a reason for judicial compliance – it is not itself something valuable that must be added to the balance of reasons for judicial obedience. Judges should obey legislative enactments only because those enactments are theoretically authoritative – that is, only because they are more likely to conform to an antecedently existing balance of reasons for governmental action than are judges' own judgments.

The Argument from Metaethical Relativism

John Ely has insisted that courts are incapable of deciphering better answers to social controversies than are legislatures, because there is no source for such answers beyond that provided by the results of democratic legislation. "[O]ur society does not, rightly does not, accept the notion of a discoverable and objectively valid set of moral principles, at least not a set that could plausibly serve to overturn the decisions of our elected representatives."[4] In a similar vein, Robert Bork has argued that when judges are called on to decide cases according to moral principles, they have no means of deciding such cases

---

[4]   John Hart Ely, *Democracy and Distrust: A Theory of Judicial Review* (Cambridge, MA: Harvard University Press, 1980), 54.

"other than by reference to some system of moral or ethical values that has no objective or intrinsic validity of its own and about which men can and do differ."[5] Thus, the only principled means by which to resolve disputes is by reference to a source other than a judge's moral principles. When the Constitution is silent, judges act morally only if they conform their decisions to the will of the majority as expressed in democratically enacted legislation.[6]

At the heart of the claims made by Ely and Bork concerning the proper scope of judicial discretion is the metaethical thesis that morality is relative to the beliefs of a majority. That is, what constitutes morality is whatever the majority of individuals within a community believe to be moral. From this thesis Ely and Bork take themselves to be in a position to argue that democratic outcomes are constitutive of what is morally true. Any judge who arrives at a view contrary to that reached by the legislature is necessarily in error. And nothing short of blind deference to the legislature can prevent such error.

Two problems confront those who are persuaded by this argument. The first problem stems from the indefensibility of the metaethical premise from which the argument proceeds. As I argued in Chapter 2, it cannot be maintained that the beliefs or preferences of a majority constitute moral facts concerning the rightness or wrongness of particular actions, and hence it cannot be argued that the beliefs of the majority concerning how judges ought to decide particular cases are themselves moral facts that provide reasons to so decide cases.

The second problem stems from the fact that, even if metaethical conventionalism were defensible, it would not support the claim that democratic results are *constitutive* of what is moral. In the conventionalist's view, morality consists in whatever the majority of a community believes to be moral. Because a group of representatives may fail to capture the majority's beliefs when they vote for legislation, legislative results may depart from what the majority would in fact prefer. Legislation thus cannot constitute majority sentiment; rather, it can only reflect it. As such, legislation can be, at most, good evidence of what the conventionalist considers moral. Accordingly, even the conventionalist must admit that it is possible for a judge to be

---

[5]   Robert H. Bork, "Neutral Principles and Some First Amendment Problems," *Indiana Law Journal* 47 (1971): 10.

[6]   Ibid., 11.

right in concluding that morality demands a departure from legislative decisions (because a judge may accurately assess majority opinion while a legislature may not).

Conventionalists might admit that legislation enacted through a process of representative democracy can, at most, evidence moral facts (i.e., the beliefs of the majority). But they might argue that legislation enacted by direct democracy (by which all citizens vote for or against all proposed enactments) is constitutive of what is moral. It truly *is* the majority opinion. They thus might conclude that judicial departures from legislative decisions born of referenda or initiatives are necessarily in error.

But such a claim would again be false. The outcome of a referendum voted on by all members of a community cannot be thought by a conventionalist to do anything more than evidence the fact that the majority believes a particular social arrangement to be moral. It is the belief of a majority – not the manifestation of that belief in a vote – that counts as the moral fact of the matter. Because voting errors can be made and beliefs can change, a judge might rightly find legislation to be in error.

While the truth of metaethical relativism would fail to establish that judicial departures from legislation are necessarily erroneous, it would nevertheless vindicate the claim that legislation is practically conclusive evidence of what is moral. As such, it would provide a reason to think that judicial departures from legislative rules are probably more frequently wrong than right. But if a judge discovers a genuine discrepancy between democratic results and majority sentiment, the argument provides no basis for insisting that the judge ought nevertheless to abide by the democratic results. Hence, the argument does not provide anything more than an epistemic reason for judges to comply with democratic results. And it further provides no basis for punishing the judge when she complies with majority sentiment rather than democratic legislation. The most that it provides is a reason to think that judicial disobedience is more frequently a product of judicial error than judicial accuracy, and thus that institution designers might be justified in punishing *all* acts of judicial disobedience as a means of reducing a disproportionate amount of unjustified judicial disobedience. But this argument for punishment is a version of the argument from error discussed in Chapter 7, and it thus provides only a pragmatic reason to punish justified judicial offenders.

The Argument from Utility

It is tempting to equate the utilitarian argument for democracy with the argument advanced by the relativist,[7] but such a temptation should be resisted. To claim that relativism entails that judges ought to maximize the satisfaction of preferences requires one of two claims: Either one must maintain that there is at least one objective (nonrelativized) moral maxim that governs adjudication, the maxim that preferences should be satisfied, or one must combine the claim that all moral maxims are relative to subjective beliefs with the empirical claim that everyone has a second-order preference for the maximal satisfaction of first-order preferences. Since relativists are typically relativists because they find the empirical persistence of profound moral disagreement to be convincing evidence that there are no objective maxims, it is extraordinarily difficult for them to advance the latter claim. Those who derive utilitarianism from relativism thus appear committed to the former self-contradictory claim. Thus, while relativism draws its intuitive strength from metaethical skepticism, a consistent theory of utilitarianism draws its strength from metaethical realism. Its claim is that utility should be maximized whether the majority believes that it should or not: Hence, majority sentiment is not constitutive of morality.

James Mill (John Stuart Mill's father) most famously articulated the utilitarian's reason to accord democratic results instrumental value. His argument runs as follows. First, "the concern of Government . . . is to increase to the utmost the pleasures, and diminish to the utmost the pains, which men derive from one another. . . ."[8] Second, individuals themselves are the best judges of what brings them pleasure and pain. That the majority prefers some course of conduct is thus compelling evidence that this course of conduct will in fact reflect what the utilitarian takes to be moral – "the greatest happiness of the greatest number."[9] Finally, because democracy enables the will of the majority to trump the will of the minority, it accomplishes, on utili-

---

[7] See John Chipman Gray, *The Nature and Sources of the Law,* 2d ed. (Boston, MA: Beacon Press, 1963), 12, 19; Robert S. Summers, *Instrumentalism and American Legal Theory* (Ithaca, NY: Cornell University Press, 1982), 43–4, 48–9; Herman Oliphant, "Current Discussions of Legal Methodology," *American Bar Association Journal* 7 (1921): 241. See also Martin P. Golding, "Realism and Functionalism in the Legal Thought of Felix S. Cohen," *Cornell Law Review* 66 (1981), 1032 (discussing Felix Cohen's derivation of utilitarianism from relativism).

[8] James Mill, "Essay on Government," in *Democracy: Theory and Practice,* ed. John Arthur (Belmont, CA: Wadsworth Pub. Co. 1992), 44.

[9] Ibid., 43.

tarian grounds, maximally good results. Thus, according to Mill, committed utilitarians should favor democracy because it provides the optimal means of tabulating the preferences that are to be maximized under a utilitarian theory of morality. By abiding by the will of the majority one is more likely to achieve maximal utility than by abiding by any other decision procedure.

Because most utilitarians, including James Mill, do not think that individuals are incorrigible in their judgments about what will bring them pleasure and reduce their pain,[10] they must admit the theoretical possibility of instances in which others may assess an individual's preferences more accurately than the individual herself. But this concession opens the door to the possibility that in certain, albeit rare, instances, individuals may better judge what is in the interests of a majority more accurately than the majority itself. In such (rare) cases, the right thing for the individual to do is to set aside the will of the majority in favor of the maximal happiness of the majority. Insofar as a judge does precisely this when she *justifiably* disobeys a legislative rule that requires the punishment of a justified offender (who *eo ipso* also rightly recognized that the interests of the majority favored disobedience of a legislatively enacted conduct rule), the utilitarian can have no principled complaint about judges who justifiably acquit justifiably disobedient citizens.

Utilitarianism would generate an exclusionary reason for judges to obey legislative rules that fail to cohere with a majority's true preferences only if it assumed the form of rule utilitarianism, and only if a rule barring all acts of judicial disobedience would produce more utility than would some alternative rule. Because there are well-known reasons to suspect that rule utilitarianism contradicts utilitarianism,[11] there are reasons to suppose that utilitarians cannot generate exclusionary reasons for judges to decide cases in ways that fail to maximize

---

[10] Although typically not thought to be a utilitarian of the Millian sort, Rousseau captured this common utilitarian assumption when he said: "Men always desire their own good, but do not always discern it; the people are never corrupted, though often deceived, and it is only then that they seem to will what is evil." Jean-Jacques Rousseau, "The Social Contract," in *The Social Contract and Discourse on the Origin of Inequality,* ed. Lester G. Crocker (New York: Washington Square Press, 1967), 30; John Stuart Mill, "Utilitarianism," in *Selected Writings of John Stuart Mill,* ed. Maurice Cowling (New York: New American Library, 1968), 252.

[11] For his now-famous argument that rule-utilitarianism must give way to act-utilitarianism to be genuinely utilitarian, see David Lyons, *Forms and Limits of Utilitarianism* (Oxford: Clarendon Press, 1965), 143–60.

utility (even if they can surmount the conceptual problems with exclusionary reasons discussed in Chapter 3). The most that they can generate are rules of thumb. And they can justifiably enforce these rules against judges who rightly calculate that such rules should be disobeyed only if they calculate that the punishment of the justified is necessary to deter a disproportionate amount of unjustified disobedience. In a world inhabited by capable practical reasoners, this rationale for punishing the justified would be unavailable. As such, utilitarianism, if defensible, can at most provide a pragmatic reason to punish justified judicial offenders.

The Argument from Institutional Competence

Even if one rejects utilitarianism, and thus rejects Mill's view that democracy yields right results because it accurately reflects what will provide for the greatest happiness of the greatest number, one might nevertheless suppose that judges are ill-equipped to second-guess legislative decisions. That is, one might plausibly think that on any moral theory, not just that of utilitarianism, the institutional constraints imposed on judges prevent them from making accurate moral assessments.

There is a set of well-rehearsed considerations that suggests that judges are institutionally ill-situated to make accurate all-things-considered moral decisions. Many of these arguments are inverted versions of those made in Chapters 5 and 6 regarding the institutional features that enable us to accord democratic decision-making bodies epistemic authority. For example, it is argued that judges are insulated from the political arena, and hence out of touch with the concerns of those whom law is to serve – concerns that on any moral theory are likely to be evidential of what is moral, if not constitutive of it. Their appointment and lengthy tenure in office render them unaccountable to those whom their decisions affect. Their understanding of the social choices with which their decisions must cohere is limited by the accidental manner in which those choices are presented on their adjudicative agenda. The constraints placed on their fact-finding facilities by hectic court schedules and restrictive rules of evidence preclude them from the sort of debate and discussion that freely inform the decisions of legislators. And the requirement that they limit their considerations to those issues that arise in the course of adjudicating particular disputes prevents them from engaging in an orderly investigation of all of the factors that speak to the pursuit of a social policy.[12] As such, courts are systemically impoverished in their ability to amass the information that is relevant to all of the things that ought to be considered when called on to make all-things-considered moral judgments.

Legislators, on the other hand, are not so impoverished. As was argued in Chapters 5 and 6, they collectively represent, at least better than does a single judge, the interests of those whom law affects. As such, they are in touch with and can make known the needs and concerns that ought to inform legal decision making. Their short tenure keeps them accountable to those they represent and thus keeps their representation genuine. They possess extensive fact-finding resources, virtually unlimited time for debate and discussion, and an open calendar as to the issues that they may consider and the order in which they may consider them. The institutional process by which social policies are formulated and enacted prevents individuals from accomplishing legislative results that are calculated only to advance personal interests. As a result of these factors, legislators are, as a group, more likely to make accurate judgments about the social policies that ought to be pursued.

It is clear on their face that these observations provide a reason to punish disobedient judges only if their disobedience in fact fails to reflect the balance of reasons for action. Insofar as these observations should prompt judges to recognize the asymmetry of information that exists between themselves and legislators, they should prompt judges to defer to legislative judgments in instances of doubt. If the considerations of institutional competence that make such deference advisable also make it true that judges will probably fail to appreciate the asymmetry of information that exists between themselves and legislators, these considerations provide compelling reasons to think that the judicial disobedience of legislative rules will, in most cases, constitute error. But when judicial departures from legislative rules are not erroneous, considerations of institutional competence only provide a

---

[12]   For a further discussion of these constraints, see Benjamin N. Cardozo, *The Nature of the Judicial Process* (New Haven, CT: Yale University Press, 1921), 113; Ronald M. Dworkin, *Taking Rights Seriously* (Cambridge, MA: Harvard University Press, 1978), 22–8; Rolf E. Sartorius, *Individual Conduct and Social Norms* (Encino, CA: Dickenson Publishing Co. 1975), 175–6; Michael S. Moore, "A Natural Law Theory of Interpretation," *Southern California Law Review* 58 (1985): 314–5; Harry H. Wellington, "Common Law Rules and Constitutional Double Standards: Some Notes on Adjudication," *Yale Law Journal* 83 (1973): 221–311.

reason for surprise; they do not provide a reason for punishment. As such, the most that judgments of institutional competence may provide in such cases is a reason to think that *other* judges are likely to err. If institution designers must punish justifiably disobedient judges to inculcate an appropriate degree of deference on the part of judges who would be unjustified in disobeying legislation, then institution designers may have a role-relative reason to punish justified judicial offenders. But such a reason is, again, only pragmatic. In the absence of judicial errors concerning how much deference is due to legislative judgments, considerations of institutional competence would fail to provide institution designers with any reason to punish justifiably disobedient judges.

The Argument from Tyranny

It has been commonly said that to delegate decision-making powers to a minority is to invite tyranny. In Lord Acton's immortal words, "Power corrupts, and absolute power corrupts absolutely." It is for this reason that classical writers maintained that "[a]ll the difficult questions of Government relate to the means of restraining those, in whose hands are lodged the powers necessary for the protection of all, from making bad use of it."[13]

Alexander Hamilton's famous solution to these difficult questions was twofold: (1) to separate legislative, executive, and judicial powers so that each might check and balance the powers of the others; and (2) to invest the legislative powers in a democratic body that internally checks the ability of individuals to pursue self-interested ends. Because each governmental branch requires for its purposes the powers accorded to the others, each governmental branch is constrained by the others in its ability to achieve its own ends. And because each individual in a democratic legislature requires for her purposes the powers accorded to other individuals, each individual is constrained by others in her ability to act self-interestedly. Under Hamilton's scheme, structural pluralism is the answer to the threat of tyranny.

> The executive not only dispenses the honors, but holds the sword of the community: The legislature not only commands the purse, but prescribes the rules by which the duties and rights of every citizen are to be regulated: The judiciary, on the contrary, has no influence over either the sword or the purse; no direction either of the strength or of the

---

[13]   Mill, *Essay on Government*, 44.

wealth of the society; and can take no active resolution whatever. It may truly be said to have neither FORCE nor WILL, but merely judgment; and must ultimately depend upon the aid of the executive arm for the efficacious exercise even of this faculty.[14]

Yet the arguments so far explored have failed to suggest that there is a principled basis on which judges can be constrained from substituting their WILL for that of the legislature in instances in which they rightly conclude that the legislature is in error. Does this not invite tyranny by a minority? Hamilton certainly thought so:

> It can be of no weight to say that the courts, on the pretence of a repugnancy, may substitute their own pleasure to the constitutional intentions of the legislature. . . . The courts must declare the sense of the law; and if they should be disposed to exercise WILL instead of JUDGMENT, the consequence would equally be the substitution of their pleasure to that of the legislative body. The observation, if it proved anything, would prove that there ought to be no judges distinct from that body.[15]

Hamilton's willingness to abolish the judicial branch before tolerating judicial disobedience rests squarely on the presupposition that if judges are licensed to break the law when they deem it in error, they will declare it to be in error when doing so advances their own interests. They will assume a "*pretense* of repugnancy" in instances in which no repugnancy in fact exists. In short, they will abuse their power.

Recognition of this fact provides a reason to be suspicious of judicial disobedience, because it provides a reason to suppose that such disobedience is motivated more by self-interest than by a concern for what is genuinely in the best interests of the community. It provides a reason to think that judicial decisions that depart from legislative decisions also depart from the real balance of reasons for action. But despite Hamilton's hope, the fear of tyranny provides no reason to punish a judge who has *accurately* assessed that the balance of reasons for action favors disobedience. At most, it provides a reason to think that if such a judge is not punished, others will be tempted to disguise their unjustified disobedience as justified disobedience – to advance disingenuous reasons for disobedience in the hope that they

---

[14] Alexander Hamilton, "The Federalist No. 78," in *The Federalist*, ed. Max Beloff (Oxford: Basil Blackwell, 1948), 396.
[15] Ibid., 399.

will escape punishment for acts that serve self-interest rather than morality. This reason to punish justified judicial offenders is probably, as a pragmatic matter, a good one. But contrary to what many defenders of structural pluralism might have thought, it is not a principled one. In the absence of temptations toward tyranny, it provides no reason to think that those who assume the constitutional perspective would be justified in punishing justified judicial offenders.

Each of the arguments canvassed so far portrays the value of democracy in instrumentalist terms. Each supposes that democracy is important because it is theoretically authoritative for judges. Because all of these arguments value moral accuracy over democracy, none of them provide a reason to punish a judge who accurately concludes that a democratic legislature is wrong in requiring the punishment of a justified private offender. The most that these arguments provide are reasons to think that any given act of judicial disobedience is more likely to be in error than not. As such, they may furnish the foundations for an argument from error that licenses the punishment of the justified as a means of curbing unjustified disobedience.

Internalist Theories of Democracy

On an internalist theory, democratic decision making is intrinsically valuable. Those who advance an internalist theory of democracy are committed to the thesis that laws enacted by a democratic legislature possess influential authority. They create new first-order content-independent reasons for acting as legislated that must be added to the balance of antecedent reasons for action.[16] Thus, the fact that a democratic legislature has reached a particular decision functions as an additional reason for judges to comply with that result. When legislation has been passed on a particular subject, judges have a reason for action that the legislature did not have, namely, the fact that a democratic body has spoken. This fact must be added to the antecedently existing reasons for obedience (which were applicable to the legislature's decision) and weighed against the antecedently existing reasons for an alternative course of conduct (which were also applicable to the legislature's decision). In the event that the inherent value of democracy provides a weighty reason for obedience, it may be sufficient to tip the balance of reasons for judicial action in favor of an action that would have been grievously erroneous on the an-

---

[16] For a reminder of the dynamics of influential authority, see the first section in Chapter 4.

tecedently existing balance of reasons for action. Hence, the internal value of democracy may make it right for judges to do what it was wrong for the legislature to legislate.

In Chapter 4 we explored four arguments in support of the claim that democratic enactments are influentially authoritative for citizens. I do not propose to resurrect those arguments here, because their problems left us with little reason to think that they would give judges (as distinct from citizens) new reasons for obedience. Instead, let me take up two new arguments which suggest that, while democratic enactments may lack influential authority for citizens, they nevertheless posses such authority for judges and institution designers.

The Argument from Participation

Carole Pateman has argued that democracy is important because political participation fosters important qualities of personal character.[17] Following in the tracks of Rousseau and John Stuart Mill, Pateman argues that there is an "interrelationship and connection between individuals, their qualities and psychological characteristics, and types of institutions; . . . that responsible social and political action depends largely on the sort of institutions within which the individual has, politically, to act."[18] Her argument proceeds as follows. First, as Mill put it, "the general mental advancement of the community, including under that phrase advancement in intellect, in virtue, and in practical activity and efficiency," depends on self-determination.[19] Second, while a benevolent despot might better achieve decisions that are in the greatest interest of the community, such a governor thwarts self-determination and thus renders it impossible for citizens to develop character traits that are crucial to their intellectual and moral development.[20] Finally, because democracy alone provides for self-determination, democracy alone guarantees intellectual advancement and the attainment of moral virtue. As Pateman puts this conclusion:

> [T]he justification for a democratic system in the participatory theory of democracy rests primarily on the human results that accrue from the participatory process. One might characterize the participatory model

---

[17] Carole Pateman, *Participation and Democratic Theory* (Cambridge: Cambridge University Press, 1970), 22–44.

[18] Ibid., 29.

[19] Ibid., 28–9 (citing John Stuart Mill, *Representative Government* (n.p.: Everyman, 1910)), 195.

[20] Ibid., 29.

as one where maximum input (participation) is required and where output includes not just policies (decisions) but also the development of the social and political capacities of each individual, so that there is "feedback" from output to input.[21]

Pateman's participatory theory provides a reason to think that democracy is inherently valuable. If valid, it provides judges with a new reason to comply with democratic results – a reason over and above the reasons for compliance that existed antecedent to the democratic decision to demand such compliance. If a course of conduct is valuable just because it has been democratically willed, then a judge who fails to add the fact of democratic enactment to the reasons to pursue that course of conduct fails to assess accurately the balance of reasons for action. If her ensuing decision to disobey the law would have been different had she added the value of democratic participation to the reasons for obedience, the judge ought to be punished, because her disobedience is unjustified.

While Pateman's argument provides a reason to think that democracy is valuable, it does not provide a reason to think that the results of democracy should be thought to give exclusionary reasons for judicial obedience. Indeed, there are good grounds to think that Pateman's argument cannot give judges even substantially weighty reasons of the sort that would compel them to treat democratic enactments "as if" they were practically authoritative. Pateman herself would admit that if democracy failed to advance individual virtue, moral action, and civic-mindedness, it would lack anything other than instrumental value. And one might plausibly argue that a democracy will fail to advance morality unless and until the individuals who participate in it are themselves, to some degree, moral. Democracies are capable of producing gravely immoral results. And it is unclear how moral virtue might be fostered in a system that requires substantial immoral conduct. While one might argue that immorality is unsustaining,[22] and that the democratic legislation of gravely immoral policies will trigger the democratic change of those policies, it appears more plausible to think that immorality breeds immoral character traits that make such change unlikely.[23] Hence, for democracy to foster virtue,

---

[21] Ibid., 43.
[22] As Fuller supposed, "coherence and goodness have more affinity than coherence and evil." Lon L. Fuller, "Positivism and Fidelity to Law: A Reply to Professor Hart," *Harvard Law Review* 71 (1958): 636.
[23] As Mill maintained, "Capacity for the nobler feelings is in most natures a very

it must seemingly require a certain amount of moral conduct, or it must not, at least, require seriously immoral conduct. Thus, a judge confronted with gravely immoral legislation will be called on to weigh the value of participation against the immorality of the legislative decisions that result from that participation. In the event that the judge concludes that those results will foster greater vice than virtue, the participatory theory of democracy will itself require that she set those results aside.

Once again, then, the value of democracy fails to provide a principled reason to think that judges should be punished for genuinely justified disobedience. As always, the fear that the systemic acquittal of justifiably disobedient judges will foster unjustified judicial disobedience serves as a reason to punish justified judicial offenders. But, again, such a reason is a pragmatic one that is premised on the fear of disproportionate judicial error.

The Argument from Autonomy

The argument from autonomy rests on the claim that autonomy is inherently valuable and hence that a decision-making process that sums autonomous choices is inherently valuable. Because democracy performs precisely this function of summing autonomous choices, its results are valuable just because they are democratic. This argument is a distant cousin of the argument from consent explored in Chapter 4, and it is so closely aligned to Pateman's argument from participation that, under some constructions, it appears to collapse into that argument. But it differs from both of these arguments when constructed as follows. Participation theorists like Pateman value political participation only because they value the results that derive from it. If a benevolent despot could advance individual virtue and civic-mindedness to a greater degree than democracy, participation theorists would no longer find democratic participation valuable. Autonomy theorists, on the other hand, value autonomy for autonomy's sake. That is, autonomy is not to be equated with moral virtue (even if it is intimately connected to it), and hence it might be the case that even if the exercise of autonomy fails to advance intellectual and moral virtue, it is nevertheless valuable. Thus, even if democracy produces results that do not contribute to the social development of citizens, its

tender plant, easily killed, not only by hostile influences, but by mere want of sustenance." Mill, *Utilitarianism*, 252. "[W]ill, like all other parts of our constitution, is amenable to habit. . . ." Ibid., 252.

241

exercise is still a source of value. There are at least two versions of the argument from autonomy – a strong one and a weak one.

The Strong Version. The strong version of the argument from autonomy runs as follows. First, for an action to have moral worth at all, it must be autonomously chosen by the actor. That is, autonomy is a necessary condition for the moral worth of an action (albeit not a sufficient condition). Only if an individual's act is both voluntary (in the sense that it is not coerced by others) and intentional (in the sense that it is the product of deliberation and choice), does that act have moral value. Under this conception, for example, a financial contribution to others will have moral value – and will thus constitute an act of charity – only if it is a product of individual choice. If it is a product of pressure by others, the act will lack moral worth. It will function like a tax, rather than a gift; it will thus have good consequences, but it will not be a good act.

Second, compliance with the law has moral worth only if the law itself is a product of the individual's choice. That is, laws constitute pressure from others – such that compliance with them lacks moral value – unless the individual autonomously endorsed their enactment.

Third, individuals within a community autonomously endorse the choice of the laws that govern their conduct only if they meaningfully participate in the democratic enactment of those laws. As we saw in Chapter 4, there is a considerable debate about what counts as meaningful participation. Suffice it to say here that if one meaningfully participates in a democracy merely by living within a territory that is ruled democratically, then the rules enacted by the government of that territory count as autonomously chosen rules. If the election of representatives is required for meaningful participation, then laws that are enacted by representative democracy count as autonomously chosen laws. If casting a ballot is required for meaningful participation, then only laws that are enacted by direct democracy (by referendum or initiative) count as autonomously chosen laws. And if casting a ballot *in favor of* the law is required for meaningful participation, then only laws for which one voted affirmatively in a direct democracy count as autonomously chosen laws.[24]

---

[24] This very stringent condition has been defended by the anarchist Robert Paul Wolff. See Robert Paul Wolff, *In Defense of Anarchism* (New York: Harper & Row, 1970), 12–14; Robert Paul Wolff, "In Defense of Anarchism," in *Is Law Dead?*, ed. E. Rostow (New York: Simon & Schuster, 1971), 110.

Fourth, to the extent that judges disobey democratic enactments and implement their own judgments concerning what citizens ought to do, they deprive citizens of the moral worth of their actions. They coerce citizens to act by enforcing laws that differ from those chosen democratically. And by so doing they defeat the possibility of moral action by citizens.

Finally, institution designers have a moral reason to punish judges who substitute their own judgments concerning what citizens ought to do for those collectively made by citizens themselves. If morality makes autonomous choice a condition of right action, and if democratically enacted laws are the only laws that are autonomously chosen, then judges cannot substitute their own judgments for democratic judgments without rendering it impossible for citizens to act morally.

If this version of the argument from autonomy were defensible, then the value of democracy would be effectively exclusionary. There would never be instances in which judges might justifiably disobey democratically enacted laws. If judges could not increase moral conduct by substituting their own judgments for those of a democracy, the separation of powers would be inviolate. Judges would be forced to recognize that, even though it might have been morally better for the legislature to have chosen a different law – because the balance of reasons for action in fact favors the pursuit of a different social policy – a judicial substitution of that policy could not accomplish morally better results, because its very imposition would deprive it of its worth. Hence, judicial disobedience of legislative rules would never be justified.

There are at least two reasons to think that this version of the argument from autonomy fails. The first is that it is self-defeating, and the second is that it is false. The argument is self-defeating because, if autonomous choice is a condition of moral action, individuals could not rationally choose to give themselves laws without threatening the moral worth of their own actions. If they then act according to their laws when absent those laws they would not so act, their actions lack moral worth. And if they act according to their laws when absent those laws they would act in just the same way, then their laws do no work and the process of their enactment appears irrational. Thus, on the strong view, the democratic enactment of action-guiding rules would be either immoral or irrational.

The strong version of the argument from autonomy appears false because, even though some acts appear to loose their moral worth if the actors who perform them have not autonomously chosen to do so, many acts (and omissions) do not appear to lose their value just because the actor would not choose to perform them without pressure from others. While charity may cease to be charity if it is coerced, truth-telling will still constitute honesty if coerced. Thus, in many instances one may not deprive others of the moral worth of their actions by pressuring them to act against their will; on the contrary, one may guarantee their moral action when they might otherwise have (autonomously) jeopardized it. As such, the strong version of the argument from participation appears too strong, because it fails to take account of the fact that many acts appear to have moral worth even when they are not autonomously chosen.

The Weak Version. A more plausible version of the argument from autonomy can be constructed with the help of the theory of autonomy developed by Joseph Raz. According to Raz, lives have greater moral worth if they are autonomously led than if they are not autonomously led.

> It is thought that what we are is, in significant respects, what we become through successive choices during our lives, that our lives are a continuous process of self-creation. . . .
>
> We regard the fact that a life was autonomous as adding value to it. We think of our own lives and the lives of others as better for having been developed autonomously.[25]

If lives are better for being autonomously chosen, then the acts that comprise those lives must be better for being autonomously chosen. Thus, the individual who chooses to save a drowning child without the promise of financial reward or the threat of punishment does an act that has greater moral worth than does the individual who saves the child because of some threat by others. This suggests, as a first step in the weak argument from autonomy, that the autonomy with which a decision is made adds moral value to that decision, although it is not a necessary condition of the moral worth of that decision.

Second, it might be the case that a decision that in fact coheres with the balance of reasons for action, but is not autonomously made, has

---

[25]   Joseph Raz, "Liberalism, Skepticism, and Democracy," *Iowa Law Review* 74 (1989): 781. See generally Joseph Raz, *The Morality of Freedom* (Oxford: Clarendon Press, 1986), 369–99.

less moral worth than does a decision that fails to cohere with the balance of reasons for action but is autonomously made. Thus, the choice to contribute to a softball team might have greater moral worth than the choice to contribute to AIDS research if the former is made autonomously while the latter is exacted through threat of sanction.

Third, insofar as democracy tabulates autonomous choices, democratic results represent choices of maximal autonomy. Hence, democratic choices possess substantial moral worth.

Fourth, even when democratic results fail to cohere with the balance of reasons for action, the value that attaches to those results by virtue of their being chosen by a majority may be sufficient, in many instances, to outweigh the value of a choice that in fact coheres with the antecedently existing balance of reasons for action. In those instances, judges ought to defer to the will of the legislature and refrain from substituting what would in fact be a better policy if (contrary to fact) the legislature had not enacted the law that it did.

Like the argument from participation, this argument provides judges with a reason to obey democratically enacted rules that should be added to the antecedently existing reasons to do what the rules require. But insofar as this argument rests on Raz's understanding of the value of autonomy, it does not purport to be exclusionary. As Raz argues:

> [W]e value autonomous choices only if they are choices of what is valuable and worthy of choice. Those who freely choose the immoral, ignoble, or worthless we judge more harshly precisely because their choice was free. . . . This shows that autonomy does not always lead to the well-being of the autonomous person. It can make his life worse if it leads him to embrace immoral or ignoble pursuits. Autonomy contributes to one's well-being only if it leads one to engage in valuable activities and pursuits.[26]

For Raz, the value of autonomy is asymmetrical. Moral acts chosen autonomously have more worth than moral acts performed accidentally or as a result of coercion. But immoral acts chosen autonomously have no moral worth at all, and thus are of less worth than moral acts performed accidentally or as a result of coercion.[27]

If Raz is right about the asymmetrical value of autonomy, then

---

[26] Ibid.
[27] To think otherwise is to think that autonomy is a sufficient condition of moral worth, even if it is not a necessary condition.

practical reason will require that judges assess the morality of democratic results. In the event that they are "immoral, ignoble, or worthless," the judge will be compelled to set them aside and to substitute a course of conduct that coheres with the balance of reasons for action. Compliance with the judicial substitution will then have some moral worth, albeit not the degree of worth that it would have if autonomously chosen. Thus, if a judge rightly concludes that democratic legislation requiring the punishment of a disobedient citizen is immoral, ignoble, or worthless, the weak version of the argument from autonomy licenses the judge to break the law and acquit the offender.

Yet, again, the only justification that a system designer would have to punish such a judge would be that such punishment is necessary to deter others from breaking the law in instances in which the law is not immoral, ignoble, or worthless. If those who assume the constitutional perspective have reason to believe that judges will fail to give due weight to democratic choices that do not suffer from these faults, and if they have reason to believe that only the wholesale punishment of *all* judicial offenders will prevent such errors, then the argument from error will provide them with a role-relative reason to punish the justified. But once again, this reason will be a pragmatic one, not a principled one.

Both the instrumentalist and the internalist arguments for democracy and the separation of powers fail to provide principled reasons to punish justified judicial offenders. At most, they provide those who assume the constitutional perspective with conditions that trigger the error-based argument from opportunity discussed in Chapter 7. That argument can now be understood as follows.

1. Judges are compelled by the demands of practical reason to assess and act on the balance of reasons for action as they see it. Hence, whenever judges conclude that legislation conflicts with the balance of reasons for action – including in that balance the reasons for obedience provided by concerns for error, self-interested bias, the rule of law values, and the inherent values of democracy – judges should break the law.
2. But judges will make errors about how much they will make errors. And judges will be self-interestedly biased about how much they are self-interestedly biased. If judges attempt to decide cases according to what is best, all things considered, they will frequently ignore or improperly weigh relevant reasons for and against action. Thus, judges would do better if they could escape the demands of

practical reason and blindly obey the law, even when the law demands things (such as the punishment of justified offenders) that are, and appear to them to be, gravely immoral. Thus, judges face a predicament.

3. Institution designers are alone capable of resolving this predicament. By parsing out matters of policy to the legislature, and by restricting judges, on pain of punishment, to the constitutional review and application of those policies, institution designers can reduce moral error. The threat of punishment will provide the judiciary with a reason to defer to the decisions of the legislature – a reason that in most instances will be sufficiently weighty to tip the balance of reasons for action in favor of complying with the legislature's judgments. Insofar as the opportunities to prevent immoral consequences provide actors with reasons for action, and insofar as the power of punishment provides institution designers with a unique ability to prevent immoral consequences, institution designers have a *prima facie* role-relative reason to punish judges who justifiably fail to punish justifiably disobedient citizens.

Yet while the fear of judicial incompetence and tyranny may provide compelling pragmatic reasons for punishing judges who are indeed justified in breaking legislatively enacted laws, it remains to be determined whether there are any principled reasons for such punishment. If judges were not susceptible to error or corruption, would there still be reasons to punish them for not punishing justified offenders? Would those who assume the constitutional perspective still have role-relative reasons to enforce the separation of powers? These are the questions that test whether morality is *necessarily* perspectival.

THE RULE OF LAW VALUES REVISITED

When contemplating the punishment or impeachment of a particular justified judicial offender, those who occupy the constitutional perspective are forced to take on the judicial perspective as well. This is because to subject a judge's conduct to scrutiny when punishment is at stake is to judge a judge. As such, the rule of law values discussed in Chapter 8 will enter the balance of reasons that determines the justifiability of decisions made by institution designers. Thus, if judges (as well as other officials or citizens) justifiably rely on the punishment of justified judicial offenders, or depend on their punishment as a means of preserving the coordination necessary to achieve collective goods such as justice, or require punishment so as to preserve equality among judges, then constitutional actors have at least *prima facie* reasons of a *principled* sort to punish justified judicial offenders.

If reliance and equality are concerns for institution designers, they may provide principled reasons for punishing judges who have justifiably determined that reliance and equality are insufficient reasons to punish justifiably disobedient citizens. That is, they may function as principled foundations for constitutional perspectivalism. If these rule of law values do vindicate a morality relative to the constitutional role, then they force us to conclude, once more, that morality is inherently paradoxical. It requires the punishment of those who do the right thing in refusing to punish those who do the right thing.

I do not propose to consider further the extent to which the rule of law values provide a principled basis for constitutional perspectivalism. Instead, let me turn to a consideration that appears to provide a principled account of role-relative morality that is unique to the constitutional perspective.

THE ARGUMENT FROM INSTITUTIONAL EFFICIENCY

Schauer maintains that, even if judges made error-free determinations, institution designers would nevertheless have reasons to encourage them to follow legislatively enacted rules in instances in which adherence to those rules would render the process of adjudication more efficient.

> When judges in courts of law are channelled by relatively precise rules into deciding cases on the basis of a comparatively small number of easily identified factors (Was the defendant driving faster than 55 miles per hour? Did the plaintiff become ill after consuming a product manufactured by the defendant?), the entire proceeding is streamlined, requiring less time and evidence than would have been necessary under a more rule-free procedure in which a wider range of factors was open for consideration (Was the defendant driving safely? Was the plaintiff's illness caused by the defendant's negligence?). A rule-based system is consequently able to process more cases, operate with less expenditure of human resources, and, insofar as rule-based simplicity fosters greater predictability as well, keep a larger number of events from being formally adjudicated at all.[28]

---

[28] Frederick F. Schauer, *Playing by the Rules: A Philosophical Examination of Rule-Based Decision-Making in Law and in Life* (Oxford: Clarendon Press, 1991), 147.

Schauer insists that we should take care "to treat efficiency as a value that is independent of the value of simplified procedures in diminishing the number of decision-maker errors."[29] That is, concern for efficiency need not collapse into concern for judicial error. This conclusion is true, but it takes some construction to see why it is true. It would be clearly true if both legislative and judicial decision making produced identical results. Then a system designer would have a reason to allocate decision-making power to the legislature if that institution could achieve those results at less expense than could the judiciary. Legislative and judicial results would be identical in two circumstances: (1) if legislatively enacted rules were never over- nor underinclusive (so that they always determined a decision that accorded with a judge's accurate assessment of the balance of reasons for action); and, conversely, (2) if the cumulative number of instances in which legislatively enacted rules were either over- or underinclusive was identical in number and weight to the cumulative number of instances in which judges failed to assess accurately the balance of reasons for action.

Neither of these circumstances obtain in the cases that concern us. Consider the first possible set of circumstances. As Chapter 1 made clear, if legislatively enacted rules were never over- nor underinclusive, then there would never be circumstances in which a citizen would be justified in disobeying legislatively enacted conduct rules, and there would never be instances in which a judge would be justified in disobeying legislatively enacted decision rules that require the punishment of citizens who break legislatively enacted conduct rules. That is, the problem of justifiably punishing the justified would not arise.

Consider now the second possible reason for identical legislative and judicial results. If judicial decision making inevitably produced the same number of errors as legislative decision making, then error would indeed drop out as a reason to prefer one decision-making institution to the other. Because institution designers would have reasons to think that the legislature would reach certain decisions (about

---

For a nice discussion of when considerations of economic efficiency favor adherence to rules as opposed to standards (by judges and citizens alike), see Louis Kaplow, "Rules Versus Standards: An Economic Analysis," *Duke Law Journal* 42 (1992): 557–629.

[29] Schauer, *Playing by the Rules*, 147. Note that Kaplow's arguments for the economic efficiency of adopting rules to govern conduct that recurs frequently are error-based. See Kaplow, "Rules Versus Standards: An Economic Analysis," 557–629.

matters of policy, for example) more cheaply than would the judiciary (given an identical error factor), efficiency would appear to give institution designers a reason to prefer legislative decision making. That is, if judicial disobedience could not accomplish a cumulative increase in morally right results, institution designers would have a principled reason to punish judicial disobedience. Punishment would deter judges from investing resources in attempts to discover whether legislatively enacted rules are either over- or underinclusive when those attempts generate as many errors at greater cost than does the blind application of those over- and underinclusive legislative rules.

But while efficiency might decide between decision-making systems that produce errors identical in weight and number, this conclusion falls short of providing us with a reason to think that institution designers should punish justified judicial offenders in circumstances in which judges are assumed to make no mistakes. The question for our purposes is whether efficiency provides a reason to punish judges for breaking legislatively enacted rules when their disobedience in fact reflects the accurate determination that those rules are over- or underinclusive. Put more bluntly, does efficiency provide a role-relative reason to punish genuinely justified judicial offenders?

For institution designers to be justified on grounds of efficiency in punishing a judge who justifiably acquitted a justified offender, it would have to be the case that the judge failed to calculate the amount of judicial resources that it was proper to expend in deciding to acquit such an offender. Take a specific case. If a judge was justified in acquitting a woman after she killed her abusive husband, then *eo ipso* the judge both accurately determined that the law of homicide was overinclusive in her case (or the law of self-defense was underinclusive in her case) and accurately calculated that the arguments from error coupled with the rule of law values and the values inherent in democracy fell short of providing sufficient reasons to punish her for her disobedience. For institution designers to be justified in punishing such a judge on grounds of efficiency, they would have to be correct in concluding that the resources spent by this judge exceeded those that should have been spent to reach an accurate decision in such a case. That is, they would have to be right in calculating that the judge spent an unjustified amount of time calculating whether the rule in the case was over- or underinclusive, and whether the arguments from error, the rule of law values, and the values inherent in democracy licensed such an acquittal.

But if institution designers rightly concluded that this judge over-calculated the likelihood of error, would this not be a reason to think that the judge made a mistake? If the costs involved in deciding that the battered wife should be acquitted exceeded the costs of punishing such an offender, then, other things being equal, is it not the case that the judge should have followed the legislatively enacted decision rule that required her to impose punishment? Efficiency provides a role-relative reason for institution designers to punish disobedient judges only if it provides judges either with no reason or with a less weighty reason to punish disobedient citizens.

There are, I think, *prima facie* grounds to suppose that efficiency provides institution designers with more of a reason to punish disobedient judges than it provides judges with a reason to punish disobedient citizens. This is because scarce resources create prisoners' dilemmas for judges. From the judicial perspective, the costs to a citizen of unjustified punishment are likely to trump the costs involved with the sort of protracted litigation that will be required to evaluate whether the applicable legislative rules are either over- or underinclusive in the citizen's case. Thus, in any given case in which a citizen's punishment is at stake, the balance of reasons will probably favor a judge's discovery and application of the background moral considerations that motivated the legislative enactment of relevant rules rather than a blind application of those rules themselves.

But if all judges in all cases second-guessed legislative decisions, the process of justice would grind to a virtual halt, and accurate decisions would be achieved at the cost of prolonged and involved litigation. Insofar as it may be more important to process many cases at the cost of a few errors than to process a few cases without errors, judges might accomplish better results if they abandoned their attempt to accomplish error-free adjudication (even in cases involving the potential punishment of morally innocent citizens) and blindly applied rules they knew to be over- and underinclusive.

But just as it appears irrational for citizens to vote because the incremental value of casting a single ballot is likely to be outweighed by the value of playing softball with their children, and just as it appears irrational to pay one's union dues because the union's activities are unlikely to be either hindered or advanced by one's small contribution, and just as it appears irrational not to take a short cut across a well-kept lawn because one's single set of footprints is unlikely to do noticeable damage, so it appears irrational for a judge to refrain from second-guessing legislative decisions because the incremental amount of systemic inefficiency that such a recalculation is likely to produce is small in comparison to the costs to a citizen of applying an overinclusive rule (even when those costs are discounted by the probability that the rule to be applied is not in fact overinclusive). Thus, even if judges recognize that the viability of the judicial system rests on the collective willingness of judges to apply legislatively enacted rules without calculating the likelihood that those rules are in error, judges will nevertheless be compelled by the demands of practical reason to calculate the likelihood of legislative error in any case in which they suspect that the costs of such error will outweigh the incremental inefficiency that their recalculation will produce.

Just as the punishment of citizens who justifiably disobey the law may rescue citizens from prisoners' dilemmas that threaten collective goods, so the punishment of judges who disobey the law may rescue them from the prisoners' dilemma that threatens the administration of justice. If the universal recalculation of legislation would contribute to the collapse of the judicial system, and if system designers can prevent that collapse by punishing judges who insist on recalculating legislation, system designers have at least a *prima facie* reason to punish judges who second-guess the legislature. And insofar as the blind application of legislatively enacted rules strikes the morally appropriate balance between rightly decided and wrongly decided cases, system designers will have a *prima facie* reason to punish judges every time judges second-guess legislation, even when judges are justified in so doing because the rule involved is in fact over- or underinclusive. Hence, the concern for efficiency would seem to provide a role-relative reason for system designers to punish justified judicial offenders.

Part IV

The Moral Case
Against Legal Perspectivalism

In the previous part, I canvassed the reasons to think that legal roles provide actors with unique reasons for action – reasons that might tip the balance of reasons for judicial action in favor of punishing a justifiably disobedient citizen, or reasons that might tip the balance of reasons for constitutional action in favor of disciplining a justifiably disobedient judge. If such arguments are persuasive, then we must conclude that the correspondence thesis as applied to punishment is false: It is not the case that the justifiability of an action makes wrong the punishment of that action. A citizen might be justified in breaking the law, but a judge might be justified in punishing her for her disobedience. Alternatively, a judge might be justified in breaking the law and acquitting a justifiably disobedient citizen, but a system designer might be justified in disciplining such judicial disobedience.

If the correspondence thesis is false as applied to punishment, then the appropriate means of resolving the dilemma of legal perspectivalism with which we began in Chapter 1 is by abandoning the principle of weak retributivism. We should admit once and for all that individuals should sometimes be blamed for acting blamelessly and punished for doing precisely what they should have done. Such a solution has the virtue of preserving the integrity of our systemic values. If judges are morally licensed to punish justifiably disobedient citizens when liberty, equality, and cooperatively achieved public goods are in jeopardy, then we need not fear that recognition of the moral justifiability of certain acts of disobedience will threaten the rule of law. And if constitutional actors are morally licensed to discipline justifiably disobedient judges to protect the institutions of democracy and the separation of powers, then we need not fear that judges will exercise powers institutionally reserved for the legislature in ways that will adversely affect structural pluralism.

But while the punishment of the justified will protect institutional

253

values, it will also encourage actors to do what they are not in fact justified in doing. It will prompt citizens to obey unjust laws that ought to be disobeyed, and it will compel judges to enforce unjust laws that ought to be overturned or ignored. While these results may be of institutional virtue, they are violative of personal virtue. The punishment of the justified thus poses personal dilemmas: In some instances, individuals must act immorally to be treated as if they had acted morally, and they must suffer the institutional blame associated with immorality if they honor their moral obligations.

Yet this paradoxical "solution" need be accepted only if the correspondence thesis as applied to acts of punishment is false. And the correspondence thesis is false only if the reasons for action explored in the previous part are in fact role-relative. While the arguments advanced in the previous part provide us with *prima facie* reasons to think that concerns about error, the rule of law, and the separation of powers are not concerns that equally affect the balance of reasons for private, judicial, and constitutional actions, there are further reasons to think that these arguments rest on one or more moral confusions. In the chapters that follow, I shall try to articulate the nature of these confusions.

In Chapter 10 I shall take up the viability of the correspondence thesis for consequential moral theories. In Chapter 11, I shall turn to deontological moral theories. While the reasons vary between the two sorts of moral theories, I shall argue in each chapter that there are compelling grounds for rejecting claims that morality is role-relative. If I am right, dissolving the moral confusions that motivate defenses of moral perspectivalism restores the viability of the correspondence thesis. And if the viability of the correspondence thesis implies that the justified cannot be justifiably punished, then the analysis in these chapters goes a substantial distance toward vindicating the principle of weak retributivism. Happily, it also reveals the means by which to reconcile that principle with our seemingly conflicting loyalties to the rule of law and structural pluralism. But we shall have to await Part V to make clear just how the marriage of these estranged principles can be made to work.

Chapter 10

Consequentialism and Moral Correspondence

Consequentialists who are inclined to embrace role-relative morality, and thereby abandon the correspondence thesis, must defend the claim that the consequences of judicial action are not consequences that enter into the balance of reasons for private action and the consequences of constitutional action are not consequences that enter into the balance of reasons for judicial action. This claim should be troubling to most consequentialists because the consequences of judicial action in a case involving a disobedient citizen are consequences that would not occur but for the citizen's disobedience, and the consequences of constitutional action in a case involving a disobedient judge are consequences that would not occur but for the judge's disobedience. That is, a citizen's disobedience is a cause-in-fact (or but-for cause) of any adverse effects on the rule of law or any disproportionate increase of erroneous acts of disobedience on the part of other citizens that occur by virtue of a judge's decision to acquit that citizen. And a judge's decision to acquit such a citizen is a cause-in-fact (or but-for cause) of any adverse effects on the separation of powers or any disproportionate increase of erroneous acts of disobedience on the part of other judges that occur by virtue of a system designer's refusal to discipline that judge. Thus, for consequentialists to defend the truth of role-relative morality, they must have grounds for maintaining that some consequences that would not occur but for a citizen's actions are consequences that do not affect the consequential calculus that determines the rightness or wrongness of that citizen's conduct. Similarly, some consequences that would not occur but for a judge's decision are consequences that do not enter into the balance of consequences that determines the morality of that judge's conduct. In short, consequentialists who reject the correspondence thesis must preserve the central consequentialist thesis that an action is right only if it produces more good consequences than bad, while maintaining the claim that some bad consequences are not to be included in the calculation that determines the rightness of actions.

Three possible approaches might be attempted by those consequentialists who do not take this project to be impossible on its face. First, consequentialists might attempt to limit the consequences that determine right action to those that are proximately caused by an action. Alternatively, consequentialists might try to limit the consequences that determine right action by confining right-making consequences to those that an actor can reasonably anticipate or predict. Third, consequentialists might seek to assign weights to right-making consequences according to their relative probability at the time of action, thereby making certain consequences more likely for some actors than for others, and thus more weighty reasons for action for some actors than for others. As I shall argue, none of these strategies succeeds: The first depends on a metaphysically indefensible conception of causation; the second and third confuse the conditions of right action with the conditions of culpability.

PROXIMATE CAUSE LIMITATIONS ON RIGHT-MAKING CONSEQUENCES

Consequentialists might attempt to limit the consequences that serve as reasons for and against an action to those that are the proximate result of that action. They might then argue that the role-relative reasons for judicial action described in Chapter 8 are not reasons for action for citizens because they do not represent values proximately affected by private conduct. Similarly, the role-relative reasons for constitutional action discussed in Chapter 9 are not reasons for action for judges because they do not represent values proximately affected by judicial conduct.

To make out these claims, consequentialists must argue that judicial action severs the causal chain between a citizen's disobedience and any increased number of erroneous acts of disobedience by other citizens or any adverse effects on the rule of law resulting from a judicial acquittal. Similarly, they must claim that constitutional action severs the causal chain between a judge's disobedient acquittal of a disobedient citizen and any increased number of erroneous acts of disobedience by other judges or any adverse effects on the separation of powers resulting from a system designer's refusal to punish the judge. In short, judicial and constitutional decisions function as the sort of voluntary intervening acts that make the prior acts of others nonproximate to any subsequent systemic consequences.

This argument draws on the intuition that currently grounds our general refusal to hold individuals legally liable for consequences that they do not proximately cause. Its implicit claim is that the legal rule reflects a deeper moral truth – that consequences that we do not proximately cause are consequences that do not bear on the rightness or wrongness of our conduct.

Notwithstanding the intuitive appeal of such an argument, there are reasons to think it an untenable foundation for a consequentialist vindication of role-relative morality. Most significantly, its defensibility rests on the ability to make the notion of proximate causation metaphysically plausible, not just morally plausible. That is, it requires one to defend the claim that voluntary, intentional human acts literally sever causal chains. The arsonist who voluntarily throws a match on a gasoline spill fully intending its subsequent explosion not only does an act that releases those who contributed to the spill from moral responsibility for the fire, but renders their acts causally inert. The judge who voluntarily and intentionally breaks the law by acquitting a disobedient citizen not only does an act that releases the citizen from moral responsibility for subsequent errors by others or subsequent adverse effects on rule of law values, but renders that citizen's disobedience causally impotent. Only if the argument is advanced as a metaphysical one, not a moral one, can the consequentialist argue that voluntary acts of judges and system designers release prior actors from causal responsibility, and not just moral responsibility, for all subsequent systemic consequences.

H.L.A. Hart and A.M. Honore were prepared to insist that such a theory of proximate causation could indeed be defended as a theory of causation, and not just a theory of moral responsibility.[1] As they argued:

[1] H.L.A. Hart and A.M. Honore, *Causation in the Law,* 2d ed. (Oxford: Clarendon Press, 1985). It is important to note, that while Hart and Honore explicitly distinguish their theory of causal responsibility from a theory of moral responsibility, they do not distinguish their thesis as a metaphysical one as distinct from a conceptual one. True to the ordinary language tradition of their day, they equate metaphysical and conceptual analysis. Yet insofar as they explicitly declare that their analysis is not limited to the linguistic issue of how the term "causation" is ordinarily employed by English speakers, ibid., they explicitly take conceptual analysis to be more than an analysis of the pragmatics of utterance. It is for this reason that I follow others in describing their theory of causation as

[A] voluntary act, or a conjunction of events amounting to a coincidence, operates as a limit in the sense that events subsequent to these are not attributed to the antecedent action or event as its consequence even though they would not have happened without it. Often such a limiting action or coincidence is thought of and described as "intervening" . . . as "superseding" or "extraneous" causes *breaking the chain of causation*.[2]

Motivated in part by a desire to make consequentialism defensible, they sought a means of answering the reductio ad absurdum that consequentialist theories have been thought to generate. That reductio can be put as follows: If the rightness or wrongness of any act is determined by the balance of its good and bad consequences, and if any act can have a virtually infinite set of consequences, then (1) the morality of virtually all acts is and will remain unsettled (the metaphysical implication), and (2) individuals must calculate an incalculable number of potential consequences to reach justified moral decisions (the epistemic implication).[3] For example, insofar as the assassination of Archduke Ferdinand of Austria triggered World War I, and insofar as that war continues to have wide-ranging effects today, the morality of that assassination remains, by this reductio, indeterminate, and its practical rationality impossible to assess.

As Hart and Honore recognized, the reductio draws its force from

a metaphysical one. See, for example, Sanford H. Kadish, "Complicity, Cause and Blame: A Study in the Interpretation of Doctrine," *California Law Review* 73 (1985): 334–5, 35. But compare Judith Thompson, "Causality and Rights: Some Preliminaries," *Chicago-Kent Law Review* 63 (1987): 473.

2   Hart and Honore, *Causation in the Law,* 71 (emphasis added).

3   Moral philosophers have insisted . . . that the consequences of human action are "infinite": this they have urged as an objection against the utilitarian doctrine that the rightness of a morally right action depends on whether its consequences are better than those of any alternative action in the circumstances. "We should have to trace as far as possible the consequences not only for the persons affected directly but also for those indirectly affected and to these no limit can be set." Hence, so the argument runs, we cannot either inductively establish the utilitarian doctrine that right acts are "optimific" or use it in particular cases to discover what is right.

Ibid., 69, quoting W.D.Ross, *The Right and the Good* (Oxford: Clarendon Press, 1954), 36. Thus, as Fumerton has maintained, "[s]ince the consequences of our actions go on and on (far beyond any point we can foresee), one can certainly sympathize with the actual consequence generic utilitarian, Moore, when he despaired of ever knowing what we ought to do." Richard A. Fumerton, *Reason and Morality: A Defense of the Egocentric Perspective* (Ithaca, NY: Cornell University Press, 1990), 105, citing G.E. Moore, *Principia Ethica* (Cambridge: Cambridge University Press, 1903), 152–3.

the claim that an act is a cause of all consequences that would not have occurred but for that act.[4] If this claim is defeasible, so too is the reductio that threatens the coherence of consequentialism. Such a claim is defeasible if the only causes of an event are proximate causes. On Hart and Honore's theory, acts cease to be proximate, and hence cease to be causes at all, when they are displaced either by the voluntary, intentional acts of another, or by a coincidental conjunction of natural events.[5] According to Hart and Honore, a voluntary action capable of breaking the chain of causation is an action that is intentional, uncoerced, and performed with knowledge of its likely consequences.[6] A coincidental conjunction of events capable of breaking the chain of causation occurs "whenever (1) the conjunction of two or more events in certain spatial or temporal relations is very unlikely by ordinary standards and (2) is for some reason significant or important, provided (3) that they occur without human contrivance and (4) are independent of each other."[7] On this analysis, one who spills gasoline is in no way a cause of a subsequent fire that is started by an arsonist who drops a match on the spill or by an unprecedented and unforeseeable bolt of lightning that strikes the spill. As Hart and Honore describe it:

> A throws a lighted cigarette into the bracken which catches fire. B, just as the flames are about to flicker out, deliberately pours petrol on them. The fire spreads and burns down the forest. A's action, whether or not he intended the forest fire, was not the cause of the fire: B's was. . . .

> Such an intervention displaces the prior action's title to be called the cause and, in the persistent metaphors found in the law, it "reduces" the earlier action and its immediate effects to the level of "mere circumstances" or "part of the history."[8]

Yet it is difficult to claim that such a theory of proximate causation is anything more than a thesis about the justified parameters of moral responsibility. Voluntary, intentional human acts and coincidental conjunctions of natural events would both have to be uncaused causes to sever causal chains so as to render causally inert many acts

---

4 Hart and Honore, *Causation in the Law*, 68–9.
5 As Hart and Honore argued, these factors function as "'new actions' (*novus actus*) or 'new causes', 'superseding', 'extraneous', 'intervening forces.' . . ." When "'the chain of causation' is broken," the initiating action is "'no longer operative', 'having worn out', *functus officio*." Ibid., 74 (footnote omitted).
6 Ibid., 76–7.   7 Ibid., 78.   8 Ibid., 74.

and events that are but-for causes of subsequent consequences. Because we have good reasons to think that there are no uncaused causes, and because we have good reasons to think that, even if there were, intentional human acts and statistically infrequent occurrences would not be among them, there appears little promise for the suggestion that a proper theory of (proximate) causation could adequately ground a consequentialist defense of role-relative morality.

This conclusion resurrects the reductio that implies that consequentialists are committed to the thesis that, because almost all actions, including the most trivial, have an infinite set of consequences, the morality of virtually all actions is indeterminate and the practical rationality of virtually all actions is incalculable. Yet consequentialists would seem to have two alternative means of resisting this reductio. They might deny that such a thesis commits them to absurdity, or they might seek an alternative means of limiting the consequences that enter into the balance of reasons that determines right action.

As I shall argue in the following sections, the latter line of argument is unavailable. But consequentialists should not find its foreclosure troublesome, because the reductio that motivates it is not, in fact, a reductio ad absurdum. As a first step, consequentialists need not conclude that the moral indeterminacy of actions precludes the practical rationality of those actions. They need not think that a defense of moral indeterminacy commits them to the claim that acts cannot be deemed practically rational in the absence of an ability to assess all of their consequences. Because consequentialists can plausibly maintain that practical rationality requires only that actors act on the balance of consequences reasonably available to them,[9] they can defend the determinacy of practical rationality while simultaneously embracing the indeterminacy of morality. And once the thesis of moral indeterminacy is divorced from a thesis about practical rationality, it should not be particularly puzzling. Indeed, it is vindicated by our affirmative answers to counterfactuals of the following sort: If those who assassinated Archduke Ferdinand could have foreseen that their assassination would trigger World War I, and if they could have foreseen that World War I would result in Hitler's rise to power and the subsequent execution of six million people, should they have considered these consequences as reasons against the as-

---

[9]   See also Moore, *Principia Ethica*, 150–9, for the argument that practical rationality consists in considering the alternatives that one thinks of, while right action may consist in an alternative that is not, and perhaps cannot be, thought of.

sassination? Because it would be the case that *if* persons possessed crystal balls that allowed them to foresee *all* of the consequences of their actions, we would consider their actions morally blameworthy if, over the long run, their actions did more harm than good, it must be the case that we consider all consequences of actions to be consequences that bear on the balance of reasons that determines the rightness of those actions.[10] It thus seems clear that our only concern with moral indeterminacy can be an epistemic one – not a metaphysical one. That the morality of actions may be indefinitely indeterminate is not itself a concern; rather, its recognition simply makes clear the degree of practical uncertainty with which we must make moral decisions. Absent a crystal ball, practical rationality requires substantial guess-work. The morality of our actions (although not their epistemic justifiability) will inevitably rest on what will seem to us to be luck.

EPISTEMIC LIMITATIONS ON
RIGHT-MAKING CONSEQUENCES

Consequentialists who are unhappy with the suggestion that morality is a matter of luck because the consequences that determine right action are indefinitely indeterminate and, in many cases, unforeseeable, might seek alternative limitations on right-making consequences. First, they might insist that it is unnecessary to construe proximacy limitations metaphysically, rather than morally. Individuals should be held responsible only for those consequences that they proximately cause, but the consequences that they proximately cause should be thought to be a function of the limits of moral responsibility, not the metaphysics of causation. Because actors cannot prevent what they cannot foresee, it is morally unfair to hold them responsible for consequences of their actions that could not be reasonably anticipated. Hence, right action should be defined as action that maximizes foreseeable good consequences or minimizes foreseeable bad consequences. Under this definition, the set of an actor's reasons for action is epistemically limited. The rightness of an individual's action is a function of the consequences that are reasonably foreseeable to the actor at the time of action. And consequences are reasonably foreseeable if the costs in time, talent, diligence, and resources required

---

10   As G.E. Moore put it, "the assertion 'I am morally bound to perform this action' is identical with the assertion 'This action will produce the greatest possible amount of good in the Universe.' . . ." Ibid., 147.

to appreciate their relative probability are less than the costs of the consequences occurring discounted by their probability.

Since a citizen who contemplates disobedience is poorly situated to judge whether the adjudication of her case will have adverse effects on others' allegiance to the law or on the systemic protection of liberty, equality, and reliance interests, the investiture of significant resources to research the likelihood of such adverse consequences is probably unreasonable. To assess accurately the likelihood of such consequences, citizens would, in effect, be forced to acquire the expertise possessed by a judge. Similarly, because a judge who contemplates the acquittal of a disobedient citizen is ill-equipped to judge whether the evaluation of her disobedience by system designers will have adverse effects on the obedience of other judges or on the separation of powers, the investiture of judicial resources to research the likelihood of those adverse consequences is probably unreasonable. Again, to calculate such consequences the judge would have to acquire the knowledge and skills of a system designer. Thus, the consequences that ensue from the adjudication of their disobedience should not be thought to affect the rightness of citizens' and judges' disobedience, because citizens and judges are epistemically constrained in their abilities to foresee those consequences.

According to this argument, the consequences that provide a judge with reasons for action are not consequences that provide a citizen with reasons for action, because, even though they are consequences that would not occur but for the citizen's (disobedient) action, they are not consequences that the citizen can reasonably predict. And the consequences that provide the system designer with reasons for action are not consequences that provide the judge with reasons for action, because, even though they are consequences that would not occur but for the judge's (disobedient) action, they are not consequences that the judge can reasonably assess. Hence, morality is role-relative, because different roles provide actors with different predictive powers. Thus, the consequences that enter into the balance of reasons that determines right action within those roles vary substantially. As such, it might be right for one actor to do what it is right for another to prevent or punish.

If successful, this argument would enable consequentialists to defend role-relative morality without embracing a metaphysically suspect theory of causation. But while this argument escapes the problem that besets the previous attempt to limit right-making consequences, it trades one metaphysical confusion for another. Instead of confusing the metaphysics of causation, it confuses the metaphysics of right action. By defining the conditions of right action to be identical to the conditions of culpability, it purports to vindicate perspectivalism as a thesis about right action. In fact, it merely establishes the relatively obvious fact that perspectivalism is true as a thesis about culpability while leaving open the truth of the correspondence thesis as a thesis about right action.

Recall the distinction drawn in Chapter 1 between right action and culpable action. An actor acts nonculpably if she justifiably believes her actions to be right. Her actions are right, however, only if they in fact conform to the objective criteria of our best normative theory. It might well be the case that a citizen is incapable of predicting that his disobedience will prompt a judge to issue a decision that adversely affects liberty, equality, and cooperatively achieved collective goods. As such, it might be true that the citizen acts nonculpably when he acts in disregard of the possibility of such consequences. But if his act in fact brings about more bad consequences than good consequences, his act is wrong, albeit nonculpable. Thus, the consequences that are epistemically available only to the judge may nevertheless be right-making for the citizen. Similarly, a judge may well be incapable of anticipating that the evaluation of her disobedience will undermine the separation of powers. As such, she may be nonculpable in failing to consider such consequences when deciding to disobey the law. But if her disobedience indeed leads a system designer to act in ways that threaten structural pluralism, her disobedience may produce more bad consequences than good. As such, her disobedience may be wrong, albeit nonculpable. The systemic consequences that serve as epistemically available reasons for action for the system designer may nevertheless be right-making for the judge, albeit epistemically unavailable to her.

Those who resist this analysis might invoke one of two rejoinders that purport to provide reasons to collapse the distinction between right action and culpability. The first attempts to demonstrate that absurd results follow from divorcing right action from culpability, because such a divorce allows for the oxymoronic possibility of culpable right action.[11] This argument runs as follows. Suppose that the year is 1930 and the place is Germany. A gunman goes to a local vegetable market where he opens fire, randomly spraying a large crowd of people with bullets. Miraculously, the only shopper he shoots is

---

[11] For one version of this argument, see Fumerton, *Reason and Morality,* 102.

the young Adolf Hitler – a man altogether unknown to the gunman. Suppose that the gunman acted out of revenge for being fired by a local merchant. He thus acted culpably, because he believed his action to be wrong, or at least unjustifiably believed it to be right. But if culpability is distinguished from right action, and if right action is defined consequentially, his action was right, at least on many versions of consequentialism. By virtue of saving millions of lives, the gunman maximized happiness, preference-satisfaction, virtue, the protection of rights, and so forth, because the millions of people saved from Hitler's forthcoming "final solution" were afforded happiness, virtue, and the exercise of rights that would otherwise have been lost to them. Thus, we must say that the gunman did the right thing.

But is this not an absurd thing to say? Is it not the case that the above scenario presents a clear counterexample to the claim that our theory of right action should be divorced from epistemic considerations about the justifiability of an actor's beliefs?[12] I think not. The claim that the gunman did the right thing only sounds absurd because we let our intuitions about culpability, our presuppositions about the appropriate conditions of punishment, and our equivocal use of the term "right" swamp our judgment.[13] The gunman was clearly culpable, and on most theories of punishment culpable action is a sufficient condition of punishment. But to see that the gunman in fact did the right act, it is useful to ask whether he should have done the same thing if he knew that Hitler was in the crowd, knew of Hitler's "final solution," knew that Hitler would be successful in implementing this

---

[12]   As Fumerton argues:

> Because the counterfactual conditionals that define rationality or reasons to act, on [this] view, ignore[s] the actual epistemic situation of the agent, it would seem to follow that it is possible for conduct to be rational despite the fact that the agent had no reason to believe that its consequences would be better (valued more) than those of its alternatives – indeed, despite the fact that the agent had every reason to believe that the consequences would be far worse. If I were to know all of the information that bears on some decision, I might well act in ways that in fact I have every reason to believe would be disastrous. But surely we want to make the rational/right course of action for me to take a function of my epistemic situation.

Ibid., 102–03.

[13]   It is just because Fumerton fails to distinguish between rational action (that is, epistemically justified action) and right action that he succumbs to this confusion. See ibid. He is surely right to make rational action a function of an actor's epistemic situation; but he is wrong to equate rational action with right action, and he is thus wrong to make right action a function of an actor's epistemic situation.

so-called "solution," and knew that he could kill Hitler without harm to anyone else. (Those with doubts that he could be so prescient or so confident in his own skills should imagine the he was a time-traveler from the twenty-first century with bullets containing homing devices programmed to impact only on Hitler). Under such circumstances, the consequentialist would have to maintain that the right thing for him to do would be to shoot Hitler. Because this is precisely what the gunman in our original hypothetical did, we must conclude that he did the right thing. But because he did it accidentally, he receives no credit for doing the right thing; indeed, because he in fact thought (or should have thought, given the evidence available to him) that he was doing the wrong thing, he acted culpably and appropriately deserves punishment. There is nothing conceptually confused about culpable right action, any more than there is something conceptually confused about nonculpable wrong action. Hence, its possibility gives us no reason to reject the distinction between right action and non-culpable action.

The second move that consequentialists might make to defend the claim that the conditions of right action should not be separated from the conditions of nonculpable action draws on the claim that, as a pragmatic matter, the moral evaluation of others turns solely on their culpability. Because the most that we can ask of people is that they act nonculpably, it is pragmatically pointless to work out a theory of right action as distinct from a theory of culpability. Because most people lack the hindsight of a time-traveler at the time that they act, they lack complete knowledge of the consequences of many of their actions. As such, the best that they can do is make educated guesses about those consequences. What sense does it make to speak of right action, when the most that people can aspire to is nonculpable action? Is it not a mere academic exercise (in the pejorative sense) to lay down the conditions of right action when those conditions are at best accidentally achieved? Moral theorists should thus concentrate on specifying the conditions of culpability and leave the conditions of right action to God.[14]

If the development of a theory of right action is pointless, then the truth of the correspondence thesis as a thesis of right action is irrelevant. We should concentrate on constructing a theory of culpability,

---

[14] There are elements of this second argument running through Fumerton's defense of an epistemically bounded theory of right action. See, for example, ibid., 107–8.

and as a feature of culpability the correspondence thesis is plainly false. Such an argument constitutes a clever strategy for those who seek to reject the correspondence thesis. It vindicates perspectivalism as a thesis about the conditions of culpability and then maintains that the conditions of culpability exhaust the subject matter of (useful) moral theory. It thus admits the possible truth of the correspondence thesis as a thesis about right action, but declares that truth irrelevant.

Tempting as this fall-back position might be, however, it too is untenable. The conditions of culpability cannot be specified without possessing an independent theory of right action. Thus the truth of the correspondence thesis as a thesis about the conditions of right action is far from pie in the sky. Under the critic's own theory, culpability is a function of belief. An actor acts nonculpably if she reasonably believes her actions to be right. But to know whether her beliefs are reasonable, we must know how close they come to being true. We must thus have a theory of when actions are in fact right. Only then can we judge whether the evidence that she employed in formulating her beliefs, and the inferences that she made in arriving at her beliefs, were reasonable. It is precisely because we think that Hitler should have been shot (at least if we are employing a consequentialist normative theory) that we are able to say that the time-traveler acted nonculpably, because it is the fact that Hitler should have been shot that makes the time-traveler's belief that he should shoot him reasonable. And it is precisely because the original gunman did not know that he would shoot only Hitler that we conclude that his actions were unreasonable. He lacked evidence from which to conclude that he would do the right thing; hence, he did the right thing culpably.

Similarly, only if we possess a theory of right action can we judge whether disobedient citizens and judges have acted nonculpably. That is, only if we know the conditions under which the law should be broken can we judge whether a citizen or judge reasonably believed that it should be broken. If the correspondence thesis is true of the conditions of justified punishment, it is significantly true because it holds that, if a citizen's act of disobedience was right, the right thing for a judge to do is to acquit the citizen. Hence, the reasonableness of a judge's belief concerning how best to decide the citizen's case is to be measured by the degree to which it approaches this truth. Alternatively, if the right thing for a judge to do is to punish a citizen for a particular act of disobedience, then that act of disobedience is wrong. Hence, the reasonableness of the citizen's belief concerning whether he should break the law is to be measured by the degree to which it approaches this truth. While reasonable belief can depart from true belief, true belief is the goal and measure of reasonable belief. Anyone concerned with the conditions of culpable action must thus admit the necessity of constructing the best possible theory of the conditions of right action. And if the correspondence thesis is part of our best theory of the conditions of right action, it is directly relevant to the project of specifying the conditions of culpability.

PROBABILITY LIMITATIONS ON RIGHT-MAKING CONSEQUENCES

In light of the above analysis, consequentialists must admit that the reasons described in the previous part as role-relative are in fact reasons for action for all actors; the fact that they are neither proximately affected by all actors nor epistemically available to all actors is irrelevant to their being right-making for all actors. Yet consequentialists might argue that this admission does not defeat a defense of perspectivalism. If the weight assigned to these reasons for action can differ as between citizens and judges, then the balance of reasons that determines right action for citizens and judges can differ. As such, it remains the case that while the values that comprise the reasons for action for citizens and judges are identical, their weight may be sufficiently different as to justify a judge in punishing a justifiably disobedient citizen. And, of course, the same can be said in defense of the possibility that a system designer will be justified in punishing a justifiably disobedient judge.

Why would we think that the weight of systemic concerns varies between citizens, judges, and institution designers? The consequentialist's answer must be that these systemic concerns differ in weight because the probability of different actors affecting them differs in value. At the time that the citizen decides to disobey the law, practical rationality dictates that the weight assigned to systemic values be discounted by the probability that the citizen will not be caught, or, if she is caught, that she will not be punished. Only if she is caught, tried, and acquitted will her disobedience result in adverse effects on liberty, equality, and reliance interests; and only if her judge is caught, tried, and acquitted will the citizen's disobedience result in adverse effects on the separation of powers. Because the probability that a citizen's disobedience will affect rule of law values is likely to be substantially less than 1.0, and the probability that such disobedience will affect the separation of powers is likely to be even less than that, rule of law values and constitutional values are appropriately assigned relatively little weight in the balance of reasons for and against private disobedience.

However, at the time the judge acts the citizen has in fact been caught and tried. The probability that an acquittal will affect rule of law values is thus substantially closer to 1.0. And the probability that the judge's disobedient acquittal of such a citizen will be detected, evaluated, and approved is significantly increased, so the probability that judicial disobedience will affect constitutional values is greater than was the probability that the citizen's private disobedience would affect those values. Thus, rule of law values and constitutional values must be assigned greater weight in the balance of reasons for and against judicial disobedience. And by the time that constitutional actors are called on to review a judge's disobedience, the probability of affecting both rule of law values and the separation of powers is quite close to 1.0. Hence, those values assume substantial weight in the balance of reasons for and against punishing the judge. Thus, by virtue of the fact that the disobedience of different actors will affect systemic values with different degrees of probability, systemic values function as reasons for action that possess different weights for different actors. The differential weights possessed by systemic values may thus make it right for a citizen to disobey the law but wrong for a judge to do so by acquitting the citizen; alternatively, they may make it right for a judge to disobey the law but wrong for system designers to ignore that disobedience.

If defensible, this argument defeats the correspondence thesis. It admits that systemic values are not themselves role-relative, but it provides reasons to think that their weight is. It thus carves out the possibility that the justified might be justifiably punished, and so provides a basis for thinking that our original dilemma should be solved by abandoning the principle of weak retributivism rather than revising our systemic convictions. Yet this argument succeeds only by smuggling epistemic considerations into the analysis of right action. As such, the argument ultimately fails for the same reason that the previous argument failed in its more explicit attempt to limit right action by epistemic constraints.

There can be little doubt that, at the time that actors act, the consequences of their actions must be assessed according to the relative probability of their occurrence. But this is because actors lack perfect knowledge of precisely what those consequences will be. They are epistemically constrained in their ability to pick out the consequences that will actually occur from among the consequences that it appears to them possible to occur. As such, the most that actors can do at the time of action is employ the data of experience to guess at the actual consequences of their conduct. They are thus practically compelled to consider all of the possible consequences of conduct that are epistemically available to them, discounting those consequences by the relative degree to which they have occurred in similar circumstances in the past.

Yet assuming the truth of physical determinism, certain consequences are destined to follow from an action while others are not. Thus, at the time of action, the actual consequences that will occur in fact possess a probability of 1.0, while the consequences that will not occur in fact possess a probability of 0. The citizen who is caught, tried, and acquitted for disobedience at a cost to certain systemic values was thus antecedently destined to affect those values. While she might have been wholly unable to know of the possibility of causing such consequences, and while she might have been wholly unable to assign a probability of 1.0 to these consequences even if their possibility was known, these consequences nevertheless enter the balance of reasons that determines the rightness of her action (as opposed to the culpability with which the action was performed) without any discount at all. On a consequentialist conception of right action, it is the actual consequences of an action that determine the rightness of the action. Because the actual consequences of action in fact have an antecedent probability of 1.0, they do not differ in their weight as right-making reasons for action. The actual probability of affecting systemic values is thus identical for citizens, judges, and system designers, even though that probability is assessed differently by these different actors by virtue of their different epistemic situations.

It thus appears that the correspondence thesis is part of our best consequentialist theory of the conditions of right action. It appears, then, that a consequentialist morality is not, in principle, paradoxical. Insofar as it embodies a commitment to the correspondence thesis, it appears reasonable to conclude that it neither requires nor permits the punishment of the morally justified. If this is the case, then the dilemma of legal perspectivalism with which we began cannot be resolved by abandoning the principle of weak retributivism.[15]

---

[15] I have put this claim tentatively here because I shall discuss in Chapter 12 a set of limiting cases that confound our ability to maintain that, under a consequentialist moral theory, the correspondence thesis is *necessarily* true of acts of

In Part V, I shall spell out how a consequentialist theory of morality that is committed to the correspondence thesis as it is applied to punishment embodies a solution to the dilemma of legal perspectivalism that squares our systemic values with the principle of weak retributivism. Before we come to this solution, however, let us take up the question of whether the correspondence thesis is also part of our best deontological theory of right action. If it is, then deontologists must join consequentialists in articulating a means of reconciling our systemic values with an uncompromising commitment to the principle of weak retributivism. If, on the other hand, the correspondence thesis is not part of our best deontological theory, then deontologists will not be committed to preserving the principle of weak retributivism. The jurisprudential question of whether to punish the justified as a means of preserving the rule of law and the separation of powers will then have to await the resolution of the normative dispute between consequentialists and deontologists.

punishment. Nevertheless, as I shall argue in that chapter, even if it is not conceptually true that a consequentialist morality makes the punishment of justified offenders unjustified, there are sound reasons to think that such a thesis is contingently true. The conclusions advanced above are thus ultimately vindicated in Part V.

Chapter 11

Deontology and Moral Correspondence

Recall that deontologists deny the consequentialist's claim that the rightness of an act consists in its maximization of good consequences. They locate the goodness of an act, not in its consequences, but in the act itself. According to a deontological theory, some act-types are intrinsically right while others are intrinsically wrong. Moral action consists in complying with agent-relative maxims that categorically prohibit or require the performance of certain acts. Individuals do not act rightly in violating the conditions of right action so as to maximize the instances in which they or others act rightly. If it is wrong to kill the innocent, then an agent is prohibited from killing an innocent person even if, by so doing, he prevents another agent from killing many innocent persons in violation of the agent-relative prohibition directed at her. If it is right to tell the truth, then an actor does wrong to lie, even if the lie will bring about substantially more truth-telling by others. And if it is wrong to punish persons who nonculpably do the right thing, then it is wrong to punish the justified even if in so doing one will dramatically reduce the instances in which the justified are punished.

In Chapter 1, I suggested that any plausible deontological theory would comply with the correspondence thesis, at least when construed in its original form as a thesis about the conditions of preventative and permissive actions. But this is not because the thesis in its original form is, as a conceptual matter, *necessarily* true of deontology. While denial of the correspondence thesis as a thesis solely about the conditions of preventative and permissive acts constitutes self-contradiction by a consequentialist, it need not constitute self-contradiction by a deontologist. It may not be logically possible for a deontological system to contain contradictory maxims (maxims that simultaneously obligate an agent to do act A and not to do act A), but it is logically possible for a deontological system to contain simultaneously binding maxims that, as a practical matter, cannot be mutually fulfilled. Hence, in a case of intrapersonal competing maxims, a deontological system might simultaneously obligate a single actor to do act A and act B, where A and B cannot both be done in the actor's circumstances. Thus, to recall Sartre's famous dilemma, a deontological morality might simultaneously provide a son with an agent-relative obligation to care for his mother and an agent-relative obligation to join the Free French, when he cannot practically fulfill both obligations simultaneously. And, in a case of interpersonal competing maxims, a deontological morality might provide one actor with an agent-relative obligation (or permission) to do an act while giving another actor an agent-relative obligation (or permission) to prevent that act. Thus, it is logically possible for a deontological system to provide an actor with an agent-relative permission to kill another if necessary to defend her life while providing others with agent-relative obligations to prevent killings, including those that are done in self-defense.

I suggested in Chapter 1 that, while the agent-relativity of competing interpersonal norms prevents them from being contradictory, it does not prevent their mutual assertion from being highly untenable. Competing interpersonal maxims would make us moral gladiators: Our successful fulfillment of our moral obligations would thwart the successful fulfillment of others' moral obligations, and their successful fulfillment of their moral obligations would thwart the successful fulfillment of our moral obligations. We would be periodically prevented from doing what we are permitted to do, and we would periodically prevent others from doing what they are permitted to do.

If it is the case that a plausible deontological theory would not pit actors against one another in moral combat by permitting or obligating some actors to prevent others from doing what they are permitted or obligated to do, then it is seemingly the case that a plausible deontological theory would not permit or obligate some actors to punish others for doing what they are permitted or obligated to do. That is, if a plausible deontological theory reflects the correspondence thesis in its maxims concerning preventative and permissive acts, it is reasonable to suppose that it also reflects the correspondence thesis in its maxims concerning acts of punishment. This is because a system that requires the punishment of the justified makes the conditions of right action gladiatorial. Citizens who have done the right thing must in some cases be treated by judges as if they have done the wrong thing. Judges who would accord citizens moral success in such cases would themselves be guilty of moral failure. A judge's moral success thus requires her to treat morally successful citizens (citizens who have been justifiably disobedient) as if they were guilty of moral failure.

In what follows I propose to explore the extent to which a plausible deontological theory is in fact committed to a nongladiatorial conception of the conditions of right action. Specifically, I propose to take up four sorts of cases that compellingly suggest the simultaneous rightness of competing interpersonal maxims. If deontologists would resist the suggestion in these cases that persons can be obligated to compete for moral success, then we have some cause to think that the correspondence thesis is naturally compatible with the most plausible deontological theory. We thus have reasonable grounds for maintaining that among the agent-relative obligations that bind actors under a deontological theory is the obligation not to punish the justified. If, on the other hand, deontologists would embrace gladiatorial maxims in these cases, then we have some reason to think that they would be untroubled by the prospect of punishing the justified, at least in cases that are analogous to these four sorts of test cases.

SPORTING COMPETITIONS

The first cases that might give deontologists pause in their incorporation of the correspondence thesis are cases of competitive sport. Consider, for example, the sport of boxing. Is it not the case that in a boxing ring it is right for each boxer to prevent what it is right for the other to do? That is, assuming for the moment that the sport of boxing is moral, is it not both morally acceptable for one boxer to throw a punch and morally acceptable for the other boxer to block that punch? It would seem that this is rather the point. But as a result, it would seem that the maxims that apply in the boxing ring defy the correspondence thesis, because the rightness of one competitor's action does not determine the rightness of the other's permission of that action. And the same can be said of the maxims that guide players in other sports: In football it is both right for a nose guard to block a punt and right for a center to block the nose guard from so doing; in basketball it is both right for a guard to shoot the hoop and right for an opposing teammate to block the shot.

Indeed, it would seem that what makes many sports sporting is that their rules suspend the correspondence thesis. But this fact, far from defeating the truth of the correspondence thesis as a metarule of deontological morality, would seem to constitute the exception that proves that rule. What is special about sports of the sort that I have mentioned is that a player's *consent* to participate in them waives the application of maxims that would otherwise apply both to his conduct and to that of others. A football player's consent turns what would be a brutal battery into an admirable tackle. It thus suspends maxims that would otherwise require the sort of peaceful interaction that makes for a poor spectator sport – maxims that would appear to embody the correspondence thesis. In the absence of a person's consent, deontological norms would surely prohibit the sort of conduct that passes for sport. That is, they would surely prohibit persons from punching an unconsenting actor, or running headlong into her, or smashing balls at her face, or jumping up and down in front of her to impede her progress. Thus, while competitive sports are competitive precisely because they impose on participants gladiatorial maxims of action (and so violate the correspondence thesis), they do so justifiably only because they do so by the consent of the participants. It is the consent of the participants that makes it morally acceptable for competitors to do to each other what they are plainly not justified in doing to others.

Sports thus provide us with a useful insight concerning the conditions under which the correspondence thesis might be plausibly suspended within a deontological morality: They suggest that acts of consent can properly suspend the otherwise proper application of the correspondence thesis. This insight has important implications in the context of punishing the disobedient. It suggests that punishment of the justifiably disobedient might be justified if, but perhaps only if, the justifiably disobedient consent to their own punishment.

This is a classic theme in the traditional literature on the conditions of justified civil disobedience.[1] Persons are thought to be justified in

---

[1] See, for example, John Rawls, *A Theory Of Justice* (Cambridge, MA: Harvard University Press, 1971), 350–98. See also Steven Bauer and Peter Eckerstrom, "The State Made Me Do It: The Applicability of the Necessity Defense to Civil Disobedience," *Stanford Law Review* 39 (1987): 1194; Carl Cohen, "Civil Disobedience and the Law," *Rutgers Law Review* 21 (1966): 6; Charles Fried, "Moral Causation," *Harvard Law Review* 77 (1964): 1269; Mulford Sibley, *Obligation to Disobey* (New York: Council on Religion and International Affairs, 1970), 26; John W. Whitehead, "Civil Disobedience and Operation Rescue: A Historical and Theoretical Analysis," *Washington and Lee Law Review* 48 (1991): 100–03; Rex J. Zedalis, "On First Considering Whether Law Binds," *Indiana Law Journal* 69 (1993): 208. But see Ronald M. Dworkin, *A Matter of Principle* (Cambridge, MA: Harvard University Press, 1985), 114–5 (advancing the case against punishing those whose disobedience is "integrity-based"); Kent Greenawalt, "A Contextual Approach to Disobedience," *Columbia Law Review* 70 (1970): 70–1 (arguing that morally justified disobedience does not necessarily require willingness to accept punish-

violating the law if, but only if, they are prepared to be punished for their disobedience. If consent to punishment were indeed a condition of *justified* disobedience, then judges would never be asked to punish the justified absent their consent to be punished. And if consent suspends the correspondence thesis, such punishment would not engender any sort of moral dilemma.

At least three things must be said about the suggestion that those who are genuinely justified have necessarily consented to their own punishment and hence have waived the application of the correspondence thesis. First, as an empirical matter, it is rarely the case that individuals can be said to consent to their own punishment – particularly when they are being punished for acts that they are morally permitted or obligated to perform. Those who are disobedient may recognize the risk that they will be punished. They may know that they will be punished. But, except in those cases in which they *seek* punishment as a means of publicly displaying its injustice,[2] they do not *intend* their own punishment. And as I have argued elsewhere, genuine consent embodies a *mens rea* requirement of specific intent vis-a-vis the actions of another.[3]

However, that justifiably disobedient citizens rarely consent to be punished might prompt theorists to claim that they *ought* to consent to their punishment, and hence that their failure to do so constitutes practical irrationality. Insofar as fully rational, fully informed actors would consent to their own punishment, the punishment of the justified is justified by the hypothetical consent of the justified. Yet hypothetical consent stands to consent the way heavy metal music stands to music. We would think it outrageous for a court to take seriously the claim of a rapist to the effect that, while his victim did not in fact consent to intercourse, she would have consented to it had she been fully rational; hence, his forced penetration did not constitute a rape. Such a case makes clear that hypothetical consent lacks just the element that makes an act of consent morally significant, namely, consent. If hypothetical consent is a morally meaningful construct, it is not because it embodies or reflects consent. Rather, it is because it refers to something that is moral, and hence it captures something to which it would be moral to consent.

ment, but citing four reasons why willingness to accept punishment may contribute to the moral justification for disobedience).

2 Recall the discussion in Chapter 7 of disobedient citizens who are motivated to be disobedient by the prospect of punishment.

3 See Heidi M. Hurd, "The Moral Magic of Consent," *Legal Theory* 2 (1996): 121–46.

This raises the third and most significant point. Consent should be thought to alter the normative environment – to grant permissions, confer rights, impose duties, and so forth – only if it is morally justifiable for it to do so. And to appeal to an individual's consent in the course of determining whether her consent should be thought to have such power is circular. As Joseph Raz has nicely argued:

> Consent . . . is an act purporting to change the normative situation. Not every act of consent succeeds in doing so, and those that succeed do so because they fall under reasons, not themselves created by consent, that show why acts of consent should, within certain limits, be a way of creating rights and duties. We cannot create reasons just by intending to do so and expressing that intention in action. Reasons precede the will. Though the latter can, within limits, create reasons, it can do so only when there is a non-will-based reason why it should.[4]

Thus, even if justifiably disobedient actors indeed consent to their own punishment, this is of no moral consequence if they ought not to do so. To resolve the question of whether those who do the right thing ought to agree to be treated as if they had done the wrong thing, we must establish, independent of arguments from consent, when, and under what circumstances, acts of consent should be thought to legitimate the practices consented to. Only then shall we be in a position to evaluate the suggestion that a justifiably disobedient actor's consent might justify his punishment.

I do not propose to engage in any detail in the quite worthy project of determining why, and under what conditions, consent should be thought to grant permissions, accord rights, or engender duties. As others have made clear, there are both instrumental and noninstrumental reasons to accord individuals the normative power to alter rights and duties. Such a power instrumentally expands liberty by creating institutions that advance useful goals and enable individuals to make long-term plans. Such a power is also noninstrumentally constitutive of certain sorts of relationships: As Julie Andrews sang it, "love isn't love 'til you give it away." Common to both an instrumental and a noninstrumental account of the proper significance of consent, however, is the claim that consent makes possible institutions and relations that are themselves morally valuable. But consent does not make institutions and relations morally valuable; it only makes morally valuable institutions and relations possible.

[4]   Joseph Raz, *The Morality of Freedom* (Oxford: Clarendon Press, 1986), 84.

Thus, as a condition of establishing that consent should operate to legitimate a particular practice, one must establish that that particular practice is itself moral or just. We think that we can do that in the case of sports (and it is just because many doubt that we succeed in the case of boxing that that sport is so morally worrisome). We do not think that we can do that in the case of slavery or murder. And it is for this reason that we do not take consent, however freely given, to legitimate a person's enslavement or murder. Can we establish that the punishment of the justified is moral or just? That is precisely the question with which we are concerned.

Just as we discovered that reliance on the punishment of the justified could not be thought to be justified unless the punishment of the justified is independently justifiable, so too, consent to the punishment of the justified cannot be thought to be justified unless the punishment of the justified is independently justifiable. We thus cannot use the possibility that justifiably disobedient persons in fact or hypothetically consent to their own punishment to ground a claim that their punishment is consistent with a plausible deontology. We must continue to seek other reasons to think that deontology would permit the punishment of the justified. If we find other reasons to suspend the correspondence thesis in cases of punishment, then it may be the case that the consent of a justifiably disobedient actor should be thought to legitimate a particular instance of punishment. It may even be the case that there will be some sense to be made of talking about hypothetical consent on the part of justifiably disobedient actors who do not in fact consent to their own punishment. But these conclusions will follow only if the punishment of the justified is justified by a plausible deontological theory. And the punishment of the justified will not be justified by a plausible deontological theory if the following cases do not vindicate the suggestion that the maxims for action that are applicable to citizens, judges, and institution designers can be gladiatorial in content.

GLADIATORS AND INNOCENT SHIELDS

A second set of cases that appears to defy the correspondence thesis involves instances in which innocent persons are forced to confront one another in life-threatening combat. Consider the true gladiators – innocent men coerced to duel until death by threats of immediate torture and execution. While the purpose of such confrontation was sporting, the sport lacked the consent of the participants. Nevertheless, was it not right for each gladiator to attempt to take the life of the other while preventing the other from taking his own life?

Consider, now, the more contemporary case of the innocent person who is forced to shield a culpable criminal in a shoot-out with an innocent police officer. In such a case, is it not right for the police officer to defend herself by shooting through the innocent shield in order to kill the criminal? And is it not simultaneously right for the innocent shield to defend herself by shooting the officer (assuming that she can do this, but cannot shoot the criminal who holds her hostage)? In cases of gladiatorial combatants and innocent human shields, it would appear that the correspondence thesis is false. The maxims of action that apply to the actors involved in such cases appear to make it right for one actor to prevent what it is right for another actor to do.

Yet deontologists need not, and should not, embrace such a conclusion. Rather, they should recognize that those who save their own (innocent) lives at the cost of an innocent life are perhaps excused, but they are not justified. Inasmuch as a deontological morality proceeds from what Thomas Nagel has called the "impersonal standpoint," it cannot contain a selfish tipping principle that allows persons to prefer their own innocent lives to the innocent lives of others.[5] Rather, all individuals are bound by an agent-relative obligation not to take an innocent life. Insofar as the actors who confront one another in these cases are equally innocent, each is obligated not to take the life of the other to save his or her own life. While this may seem to the actors involved to require an impossible kind of heroism, this is a reason merely to excuse them for the innocent deaths that they cause; it is not a reason to think them justified in causing those deaths.

This rejoinder affirms the correspondence thesis by making it wrong for innocent actors to preserve their own lives at the cost of other innocent lives. In the event that an innocent actor violates his obligation not to use deadly force against another innocent actor, he looses his innocence. It then becomes right for the other to defend herself,

---

[5] As Nagel argues, the rejection of a selfish tipping principle follows from the assumption of "the impersonal standpoint" – the standpoint from which each actor must recognize that "[e]veryone's life matters as much as his does, and his matters no more than anyone else's." Thomas Nagel, *Equality and Partiality* (Oxford and New York: Oxford University Press, 1991), 14. See also Thomas Nagel, *The View from Nowhere* (New York: Oxford University Press, 1986), 152–4; Thomas Nagel, *The Possibility of Altruism* (Princeton, NJ: Princeton University Press, 1978), 90–5; Derek Parfit, *Reasons and Persons* (Oxford: Clarendon Press, 1984), 143.

because in so doing she is not violating the maxim against taking the life of an innocent person. Thus, neither gladiator may initiate combat against the other; but if one does, the other acts rightly in defending himself. And neither a police officer nor an innocent shield may initiate the use of deadly force against the other; but if one does, the other acts rightly in defending herself. The rightness of one actor's conduct (in refusing to use deadly force against an innocent person) thus determines the rightness of the other's permission of that conduct (that is, the rightness of not initiating the use of deadly force). And the wrongness of one actor's conduct (in initiating deadly force) determines the rightness of the other's prevention of that conduct (that is, the rightness of using deadly force in self-defense).

It thus appears that deontologists should not give up the correspondence thesis when confronted with genuine cases of gladiatorial confrontation, because they should not think that gladiatorial maxims apply to gladiators.

SELF-DEFENSE

Deontologists preserve the correspondence thesis in cases involving gladiators and human shields by construing such cases as traditional cases of self-defense: Both actors are wrong in such cases to initiate combat, but, in the event that one actor does the wrong thing, the other does the right thing in employing deadly force in self-defense. There are those, however, who may doubt that a proper deontological account of self-defense reflects the correspondence thesis. They may argue that, even in classic cases of self-defense, in which an innocent victim confronts a culpable aggressor, right action is defined by compliance with competing maxims. In such cases, actors rightly defend themselves only in the sense that they do what they are permitted to do. And while the correspondence thesis may be true as a thesis about obligations, it is false as a thesis about permissions. Hence, while an actor may be permitted to defend herself, another actor may be permitted, or obligated, to prevent her from defending herself. There are at least three possible motivations for this position, all of which, I shall argue, are misconceived.

The Argument from Competing Permissions

First, it may be tempting to think that, while obligations cannot conflict, permissions can conflict. One individual may be permitted to do what another is permitted to prevent.[6] But, as we saw in Chapter 2, permissions are classically thought to constitute rights. If one has a permission to do an act, one has a right to do it.[7] And if one has a right to do an act, then others have a duty not to interfere with one's performance of that act.[8] Hence, others cannot be permitted to prevent what one has a permission to do. To maintain both that permissions are rights and that permissions can conflict is thus incoherent. If another has a permission to interfere with one's performance of an act, then that actor has a right that one not interfere with her interference. But if she has a right that one not interfere with her act, then one has a duty not to interfere with her act. One thus cannot have a right to do the act with which she is permitted to interfere, because one cannot have both a right to do an act and a duty not to prevent others from preventing one's performance of that act.

The Argument from Hohfeldian Privileges

The second motivation for abandoning the correspondence thesis as a thesis about permissions might derive from a willingness to abandon the claim that permissions are best thought of as rights. If, instead, permissions are thought of as Hohfeldian privileges or liberties, then it would seem that permissions could conflict. If one has a Hohfeldian privilege to do an act, it is not the case that others have a duty not to interfere with that act; it is merely the case that others have no right that one not do that act.[9] But if others simply have no right that

---

6   This argument, and the argument to which the following section is devoted, were first advanced in the second section of Chapter 2, by moral relativists claiming that when actions are of an incommensurate value, persons have permissions or privileges to engage in them, regardless of whether they thwart the justified actions of others. The responses that follow here are reminiscent of those I advanced in Chapter 2 to demonstrate the indefensibility of such claims.

7   In this subsection I am taking permissions to be distinct from what Wesley Hohfeld called "privileges" or "liberties." Hohfeld maintained that it is important to keep "the conception of a right (or claim) and the conception of a privilege quite distinct. . . ." Wesley Newcomb Hohfeld, *Fundamental Legal Conceptions*, ed. W.W. Cook (New Haven, CT: Yale University Press, 1919), 39. According to Hohfeld, when one has a privilege to do an act, it is not the case that one has a right to do the act (in the sense that others have a duty not to interfere with one's doing the act); it is rather the case that others have no right that one not do the act. Ibid., 35–50. I discuss the understanding of permissions as Hohfeldian privileges in the next subsection. In this subsection, I am concerned with the more common understanding of permissions as rights. Under this conception, permissions count as a combination of both Hohfeldian claim rights and Hohfeldian privileges. See ibid., 39.

8   Ibid., 36–8.   9   Ibid., 38–9.

one not do the act, they may have a Hohfeldian privilege to prevent one from doing the act.[10] Yet if they have such a liberty, then one does not have a right that they not prevent one from doing the act. They thus have no right that one not do the act; but one has no right that they not prevent one from doing the act. The correspondence thesis appears to be in jeopardy, because the liberty that licenses one's act does not imply an absence of a liberty on the part of another actor to prevent that act.

This argument effectively admits that the correspondence thesis is true of obligations and permissions (as those are commonly understood) but denies that it is true of privileges or liberties. There are two lexically ordered points to be made in response to this argument. First, the argument can easily be admitted by a deontologist. As we saw in Chapter 2, if there are liberties of the Hohfeldian sort, they define arenas of amoral action. Actors within such arenas are not bound by any maxims of action – they are genuinely at liberty. It is not the case that they are obligated to act in certain ways, but it is also not the case that they have rights (or commonly understood permissions) to act in certain ways (because, on this argument, a liberty is not a right). Hence, actors operating under Hohfeldian liberties are untouched by deontological norms. That their actions may conflict is thus of no normative importance, because their actions are of no normative importance. They are the actions of those in a moral state of nature. Because the correspondence thesis is a thesis about the conditions of moral action, it is hardly worrisome that it does not apply in such a state of nature.

Second, insofar as Hohfeldian liberties define amoral actions, they do not appear to capture the nature of acts done in self-defense or acts done in violation of the law. As a matter of substantive morality, such acts appear to be of moral significance. A plausible moral theory may obligate an actor to employ self-defense, permit an actor to employ self-defense, or obligate an actor not to employ self-defense, but it at least speaks to the question of self-defense. Similarly, a plausible moral theory may obligate an actor to disobey the law, permit an actor to disobey the law, or obligate an actor not to disobey the law, but it at least speaks to the question of disobedience. Thus, while the correspondence thesis may be inapplicable in cases involving amoral acts (acts licensed by liberties), this does not make it inapplicable in cases involving self-defense or disobedience, because such acts are not amoral.

[10] Ibid., 41.

The Argument from Permissions to do Wrong

The third motivation for rejecting the correspondence thesis as a thesis about permissions derives from the view that deontological norms of morality are exceptionless maxims, for example, "Do not kill." Justifications for violating such maxims are agent-relative permissions to do the wrong thing, for example, "You are permitted to kill in circumstances of self-defense." Such permissions do not remove the wrongness of violating moral maxims; they only entitle one to do what it is wrong to do (while making it virtuous to do what it is right to do, namely, to abide by the maxims in question). On this view, all permissions function like the permission that many theorists accord women concerning abortion: Women's liberty interests are sufficiently great as to permit them to make wrong decisions about abortion (for example, to have periodic abortions rather than to use birth control).

According to this understanding of the content of deontological morality, an actor may be permitted to do the wrong thing while others are at least permitted, if not obligated, to do the right thing. Insofar as it is wrong for an actor to do what he is permitted to do, it must be right for others to prevent him from doing that act. Thus, an innocent actor whose life is in peril is permitted to kill a culpable aggressor in self-defense; but insofar as this act is a wrong one, albeit a permitted one, others are permitted, or perhaps obligated, to prevent this act. Hence, the correspondence thesis is false: The rightness of an act does not determine the rightness of not preventing that act, because an act may be right only in the sense of being a permitted wrong, and it can be right to prevent a permitted wrong.

Deontologists might be particularly tempted to advance this analysis because of the payoffs that it might seem to offer in cases involving the punishment of citizens who disobey immoral laws. This analysis suggests the following. Citizens are subject to the exceptionless maxim, "Obey the law." In cases in which the law conflicts with other deontological maxims, citizens are permitted to disobey the law. But such a permission does not remove the wrongness of their disobedience. Insofar as such disobedience remains wrong, judges remain obligated to punish that disobedience. Hence, the correspondence thesis is false in cases of punishment: The rightness of a disobedient act does not determine the rightness of not punishing that act, because a disobedient act may be right only in the sense of being a permitted wrong, and, as was previously suggested, it can be right to punish a permitted wrong.

Two rejoinders are available in response to those who invoke this argument to defend the morality of preventing permitted acts. First, the argument fails for the same reason that the first argument failed: It is committed to the incoherent conclusion that permissions are rights, but that those to whom they apply are simultaneously under duties not to interfere with the attempts of others to prevent the exercise of those rights. If an actor has a right – even a right to do wrong – then others have a duty not to interfere with the actor's exercise of that right. Thus, even if permissions simply license wrong acts, rather than make otherwise wrong acts right, they generate duties on the part of others that are inconsistent with having rights of interference. Thus, the correspondence thesis in its original form remains intact: The permission of an act entails the rightness of not preventing that act.

Second, while autonomy rights, such as those of women concerning reproductive decisions, may be plausibly characterized as agent-relative permissions to do wrong, the justification of self-defense is quite implausibly described as an agent-relative permission to do wrong. Defending oneself against a culpable aggressor does not appear to be the wrong thing to do (albeit a permitted thing to do); it appears, rather, to be the right thing to do. If this is so, then acts that prevent self-defense are not acts that prevent wrong action; they are acts that prevent right action. Even if critics could escape the conclusion that the correspondence thesis applies even to permissions to do wrong acts, they could not escape the correspondence thesis in cases of self-defense.

The same is all the more true in cases of justified disobedience of the law. In cases of justified disobedience, the law conflicts with certain agent-relative obligations or permissions. Disobedience cannot constitute a permitted wrong in such cases; indeed, it cannot constitute a wrong at all, because such a conclusion would commit the deontologist not just to maxims that are gladiatorial, but to maxims that are genuinely contradictory. An actor would be simultaneously obligated both to obey the law and to disobey the law. If the content of deontology is at least constrained by the requirement that it not be flatly contradictory, then a deontological theory cannot both impose an exceptionless obligation to obey the law and require citizens to sometimes break the law. Insofar as it obligates citizens to break the law, a citizen's fulfillment of such an obligation must thus constitute the right thing to do; it cannot simply serve as a permitted wrong thing to do. Hence, a judge's punishment of such an act cannot be the punishment of a wrong (albeit permitted) act; it must be the punishment of a right act. And if the remaining cases convince us that deontologists should consider cases of punishment to be analogous to cases of prevention, then, even if critics could escape the correspondence thesis in cases that involve permissions to do wrong, they could not escape it in cases that involve the punishment of the justifiably disobedient.

STATUS-BASED RELATIONSHIPS
AND CONTRACTUAL ROLES

Rather than stymieing the ability of deontologists to defend the correspondence thesis, the previous examples have illustrated the viability of that thesis for a deontological morality. But this conclusion meets its most compelling counterexamples in cases such as the following.

Imagine two mothers, each of whom has a small baby and neither of whom can swim. They find themselves aboard a sinking ship that has only one life vest. If each mother cannot secure that life vest for her own baby, her baby will surely drown. Is it not the case that each mother does the right thing in attempting to obtain the life vest for her own child, even when this amounts to preventing the other from saving her child?[11] If so, the correspondence thesis is false, because the rightness of one mother's actions does not determine the rightness of the other mother's permission of those actions.

This sort of case tests the suggestion that individuals are entitled to prefer the welfare of those who are close to them to the welfare of strangers. Such a claim is thought to be most at home within a deontological morality. In light of the consequentialist requirement that all persons' interests be considered equally (that each count for one and only one), consequentialists have difficulty justifying why one might be morally justified in aiding a loved one in circumstances in which the interests of strangers are of equal or greater weight. Deontologists, on the other hand, would seem to be in a position to maintain that actors have agent-relative permissions or obligations to favor the interests of loved ones over the interests of strangers. But if the most plausible deontological morality contains such agent-relative permissions or obligations, the correspondence thesis is in jeopardy, because morality may then pit us against one another in gladiatorial moral combat.

It is possible to distinguish at least five deontological views concerning the content of the maxims that apply to actors in circumstances of the sort raised by the two mothers on the sinking ship. Some

---

[11]   This example is drawn from Nagel, *Equality and Partiality*, 172.

of these views falsify the correspondence thesis while others preserve it. Let us work through these five views to determine how likely it is that deontologists will consider themselves compelled to abandon the correspondence thesis to vindicate the intuitive claim that we may accord preferential treatment to those we love. Throughout this discussion we should not lose sight of our ultimate goal: to determine whether the correspondence thesis is implied by our most plausible deontological theory so as to assess whether or not our most plausible deontological theory would license the punishment of the justified.

The Argument from Agent-Relative Obligations/Permissions of Preference

On the first view, actors are obligated, or at least permitted, to give aid to those with whom they share special relationships, as opposed to those with whom they share no relationship. Thus, when a choice must be made, parents are obligated (or permitted) to aid their children, friends are obligated (or permitted) to aid friends, husbands are obligated (or permitted) to aid wives, sisters are obligated (or permitted) to aid brothers, security guards are obligated (or permitted) to aid those who have contracted for their services, lawyers are obligated (or permitted) to aid their clients, and doctors are obligated (or permitted) to aid their patients.

This view flatly contradicts the correspondence thesis because it makes agent-relative obligations and permissions role-relative. The role of a mother is in part defined by the obligation (or permission) to administer preferential aid to her own children. The role of a lawyer is in part defined by the obligation (or permission) to provide special services to his clients.[12] Insofar as role-relative obligations and permissions can conflict, the correspondence thesis is false as a thesis about the conditions under which one actor must permit the acts of another. Just as in the case of the two mothers who must compete for one life jacket, it may be right for an actor in one role to prevent what it is right for an actor in another role to do.

Deontologists who are persuaded that certain roles create agent-relative obligations (or permissions) to administer preferential treatment may be inclined to think that they are committed to a slippery

---

[12]   For a defense of the claim that citizenship constitutes a unique role characterized by unique rights and duties, see Leslie Green, "Law, Legitimacy and Consent," *Southern California Law Review* 62 (1989): 818–25. See also Chapter 4, note 27, for a discussion of Green's role-relative conception of the duties of citizenship.

slope that forces them to admit the possibility that other roles will create other sorts of agent-relative obligations and permissions. If mothers have agent-relative obligations to aid their children, then police officers may have agent-relative obligations to apprehend criminals and judges may have agent-relative obligations to punish all citizens who violate the law (even those who do so justifiably).

Yet deontologists need not slide down such a slippery slope. Deontologists must recognize at least a *prima facie* distinction between two different sorts of roles: those that arise by virtue of a person's status (for example, the status of being a mother or a brother) and those that arise by virtue of a person's promise or contract (for example, a promise to provide security or a contract to perform legal services). Deontologists may plausibly believe that the only reason that contractual roles create certain agent-relative obligations of preferential aid is because these obligations are part of what persons have contracted for in taking on such roles. The agent-relative obligations that define such roles are thus special cases of the agent-relative obligation to keep promises. Thus, the agent-relative obligations that define contractual roles are given by the contracts in question. The reason that a lawyer has a duty to provide preferential treatment to her clients is because she entered into a contract to do so. The reason that a husband has an obligation to provide aid to his wife is because his marriage oath embodied such a promise. Similarly, the reason that roles create other sorts of obligations is because those obligations have been voluntarily undertaken. Thus, the reason that a police officer is obligated to apprehend criminals is because he entered into an employment contract to do so. And the reason that judges must punish all individuals who violate the law, including those who do so justifiably, is because their oath of office is rightly interpreted to include a promise to do so.

But if deontologists impose agent-relative obligations on certain actors just because actors have promised to fulfill those obligations, then deontologists must have a theory that specifies the conditions under which individuals have the power to contract into certain obligations. Just as in the case of consent discussed earlier, individuals should be accorded the power to promise to do certain actions only if it is normatively justifiable for them to do so. On pain of circularity, the fact that an actor has made a promise cannot be a reason to maintain that he should fulfill that promise. We must have some reason, independent of his promise, to think that his promise is binding, and hence that it entails certain role-relative obligations. As in the case of consent, there are reasons to think that certain promises make possible certain morally valuable institutions and relations. But then the bindingness of a promise, like the scope of an actor's consent, is relative to the morality of the institutions and relations that it makes possible.

We have reasons to think that a promise to provide security services makes possible morally valuable relations. But we also have reasons to think that such a promise loses its normative power when it is made by a contract killer who takes security services to include the execution of an employer's political enemies. We have reasons to think that a promise to provide legal defense services makes possible certain morally valuable relations. But we also have reasons to think that defense lawyers properly lack the power to promise to destroy incriminating evidence. We have reasons to think that a judge's oath of office makes possible certain morally valuable institutions. But do we have reasons to think that that oath can include a binding promise to punish the justified? This is, once again, the question we are trying to answer.

Just as deontologists could not use the possibility that justifiably disobedient persons would consent to their own punishment as a reason to think that their punishment is consistent with a plausible deontology, so deontologists cannot use the judicial oath of office to establish that judges have agent-relative obligations to punish the justified. Only if deontologists have *other* reasons to think that the punishment of the justified is itself justified will they have good cause to consider judges obligated to punish the justified if their oath of office includes such a promise.

This discussion makes clear that deontologists must be discriminating with respect to the sorts of agent-relative obligations that attach to particular roles. In cases in which deontologists ascribe agent-relative obligations to actors solely because those actors have assumed those obligations by promise or contract, they must be clear that those agent-relative obligations are not obligations just because they have been assumed by promise or contract. If, as I suspect, the conditions that justify contractually based agent-relative obligations embody the correspondence thesis, then actors may not promise to do acts that prevent other actors from doing what it is right for them to do.

Thus, a plausible deontological theory might contain status-based agent-relative obligations that violate the correspondence thesis without containing contractually based agent-relative obligations that violate the correspondence thesis. Recognizing this allows deontologists to have what they may consider the best of both worlds. They can vindicate our deep-seated conviction that the role of a mother includes the obligation to prefer the welfare of her own children to the welfare of other children (because they can insist that deontological morality contains certain status-based agent-relative obligations that violate the correspondence thesis). But they can deny that this commits them to a morality that empowers judges to create contractual obligations to punish the justified (because they can deny that deontological morality contains contractually based agent-relative obligations that violate the correspondence thesis).

The Argument from the Denial of Agent-Relative Obligations/Permissions of Preference

Some deontologists may find the above analysis altogether unsatisfying. First, they may be unhappy with the implications of the analysis in the case of the two mothers aboard the sinking ship. The above analysis admits (at least for the sake of argument) that, in such a case, both mothers confront each other as moral gladiators. Each does right to attempt to save her own child, even though this means that the other mother will fail and her child will drown. Second, deontologists may refuse the suggestion that they can suspend the correspondence thesis in cases such as this without suspending it in cases that present judges with a decision about whether to punish the justified. They may subscribe to one of two claims: (1) that actors in contractually based roles also have agent-relative obligations (or permissions) that are status-based, so that actors in such roles may be right to prevent what it is right for others to do;[13] or (2) that the theory that grounds gladiatorial status-based obligations will speak in favor of a theory that allows individuals to create by contract gladiatorial obligations that make it right to prevent others from doing what it is right for them to do.

To alleviate these concerns, deontologists must reject the claim that there can be any agent-relative obligations or permissions that violate the correspondence thesis. That is, they must deny that mothers have obligations or permissions to aid their own children when doing so will prevent others from aiding other children. There are grounds for thinking such a denial deontologically defensible. The discussion

---

[13] See Green's defense of the claim that voluntarily adopted roles can, and typically do, carry nonvoluntary duties – that is, duties that are not themselves subject to individual alteration. Ibid.

concerning gladiators and human shields made plausible the view that morality does not contain a selfish tipping principle that makes it right to prefer one's own innocent life to the innocent life of another. The same might be said of cases in which persons prefer the innocent lives of their loved ones to the innocent lives of strangers: Neither mother on the sinking ship is morally entitled to prefer the life of her own child to the life of the other mother's child. If one of these mothers finds this conclusion to be too difficult to bear, and so seizes the life jacket for her own child, we may find grounds for thinking her excused, but she is not justified. Like the gladiator who takes up arms or the police officer who shoots through an innocent shield, the mother who seizes the life jacket may act understandably, but she does not act rightly.

If this analysis of cases in which persons are tempted to provide preferential treatment to loved ones is the better of the two here considered, then we have grounds to think that the correspondence thesis is secure as a thesis about preventative acts. This provides us with a further reason to suppose that, as a general matter, roles (of either the status-based or contractually based sort) cannot call on those who occupy them to prevent others from doing what it is right for them to do. It thus gives us grounds on which to maintain that official oaths of office cannot include promises to punish the justified that generate agent-relative permissions or obligations to do so.

Deontologists who paradoxically find both of the above accounts compelling may continue to seek a middle ground from which to defend both the claim that morality does not provide role-relative permissions or obligations to provide aid to loved ones before strangers and the claim that morality does not prohibit such preferential treatment in all cases. Three compromise positions present themselves.

The Argument from Hohfeldian Liberties of Preference
The first such compromise is provided by the claim that morality runs out in circumstances in which we find ourselves forced to choose between aiding a loved one and aiding a stranger. In such circumstances, we are genuinely at liberty to give preferential treatment to our loved ones because, while we have neither an obligation nor a permission to prefer our loved ones to strangers, strangers have no right that we not do so. To maintain this, one must maintain that such circumstances of third-party defense are amoral. This was hard to believe in the case of self-defense, and it seems all the harder to believe in these cases. However, as was previously argued, if these cases of

third-party defense suspend the correspondence thesis by constituting instances in which agents possess Hohfeldian liberties, then they do not pose a reason to reject the correspondence thesis in cases of punishment. This is because, while these cases may be beyond the reach of moral maxims, cases of punishing others are not.

The Argument from Preferential Killings vs. Preferential Omissions to Save

A second compromise might be struck by deontologists who similarly admit that there are no obligations or permissions to prefer the welfare of loved ones to the welfare of strangers, but who also argue that, while persons have agent-relative obligations not to kill, they do not have agent-relative obligations to save.[14] In the case of the two mothers aboard the sinking ship, this would imply that neither mother has a right to seize the life jacket if it is already in the possession of the other, because to do so is to *cause* the death of that mother's child, and so to violate the obligation not to kill. But neither mother has an obligation to give up the life jacket if it is already in her possession, because to refuse to transfer the life jacket from her own child to the other mother's child is simply to omit to save that child, it is not to kill that child.

This thesis entails that if neither mother has previous possession of the life jacket, then neither mother is entitled to take the life jacket at the time of crisis. To do so would violate the maxim against killing by affirmatively causing the death of the other mother's child. Hence, if the life jacket is not already in the possession of one of the two mothers, both mothers do the right thing only if each refuses to grab the jacket. While both children will die, they will not have been killed; they will simply not have been saved. This position preserves the correspondence thesis, because the maxims that apply to each mother obligate the other not to interfere with their fulfillment. If one mother

---

14   For a defense of this position, see Leo Katz, *Ill-Gotten Gains* (Chicago, IL: University of Chicago Press, 1996), 46; John Finnis, *Natural Law and Natural Rights* (Oxford: Clarendon Press, 1980), 118–25; Richard A. Epstein, "A Theory of Strict Liability," *Journal of Legal Studies* 2 (1973): 198–200; Richard Epstein, "Causation and Corrective Justice, A Reply to Two Critics," *Journal of Legal Studies* 8 (1979): 477; Michael S. Moore, "Torture and the Balance of Evils," *Israel Law Review* 23 (1989): 299–300, 308–12. For a critique of this view, see Peter Singer, *The Expanding Circle: Ethics and Sociobiology* (Oxford: Clarendon Press, and New York: Farrar, Straus, and Giroux, 1981), 149–53; Richard A. Posner, "Epstein's Tort Theory: A Critique," *Journal of Legal Studies* 8 (1979), 460; Ernest J. Weinrib, "The Case for a Duty to Rescue," *Yale Law Journal* 90 (1980): 247.

possesses the life jacket, the other does right not to take it from her. If neither mother possesses the life jacket, each does right only if neither takes it. Thus, on this account of the content of morality, one actor is never justified in preventing what the other actor is justified in doing. If this constitutes the best analysis of these sorts of cases, then this analysis, like the second one advanced above, provides a basis for thinking that the correspondence thesis should be preserved in cases of punishment.

This position constitutes a compromise between the first two views with which we began, because, while it denies that there are obligations and permissions of preference, it makes room for circumstances in which persons can pursue the welfare of their loved ones over the welfare of others; that is, in those circumstances in which their aid to loved ones does not cause harm to strangers (although it may constitute a failure to save strangers from harm). But this compromise commits its defenders to maintaining that, in the original case of the two mothers aboard the sinking ship, both of their children should be sacrificed when one can be saved. While deontologists cannot permit consequential calculations to dictate the content of their morality, they may nevertheless find that a plausible deontological theory would not contain maxims that commit them to such a troubling conclusion. They thus may search further for a compromise.

The Argument from the Intent with Which Preferential Treatment Is Bestowed

The third compromise that might be attempted follows the previous two in admitting that there are no obligations or permissions that make it right to prefer loved ones to strangers. It also incorporates the claim that individuals are obligated not to kill but are not obligated to save. It denies, however, that actors violate the obligation not to kill in circumstances in which they cause death without a direct intention to do so.[15] If applied to our previous hypothetical, each mother may save

---

[15] This thesis takes its leave from what I call "intentional deontology" – the view that the maxims of morality concern themselves not with actions but with intentions. I have elsewhere identified other deontologies, in addition to intentional deontology, which similarly assume that deontological norms permit or prohibit certain mental states, rather than completed, causally complex actions – e.g., motivational deontology (that is concerned with actors' motives for action); deliberational deontology (that requires or prohibits certain deliberational processes); and attempted act deontology (that concerns itself with what persons try to do, rather than with what they succeed at doing). See Heidi M. Hurd, "What in the World Is Wrong?," *Journal of Contemporary Legal Issues* 5 (1994):

her own child by seizing the life jacket from the other or from some neutral resting place, because by so doing she does not directly intend the death of the other mother's child; she simply knows that that death will come about if she is successful.

This view constitutes a compromise because, like the previous position, it both denies the existence of obligations or permissions that make it right to prefer the welfare of loved ones to strangers while carving out circumstances in which the exercise of such a preference does not violate any agent-relative maxims. By licensing the rescue of one life when both cannot be saved, this view escapes the troubling conclusion to which the previous compromise position was committed. If plausible, this position also implies that we must abandon the correspondence thesis in cases of the sort represented by the two mothers aboard the sinking ship, because in such cases one actor does not do wrong in preventing the other from doing what is right.

Yet this argument is guilty of the same confusion that beset previous consequentialist attempts to limit right-making consequences on epistemic grounds: It smuggles considerations of culpability into the specification of the conditions of right action. Actors who only knowingly violate moral maxims may indeed be less culpable than actors who intend to violate moral maxims, but before we can engage in this discussion we must have some independent understanding of the content of moral maxims. We must have some theory of right action over which intentions can range. If it is wrong to kill one innocent child to save another, then it is wrong to do so negligently, recklessly, knowingly, or intentionally – although it may not be as culpable to do so negligently as knowingly, or to do so knowingly as intentionally. It is even wrong to do so innocently, that is, on a reasonable belief that it is not wrong, although such wrongdoing is wholly nonculpable.

Thus deontologists cannot avail themselves of this compromise without confusing the metaphysics of right action with the conditions of culpability. Since this compromise violates the correspondence thesis precisely because it commits such a confusion, this compromise

157–216. Any one of these deontologies might be appealed to as a means of licensing gladiatorial competition in circumstances such as those of the two women on the sinking ship, because they respectively entail that one does not violate the maxim against killing if one is not motivated to kill; does not deliberate about killing; or does not try to kill.

Insofar as each of these deontologies is subject to the problem that defeats the use of intentional deontology in this context, none provide a more promising means of vindicating preferential treatment of loved ones in defiance of the correspondence thesis.

poses no threat to the viability of the correspondence thesis for a plausible deontological theory of right action.

Where does this leave us? We have worked through a series of cases that on their face appear to function as counterexamples to the claim that a viable deontological moral theory would embody the correspondence thesis. We have found that, with regard to all of these cases, deontologists can plausibly adopt one of two responses: They can deny that the maxims that are properly applicable to actors in these cases violate the correspondence thesis by being gladiatorial in content, or they can admit that the maxims that are properly applicable to actors in these cases violate the correspondence thesis but deny that such a violation serves as a precedent for suspending the thesis in cases involving punishment. These responses give us good reasons to suppose that a plausible deontological theory embraces the correspondence thesis in cases that raise the question of whether or not to punish the justified.

When coupled with the general conclusion reached in the previous section, this result prompts the conclusion that our moral obligations – be they consequentialist or deontological – cannot be role-relative. If this is true, then justifiably disobedient citizens and the judges who judge them cannot be thought to be moral gladiators. The rightness of a citizen's disobedience must make right both the citizen's acquittal and the acquittal of the judge who breaks the law by acquitting the citizen. We must seek to resolve the dilemma of legal perspectivalism by means other than abandoning the principle of weak retributivism.

But if the principle of weak retributivism is in genuine conflict with the rule of law in cases that call on judges to adjudicate justified acts of private disobedience, then it would appear that judges must sacrifice the rule of law. And if the principle of weak retributivism is in genuine conflict with the principle of democracy and the separation of powers in cases that call on system designers to adjudicate justified acts of judicial disobedience, then it would appear that system designers must sacrifice structural pluralism. If the correspondence thesis indeed applies to acts of punishment, then morality does not permit the sacrifice of the principle of weak retributivism.

In the next and final part, we shall take up the question of whether the dilemma of perspectivalism can be solved without either giving up the principle of weak retributivism to which this part has lent substantial support or trivializing the systemic values that have long been held jurisprudentially dear.

Part V

Resolving the Dilemma
of Legal Perspectivalism

In the previous part, we explored reasons to think that our best moral theory – be it consequentialist or deontological – would not impose role-relative duties on actors in a manner that would pit them against one another in moral combat. If this is the case, then we have good reason to believe that the justified cannot be justifiably punished. That is, we have grounds for concluding that the morality of a citizen's disobedience makes right the citizen's acquittal, and the morality of acquitting the citizen makes right the refusal of a system designer to sanction the citizen's judge.

But if, by virtue of the analysis in the previous part, we must consider the principle of weak retributivism inviolate, then the dilemma of legal perspectivalism can be solved only by subjugating our commitments to the rule of law and democracy to that principle. It remains for us to explore whether such a solution can be viably advanced. If it cannot, we will be forced to conclude that our jurisprudence is irreconcilably conflicted: It both does not permit the punishment of the innocent and depends on it as a means of protecting our most basic systemic values.

Chapter 12

Legal Practices Without Moral Combat

If our best moral theory commits us to the correspondence thesis as applied to acts of punishment, then we cannot resolve the dilemma of perspectivalism by abandoning the principle of weak retributivism. We must conclude that justified offenders cannot be justifiably punished. But if the demands of morality require judges to set aside the law whenever its application will work an injustice, what becomes of our commitment to the rule of law, democracy, and the separation of powers? We are not governed by rules, the majority does not give itself its own laws, and powers are not checked and balanced if individual judges are ultimately entitled to set aside democratic enactments whenever their application would be unwise or immoral.

If judicial anarchy is the price that we must pay for the preservation of the principle of weak retributivism, we indeed have cause to rethink the inviolability of that principle. But the work done in the previous chapters has put us in a position to articulate both consequentialist and deontological solutions to the dilemma of legal perspectivalism that preserve our systemic commitments without sacrificing the principle that the innocent should not be punished. While the previous chapters strongly suggested that we must give up our philosophical attachment to the notion that legal officials have role-relative obligations to obey the law of the sort that assure the rule of law and democracy, they also gave us good grounds to believe that morality itself precludes significant judicial activism. In this chapter, I shall spell out the arguments that follow from the previous chapters concerning how an uncompromising application of the principle of weak retributivism can be reconciled with a robust commitment to structural pluralism without resorting to claims of role-relative morality.

In the first section, I shall articulate the means of solving the dilemma that is available to consequentialists who do not attempt to limit right-making consequences either metaphysically or epistemically. In the second section, I shall turn to four distinct deontological theories, each of which promises to reconcile our systemic principles with an agent-relative obligation to abide by the principle of weak retributivism. In the third section, I shall recall the reasons uncovered in previous chapters to think that when our systemic values are not morally compelling, they are epistemically important, so that their consideration will (epistemically) obligate judges under either a consequentialist or deontological moral theory. And finally, in the last section, I shall conclude with a brief discussion of some of the jurisprudential implications of denying role-relative obligations and resolving the dilemma of legal perspectivalism in favor of the principle of weak retributivism.

THE CONSEQUENTIALIST SOLUTION
TO THE DILEMMA OF LEGAL PERSPECTIVALISM

Systemic Values as Right-Making Consequences

In Chapter 10, I argued that consequentialists cannot defend role-relative morality by limiting the consequences that function as reasons for action to those that are proximately caused by an actor or those that are epistemically available to an actor. To invoke proximate cause limitations confuses the metaphysics of causation. To employ epistemic limitations confuses the metaphysics of right action. If these conclusions are right, then the consequentialist must admit that *all* of the consequences of an action enter into the balance of reasons that determines the rightness of that action. It follows that if the systemic consequences of a judge's decision are also consequences of the actions performed by the citizen whose case is decided by the judge, then those systemic consequences are part of the set of consequences that determines the rightness of the citizen's actions. Similarly, if the institutional consequences of a system designer's decision are also consequences of the adjudicatory result reached by the judge whose case is evaluated by the system designer, then those institutional consequences are among the consequences that determine the rightness of the judge's decision and the rightness of the citizen's decision that caused the judge's decision.

A consequentialist morality unfettered by proximate cause and epistemic constraints thus appears to embody a straightforward solution to the dilemma of legal perspectivalism. While a citizen's disobedience might not be as visible as a judge's disobedience, and hence might not itself generate a disproportionate amount of unjustified disobedience on the part of others, the fact that a judge's subsequent acquittal of such a citizen is a consequence of the citizen's disobedience makes it the case that the disproportionate amount of unjustified disobedience that the judge's highly visible disobedience generates is in fact a consequence of the citizen's disobedience. As such, that consequence does not merely affect the rightness of the judge's acquittal; it also enters into the balance of reasons that determines the rightness of the citizen's original disobedience. Similarly, while a citizen's refusal to cooperate with a legally established cooperative strategy to a prisoners' dilemma will not itself lead to the dissolution of that strategy (and the subsequent loss of an important collective good), the fact that a judge's subsequent acquittal of that citizen is a consequence of that citizen's disobedience makes it the case that any adverse effects on the cooperative strategy generated by the judge's disobedience are consequences of the citizen's disobedience. As such, those adverse effects are reasons that enter into the balance of reasons that determines the rightness of the citizen's disobedience to begin with; they are not just consequences that enter into the balance of reasons that determines the rightness of the judge's disobedience.

The same sort of analysis establishes that the institutional effects of constitutional decisions are consequences that affect not just the rightness of constitutional decisions, but also the rightness of judicial decisions and the rightness of private decisions. While the disobedience of a citizen, and the acquittal of that citizen by a judge, are acts that are by themselves unlikely to affect the efficient separation of governmental powers, the fact that a system designer's subsequent decision to ignore such disobedience is a consequence of both the citizen's disobedience and the judge's disobedience makes it the case that any adverse effects of such a decision on structural pluralism are consequences of both the citizen's disobedience and the judge's disobedience. As such, those institutional consequences affect the rightness of both the citizen's conduct and the judge's conduct, as well as the system designer's conduct.

Thus, none of the reasons characterized in Part III as role-relative are in fact role-relative on a consequentialist understanding of morality. The rule of law values of liberty, equality, and the protection of reliance interests are reasons for action for citizens as well as for judges, and the institutional values of structural pluralism are reasons for action for citizens and judges as well as for system designers. While some actors may be epistemically ill-situated to evaluate the degree to which their actions will affect the values discussed in the chapters of Part III, the consequential effects of their actions on those values nevertheless enter into the determination of the rightness of their actions.

Consider again the case of the battered wife who violates the law by preemptively killing her abusive husband after he threatens her life and the lives of her children. Suppose that the consequences of her disobedience, including the adverse systemic consequences caused by her acquittal and the acquittal of her judge (i.e., including all of the adverse effects on the obedience of others, the rule of law values, and the separation of powers), are not as bad as are the consequences of her obedience. Under such circumstances the wife's disobedient action is the right action. And it is the right action not just for her, but for her judge and her judge's judge, because the balance of reasons that determines the rightness of her disobedience is identical to the balance of reasons that determines the rightness of their disobedience. Hence, if her disobedience is right, then their disobedience must be right. Thus, her judge does the right thing in acquitting her, and her judge's judge does the right thing in acquitting him. Included in the calculus that makes her act right is the fact that an acquittal of her by her judge, and an acquittal of her judge by a system designer, will not disproportionately encourage unjustified acts of disobedience on the part of other citizens or judges, and will not unduly affect the rule of law or the separation of powers. As such, the rightness of her act determines both the rightness of a judge's decision to acquit her and the rightness of a system designer's decision to acquit her judge.

It would appear, then, that the dilemma of legal perspectivalism is elegantly solved by a consequentialist morality, once it is recognized that such a morality makes *all* of the consequences of an action rightmaking. Actors are justified in disobeying the law only if the consequences of their actions, including *all* of those systemic consequences that they cannot predict or accurately weigh, favor disobedience.[1] If the consequences of their disobedience, including all of those sys-

---

[1] It may be tempting to invoke Derek Parfit's clever solution to what he calls "small effect cases" to argue that there will be so negligible a number of situations in which the consequences of disobedience, however small, favor the violation of the law that we need not worry about justified disobedience under a consequentialist theory. See Derek Parfit, *Reasons and Persons* (Oxford: Clarendon Press, 1984): 75. For a rebuttal of Parfit's theory that consequentialists can defend a general obligation to obey the law, even in the face of instances in which violations will have small (or imperceptible) effects, see George Klosko, "Parfit's Moral Arithmetic and the Obligation to Obey the Law," *Canadian Journal of Philosophy* 20 (1990): 191–214.

temic consequences that are epistemically unavailable to them, are worse than the consequences of their obedience, they are wrongdoers who are not in fact justified in disobeying the law. The refusal to punish justified offenders can be reconciled with a commitment to the systemic values that have long been thought to define the offices of legal officials by recognizing that one must take into account those systemic values when assessing whether an offender is indeed justified. Thus, our commitment to the rule of law and democracy will not be dangerously jeopardized by the (illegal) acquittal of those who justifiably violate the law, because those who violate the law only do so justifiably if their acquittal will not dangerously jeopardize the rule of law and democracy.

Yet it is hasty to conclude that this understanding of consequentialism yields a solution to the dilemma of legal perspectivalism that is altogether philosophically unproblemmatic. This is because there is a special set of limiting cases that confounds our ability to generalize the truth of the correspondence thesis to all cases that involve the punishment of those who violate the law. Such cases resurrect the dilemma of legal perspectivalism for a consequentialist moral theory.

Limiting Cases: Self-Referential Right-Making Consequences

While the rejection of proximate cause and epistemic limitations enables the consequentialist to advance a satisfyingly clear solution to the dilemma of legal perspectivalism, there appear to be some special cases that limit the scope of that solution. These cases are not generated by conceptual confusions about the metaphysics of causation or the metaphysics of right action. As such, they provide a basis for thinking that consequentialism may fail to reconcile our systemic values with the principle of weak retributivism in all cases in which those principles are in competition.

Suppose it is the case that, if a battered wife is acquitted for the murder of her abusing husband, there will be a substantial increase in the instances in which other women will invoke this "solution" in circumstances in which it is quite unjustified (e.g., in circumstances in which it is simpler or more lucrative than divorce). Suppose further that such an acquittal will have significant adverse effects on liberty, equality, and certain cooperatively achieved collective goods. Together, these bad consequences outweigh the good consequences that come of her action. While the killing will save three innocent lives, more than three innocent lives will be taken by others who copycat the killing in unjustified circumstances. While the killing will relieve the psychological torment of the battered wife and her children, it will trigger a disproportionate amount of anguish on the part of those whose loved ones are killed unjustifiably, and it will engender a disproportionate amount of insecurity among those who fear that they or those they love will be the targets of future unjustified killings. According to the analysis in the previous section, the battered wife's disobedient action is unjustified: The consequences that function as reasons for and against action favor the decision not to kill her husband.

But suppose that her punishment would alleviate most of the adverse systemic effects of her killing – so many, indeed, that her act would then produce more good consequences than bad consequences. Her punishment would deter other women from killing their husbands in circumstances in which such killings would be unjustified, and it would protect rule of law values that would otherwise be adversely affected by her disobedience. Under such circumstances, it appears that her punishment would *make* her action right. It would make it the case that she has saved three innocent lives without causally contributing to the loss of a greater number of innocent lives.

Such a case is deeply puzzling. In the absence of punishment, the battered wife does the wrong thing to save her own life and the lives of her children, because by so doing she causes others to take more than three innocent lives. Thus, an acquittal makes her a wrong-doer. It treats as blameless a person who is morally blameworthy – a wrong-doer whose punishment would not constitute punishment of the justified. Yet if punished, she is a right-doer. Her punishment has the happy consequence of making right an act that is otherwise wrong. But by virtue of making her conduct right, her punishment treats as blameworthy a person who is now morally blameless. For the price of punishment, this actor saves three lives without causing the sort of bad consequences that would make her a wrong-doer deserving of punishment.

By demonstrating the conceptual possibility of actions that are morally justified if and only if punished, this scenario poses a powerful counterexample to the truth of the correspondence thesis as a consequentialist thesis about the conditions of punishment. Given the self-referential nature of the consequences involved, the rightness of the citizen's action does not determine the rightness of not punishing that action. Indeed, the rightness of the citizen's action depends on its punishment.

Because this case does not smuggle in considerations of culpability or considerations of proximate causation, it cannot be dismissed as conceptually confused. But there are a set of reasons to think that such a case is quite special – so special, in fact, that its possibility need not defeat the general viability of the correspondence thesis as a consequentialist thesis about the conditions of punishment.

First, it is crucial to recognize that, while the conceptual possibility of self-referential consequences defeats the claim that the correspondence thesis is necessarily true as a thesis about the conditions of punishment, it does not defeat the claim that the correspondence thesis is necessarily true as a thesis about the conditions of preventative or permissive actions. Cases involving preventative or permissive actions do not permit self-referential consequences. Hence, the correspondence thesis as it was originally stated remains necessarily true for consequentialism. Let me explain.

Recall that, as it was originally stated in Chapter 1, the correspondence thesis held that the rightness of an action determines the rightness of permitting that action. Cases involving self-referential consequences do not affect the truth of this original thesis. As Chapter 10 made clear, if it is right for an individual to do an act, it must be the case that that act will produce more good consequences than bad consequences, *all consequences considered*. An act that prevents a right act prevents not only its bad consequences, but also its good consequences. Thus, if the good consequences of the act outweigh the bad consequences of the act, a preventative act fails to maximize good consequences. Hence, if an act is right, its prevention must be wrong.

Those who would doubt that the morality of an act and its prevention cannot be self-referential might toy with the following sort of counterexample. Suppose that a preventative act would turn a completed act into a mere attempt. Is it not possible that the attempt would be right, but that its completion would be wrong and hence that the prevention of its completion would be right? Consider the case in which a nation builds a nuclear bomb as a means of deterring another nation from waging war against it. Suppose that those who control the bomb would not be justified in deploying it (because, for example, it would kill far more civilians in enemy territory than would be lost domestically should war be declared by the enemy nation). But suppose further that, in the event of escalating violence, the only way to convince the enemy nation that the bomb will be used is by commencing the procedures that will deploy the bomb. In such circumstances, is it not both right for one individual to act so as to deploy the bomb and right for another individual to prevent the successful completion of that task?

While this scenario appears to make self-referential the rightness of an act and the rightness of its prevention, it fails to defeat the truth of the original correspondence thesis. If an attempt is right, then anyone who thwarts the attempt at the stage of mere preparation acts wrongly. And if the completion of that attempt is wrong, then the attempter acts wrongly at the point at which he does not abort the attempt so as to prevent its completion. Hence, another's prevention of his attempt at that point will be right. In both cases, the rightness of an act determines the wrongness of its prevention, and the wrongness of an act determines the rightness of its prevention. The correspondence thesis thus looks airtight in any case that involves an act and its prevention or permission.

But punishment is special.[2] While an act of punishment prevents future acts of just the sort for which the actor is punished, it does not prevent that actor's past act. Thus, unlike an act of prevention, an act of punishment has the capacity to both preserve the good consequences of the punished act and prevent at least some of the bad consequences of that act. Thus, the punishment of a battered wife who has preemptively killed her husband does not take away the good consequences of that act (i.e., the lives saved). It also does not take away a number of its bad consequences (i.e., the loss of the husband's life, the grief of the children at losing their father, the emotional trauma of the wife at taking a life). But it does take away, or at least reduce, the bad consequences that that act has on future actors and on systemic values (i.e., its precedential effect on others who would kill in unjustified circumstances and its adverse effects on liberty, equality, and cooperatively achieved collective goods). If punishment reduces the bad consequences of such an act to the point at which the good consequences of the act outweigh its remaining bad consequences, then punishment can make that act right.

Does this conclusion force us to confine the correspondence thesis to acts of prevention and permission? As a conceptual matter, yes. But this admission need not defeat the consequentialist's defense of the thesis as contingently true of punishment, because there are empirical reasons to think both that the correspondence thesis is contin-

---

[2] Recall the preliminary discussion of this claim in the second section of Chapter 1.

gently true in the vast majority of cases involving punishment and that it could and should be made true in all remaining cases.

First, as an empirical matter, the class of cases in which punishment can make an otherwise wrong act right appears to be very small. It includes only those cases in which most of the bad consequences of a disobedient act are the product of the institutional adjudication of that act. That is, it includes only those cases in which citizens would be justified in breaking the law were it not for the fact that their disobedience would cause judicial publication of their behavior. For only in such cases do judges have the ability to affect the bad consequences of citizens' private acts. That is, only when a judge will be causally responsible for the disproportionate number of bad consequences of a citizen's disobedience will the judge have the power to alleviate those bad consequences so as to make it the case that the citizen's actions produce a disproportionate number of good consequences.

Second, there are reasons to think that this small class of cases would dwindle to zero over the long run if judges refused to punish persons in all of these cases. If judges were to consistently refuse to punish battered wives who have killed their abusing husbands so as to save their own lives, sufficient decisions would be amassed to make clear both the conditions under which spousal killings are justified and the conditions under which spousal killings are unjustified. With the multiplication of such cases, the number of erroneous killings would dwindle to the point at which otherwise justified killings would not trigger a disproportionate number of unjustified killings. From that point forward, more innocent lives would be saved than lost by acquitting battered wives who killed their husbands as a necessary means to saving their own lives and the lives of their children. Thus, from that point forward, punishment would deter more justified killings than unjustified ones. So long as more innocent lives are saved after this point than are lost prior to this point, the right thing for judges to do is to acquit battered wives prior to this point. Put simplistically, while the first acquittal of a battered wife who saves three by killing an abusive husband may trigger ten unjustified killings, the second is likely to trigger fewer unjustified killings, because it makes more clear the conditions under which killings are justified and unjustified. And the third is likely to trigger still fewer unjustified killings, as are the fourth and the fifth. At the point at which an acquittal triggers fewer unjustified killings than justified killings, battered wives no longer act wrongly (in the absence of punishment) in killing their abusive husbands to save their lives. From that point forward, acquittals will encourage more right action than wrong action while relieving right actors of the harm of punishment. Hence, so long as there will be more cases after that point than there are cases prior to that point, the right thing for judges to do is to acquit disobedient actors prior to that point.

Thus, just as all consequences enter into the balance of consequences that determines the rightness of a citizen's disobedience, so all consequences enter into the balance of consequences that determines the rightness of a judge's act of punishment. If an acquittal will in the long run maximize good consequences, then the right thing for a judge to do is to issue an acquittal. And in cases in which a citizen's action is deemed wrong because of its bad systemic consequences, there are grounds for thinking that her acquittal is right. For her acquittal, coupled with the successive acquittals of those like her that will follow out of deference to the value of equality, will reduce over the long run the bad systemic consequences of actions like hers. At some point those actions will become right, because their bad systemic consequences will be outweighed by their good consequences. With the multiplication of such cases, the earlier acts of disobedient citizens are made right. And the rightness of those earlier acts thus makes it right that the citizens who performed them were acquitted.

This argument does not make the correspondence thesis necessarily true as a consequentialist thesis about the conditions of justified punishment. But it makes its contingent truth enormously plausible. It remains possible to construct cases in which the consequences of certain private acts and their punishment remain permanently self-referential (because, for example, persons remain oblivious to the theoretical authority of judicial decisions and so fail to learn the conditions of justified disobedience from successive acquittals of disobedient actors). And in such cases, the correspondence thesis will remain false. But such cases are likely to be the product of academic fancy. So long as we think that the law possesses theoretical authority so as to guide persons toward right action, we have reason to think that persons should be acquitted when their actions are made wrong only by the fact that the law (temporarily) lacks the clarity to succeed perfectly at this task.[3]

---

[3] For criticism of this solution to the problem posed by cases of self-referential consequences, see Larry Alexander and Emily Sherwin, "The Deceptive Nature of Rules," 142 *University of Pennsylvania Law Review* 142 (1994), 1199 n.18.

The class of limiting cases that I have described here thus should not ultimately limit the scope of the consequentialist solution to the dilemma of legal perspectivalism. It remains as clean as the previous section promised. Our systemic commitments to the rule of law, democracy, and the separation of powers are made compatible with the principle of weak retributivism by the recognition that the effects on them that are generated by an act of disobedience must be calculated in evaluating whether a person who is threatened with punishment is indeed a justified offender. If our institutional values are of great concern, then they weigh heavily in the assessment of the justifiability of an actor's disobedience. But if, after our systemic commitments are given their due weight in the calculus of consequences, a disobedient actor is deemed to have caused more good consequences than bad, that actor's disobedience should be considered to have been justifiable. And on pain of preventing the disproportionately good consequences that will necessarily follow from his disobedience if it is indeed justifiable, that actor must not be punished. An uncompromising application of the principle of weak retributivism is thus made compatible with our jurisprudential loyalty to the rule of law and the institutional demands of democracy.

DEONTOLOGICAL SOLUTIONS TO THE DILEMMA OF LEGAL PERSPECTIVALISM

A deontologist cannot score the same sort of victory over the dilemma of legal perspectivalism that a consequentialist can boast. Unlike consequentialists, deontologists are not conceptually committed to viewing the systemic values of the rule of law and democracy as values that must be taken into consideration when assessing the justifiability of an individual's disobedience. Our best deontological theory might, for example, make the principle of weak retributivism the object of agent-relative maxims while assigning no deontological status to our systemic principles. Such a theory would solve the dilemma of legal perspectivalism simply by declaring it to be no dilemma at all: Judges should pay no heed to the rule of law values when confronted with the prospect of punishing those who have justifiably broken the law, and system designers should pay no heed to the importance of democracy when called on to judge a judge's justified disobedience. Inasmuch as this solution can be articulated by a deontologist without fear of the conceptual confusions that would beset a consequentialist who advanced such a solution, a deontological moral theory

cannot guarantee that a commitment to the principle of weak retributivism will not spell the complete sacrifice of our traditional jurisprudential values.[4]

Nevertheless, there are at least four philosophical moves that deontologists might make in an effort to reconcile an agent-relative obligation to honor the principle of weak retributivism with the institutional values to which we give such weight. As I shall argue, while
the first two moves are ultimately unpromising, the latter two provide viable theoretical means of honoring our jurisprudential values
while sustaining an unwavering commitment to the principle of weak
retributivism.

Systemic Values as Self-Referential Maxims

In an attempt to make the systemic values integral to the assessment
of a citizen's justified disobedience, a deontologist might maintain
that persons are justified in violating the law if and only if they will
be punished for their disobedience. Thus, a citizen has an agent-
relative obligation (or permission) to violate the law if and only if she
will be punished for so doing, and a judge has an agent-relative obligation (or permission) to violate the law and acquit a justified offender if and only if he will be punished by a system designer for his
disobedience.

Such a deontology pays homage to the principle of weak retributivism by imposing on judges an agent-relative obligation to punish
the unjustified and acquit the justified. It then purports to solve the
dilemma of perspectivalism by making the protection of our systemic
values – via the punishment of those who are disobedient – a condition of justified disobedience.

Such a solution, however, is extraordinarily paradoxical. Most ob-

---

[4]   As I have elsewhere argued, deontologists can and should maintain that, in the
    absence of obligations imposed by deontological maxims, the right thing to do
    is to maximize good consequences. See Heidi M. Hurd, "What in the World Is
    Wrong?," *Journal of Contemporary Legal Issues* 5 (1994): 164–5; Heidi M. Hurd,
    "The Deontology of Negligence," *Boston University Law Review* 76 (1996): 252–4.
    Hence, deontologists should at least consider the rule of law, democracy, and the
    separation of powers important for consequential reasons, even if they do not
    make the protection of these institutions the objects of agent-relative obligations.
    Because consequential considerations are subjugated to agent-relative obliga-
    tions, however, a deontologist who merely gives consequential importance to
    our systemic values while construing the principle of weak retributivism as a de-
    ontological side-constraint cannot offer a solution to the dilemma of legal per-
    spectivalism that will appease those who worry that we cannot protect the rule
    of law and democracy without punishing the innocent.

viously, a moral theory that requires us to do things for which it requires our punishment is, at the least, a cruel joke. Worse yet, it is likely a contradictory moral theory because, if a democracy can enact a law that requires the violation of some (other) deontological duty (by requiring, for example, the killing of an innocent person), and if a citizen's violation of that law can for one reason or another go unpunished, then that citizen can be obligated both to violate the law (by the agent-relative obligation imposed by the maxim with which the law conflicts) and to follow that law (by the fact that her disobedience will go unpunished).

Moreover, even if such a deontology could escape contradiction, it would inevitably confront officials with conflicting obligations and resurrect the prospect of moral combat between officials and citizens. Under such a deontological system, a judge's punishment could make a citizen's disobedience right, and so violate the agent-relative prohibition against punishing the justified. But a judge's refusal to punish the citizen could make the citizen's action wrong, and so violate the obligation to punish the unjustified. A judge might thus be bound by conflicting obligations. She might be obligated to punish a disobedient citizen when so doing would result in being obligated not to punish that citizen. Similarly, inasmuch as this deontological solution implies that the rightness of one actor's conduct can make another actor's conduct wrong, this deontology returns us to moral combat. If the previous chapter gave us sound reasons to think that a plausible deontology would not force actors to compete with one another to fulfill their moral obligations, then this solution to the dilemma of perspectivalism is no solution at all.

Systemic Values as Absolute Agent-Relative Obligations

Deontologists might maintain that, just as our agent-relative obligations include the obligation not to punish the innocent, so they include the obligation not to act in ways that will threaten the rule of law and majoritarian self-determination. That is, deontologists might characterize our systemic values as the objects of categorical deontological maxims that bear the same status as the principle of weak retributivism. Such a deontological theory would reconcile the principle of weak retributivism with our systemic principles, and so solve the dilemma of legal perspectivalism, by refusing to permit us either to sacrifice our institutional principles for the principle of not punishing the innocent or to sacrifice the principle of not punishing the innocent for the principles of the rule of law and structural pluralism.

309

Yet, like the last solution, such a deontology would solve the dilemma of legal perspectivalism only by inviting moral contradiction and countenancing moral conflict. First, if persons have agent-relative obligations to protect the rule of law, democracy, and structural pluralism, then they must seemingly obey democratically enacted laws (including their exceptions) without exception. If the rule of law requires that individuals act in accordance with legal rules, then any instance of disobedience would appear to violate the agent-relative obligation to honor the rule of law. And if democracy depends on obeying the rules legislated by a majority, then any instance of disobedience would appear to violate an agent-relative obligation to honor majoritarian decisions. Yet if majorities can democratically enact laws that mandate the violation of other deontological maxims, such a theory opens itself to contradiction. One might, for example, be obligated to obey laws requiring that one kill innocent persons, take the property of others, or enslave a race while being simultaneously subject to agent-relative obligations prohibiting murder, theft, and slavery.

Second, even if such a deontology could be rescued from moral contradiction, it would nevertheless imply the possibility of moral conflict. Even if agent-relative obligations to protect the rule of law, democracy, and the separation of powers did not imply a categorical obligation to obey the law, a legal official's satisfaction of those obligations might nevertheless depend on punishing the justified. Like Sartre's example of the son who was simultaneously obligated both to join the Free French and to stay home to take care of his mother, a judge might be obligated both to act in ways that promote rule-governed behavior by others and to acquit individuals who violate rules in morally justified circumstances. While these obligations may not contradict one another, Part III gave us plausible reasons to think that sometimes they cannot be simultaneously satisfied. As such, a deontology that characterizes both the principle of weak retributivism and the systemic principles behind the rule of law and democracy as the objects of deontological maxims implies the possibility of moral conflict.

Inasmuch as a morality that subjects individuals to conflicting obligations appears Kakfaesque, we have reason to seek a deontology that does not preclude our ability to satisfy its duties. Let us turn, then, to two more plausible ways by which deontologists might reconcile the refusal to punish the innocent with the systemic values that such a refusal implicates.

Systemic Values as Less Weighty Agent-Relative Obligations or as Agent-Relative Exceptions

There are two conceptually distinct but similar sorts of deontological theories that permit the reconciliation of our jurisprudential principles without moral combat, conflict, or contradiction. One is a deontology that rejects the view that moral obligations are absolute, instead according our duties differential weights. On such a deontology, the incompatibility of two moral duties is merely apparent, because, when examined carefully, one obligation will inevitably trump the other. On this form of deontology, to discover that one has an obligation is not yet to discover what one should do. Rather, obligations give reasons for action (of a particular weight), and it is the task of practical reason to weigh those obligations against one another to determine the conduct prescribed by the balance of reasons for action.

The other sort of deontological theory retains the more orthodox view that obligations bind categorically, but rejects the possibility of their conflict. On such a view, obligations possess interlocking exceptions, so that when two duties appear to conflict, one in fact bears an exception for the application of the other. To discover what one ought to do is thus to discover the obligation that alone applies, but doing so may require that one work through exceptions to a general maxim to determine its true applicability.

It is entirely realistic to think that the maxims of morality do not bind us in the way that the Ten Commandments suggest – that is, as exceptionless injunctions applicable absolutely in all contexts. Just as the obligation not to kill surely permits an exception, or is overridden, in instances requiring self-defense and the defense of innocent others, and just as the obligation not to lie plausibly contains an exception, or is overridden, in the case of the man who is asked by a contract killer to reveal the location of his would-be victim, so our systemic obligations and our obligation to honor the principle of weak retributivism plausibly contain exceptions that limit their application, or are weighted so as to permit their override.

I shall not pause at this point to take up the philosophical merits of these two theories concerning the structure of morality. For our purposes, it is enough to recognize that both theories provide deontologists with a means of resolving the dilemma of legal perspectivalism. On the first view, deontologists can declare both the set of systemic principles and the principle of weak retributivism to be the objects of agent-relative obligations, but assign such principles weights that enable one to trump the other. One such deontology

311

would weight our systemic obligations so that they trumped our obligation not to punish the innocent. An alternative theory would weight the obligation not to punish the innocent so that it trumped the obligations to protect the rule of law and structural pluralism.

On the view of deontology that conceives of obligations as absolute in weight, but interlocking in content, one can either think that the obligation to protect our systemic values is the exception to the obligation to honor the principle of weak retributivism, or vice versa. On the first version, legal officials would be obligated not to punish the justified *unless* so doing would seriously implicate the rule of law, democracy, and the separation of governmental powers. On the second version, legal officials would be obligated to protect our systemic values *unless* so doing would result in the punishment of the justified.

Certainly our systemic values are accorded maximal protection if they are conceived of as more weighty than the principle of weak retributivism or as exceptions to that principle. Yet, if the arguments advanced in Chapter 11 persuade deontologists that adherence to the correspondence thesis bars the violation of the principle of weak retributivism, then deontologists must either rank our systemic obligations less heavily than the obligation to acquit the justified or construe the obligation to acquit the justified as the exception to our systemic obligations. They must thus reconcile our jurisprudential commitments by maintaining that citizens and officials have an equally weighty general duty to protect the rule of law, but when, for example, a citizen is subject to a more weighty obligation (say, the obligation not to kill an innocent person), the citizen must violate the law, and the citizen's judge must honor the principle of weak retributivism by acquitting him.

While deontologies that weight our systemic obligations less heavily than the obligation to honor the principle of weak retributivism (or make the latter an exception to the former) do not solve the dilemma of legal perspectivalism in favor of our systemic commitments, they nevertheless reconcile our jurisprudential values in ways that accord significant protection to the rule of law and structural pluralism. Our systemic values are safe on these theories because a citizen who jeopardizes them in the name of satisfying a less weighty agent-relative obligation (or an obligation to which the duty to protect the rule of law and democracy is an exception) does not act justifiably and hence can be justifiably punished. Only when the law requires citizens to violate more important agent-relative duties (as did Nazi law, for example) will adherence to it in the name of systemic values be threatened. But as Chapter 3 argued, those who would defend obligations to obey the law should surely refuse to do so when the law requires conduct more immoral than disobedience.

The most serious general objection to the above means of resolving the dilemma of legal perspectivalism will derive from the fear that theorists who defend these positions are consequentialists in deontological clothing. Take, for example, the view that deontological maxims possess exceptions. While the maxims of our best deontological theory are likely to be long and complex, rather than short and snappy, the philosophical suspicion that this solution legitimately inspires is that maxims will be found to have exceptions in all cases in which good consequences will be achieved by their suspension. On pain of collapsing deontology into consequentialism, one cannot find an exception to a rule whenever its application would fail to produce a net balance of good consequences. Similarly, while some obligations may be more or less important than others, one should worry that the relative importance of duties will be weighted, by those who defend the first sort of deontology here considered, so as to enable persons to act in ways that achieve consequentially ideal results. Those fearful that the above solutions simply give up deontology for consequentialism may thus continue to seek an exceptionless means of squaring the principle of weak retributivism with an intuitively plausible conception of the role of our systemic values.

Systemic Values as Threshold Triggers in a Threshold Deontology

There will undoubtedly remain those who are appalled at the claim that our systemic values can never take precedence over the principle of weak retributivism. Surely, they will argue, the western world need not collapse before a lie can be told, a prisoner can be tortured, or an innocent person can be punished. While, as a general matter, our systemic values should give way to the refusal to punish those who are morally justified in breaking the law, we cannot sensibly defend a refusal to punish the justified when that refusal will spell the demise of liberal democracy.

Those who would make this argument while maintaining their allegiance to a deontological moral theory are likely to characterize themselves as threshold deontologists – deontologists who believe that, at some point, the bad consequences of abiding by deontological maxims can become so severe as to justify the violation of those maxims. These deontologists might seek to solve the dilemma of legal

313

perspectivalism by arguing that the obligations imposed by the principle of weak retributivism can be violated when the systemic consequences of abiding by that principle are so grave as to seriously threaten the rule of law, democracy, and the separation of powers.

Yet theorists who invoke threshold deontology to make this argument fail to understand the implications of their own theory. Deontologists who claim that the principle of weak retributivism can be set aside to prevent the demise of just institutions must presumably claim that whatever obligations might prompt a citizen to violate the law in these cases are overridden by the bad systemic consequences caused by so doing. Hence, a citizen whose disobedience seriously threatens the rule of law and structural pluralism (by setting a dangerous example for others, for example, or by causing her judge and her judge's judge to issue decisions threatening liberty, equality, and the protection of reliance interests) is not justifiably disobedient. The principle of weak retributivism remains inviolable, because there can never be a circumstance in which a citizen is genuinely justified in disobeying the law while a judge is forced to set aside the principle of weak retributivism in the name of good systemic consequences.

Threshold deontology thus provides a solution to the dilemma of legal perspectivalism, but not the one that those who advance it might initially suppose. The solution that it provides is that of the consequentialist, made possible by the belief that deontology must give way to consequentialism once a certain threshold of bad consequences is reached. Thus, if bad systemic consequences would compel a judge to violate the obligation imposed by the principle of weak retributivism, then (at least if the arguments in Chapter 11 persuasively eliminate the possibility of role-relative obligations) they must compel the violation of the maxims that would otherwise require the citizen's violation of the law to begin with. A threshold deontology thus makes a robust commitment to the protection of our systemic values compatible with the view that the principle of weak retributivism is absolute.

SYSTEMIC VALUES AS EPISTEMIC HEURISTICS

The above sections have demonstrated that both consequentialist and deontological moral theories can resolve the dilemma of legal perspectivalism without either resorting to the claim that morality is role-relative or sacrificing any of our fundamental jurisprudential principles. According to both sorts of moral theories, if our rule of law values are moral ones, then they serve as reasons for action for citizens as well as for officials. That is, if our systemic values are right-making, then they are right-making for all actors. A citizen, judge, or system designer is genuinely justified in violating the law only if her violation reflects due consideration of the impact of her acquittal on the rule of law and structural pluralism. Hence, a refusal to punish those who are justified will not unduly jeopardize our systemic values, because those who violate the law do so justifiably only if their acquittal will not unduly jeopardize the protection of our systemic values.

Part III, however, gave us a host of reasons to think that, even when our systemic values cannot be thought to be moral values (because they are not, in fact, right-making), they may nevertheless be epistemic values – heuristic guides to those reasons for action that are in fact right-making. If this is the case, then we have further grounds to think that by resolving the dilemma of legal perspectivalism in favor of an exceptionless commitment to the principle of weak retributivism we shall not license a worrisome amount of judicial disobedience. Judges will not be entitled to set aside the law in favor of their own moral judgments without taking seriously that the law constitutes sound theoretical authority concerning the content of the obligations that bind them. While I do not propose to revisit in any detail the arguments made in Part III concerning the epistemic reasons that citizens, judges, and system designers have to abide by laws that legislators should not have enacted, their summary here may further content those who fear that the upshot of the solution to the dilemma of legal perspectivalism that I have advanced permits judges to suspend the law whenever they deem it unjust.

First, for all of the reasons explored in Chapters 5, 6, and 9, judges should fear that, relative to legislators, they are ill-situated to evaluate the merits of a law. If democratically enacted laws must be thought to be theoretically authoritative by virtue of the institutional competence of the legislatures that enact them, then, as I argued in Chapters 6 and 9, even if such laws are not morally binding, judges are epistemically obligated to defer to them in instances of doubt.

Second, inasmuch as democratically enacted laws are thought to possess theoretical authority, citizens can be expected to rely on them both as a means of determining their moral obligations and as salient solutions to coordination problems. As we concluded in Chapter 8, to the extent that concerns for fairness and the encouragement of industry require the protection of such reliance interests, judges have a reason to apply laws that the legislature lacked good reason to enact.

Third, if equal treatment is a value, and if judges can accomplish comparative proportionality in punishment only by applying laws without (significant) exception, then, as Chapter 8 argued, judges will have a reason to defer to laws with which they bear substantial disagreement. Put differently, if the law is deemed theoretically authoritative for the above reasons, then the law will provide the best evidence of the basis on which past cases have been adjudicated and will thus provide the best evidence of how like cases can be treated alike in the future.

Finally, if a judge's disobedience would set an example for others who would follow it in unjustified circumstances, or if in being disobedient a judge would lose an opportunity to reinforce the willingness of others to appeal to the law when so doing would assist them in acting morally, then a judge should abide by the law even if, absent the moral error that his disobedience would cause or fail to prevent, the right thing to do would be to break the law.

Of course, we can now appreciate that all of these arguments serve equally as epistemic reasons for citizens, judges, and system designers to abide by the law. I have emphasized here their role in judicial reasoning as a means of answering those who are especially fearful that the solution to the dilemma of legal perspectivalism that I have advanced gives judges a license to be legislators. Inasmuch as citizens, judges, and system designers will continue to have both moral and epistemic reasons to abide by bad laws, one need not conclude that a refusal to let law trump morality spells a philosophical dismissal of values as profound as the rule of law, democracy, and the separation of governmental powers.

JURISPRUDENTIAL IMPLICATIONS

I should like to conclude with two general jurisprudential remarks. The first denies an implication that has been commonly attributed to my theory, while the second traces an implication that is likely to be surprising.

First, jurisprudence and political theory are undoubtedly two legs of the same pair of trousers. Just as one must put on trousers one leg at a time, so those engaged in these two disciplines have been forced to hold constant the assumptions of the other as a means of examining the principles that comprise their own subject matter. Political theorists, for example, have generally been unconcerned with the question of what law *is*, inquiring instead into whether whatever it is can obligate us. Jurisprudes, on the other hand, have been principally occupied with the question of what law is, holding fixed the assumption that, in some sense, it obligates.

My project has been that of the political theorist, not the jurisprude. I have said nothing about the nature of law, nor have I advanced any argument that stakes out a position in the defining debate in jurisprudence between the positivist and the natural lawyer. Like political theorists, I have sought to examine the bindingness of law by simply assuming a fairly simplistic positivism. Throughout the discussion, the term "law" has been given its meaning in ordinary English – a meaning that reflects the view that law is whatever a society's rule of recognition declares it to be (which, in our society, is whatever legal institutions – legislatures, courts, and constitutional conventions – formally announce). My use of the ordinary meaning of the term "law" has not, however, entailed that I am, or am committed to being, a positivist about the nature of law. It rather reflects a more spare commitment to there being *some* theory of the nature of law according to which statutes will be considered law – a commitment that positivists and most natural law theorists can make alike.

By the same token, while I am flattered to have had a sophisticated natural law theory attributed to me by those who have studied my previous work,[5] nothing I have written here or elsewhere constitutes a defense of such a view. While the answer advanced in the first half of the book is that nothing obligates but morality, the question to which it is an answer is that of the political theorist, not the jurisprude. I have argued that only morality can obligate, not that only what is moral can be law.

I would be committed to a natural law theory only if legal positivism necessarily rejected the view that only morality can obligate. Some versions of legal positivism do appear to reject this view. Bentham and Austin, for example, appeared to believe that legal obligations are not a species of moral obligations but, rather, constitute a genus of obligations all their own. But other forms of positivism do not so abuse the meaning of "obligation." On H.L.A. Hart's theory, legal

---

5   See, for example, William N. Eskridge, *Dynamic Statutory Interpretation* (Cambridge, MA and London, England: Harvard University Press, 1994), 179–83; Kent Greenawalt, *Law and Objectivity* (New York and Oxford: Oxford University Press, 1992), 283 n.3.

obligations are a specific kind of moral obligation, *viz* moral obligations with respect to the content of valid legal rules. And even more clearly, on Joseph Raz's version of legal positivism, only morality (practical reason) can obligate: Legal obligations are simply moral obligations with respect to valid laws.

I am thus committed only to rejecting certain extreme versions of natural law and legal positivism. My assumption that institutionally enacted rules are law precludes a pure natural law view, according to which the content of law is fully congruent with the content of morality, and the content of morality is not affected by institutional history. My argument that only morality obligates precludes any forms of legal positivism that deny this. But more moderate versions of natural law and positivism remain open to me.

Were I to put on the jurisprudential leg of this pair of trousers, nothing I have said herein would prevent me from defending either positivism or natural law. I would be free to maintain that the concept of law is descriptively best characterized by a positivist theory, and that there are sound normative reasons for pedigreeing law by its institutional genesis. I would be similarly free to maintain that law is descriptively equated with whatever is obligatory (which on the view advanced herein is only morality), and that we have sound normative reasons to embrace some version of the thesis that law should not be thought to be law at all if it departs from what is obligatory. While I would be pleased to take credit for having already advanced a defense of one of these views, honesty compels me to deny that anything I have argued for here or elsewhere merits such an implication.

Second, while I have not advanced a theory of law, I have advanced claims that bear on the methodology of those who do take up this task. If I am right that morality is not role-relative, it follows that the role of the judge should not continue to preoccupy those who do jurisprudence. While I surely cannot satisfy those whose jurisprudence is affected by this implication, let me close by giving a cursory sketch of its significance.

H.L.A. Hart once complained that American jurisprudence is "obsessed" with judges and how they reason.[6] Hart was explicitly referring to the work of Oliver Wendell Holmes and the Legal Realists who followed him in thinking that the law is a prediction of judicial

---

6   H.L.A. Hart, "American Jurisprudence Through English Eyes: The Nightmare and the Noble Dream," *Georgia Law Review* 11 (1977): 969.

behavior.[7] Jurisprudence in such hands is, indeed, a study of what guides judicial decisions specifically.

Yet this is not the judge-centered jurisprudence affected by the central thesis of this book. Such jurisprudence is not concerned with judicial obligation, and thus is unaffected by the truth that the obligations of judges do not differ from those of citizens. Rather, even if the thesis advanced by this book is correct, such jurisprudence will justifiably continue its focus on judicial behavior. After all, such jurisprudence makes central the question asked by Holmes' "bad man": When will legal sanctions be visited on me? Because judges are the ones (by and large) who attach legal sanctions to individual behavior, such (external and predictive) jurisprudence has every reason to continue its "obsession" with judicial behavior.

The jurisprudence that *is* affected by the claims of this book is the kind that Hart himself both practiced and inspired in others. Hart's concept of law centrally involves judges, because it is judges whose "internal attitude" toward the rule of recognition is crucial for there to be law at all. Hart thought that our concept of when a society is ruled by law – when, in other words, a legal system exists – centrally requires judges to accept a rule that recognizes other rules as valid and, hence, binding on them.[8]

Joseph Raz's jurisprudence modifies this judicial focus only slightly. According to Raz, judges must accept the rule of recognition for more specific reasons than those allowed by Hart. Judicial obligation only becomes comprehensible for Raz when judges accept the rule of recognition *because* they consider it just.[9] That judges regard the rule of recognition as just does not, according to Raz, commit one who adopts his jurisprudence to believing that such a rule is just. One can make a "detached normative statement," observing that judges

---

[7] In Holmes' famous words: "The prophecies of what the courts will do in fact, and nothing more pretentious, is what I mean by the law." Oliver Wendell Holmes, "The Path of the Law, *Harvard Law Review* 10 (1897): 461. "If you want to know the law and nothing else, you must look at it as a bad man, who cares only for the material consequences which such knowledge enables him to predict, not as a good one, who finds his reasons for conduct, whether inside the law or outside of it, in the vaguer sanctions of conscience." Ibid., 459. And as Karl Llewellyn once regretted saying: "What these officials [i.e., judges] do about disputes, is, to my mind, the law itself." Karl Llewellyn, *The Bramble Bush* (1930): 3. (See the second edition for his partial retraction of this view.)

[8] See generally, H.L.A. Hart, *The Concept of Law* (Oxford: Clarendon press, 1961).

[9] See particularly Joseph Raz, *The Concept of a Legal System* (Oxford: Clarendon Press, 1970), 234–8.

within a system believe that their rule of recognition is a just one. This is what saves Raz's jurisprudence from becoming a natural law theory.

Despite their differences, both Hart and Raz address themselves to the question of when a legal system exists. And both answer this question in terms of when judges believe themselves obligated by a rule of recognition and the rules that it validates. Neither Hart nor Raz adopts the natural lawyer's view that these rules must in fact obligate judges to be law at all; it is enough for their positivist views that judges believe themselves obligated. The moral thesis advanced herein does not impact on this descriptive thesis concerning the concept of law. Still, I suspect that if my moral claim is true – that the obligations of judges do not differ from those of the citizens they judge – it affects the attractiveness of the positivist theories advanced by Hart and Raz. If my moral thesis is right, then our concept of law (as analyzed by Hart and Raz) rests on a moral mistake. Both the judges whose beliefs are made crucial by this concept of law, and we ourselves in embracing this concept, believe something false, *viz*, that the role of a judge gives judges reasons to abide by the law that citizens do not share. According to the brand of positivism advanced by Hart and Raz, it is this (false) belief that makes judges so important to there being law at all.

That the theories defended by Hart and Raz rest on a moral mistake does not prove false their descriptive claims about our concept of law. It could be the case that we in fact share a concept built on false presuppositions. After all, we undoubtedly share a number of such concepts, and the concept of law could be among them. But such a moral mistake should impact on the normative versions of Hart's and Raz's jurisprudence. That is, if we leave the descriptive question of what our concept of law is for the normative question of what our concept of law should be, then the fact that the concept of law articulated by Hart and Raz depends on a moral mistake gives us a good reason to reject it in favor of one that pays no special heed to judicial obligation.

Even more plainly affected by the central thesis of this book are the natural law theories advanced by Ronald Dworkin and Michael Moore. Both of these theories not only pay special attention to judicial obligations, but they do so in a way that makes those obligations even more central to the concept of law than they are in the hands of positivists like Hart and Raz.

The theories advanced by Dworkin and Moore are both exercises in internal jurisprudence. That is, they both address the question of what law is from the perspective of a judge within our legal system.

When Dworkin asks whether a principle (such as the principle that no one should profit from his own wrong) is a *legal* principle, the answer turns on whether its application by judges is obligatory or discretionary. Dworkin's assumption is that judges' obligations vis-a-vis a particular standard fully determines whether that standard is part of the law.[10] Similarly, when Moore theorizes about how law is to be interpreted, he does so explicitly in terms of the judicial role. The role of a judge is defined by the rule of law values, and it is the proper exercise of that role which determines whether a particular legal interpretation is correct.[11]

Inasmuch as it is the actual obligations of judges (not the believed obligations of judges) that determine whether a proposition is law, both Dworkin and Moore advance theories that are squarely within the natural law tradition. Yet, if the actual obligations of judges do not differ from those of citizens (or police officers, lawyers, prosecutors, jurors, system designers, etc.), then natural law jurisprudence of the sort defended by Dworkin and Moore is mistaken in picking out judicial obligations as the touchstone of law. Natural law jurisprudence must return to that of Aquinas. Law must morally obligate to be law at all, but, inasmuch as there are no role-relative moral obligations, the moral obligations of judges merit no more attention than do the moral obligations of waitresses and truck drivers. Contemporary natural law theorists can continue to speak of the obligations of judges if so doing is a useful means of articulating the obligations to which we are all subject, or if so doing otherwise has particular rhetorical value. But they cannot claim anything more on behalf of the judicial role, because the obligations of judges are simply the obligations of all of us.

To discover that morality cannot make us gladiators thus implies that our jurisprudence cannot pronounce legal officials the necessary victors in instances in which their duties are in apparent conflict with those of citizens. While this implication may force us to revise some of our most basic jurisprudential and political assumptions, it puts to rest the fear that our legal institutions can make one person's moral success turn on another's moral failure. We must conclude that law does not require, and cannot permit, moral combat.

---

[10] See particularly Ronald Dworkin, "The Model of Rules," *University of Chicago Law Review* 35 (1967): 14–54.

[11] See Michael S. Moore, "A Natural Law Theory of Interpretation," *Southern California Law Review* 58 (1985): 277–398.

Bibliography

Acton, Harry B. *Kant's Moral Philosophy*. London: Macmillan & Co., 1970.

Alexander, Larry. "Constrained by Precedent." *Southern California Law Review* 63 (1989): 1–64.

"The Gap." *Harvard Journal of Law and Public Policy* 14 (1991): 695–701.

"Law and Exclusionary Reasons." *Philosophical Topics* 18 (1990): 5–22.

"Painting Without the Numbers: Noninterpretive Judicial Review." *University of Dayton Law Review* 8 (1983): 447–63.

"Pursuing the Good – Indirectly." *Ethics* 95 (1985): 315–32.

Alexander, Larry and Ken Kress. "Against Legal Principles." In *Law and Interpretation*, ed. Andrei Marmor, 279–327 (Oxford: Clarendon Press, 1995).

Alexander, Larry and Emily Sherwin. "The Deceptive Nature of Rules." *University of Pennsylvania Law Review* 142 (1994): 1191– 1225.

American Law Institute. *Model Penal Code*. Proposed Official Draft. Philadelphia, PA: 1962.

Restatement (Second) of Torts. Philadelpha, PA: 1965.

Aquinas, Saint Thomas. *Summa Theologica*. In *Basic Writings of Saint Thomas Aquinas*, vol. 2, ed. A.C. Pegis. New York: Random House, 1945.

Arendt, Hannah. "What Was Authority?" In *Nomos I: Authority*, ed. Carl J. Friedrich, 81–112. Cambridge, MA: Harvard University Press, 1958.

Aristotle. *Eudemian Ethics*. In *The Complete Works of Aristotle*, vol. 2, ed. Jonathan Barnes, trans. J. Solomon. Princeton, NJ: Princeton University Press, 1984.

Nicomachean Ethics. In *The Complete Works of Aristotle*, ed. Jonthan Barnes, trans. David Ross, rev'd by J.O. Urmson. Princeton, NJ: Princeton University Press, 1984.

The Politics. In *The Complete Works of Aristotle*, vol. 2, ed. Jonthan Barnes, trans. Benjamin Jowett. Princeton, NJ: Princeton University Press, 1984.

Arrington, Robert L. *Rationalism, Realism and Relativism: Perspectives in Contemporary Moral Epistemology*. Ithaca, NY: Cornell University Press, 1989.

Arthur, John, ed. *Democracy: Theory and Practice*. Belmont, CA: Wadsworth Pub. Co. 1992.

Atiyah, P.S., *Promises, Morals and Law*. Oxford: Clarendon Press, 1981.

Baier, Kurt. *The Moral Point of View*. Ithaca, NY: Cornell University Press, 1958.

Bibliography

Bauer, Steven and Peter Eckerstrom, "The State Made Me Do It: The Applicability of the Necessity Defense to Civil Disobedience." *Stanford Law Review* 39 (1987): 1173–1200.

Bennett, Robert W. "Mere Rationality in Constitutional Law: Judicial Review and Democratic Theory." *California Law Review* 67 (1979): 1049–1103.

Bentham, Jeremy. *A Fragment of Government and An Introduction to the Principles of Morals and Legislation,* ed. Wilfred Harrison. Oxford: Oxford University Press, 1948.

Bice, Scott H. "Rationality Analysis in Constitutional Law." *Minnesota Law Review* 65 (1980): 1–62.

Bingham, Joseph W. "The Nature of Legal Rights and Duties." *Michigan Law Review* 12 (1913): 1–26.

Blackburn, Simon. *Spreading the Word.* Oxford: Clarendon Press, 1984.

Boas, Franz. "The Mind of Primitive Man." *Journal of American Folklore* 14 (1901): 1–11.

Bork, Robert H. "Neutral Principles and Some First Amendment Problems." *Indiana Law Journal* 47 (1971): 1–35.

Brandt, Richard B. *Ethical Theory: The Problems of Normative and Critical Ethics.* Englewood Cliffs, NJ: Prentice-Hall, 1959.

Broad, C.D. *Five Types of Judicial Theory.* New York: Harcourt, Brace, 1930.

Buchanan, James M. "Politics Without Romance: A Sketch of Positive Public Choice Theory and Its Normative Implications." In *The Theory of Public Choice II,* eds. James M. Buchanan and Robert D. Tollison, 11–32. Ann Arbor: University of Michigan Press, 1984.

Buchanan, James M. and Gordon Tullock. *The Calculus of Consent: Logical Foundations of Constitutional Democracy.* Ann Arbor: University of Michigan Press, 1962.

Burton, Steven J. "Particularism, Discretion, and the Rule of Law." In *Nomos XXXVI: The Rule of Law,* ed. Ian Shapiro, 178– 201. New York and London: New York University Press, 1994.

Cardozo, Benjamin N. *The Nature of the Judicial Process.* New Haven, CT: Yale University Press, 1921.

Cauthen, Kenneth. *The Passion for Equality.* New Jersey: Rowman and Littlefield Pub., 1987.

Christie, George C. "On the Moral Obligation to Obey the Law." *Duke Law Journal* 1990 (1990): 1311–36.

Cohen, Carl. "Civil Disobedience and the Law." *Rutgers Law Review* 21 (1966): 1–42.

Cohen, Marshall. "Law, Morality and Purpose." *Villanova Law Review* 10 (1965): 640–654.

Coleman, Jules. *Markets, Morals and the Law.* Cambridge and New York: Cambridge University Press, 1988.

"Moral Theories of Torts: Their Scope and Limits: Part II." *Law and Philosophy* 2 (1983): 5–36.

Bibliography

Cooper, John. *Reason and the Human Good in Aristotle.* Cambridge, MA: Harvard University Press, 1975.

Corry, J.A. "Administrative Law and the Interpretation of Statutes." *University of Toronto Law Journal* 1 (1936): 286–312.

Culler, Jonathan. *On Deconstruction: Theory and Criticism After Structuralism.* Ithaca, NY: Cornell University Press, 1982.

Dahl, Robert A. *Preface to Democratic Theory.* Chicago, IL: University of Chicago Press, 1956.

D'Amato, Anthony. "Can Legislatures Constrain Judicial Interpretation of Statutes?" *Virginia Law Review* 75 (1989): 561–603.

Dan-Cohen, Meir. "Decision Rules and Conduct Rules: On Acoustic Separation in Criminal Law." *Harvard Law Review* 97 (1984): 625– 77.

Darwall, Stephen. *Impartial Reason.* Ithaca, NY: Cornell University Press, 1983.

Daube, David. *Forms of Roman Legislation.* Oxford: Clarendon Press, 1956.

Davidson, Donald. *Essays on Actions and Events.* Oxford: Clarendon Press, 1980.

DeCrew, Judith Wagner. "Moral Conflicts and Ethical Relativism." *Ethics* 101 (1990): 27–41.

DeGeorge, Richard T. "The Nature and Function of Epistemic Authority." In *Authority: A Philosophical Analysis,* ed. R. Baine Harris, 76–93. University: University of Alabama Press, 1976.

Dickerson, Reed. *The Interpretation and Application of Statutes.* Boston, MA: Little, Brown, 1975.

Donagan, Alan. *The Theory of Morality.* Chicago, IL: University of Chicago Press, 1977.

Dreier, James. "Internalism and Speaker Relativism." *Ethics* 101 (1990): 6–26.

Dworkin, Ronald M. *A Matter of Principle.* Cambridge, MA: Harvard University Press, 1985.

  Law's Empire. Cambridge, MA: Harvard University Press, 1986.

  Taking Rights Seriously. Cambridge, MA: Harvard University Press, 1978.

  "The Elusive Morality of Law." *Villanova Law Review* 10 (1965): 631–39.

Easterbrook, Frank H. "Statutes' Domains." *University of Chicago Law Review* 50 (1983): 533–52.

Elster, Jon. *Ulysses and the Sirens: Studies in Rationality and Irrationality.* New York: Cambridge University Press, 1979.

Ely, John Hart. *Democracy and Distrust: A Theory of Judicial Review.* Cambridge, MA: Harvard University Press, 1980.

Epstein, Richard A. "Causation and Corrective Justice, A Reply to Two Critics." *Journal of Legal Studies* 8 (1979): 477–504.

  "A Theory of Strict Liability." *Journal of Legal Studies* 2 (1973): 151–221.

Eskridge, William N. *Dynamic Statutory Interpretation.* Cambridge, MA, and London: Harvard University Press, 1994.

  "Dynamic Statutory Interpretation." *University of Pennsylvania Law Review* 135 (1987): 1479–1555.

Falk, W.D. "Morality, Self, and Others." In *Ethics,* eds. Judith J. Thomson and
    Gerald Dworkin, 349–62. New York: Harper and Row, 1968.
Feldman, Fred. *Introductory Ethics.* Englewood Cliffs, NJ: Prentice-Hall,
    1978.
Finnis, John M. *Fundamentals of Ethics.* Oxford: Oxford University Press, and
    Washington, DC: Georgetown University Press, 1983.
    Natural Law and Natural Rights. Oxford: Clarendon Press, 1980.
    "The Authority of Law in the Predicament of Contemporary Social The-
    ory." *Notre Dame Journal of Law, Ethics and Public Policy* 1 (1984): 115–37.
    "Law as Co-ordination." *Ratio Juris* 2 (1989): 97– 104.
Finnis, John M., J. Boyle and G. Grisez. *Nuclear Deterrence, Morality and Real-
    ism.* Oxford: Clarendon Press, 1987.
Flanagan, Owen and Amelie Oksenberg Rorty, eds. *Identity, Character and
    Morality: Essays in Moral Psychology.* Cambridge, MA, and London: MIT
    Press, 1990.
Flathman, Richard E. *The Practice of Political Authority.* Chicago, IL: Univer-
    sity of Chicago Press, 1980.
    Political Obligation. New York: Atheneum Press, 1972.
Fletcher, George P. *Basic Concepts of Legal Thought.* New York and Oxford:
    Oxford University Press, 1996.
    "Fairness and Utility in Tort Theory." *Harvard Law Review* 85 (1972): 537–
    573.
Foot, Philippa. "Moral Relativism." In *Relativism: Cognitive and Moral,* eds.
    Michael Krausz and Jack W. Meiland. Notre Dame, IN: University of
    Notre Dame Press, 1982.
    "Morality as a System of Hypothetical Imperatives." *The Philosophical Re-
    view* 84 (1972): 305–16.
Frankena, William K. "The Concept of Social Justice." In *Social Justice,* ed.
    Richard Brandt. Englewood Cliffs, NJ: Prentice- Hall, 1962.
    Ethics. Englewood Cliffs, NJ: Prentice-Hall, 1963.
    Ethics, 2d ed. Englewood Cliffs, NJ: Prentice-Hall, 1973.
Fried, Charles. "Moral Causation." *Harvard Law Review* 77 (1964): 1258–70.
Friedman, Richard. "On the Concept of Authority in Political Philosophy."
    In *Concepts in Social and Political Philosophy,* ed. Richard E. Flathman,
    124–43. New York: Macmillan, 1973.
Friedrich, Carl. *Tradition and Authority.* London: Pall Mall Press, 1972.
Fuller, Lon L. *The Morality of Law,* rev. ed. New Haven, CT: Yale University
    Press, 1969.
    "A Rejoinder to Professor Nagel." *Natural Law Forum* 3 (1958): 83–104.
    "Human Interaction and the Law." *American Journal of Jurisprudence* 14
    (1969): 1–36.
    "Human Purpose and Natural Law." *Journal of Philosophy* 53 (1956):
    697–705. Reprinted in *Natural Law Forum* 3 (1958): 68-76.
    "Positivism and Fidelity to Law – A Reply to Professor Hart." *Harvard Law
    Review* 71 (1958): 630–72.

Bibliography

Fumerton, Richard A. *Reason and Morality: A Defense of the Egocentric Perspective*. Ithaca, NY: Cornell University Press, 1990.

Gans, Chaim. *Philosophical Anarchism and Political Disobedience*. Cambridge: Cambridge University Press, 1992.

"The Normativity of Law and its Co-ordinative Function." *Israel Law Review* 16 (1981): 333–55.

Gauthier, David P., ed. *Morality and Rational Self-Interest*. Englewood Cliffs, NJ: Prentice-Hall, 1970.

Morals by Agreement. Oxford: Oxford University Press, 1986.

Gewirth, Alan. "Political Justice." In *Social Justice*, ed. Richard B. Brandt, 119–69. Englewood Cliffs, NJ: Prentice-Hall, 1962.

Gilmore, Grant. *The Ages of American Law*. New Haven, CT: Yale University Press, 1977.

Godwin, William. *Enquiry Concerning Political Justice*, ed. K. Codell Carter. Oxford: Clarendon Press, 1971.

Golding, Martin P. "Realism and Functionalism in the Legal Thought of Felix S. Cohen." *Cornell Law Review* 66 (1981): 1032– 1057.

Goldstein, Abraham. *The Insanity Defense*. New Haven, CT: Yale University Press, 1967.

Gough, J.W., *John Locke's Political Philosophy* 2d ed. Oxford: Clarendon Press, 1972.

Gowans, Christopher W., ed. *Moral Dilemmas*. New York: Oxford University Press, 1987.

Gray, John Chipman. *The Nature and Sources of the Law*, 2d ed. Boston, MA: Beacon Press, 1963.

Green, T.H. "The Principles of Political Obligation." In *The Political Theory of T.H. Green*, ed. John R. Rodman. New York: Appleton-Century-Crofts, 1964.

Green, Leslie. *The Authority of the State*. Oxford: Clarendon Press, 1990.

"Law, Co-ordination, and the Common Good." *Oxford Journal of Legal Studies* 3 (1983): 299–324.

"Law, Legitimacy and Consent." *Southern California Law Review* 62 (1989): 795–825.

Greenawalt, Kent. *Conflicts of Law and Morality*. New York and Oxford: Oxford University Press, 1987.

Law and Objectivity. New York and Oxford: Oxford University Press, 1992.

"A Contextual Approach to Disobedience." *Columbia Law Review* 70 (1970): 48–80.

"Comment." In *Issues in Contemporary Legal Philosophy*, ed. Ruth Gavison, 156–164. Oxford: Oxford University Press, 1987.

"The Natural Duty to Obey the Law." *Michigan Law Review* 84 (1985): 1–62.

"The Perceived Authority of Law in Judging Constitutional Cases." *University of Colorado Law Review* 61 (1990): 783–93.

"Promise, Benefit and Need: Ties That Bind Us to the Law." *Georgia Law Review* 18 (1984): 727–70.

Grice, H.P. "Meaning." In *Readings in the Philosophy of Language,* eds. Jay F. Rosenberg and Charles Travis, 436–48. Englewood Cliffs, NJ: Prentice-Hall, 1971.

Hall, Jerome. *General Principles of Criminal Law.* 2d ed. Indianapolis, IN: Bobbs-Merrill, 1947.

Hamilton, Alexander. *The Federalist No. 78.* In *The Federalist,* ed. Max Beloff. Oxford: Basil Blackwell, 1948.

Hampshire, Stuart. *Morality and Conflict.* Cambridge, MA: Harvard University Press, 1983.

Hand, Learned. *The Bill of Rights.* Cambridge, MA: Harvard University Press, 1958.

Harman, Gilbert. *The Nature of Morality.* New York: Oxford University Press, 1977.

"Moral Relativism Defended." *The Philosophical Review* 84 (1975): 3–22.

Harris, Charles E. *Applying Moral Theories.* Belmont, CA: Wadsworth Publishing Co., 1986.

Edward A. Harris, "From Social Contract to Hypothetical Agreement: Consent and the Obligation to Obey the Law." *Columbia Law Review* 92 (1992): 651–83.

Harrison, Geoffrey. "Relativism and Tolerance." In *Relativism: Cognitive and Moral,* eds. Michael Krausz and Jack W. Meiland, 229–43. Notre Dame, IN: University of Notre Dame Press, 1982.

Hart, H.L.A. *The Concept of Law.* Oxford: Clarendon Press, 1961.

Essays on Bentham. Oxford and New York: Oxford University Press, 1982.

"American Jurisprudence Through English Eyes: The Nightmare and the Noble Dream." *Georgia Law Review* 11 (1977): 969–89.

"Are There Any Natural Rights?" *The Philosophical Review* 64 (1955): 175–91.

"Book Review." *Harvard Law Review* 78 (1965): 1281– 1296.(Reviewing Lon L. Fuller. *The Morality of Law.* New Haven, CT: Yale University Press, 1964.)

"Positivism and the Separation of Law and Morals." *Harvard Law Review* 71 (1958): 593–629.

Hart, H.L.A. and A.M. Honore. *Causation in the Law,* 2d ed. Oxford: Clarendon Press, 1985.

Hart, Henry M. and Albert M. Sacks. *The Legal Process: Basic Problems in the Making and Application of Law,* eds. William N. Eskrdige and Philip P. Frickey. Westbury, NY: Foundation Press, 1994.

Hayek, F.A. *The Constitution of Liberty.* London and Chicago, IL: Routledge and Kegan Paul, 1960.

The Road to Serfdom. Chicago, IL: University of Chicago Press, 1944.

Hendel, Charles W. "An Exploration of the Nature of Authority." In *Nomos I: Authority,* ed. Carl J. Friedrich, 3–27. Cambridge, MA: Harvard University Press, 1958.

Henry, Nannerl O. "Political Obligation and Collective Goods." In *Nomos XII: Political and Legal Obligation,* eds. J. Roland Pennock and John W. Chapman, 263–89. New York: Atherton Press, 1970.

Herman, Barbara. "Obligation and Performance: A Kantian Account of Moral Conflict." In *Identity, Character, and Morality: Essays in Moral Psychology,* eds. Owen J. Flanagan and Amelie Oksenberg Rorty, 311–37. Cambridge, MA, and London: MIT Press, 1990.

"The Practice of Moral Judgment." *The Journal of Philosophy* 82 (1985): 414–36.

Herskovits, Melville J. *Cultural Relativism: Perspectives in Cultural Pluralism.* New York: Random House, 1972.

Man and His Works: The Science of Cultural Anthropology. New York: A.A. Knopf, 1948.

Hobbes, Thomas. *Leviathan,* ed. Michael J. Oakeshott. Oxford: Basil Blackwell, 1946.

Hocutt, Max. "Must Relativists Tolerate Evil?" *The Philosophical Forum* 17 (1986): 188–200.

Hohfeld, Wesley Newcomb. *Fundamental Legal Conceptions,* ed. W.W. Cook. New Haven, CT: Yale University Press, 1919.

Holmes, Oliver Wendell. "Natural Law." *Harvard Law Review* 32 (1918): 40–44.

"The Path of the Law." *Harvard Law Review* 10 (1897): 457–78.

Hospers, John. *Libertarianism: A Political Philosophy for Tomorrow.* Los Angeles, CA: Nash Publishers, 1971.

"What Libertarianism Is." In *The Libertarian Alternative,* ed. Tibor Machan. Chicago, IL: Nelson Hall Co., 1974.

Hugly, Philip and Charles Sayward, "Moral Relativism and Deontic Logic." *Synthese* 85 (1990): 139–52.

Hume, David. "Of the Original Contract." In *Social Contract: Essays by Locke, Hume and Rousseau,* ed. Sir Ernest Barker, 147– 66. Westport, CT: Greenwood Press, 1980.

Hurd, Heidi M. "Challenging Authority." *Yale Law Journal* 100 (1991): 1611–77.

"Correcting Injustice to Corrective Justice." *Notre Dame Law Review* 67 (1991): 51–96.

"Interpreting Authorities." In *Law and Interpretation,* ed. Andrei Marmor, 405–32. Oxford: Clarendon Press, 1995.

"Justifiably Punishing the Justified." *Michigan Law Review* 90 (1992): 2203–2324.

"Relativistic Jurisprudence: Skepticism Founded on Confusion." *Southern California Law Review* 61 (Note 1988): 1417–1509.

"Sovereignty in Silence." *Yale Law Journal* 99 (1990): 945–1028.

"The Levitation of Liberalism" *Yale Law Journal* 105 (1995): 795–824. (Reviewing John Rawls. *Political Liberalism.* New York: Columbia University Press, 1993.)

"The Moral Magic of Consent." *Legal Theory* 2 (1996): 121–46.

"What in the World is Wrong?" *Journal of Contemporary Legal Issues* 5 (1994): 157–216.

Idleman, Scott C. "A Prudential Theory of Judicial Candor." *Texas Law Review* 73 (1995): 1307–1417.

Kadish, Sanford H. "Complicity, Cause and Blame: A Study in the Interpretation of Doctrine." *California Law Review* 73 (1985): 323–410.

"Methodology and Criteria in Due Process Adjudication: A Survey and Criticism." *Yale Law Journal* 66 (1957): 319–63.

Kalin, Jesse. "In Defense of Egoism." In *Ethical Theory: Classical and Contemporary Readings,* ed. Louis P. Pojman. Belmont, CA: Wadsworth Publishing Co., 1989.

Kant, Immanuel. *Critique of Practical Reason,* trans. Lewis W. Beck. New York: MacMillan Publishing Co., 1956.

Foundations of the Metaphysics of Morals, trans. Lewis W. Beck. Indianapolis, IN: Bobbs-Merrill, 1959.

The Metaphysics of Morals, ed. Mary Gregor. Cambridge: Cambridge University Press, 1991.

Metaphysical Elements of Justice, trans. John Ladd. Indianapolis, IN: Bobbs-Merrill, 1965.

"On the Common Saying: 'This May be True in Theory, But it Does Not Apply in Practice.'" In *Kant's Political Writings,* ed. Hans S. Reiss, trans. H.B. Nisbet, 61–92. Cambridge and New York: Cambridge University Press, 1970.

Lectures on Ethics, trans. Louis Infield. London: Methuen, 1979.

Kaplow, Louis. "Rules Versus Standards: An Economic Analysis." *Duke Law Journal* 42 (1992): 557–629.

Katz, Leo. *Ill-Gotten Gains.* Chicago, IL: Chicago University Press, 1996.

Keeton, Robert E. *Venturing to Do Justice: Reforming Private Law.* Cambridge, MA: Harvard University Press, 1969.

Kelman, Mark. "On Democracy-Bashing: A Skeptical Look at the Theoretical and 'Empirical' Practice of the Public Choice Movement." *Virginia Law Review* 74 (1988): 199–273.

Kelman, Steven. *Making Public Policy: A Hopeful View of American Government.* New York: Basic Books, 1987.

"'Public Choice' and Public Spirit." *The Public Interest* 87 (1987): 80–94.

Kelsen, Hans. *General Theory of Law and State.* Cambridge, MA: Harvard University Press, 1945.

Kennedy, Duncan. "Form and Substance in Private Law Adjudication." *Harvard Law Review* 89 (1976): 1685-1778.

Klosko, George. "Parfit's Moral Arithmetic and the Obligation to Obey the Law." *Canadian Journal of Philosophy* 20 (1990): 191– 214.

"Political Obligation and Gratitude." *Philosophy and Public Affairs* 18 (1989): 352–59.

Kruschwitz, R. and R. Roberts, eds. *The Virtues: Contemporary Essays on Moral Character.* Belmont, CA: Wadsworth Publishing Co., 1987.

Ladd, John. "The Issue of Relativism." In *Ethical Relativism,* 107–29. Belmont, CA: Wadsworth Publishing Co., 1973.

"Legal and Moral Obligation." In *Nomos XII: Political and Legal Obligation,* eds. J. Roland Pennock and John W. Chapman, 3–35. New York: Atherton Press, 1970.

Lesnick, Howard. *Listening for God: Religion and Moral Discernment.* New York: Fordham University Press, 1998.

Lewis, David K. *Convention: A Philosophical Study.* Cambridge, MA: Harvard University Press, 1969.

Lewis, H.D. "Ethical Theory and Utilitarianism." In *Contemporary British Philosophy,* ed. H.D.Lewis, 4th series. London: George Allen & Unwin, 1976.

Lippman, Matthew. "Civil Resistance: Revitalizing International Law in the Nuclear Age." *Whittier Law Review* 13 (1992): 17–105.

"Liberating the Law: The Jurisprudence of Civil Disobedience and Resistance." *San Diego Justice Journal* 2 (1994): 299–394.

Llewellyn, Karl. *The Bramble Bush.* New York, NY: 1930.

Locke, John. *The Second Treatise of Government,* ed. J.W. Gough. Oxford: Basil Blackwell, 1976.

Louden, Robert B. "Some Vices of Virtue Ethics." *American Philosophy Quarterly* 21 (1984): 227–36.

Lyons, David. *Ethics and the Rule of Law.* Cambridge and New York: Cambridge University Press, 1984.

Forms and Limits of Utilitarianism. Oxford: Clarendon Press, 1965.

"Ethical Relativism and the Problem of Incoherence." In *Relativism: Cognitive and Moral,* eds. Michael Krausz and Jack W. Meiland, 209–25. Notre Dame, IN: University of Notre Dame Press, 1982.

"Need, Necessity and Political Obligation." *Virginia Law Review* 67 (1981): 63-77.

MacCallum, Gerald C. "Legislative Intent." *Yale Law Journal* 75 (1966): 754–787.

MacCormick, Neil. *Legal Right and Social Democracy.* Oxford: Clarendon Press, 1982.

Macdonald, Margaret. "The Language of Political Theory." In *Essays on Logic and Language,* ed. (1st series) Antony G.N. Flew, 16–86. Oxford: Basil Blackwell, 1952.

Machan, Tibor R. *Individuals and Their Rights.* La Salle, IL: Open Court Publishers, 1989.

MacIntyre, Alasdair C. *After Virtue.* Notre Dame, IN: University of Notre Dame Press, 1981.

"Egoism and Altruism." In *The Encyclopedia of Philosophy,* ed. Paul Edwards, vol. 2, 462–66. New York: Macmillan, 1967.

Mackie, John L. "Obligations to Obey the Law." *Virginia Law Review* 67 (1981): 143–58.

Marmor, Andrei. *Interpretation and Legal Theory.* Oxford: Clarendon Press, 1992.

Mayo, Bernard. *Ethics and the Moral Life.* New York: St. Martin's Press, 1958.

331

McMorrow, Judith A. "Civil Disobedience and the Lawyer's Obligation to the Law." *Washington and Lee Law Review* 48 (1991): 139–63.

Meiklejohn, Alexander. *Free Speech and Its Relation to Self Government.* New York: Harper, 1948.

Mill, James. *Essay on Government.* In *Democracy: Theory and Practice,* ed. John Arthur, 43–49. Belmont, CA: Wadsworth Pub. Co., 1992.

Mill, John Stuart. *On Liberty.* In *Selected Writings of John Stuart Mill,* ed. Maurice Cowling, 121–229. New York: New American Library, 1968.

   Representative Government. In *Utilitarianism, Liberty, and Representative Government,* 235–532. New York: E.P. Dutton and Co., 1951.

   Utilitarianism. In *Selected Writings of John Stuart Mill,* ed. Maurice Cowling, 243–304. New York: New American Library, 1968.

Miller, Geoffrey P. "Pragmatics and the Maxims of Interpretation." *Wisconsin Law Review* 1990 (1990): 1179–1227.

Miller, H. and W. Williams, eds. *The Limits of Utilitarianism.* Minneapolis: University of Minnesota Press, 1982.

Minnow, Martha A. "Breaking the Law: Lawyers and Clients in Struggles for Social Change." *University of Pittsburgh Law Review* 52 (1991): 723-51.

Montague, Phillip. "Comparative and Non-Comparative Justice." *The Philosophical Quarterly* 30 (1980): 131–140.

Moore, G.E. *Ethics.* Cambridge: Cambridge University Press, 1912.

   Principia Ethica. Cambridge: Cambridge University Press, 1903.

Moore, Michael S. *Law and Psychiatry: Rethinking the Relationship.* Cambridge: Cambridge University Press, 1984.

   Placing Blame: A Theory of Criminal Law. Oxford: Clarendon Press, 1997.

   "Authority, Law, and Razian Reasons." *Southern California Law Review* 62 (1989): 827–96.

   "The Moral Worth of Retribution." In *Responsibility, Character, and the Emotions,* ed. Ferdinand Shoeman, 179–219. Cambridge: Cambridge University Press, 1987.

   "A Natural Law Theory of Interpretation." *Southern California Law Review* 58 (1985): 277–398.

   "The Need for a Theory of Legal Theories: Assessing Pragmatic Instrumentalism." *Cornell Law Review* 69 (1984): 988–1013.(Reviewing Robert S. Summers, *Instrumentalism and American Legal Theory.* Ithaca, NY: Cornell University Press, 1982.)

   "The Semantics of Judging." *Southern California Law Review* 54 (1981): 151–294.

   "Torture and the Balance of Evils." *Israel Law Review* 23 (1989): 280–344.

Murdoch, Iris. *The Sovereignty of Good.* London: Routledge & Kegan Paul, 1970.

Murphy, Jeffrie G. and Jules L. Coleman. *Philosophy of Law: An Introduction to Jurisprudence.* Totowa, NJ: Rowman & Allanheld, 1984.

Nagel, Thomas. *Equality and Partiality.* New York and Oxford: Oxford University Press, 1991.

   The Last Word. New York and Oxford: Oxford University Press, 1997.

Mortal Questions. New York: Cambridge University Press, 1979.

The Possibility of Altruism. Oxford: Clarendon Press, 1970.

The View From Nowhere. New York: Oxford University Press, 1986.

Nelson, William N. *On Justifying Democracy.* London and Boston: Routledge & Kegan Paul, 1980.

Nielson, Kai. "Against Moral Conservatism." *Ethics* 82 (1972):219–31.

Nozick, Robert. *Anarchy, State and Utopia.* New York: Basic Books, 1974.

Oliphant, Herman. "Current Discussions of Legal Methodology." *American Bar Association Journal* 7 (1921): 241–43.

Parfit, Derek. *Reasons and Persons.* Oxford: Clarendon Press, 1984.

Pateman, Carole. *Participation and Democratic Theory.* Cambridge: Cambridge University Press, 1970.

Pence, Gregory E. "Recent Work on Virtues." *American Philosophy Quarterly* 21 (1984): 281–97.

Perry, Michael J. *Morality, Politics and Law.* New York: Oxford University Press, 1988.

Perry, Stephen R. "Judicial Obligation, Precedent and the Common Law." *Oxford Journal of Legal Studies* 7 (1987): 215–57.

Plamenatz, John. *Consent, Freedom and Political Obligation,* 2d ed. London and New York: Oxford University Press, 1968.

Man and Society. Vol. 1. London: Longmans, Green and Co., 1963.

Plato. *Crito.* In *The Collected Dialogues of Plato,* eds. Edith Hamilton and Huntington Cairns, trans. Hugh Tredennick, 27–39. Princeton, NJ: Princeton University Press, 1961.

Laws. In *The Collected Dialogues of Plato,* eds. Edith Hamilton and Huntington Cairns, trans. A.E. Taylor, 1225–1513. Princeton, NJ: Princeton University Press, 1961.

The Republic. In *The Collected Dialogues of Plato,* eds. Edith Hamilton and Huntington Cairns, trans. Paul Shorey, 575–844. Princeton, NJ: Princeton University Press, 1961.

Pojman, Louis P. "Gilbert Harman's Internalist Moral Relativism," *The Modern Schoolman* 68 (1990): 19–39.

Posner, Richard A. *Law and Literature: A Misunderstood Relation.* Cambridge, MA: Harvard University Press, 1988.

"Epstein's Tort Theory: A Critique." *Journal of Legal Studies* 8 (1979): 457–475.

Postema, Gerald J. "Coordination and Convention at the Foundations of Law." *Journal of Legal Studies* 11 (1982): 165–203.

Quinton, Anthony. *Utilitarian Ethics.* London: Macmillan, 1973.

Rachels, J. *The Elements of Moral Philosophy.* Philadelphia, PA: Temple University Press, 1986.

Radin, Margaret Jane. "Reconsidering the Rule of Law." *Boston University Law Review* 69 (1989): 781–819.

Railton, Peter. "Alienation, Consequentialism, and the Demands of Morality." *Philosophy and Public Affairs* 13 (1984): 134–71.

Bibliography

Raphael, D.D. *Moral Philosophy*. New York: Oxford University Press, 1981.

Rawls, John. *A Theory of Justice*. Cambridge, MA: Harvard University Press, Belknap Press, 1971.

Political Liberalism. New York: Columbia University Press, 1993.

"Justice as Fairness." *The Philosophical Review* 67 (1958): 164–94.

"Two Concepts of Rules." *The Philosophical Review* 64 (1955): 3–32.

Raz, Joseph. *The Authority of Law: Essays on Law and Morality*. Oxford: Clarendon Press, 1979.

The Concept of a Legal System. Oxford: Clarendon Press, 1970.

The Morality of Freedom. Oxford: Clarendon Press, 1986.

Practical Reason and Norms, 2d ed. London: Hutchinson & Sons, 1990.

"Authority and Consent." *Virginia Law Review* 67 (1981): 103–31.

"Authority and Interpretation in Constitutional Law: Some Preliminaries." In *Objectivity in Constitutional Law*, ed. Larry Alexander. Cambridge: Cambridge University Press, 1998.

"Authority, Law and Morality." *Monist* 68 (1985): 295–324.

"Dworkin: A New Link in the Chain." *California Law Review* 74 (1986): 1103–19. (Reviewing Ronald Dworkin, *A Matter of Principle*. Cambridge, MA: Harvard University Press, 1985.)

"Liberalism, Skepticism, and Democracy." *Iowa Law Review* 74 (1989): 761–86.

"Promises and Obligations." In *Law, Morality, and Society*, eds. P.M.S. Hacker and Joseph Raz, 210–28. Oxford: Clarendon Press, 1977.

"Reasons for Action, Decisions and Norms." In *Practical Reasoning*, ed. Joseph Raz, 128–43. Oxford and New York: Oxford University Press, 1978.

"Voluntary Obligations and Normative Powers." *Aristotelian Society Proceedings* 46 (Supp. 1972): 79–102.

Regan, Donald H. "Authority and Value: Reflections on Raz's *The Morality of Freedom*." *Southern California Law Review* 62 (1989): 995–1095.

"Law's Halo." In *Philosophy and Law*, eds. Jules Coleman and Ellen Frankel Paul, 15–30. Oxford: Basil Blackwell, 1987.

Utilitarianism and Co-operation. Oxford: Clarendon Press, 1980.

Reiman, Jeffrey H. *In Defense of Political Philosophy*. New York: Harper, 1972.

Riker, William H. *The Theory of Political Coalitions*. New Haven, CT: Yale University Press, 1962.

Ross, Alf. *Why Democracy?* Cambridge, MA: Harvard University Press, 1952.

Ross, W.D. *Kant's Ethical Theory*. Oxford: Clarendon Press, 1954.

The Right and the Good. Oxford: Clarendon Press, 1930.

Rothbard, Murray N. *The Ethics of Liberty*. Atlantic Highlands, NJ: Humanities Press, 1982.

For a New Liberty: A New Manifesto. New York: Collier Books, 1978.

Rousseau, Jean-Jacques. *The Social Contract*. In *Social Contract*, ed. Sir Ernest Barker, trans. G. Hopkins. Westport, CT: Greenwood Press, 1980.

Russell, Bertrand. *My Philosophical Development*. New York: Simon & Schuster, 1959.

"On Denoting." *Mind* New Series 14 (1905): 479–93.

Bibliography

Sadurski, Wojciech. "Harman's Defence of Moral Relativism." *Philosophical Investigations* 12 (1989): 33–51.

Sartorius, Rolf E. *Individual Conduct and Social Norms.* Encino, CA: Dickenson Publishing Co., 1975.

  "Political Authority and Political Obligation." *Virginia Law Review* 67 (1981): 3–17.

Sayward, Charles. "System Relativity." *Ratio* 1 (1988): 163–75.

Schauer, Frederick F. *Playing by the Rules: A Philosophical Examination of Rule-Based Decision-Making in Law and in Life.* Oxford: Clarendon Press, 1991.

  "Easy Cases." *Southern California Law Review* 58 (1985): 399–440.

  "Formalism." *Yale Law Journal* 97 (1988): 509–48.

  "Judicial Self-Understanding and the Internalization of Constitutional Rules." *University of Colorado Law Review* (1990): 749–71.

  "Statutory Construction and the Coordinating Function of Plain Meaning." *The Supreme Court Review* 7 (1990): 231–56.

  "The Practice and Problems of Plain Meaning: A Response to Aleinikoff and Shaw." *Vanderbilt Law Review* 45 (1992): 715–41.

  "Rules and the Rule of Law." *Harvard Journal of Law & Public Policy* 14 (1991): 645–94.

Scheffler, Samuel. *The Rejection of Consequentialism.* Oxford: Clarendon Press, 1982.

Schelling, Thomas C. *Micromotives and Macrobehavior.* New York: Norton, 1978.

  The Strategy of Conflict, rev. ed. Cambridge, MA: Harvard University Press, 1980.

Sen, Amartya and Bernard A.O. Williams, eds. *Utilitarianism and Beyond.* New York: Cambridge University Press, 1982.

Shiner, Roger. "Law and Authority." *Canadian Journal of Law and Jurisprudence* 2 (1989): 3–18.

Sibley, Mulford. *Obligation to Disobey.* New York: Council on Religion and International Affairs, 1970.

Sidgwick, Henry. *The Methods of Ethics.* Indianapolis, IN: Hackett Publishing Co., 1981.

Silving, Helen. "A Plea for a Law of Interpretation." *University of Pennsylvania Law Review* 98 (1950): 499–529.

Simon, Yves Rene Marie. *A General Theory of Authority.* Notre Dame, IN: University of Notre Dame Press, 1962.

Simmons, A. John. *Moral Principles and Political Obligations.* Princeton, N.J.: Princeton University Press, 1979.

  "Consent, Free Choice, and Democratic Government." *Georgia Law Review* 18 (1984): 791–819.

Sinclair, M.B.W. "Law and Language: The Role of Pragmatics in Statutory Interpretation." *University of Pittsburgh Law Review* 46 (1985): 373–420.

Singer, Peter. *Democracy and Disobedience.* Oxford: Clarendon Press, 1973.

  The Expanding Circle: Ethics and Sociobiology. Oxford: Clarendon Press, 1981; New York: Farrar, Straus, and Giroux, 1981.

Bibliography

Practical Ethics. Cambridge and New York: Cambridge University Press, 1979.

Smith, Holly M. "Two-Tier Moral Codes." In *Foundations of Moral and Political Philosophy,* eds. Ellen Frankel Paul, Fred D. Miller, and Jeffrey Paul, 112–32. Oxford and Cambridge, MA: Basil Blackwell, 1990.

Smith, M.B.E. "Is There A Prima Facie Obligation to Obey the Law?" *Yale Law Journal* 82 (1973): 950-76.

Smith, Steven D. "Radically Subversive Speech and the Authority of Law." *Michigan Law Review* 94 (1995): 348-70.

"Skepticism, Tolerance, and Truth in the Theory of Free Expression." *Southern California Law Review* 60 (1987): 649–731.

Sommers, Christina Hoff. *Vice and Virtues in Everyday Life.* New York: Harcourt, Brace, Jovanovich, 1985.

Soper, Philip. *A Theory of Law.* Cambridge, MA: Harvard University Press, 1984.

"Law's Normative Claims." In *The Autonomy of Law,* ed. Robert George. Oxford: Oxford University Press, 1996.

"Legal Theory and the Claim of Authority." *Philosophy and Public Affairs* 18 (1989): 209–37.

"The Moral Value of Law." *Michigan Law Review* 84 (1985): 63–86.

Stace, Walter Terence. *The Concept of Morals.* New York: Macmillan Co., 1937.

Stigler, George J. "The Theory of Economic Regulation." *The Bell Journal of Economics and Management Science* 2 (1971): 3–21.

Strawson, Peter. "On Referring." *Mind* New Series 59 (1950): 320–44.

Sturgeon, Nicholas. "Moral Disagreement and Moral Relativism." *Social Philosophy and Policy* 11 (1994): 80–115.

Summers, Robert S. *Instrumentalism and American Legal Theory.* Ithaca, NY: Cornell University Press, 1982.

Taylor, Richard. *Ethics, Faith, and Reason.* Englewood Cliffs, NJ: Prentice Hall, 1985.

Tennyson, Alfred Lord. "The Charge of the Light Brigade." In *The Poetical Works of Tennyson,* ed. G. Robert Strange, 226–27. Boston, MA: Houghton Mifflin, 1974.

Thomson, Judith Jarvis. "Causality and Rights: Some Preliminaries." *Chicago-Kent Law Review* 63 (1987): 471–96.

Thoreau, Henry David. "Civil Disobedience." In *Civil Disobedience: Theory and Practice,* ed. Hugo A. Bedau, 27–48. New York: Pegasus, 1969.

Trianosky, Gregory W. "Supererogation, Wrongdoing, and Vice: On the Autonomy of the Ethics of Virtue." *The Journal of Philosophy* 83 (1986): 26–40.

Tullock, Gordon. "Problems of Majority Voting," *Journal of Political Economy* 67 (1959): 571–79.

Ullmann-Margalit, Edna. *The Emergence of Norms.* Oxford: Clarendon Press, 1977.

Von Leyden, Wolfgang. *Aristotle on Equality and Justice: His Political Argument.* New York: St. Martin's Press, 1985.

Waldron, Jeremy. "The Irrelevance of Moral Objectivity." In *Natural Law The-ory*, ed. Robert P. George, 158–87. Oxford: Clarendon Press, 1992.
  "Legislators' Intentions and Unintentional Legislation." In *Law and Inter-pretation*, ed. Andrei Marmor, 329–56. Oxford: Clarendon Press, 1995.
Walker, A.D.M. "Political Obligation and the Argument from Gratitude." *Philosophy and Public Affairs* 17 (1988): 191–211.
  "Obligations of Gratitude and Political Obligation." *Philosophy and Public Affairs* 18 (1989): 359–64.
Wallace, James D. *Virtues and Vices*. Ithaca, NY: Cornell University Press, 1978.
Warnock, G.J. *The Object of Morality*. London: Methuen, 1971.
Weinrib, Ernest J. "The Case for a Duty to Rescue." *Yale Law Journal* 90 (1980): 247–93.
Weiss, Paul. "The Right to Disobey." In *Law and Philosophy*, ed. Sydney Hook, 98-101. New York: New York University Press, 1964.
Wellington, Harry H. "Common Law Rules and Constitutional Double Stan-dards: Some Notes on Adjudication." *Yale Law Journal* 83 (1973): 221–311.
Westen, Peter. "The Empty Idea of Equality." *Harvard Law Review* 95 (1982): 537–96.
  Speaking of Equality. Princeton, NJ: Princeton University Press, 1990.
Westermarck, Edward, *Ethical Relativity*. New York: Harcourt, Brace & Co., 1932.
Westphal, Kenneth R. "Kant on the State, Law, and Obedience to Authority in the Alleged 'Anti-Revolutionary'" Writings." *Journal of Philosophical Research* 17 (1992): 383–426.
Whitehead, John W. "Civil Disobedience and Operation Rescue: A Historical and Theoretical Analysis." *Washington and Lee Law Review* 48 (1991): 77–122.
Wiles, Anne M. "Harman and Others on Moral Relativism." *Review of Meta-physics* 42 (1989): 783–95.
Williams, Bernard A.O. *Ethics and the Limits of Philosophy*. London: Fontana Press/Collins, 1985.
  Morality: An Introduction to Ethics. New York: Harper & Row, 1972.
  "A Critique of Utilitarianism." In *Utilitarianism: For and Against*, eds. J.J.C. Smart and Bernard Williams, 77– 150. New York: Cambridge University Press, 1973.
  "The Truth in Relativism." *Proceedings of the Aristotelian Society* 75 (1974-75): 215-28.
Wolf, Susan. "Moral Saints." *The Journal of Philosophy* 79 (1982): 419–39.
Wolff, Robert Paul. *The Autonomy of Reason: A Commentary on Kant's "Ground-work of the Metaphysic of Morals."* New York: Harper and Row, 1973.
  In Defense of Anarchism. New York: Harper and Row, 1970.
  "In Defense of Anarchism." In *Is Law Dead?* ed. E. Rostow, 110–33. New York: Simon & Schuster, 1971.
Wollheim, Richard. "A Paradox in the Theory of Democracy." In *Philosophy,*

Politics and Society, eds. Peter Laslett and W.G. Runciman, 71–87, 2d series. Oxford: Basil Blackwell, 1962.

Wong, David B., *Moral Relativity.* Berkeley, CA: University of California Press, 1984.

Wright, R. George. "Legal Obligation and the Natural Law." *Georgia Law Review* 23 (1989): 997–1020.

Zedalis, Rex J. "On First Considering Whether Law Binds." *Indiana Law Journal* 69 (1993): 137–214.

Ziff, Paul. "On H.P. Grice's Account of Meaning." *Analysis* 28 (1967): 1–8.

Index

action *See also* amoral action; judicial action; reasons for action; right action: based on content-dependent and -independent reasons, 71–2; based on epistemic authority, 125–6; based on first- and second-order reasons, 71–94; consenting to exercise of influential authority, 118–19; in consequentialist thesis, 255–6; content-dependent reasons for (Raz), 80–1; Hohfeldian privilege for, 280–1; of incommensurate value, 31–4; moral action of correspondence thesis, 33; moral worth of, 242; promises as predictors of, 118; right and morally right (Hocutt), 40; role-relative reasons for, 10–16; rule of law values as reason for, 299; as sign of consent, 116; of tacit consent (Locke), 115–16

Acton, John (lord), 236

advice: difference in effect from request, 65–6; from epistemic authority, 63–5, 67; as evidence, 131

advisory authority: conditions for someone to be deemed, 132–3; exercised only by persons, 126–7; function of, 63n2; indicator rules (Regan), 126, 128; theory of legal authority as epistemic authority under, 125; utterances as signals, 130

advisory authority theory: advice evaluated by non-advisory authority, 127, 132–3; difference from theoretical authority theory, 156; lawmakers as moral observers, 127, 133–40; modified, 129–30; potential for paradox, 127–32; requires commitment to intentionalist theory of interpretation, 127–8, 140–6

agreement, syntactic theory, 60–1

Alexander, Larry, 14n14, 172–3, 186–7, 189, 190–1, 195n12, 197n14

amoral action: correspondence thesis not applicable to, 33; defined by Hohfeldian liberties, 281

Aristotle, xx, 217n20, 223n22

authority. *See* advisory authority; epistemic authority; influential authority; practical authority; theoretical authority.

autonomy: internalist theories of democracy argued from, 241–7; value of, 241

beliefs: advisory authority affects reasons for, 128; belief sets of individuals, 45; concerning right action, 155; false, 197–9; justified, 209; rational and irrational, 129; reason for, 73–4

Bentham, Jeremy, 10n9, 317

339

reliance interests: protection in argument from coordination, 214–21; protection in argument from fairness, 208–13; protection in argument from industry, 213–14; rule of law value to protect, 207–13

request: difference in effect from advice, 65–6; by influential authority, 68; reasons in support of authority of, 98–9

responsibility, causal (Hart and Honore), 257–9

right action: conditions of, 265; consequential conception of, 255–70; of consequentialism, 8; in coordination problems, 169–76; under correspondence thesis, 4–7; defined, 261; deontologist interpretation, 271–93; distinct from culpable action, 263–5; intuition for, 192; reasons for, 261–3; theory of, 266

Rousseau, Jean-jacques, 233n10

rule of law: conditions for legal system to accomplish (Fuller), 203; incompatibility with principles of weak retributivism, democracy and separation of powers, 1, 3–23; individual liberty as value of, 205–7; judgment based on values of, 203–4; protection of equality as value of, 221–5; protection of reliance interests as value of, 207–13; values, 204, 299; when demands of morality substutue for demands of law, 182

rule of law principle, 1

rules: comparison of legal to moral rules, 21–2; rule of recognition (Hart), 59

rules, majority-enacted: behavior consistent with, 101–2; natural duty of justice theory, 120–4; as reasons for action, 102–20; theory

of consent, 112–20; theory of gratitude, 107–12; theory of reciprocity, 102–7

Russell, Bertrand, 47

Sacks, Albert, 148n39

sanctions: to induce compliance, 216; influence on reasons for action, 178–83; judges power to levy, 196; in real legal systems (Green), 169, 180; theoretical authority of law to impose, 178

Sartorius, Rolf E., 12n12, 14n14, 203n3

Sartre's dilemma, 272, 310

Sayward, Charles, 41n27, 44n31, 59n60

Schauer, Frederick, 186–7, 195n11, 222n21, 226, 248–9

Schauer, Frederick F., 21–2

self-defense: argument from competing permissions, 279–80; argument from Hohfeldian privileges, 280–1; argument from permissions to do no wrong, 282–4

semantic relativists. *See* relativism.

separation of powers: arguments for democracy and, 227–48; Hamilton's solution to potential tyranny, 236–7; in principle of democracy, 1, 3–23

Simmons, John, 101n4, 110

Singer, Peter, 102n6, 122n34

Smith, Holly, 195n10, 198, 199–200

Smith, Steven, 42n29, 117n28

Soper, Philip, 68n10, 112n16, 204n6

standards: in meaning of moral judgments, 45; rule of recognition to identify (Hart), 59

Strawson, Peter, 47–8

Sturgeon, Nicholas, 38n18

subjectivism: conditions for collapse of relativism into, 42; of moral relativists, 58–61; of post-structuralism, 166